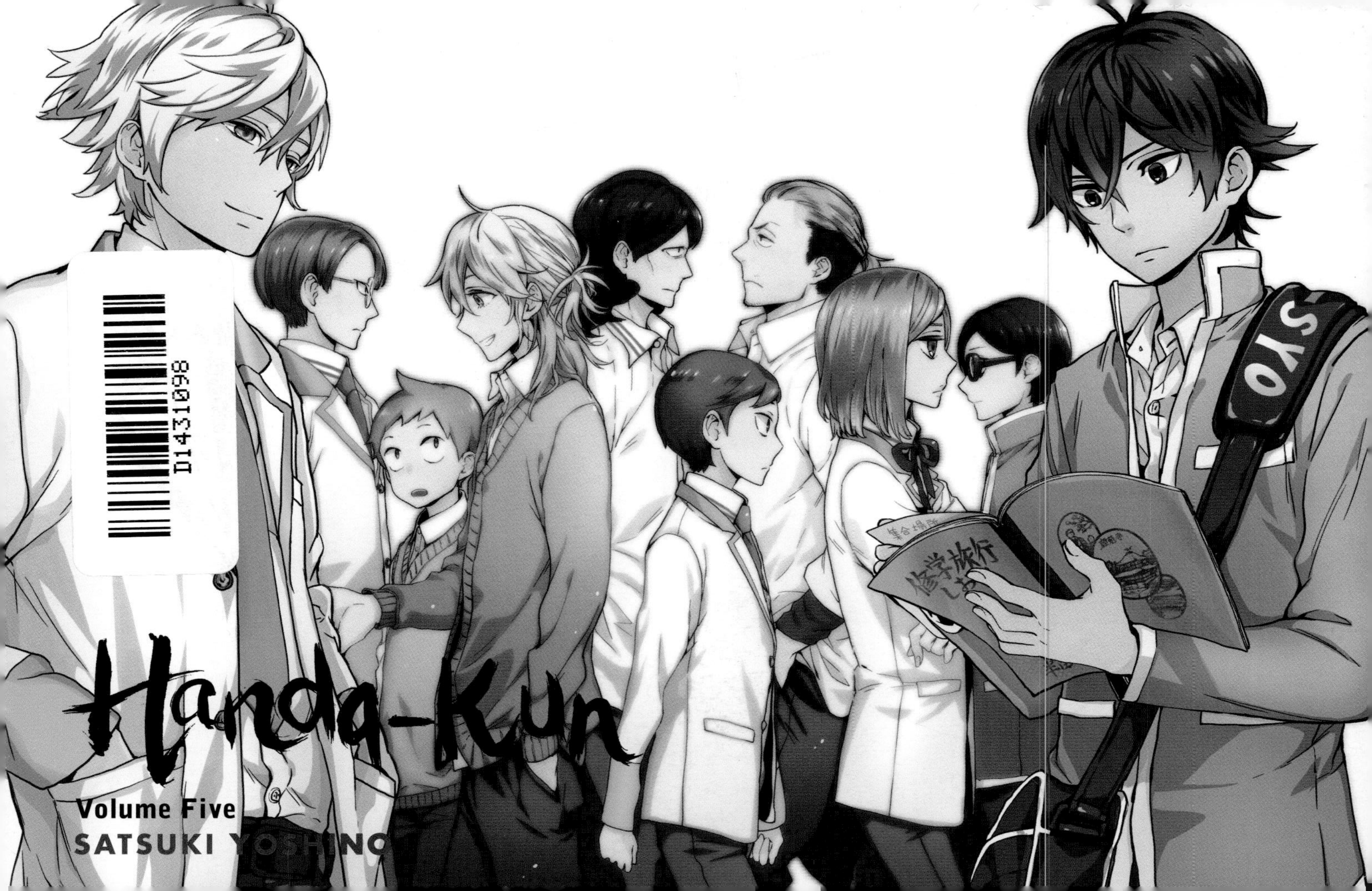
Handa-Kun
Volume Five
SATSUKI YOSHINO
SYO

Contents

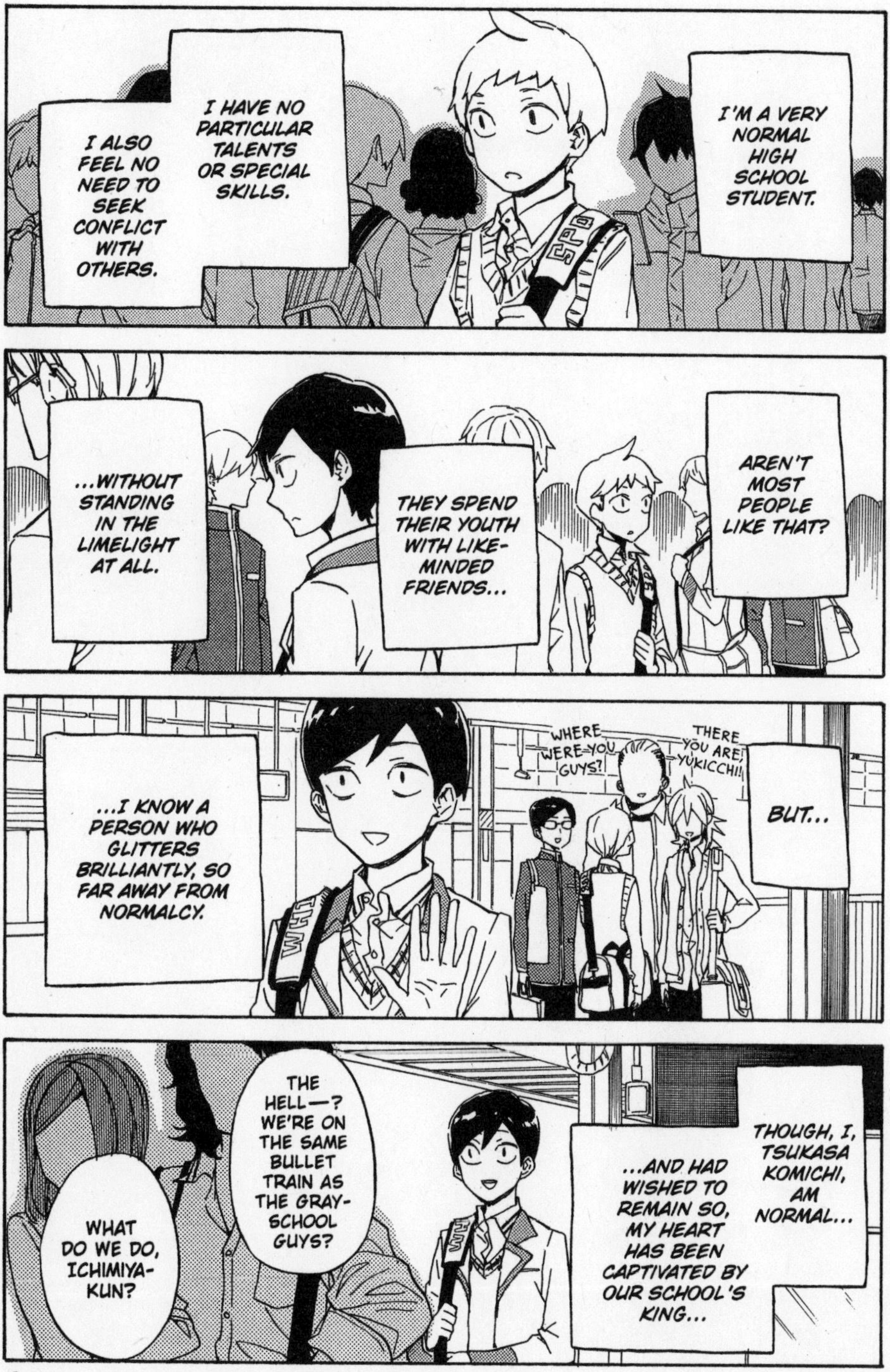
I'M A VERY NORMAL HIGH SCHOOL STUDENT.
I HAVE NO PARTICULAR TALENTS OR SPECIAL SKILLS.
I ALSO FEEL NO NEED TO SEEK CONFLICT WITH OTHERS.
AREN'T MOST PEOPLE LIKE THAT?
THEY SPEND THEIR YOUTH WITH LIKE-MINDED FRIENDS...
...WITHOUT STANDING IN THE LIMELIGHT AT ALL.
BUT...
THERE YOU ARE, YUKICCHI!!
WHERE WERE YOU GUYS?
...I KNOW A PERSON WHO GLITTERS BRILLIANTLY, SO FAR AWAY FROM NORMALCY.
THOUGH, I, TSUKASA KOMICHI, AM NORMAL...
...AND HAD WISHED TO REMAIN SO, MY HEART HAS BEEN CAPTIVATED BY OUR SCHOOL'S KING...
THE HELL—? WE'RE ON THE SAME BULLET TRAIN AS THE GRAY-SCHOOL GUYS?
WHAT DO WE DO, ICHIMIYA-KUN?

Chapter 21: Handa-kun & the Class Trip, Day 1

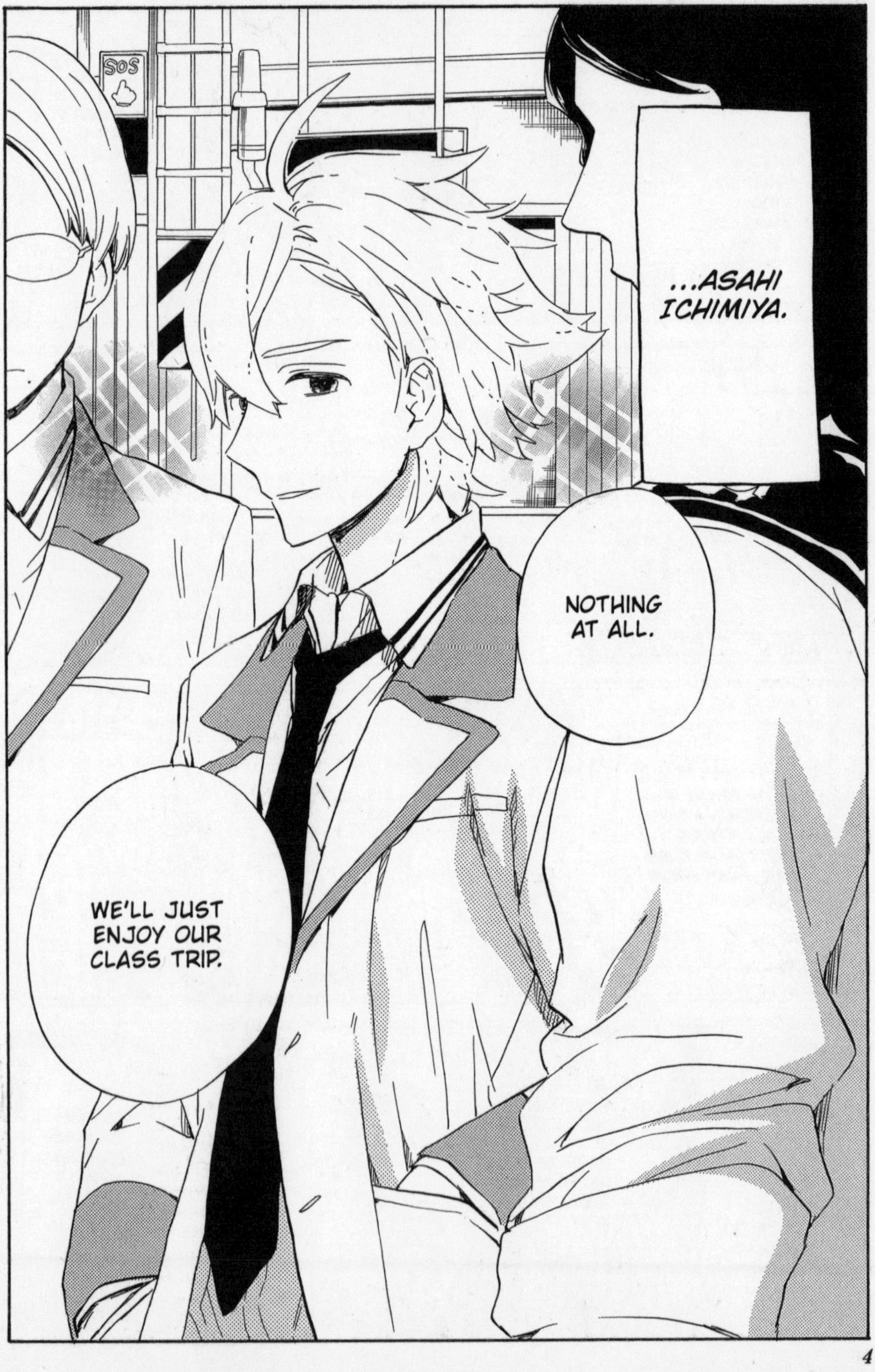
...ASAHI ICHIMIYA.
SOS
NOTHING AT ALL.
WE'LL JUST ENJOY OUR CLASS TRIP.

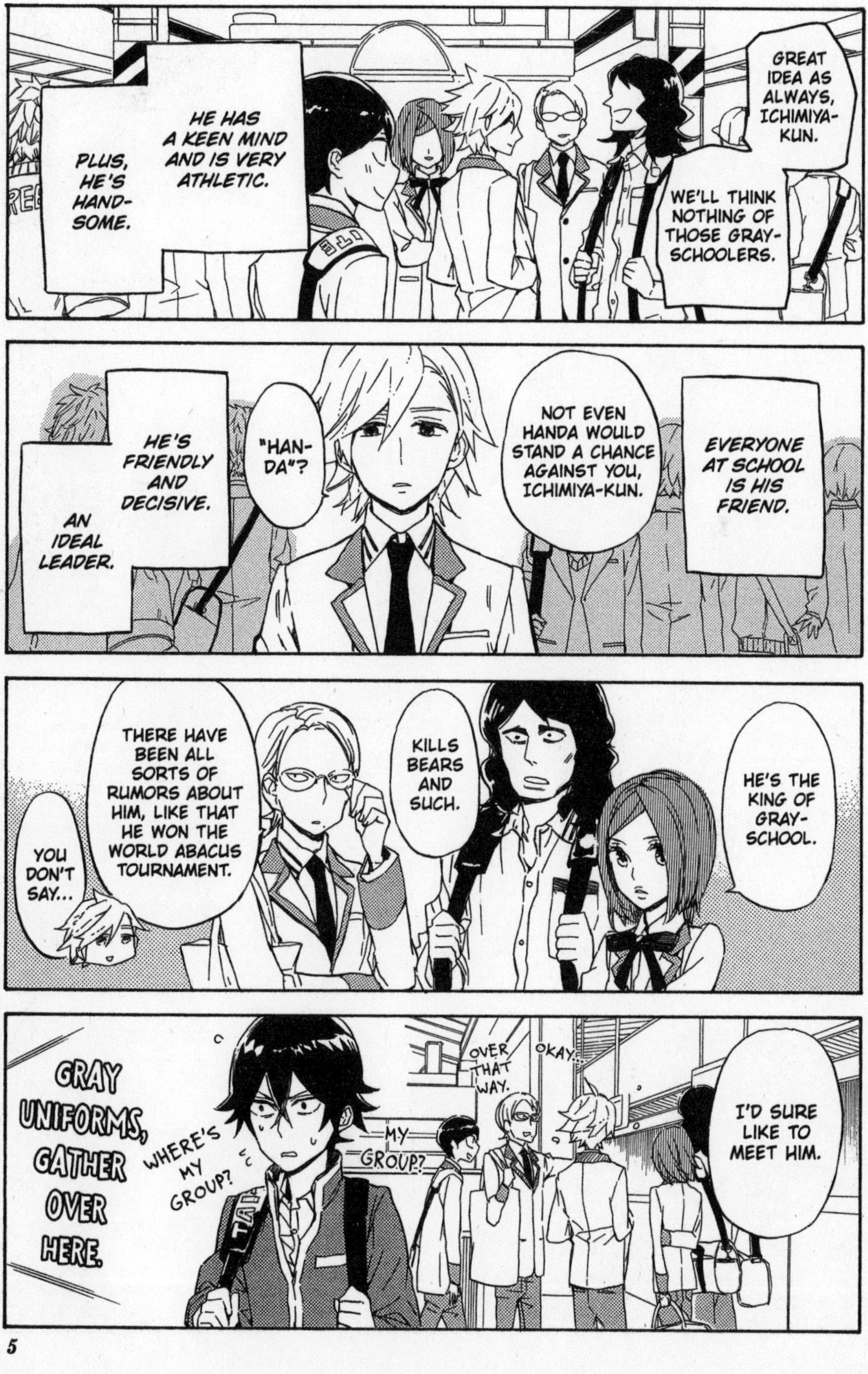
GREAT IDEA AS ALWAYS, ICHIMIYA-KUN.
WE'LL THINK NOTHING OF THOSE GRAY-SCHOOLERS.
HE HAS A KEEN MIND AND IS VERY ATHLETIC.
PLUS, HE'S HANDSOME.
EVERYONE AT SCHOOL IS HIS FRIEND.
NOT EVEN HANDA WOULD STAND A CHANCE AGAINST YOU, ICHIMIYA-KUN.
"HAN-DA"?
HE'S FRIENDLY AND DECISIVE.
AN IDEAL LEADER.
HE'S THE KING OF GRAY-SCHOOL.
KILLS BEARS AND SUCH.
THERE HAVE BEEN ALL SORTS OF RUMORS ABOUT HIM, LIKE THAT HE WON THE WORLD ABACUS TOURNAMENT.
YOU DON'T SAY...
I'D SURE LIKE TO MEET HIM.
OKAY...
OVER THAT WAY.
MY GROUP?
WHERE'S MY GROUP?
GRAY UNIFORMS, GATHER OVER HERE.

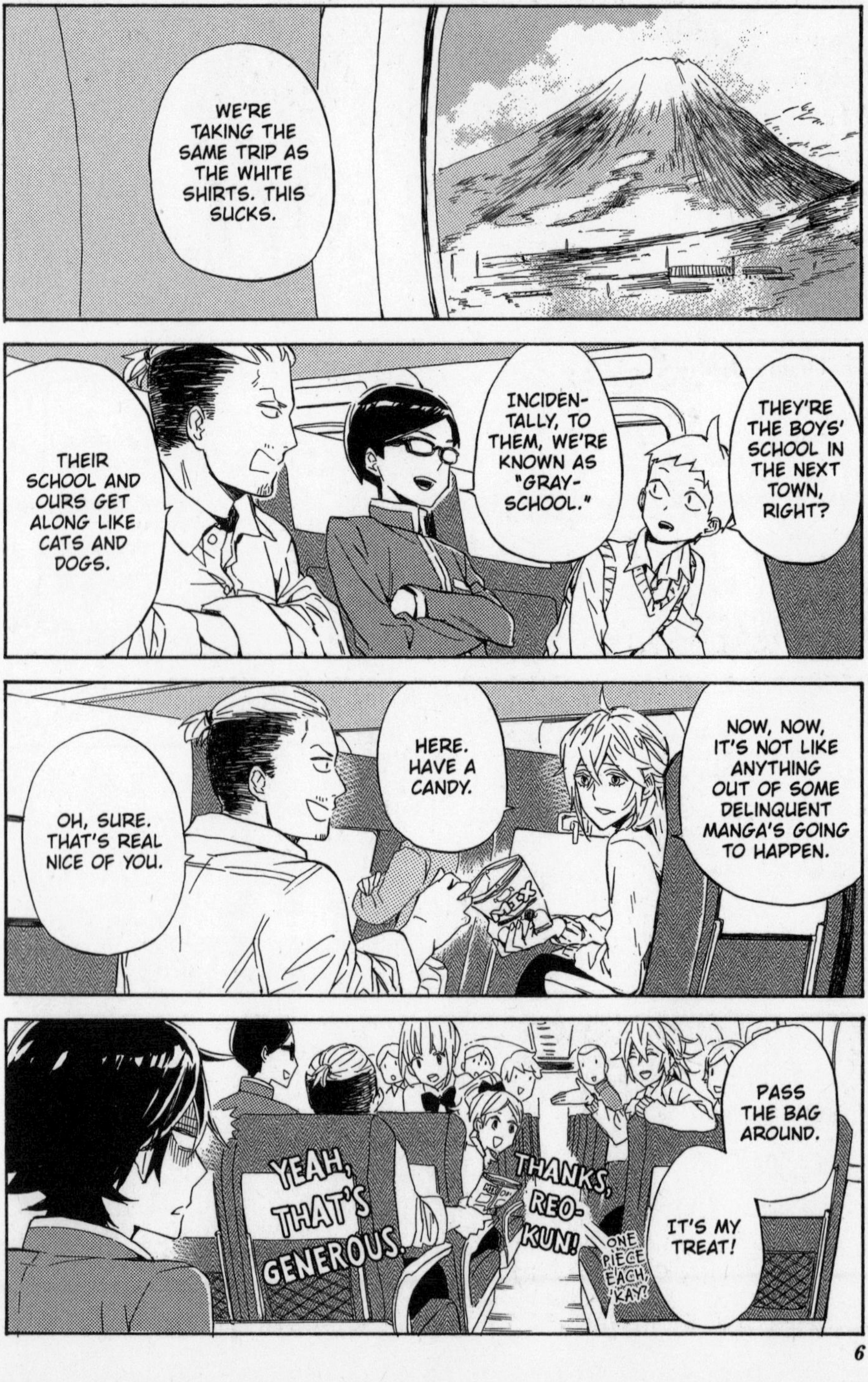
WE'RE TAKING THE SAME TRIP AS THE WHITE SHIRTS. THIS SUCKS.
THEY'RE THE BOYS' SCHOOL IN THE NEXT TOWN, RIGHT?
INCIDEN-TALLY, TO THEM, WE'RE KNOWN AS "GRAY-SCHOOL."
THEIR SCHOOL AND OURS GET ALONG LIKE CATS AND DOGS.
NOW, NOW, IT'S NOT LIKE ANYTHING OUT OF SOME DELINQUENT MANGA'S GOING TO HAPPEN.
HERE. HAVE A CANDY.
OH, SURE. THAT'S REAL NICE OF YOU.
PASS THE BAG AROUND.
IT'S MY TREAT!
ONE PIECE EACH, 'KAY?
THANKS, REO-KUN!
YEAH, THAT'S GENEROUS.

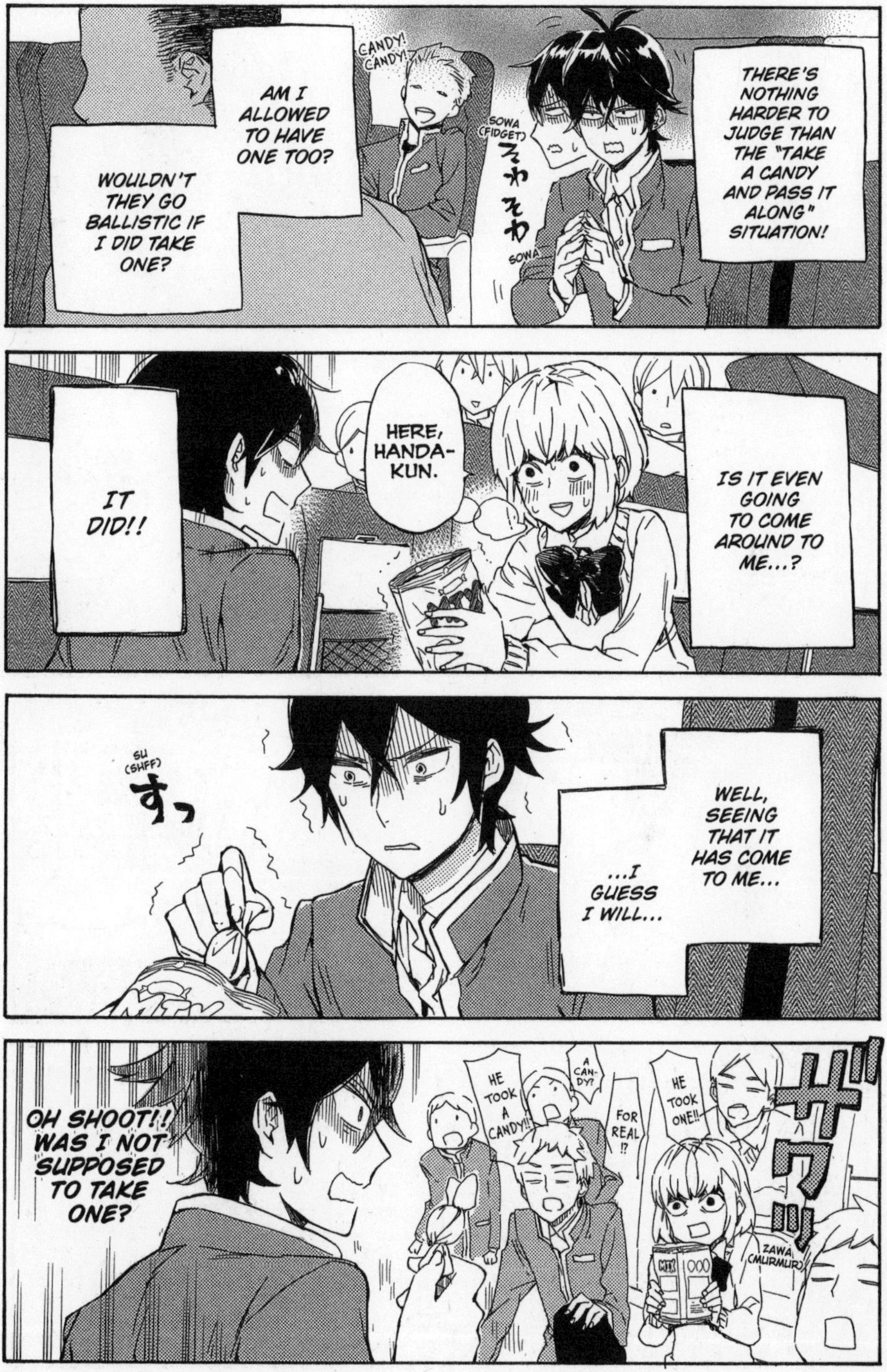
THERE'S NOTHING HARDER TO JUDGE THAN THE "TAKE A CANDY AND PASS IT ALONG" SITUATION!
SOWA (FIDGET)
そわそわ
SOWA
CANDY! CANDY!
AM I ALLOWED TO HAVE ONE TOO?
WOULDN'T THEY GO BALLISTIC IF I DID TAKE ONE?
IS IT EVEN GOING TO COME AROUND TO ME...?
HERE, HANDA-KUN.
IT DID!!
WELL, SEEING THAT IT HAS COME TO ME...
...I GUESS I WILL...
SU (SHFF)
すっ
ザワッ
ZAWA (MURMUR)
HE TOOK ONE!!
FOR REAL!?
A CANDY?
HE TOOK A CANDY!!
OH SHOOT!! WAS I NOT SUPPOSED TO TAKE ONE?

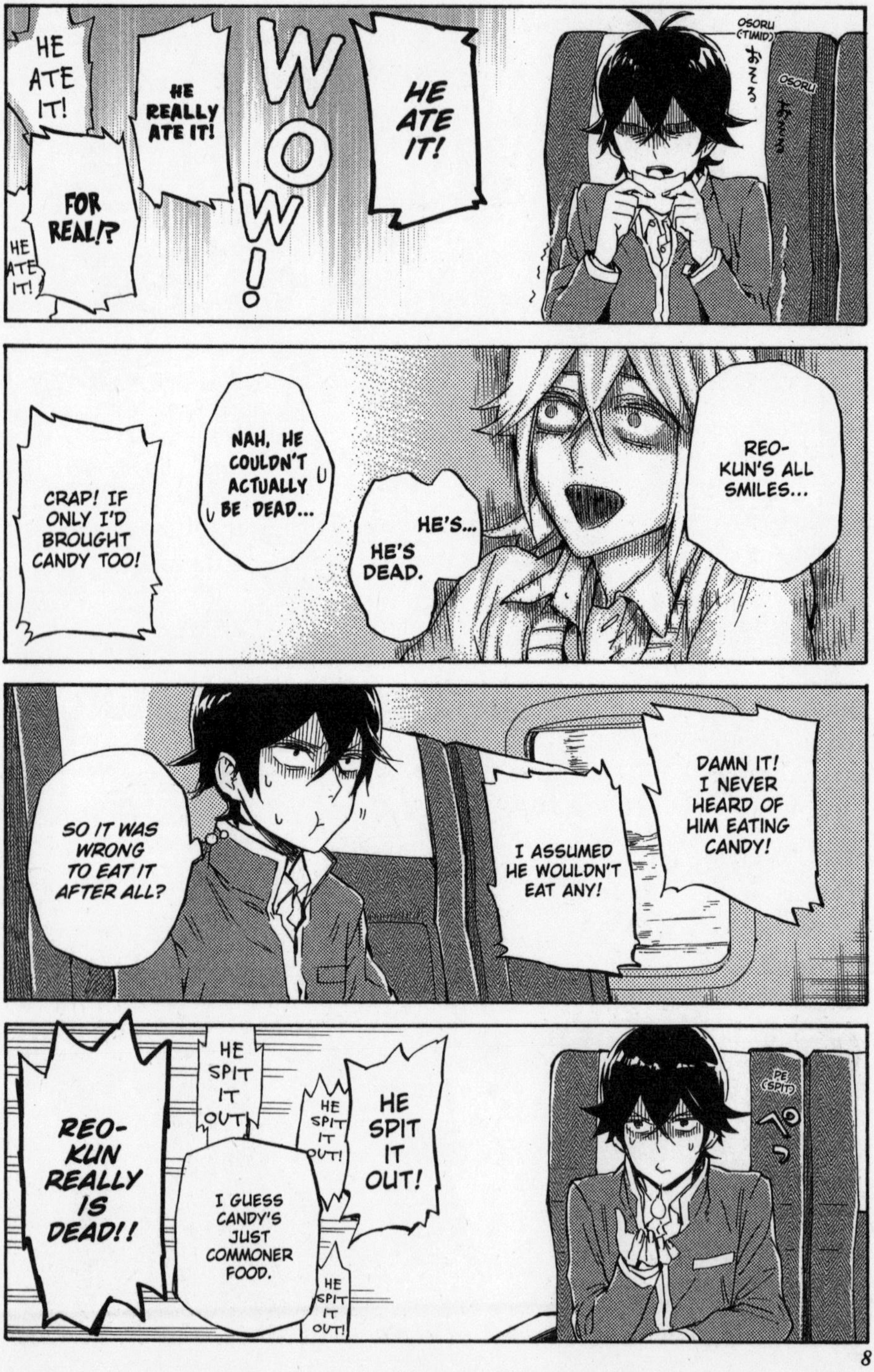
OSORU (TIMID)
おそる
OSORU
おそる
HE ATE IT!
WOW!
HE REALLY ATE IT!
HE ATE IT!
FOR REAL!?
HE ATE IT!
REO-KUN'S ALL SMILES...
HE'S... HE'S DEAD.
NAH, HE COULDN'T ACTUALLY BE DEAD...
CRAP! IF ONLY I'D BROUGHT CANDY TOO!
DAMN IT! I NEVER HEARD OF HIM EATING CANDY!
I ASSUMED HE WOULDN'T EAT ANY!
SO IT WAS WRONG TO EAT IT AFTER ALL?
PE (SPIT)
ぺっ
HE SPIT IT OUT!
HE SPIT IT OUT!
HE SPIT IT OUT!
I GUESS CANDY'S JUST COMMONER FOOD.
HE SPIT IT OUT!
REO-KUN REALLY IS DEAD!!

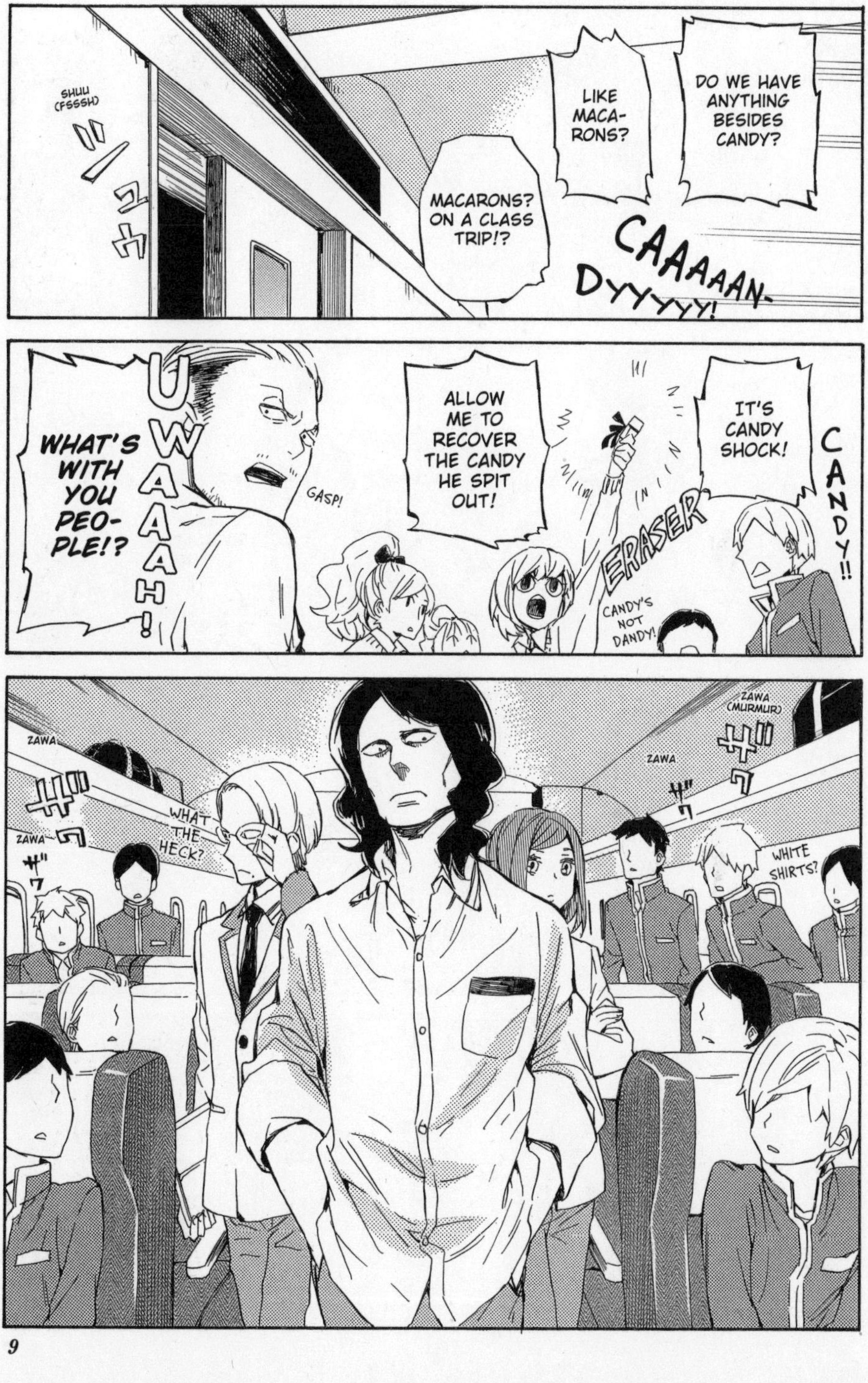
DO WE HAVE ANYTHING BESIDES CANDY?
LIKE MACARONS?
MACARONS? ON A CLASS TRIP!?
CAAAAAN-DYYYYY!
SHUU (FSSSH)
CANDY!!
IT'S CANDY SHOCK!
CANDY'S NOT DANDY!
ERASER
ALLOW ME TO RECOVER THE CANDY HE SPIT OUT!
GASP!
UWAAAAH!
WHAT'S WITH YOU PEO-PLE!?
ZAWA (MURMUR)
ZAWA
WHITE SHIRTS?
WHAT THE HECK?
ZAWA
ZAWA

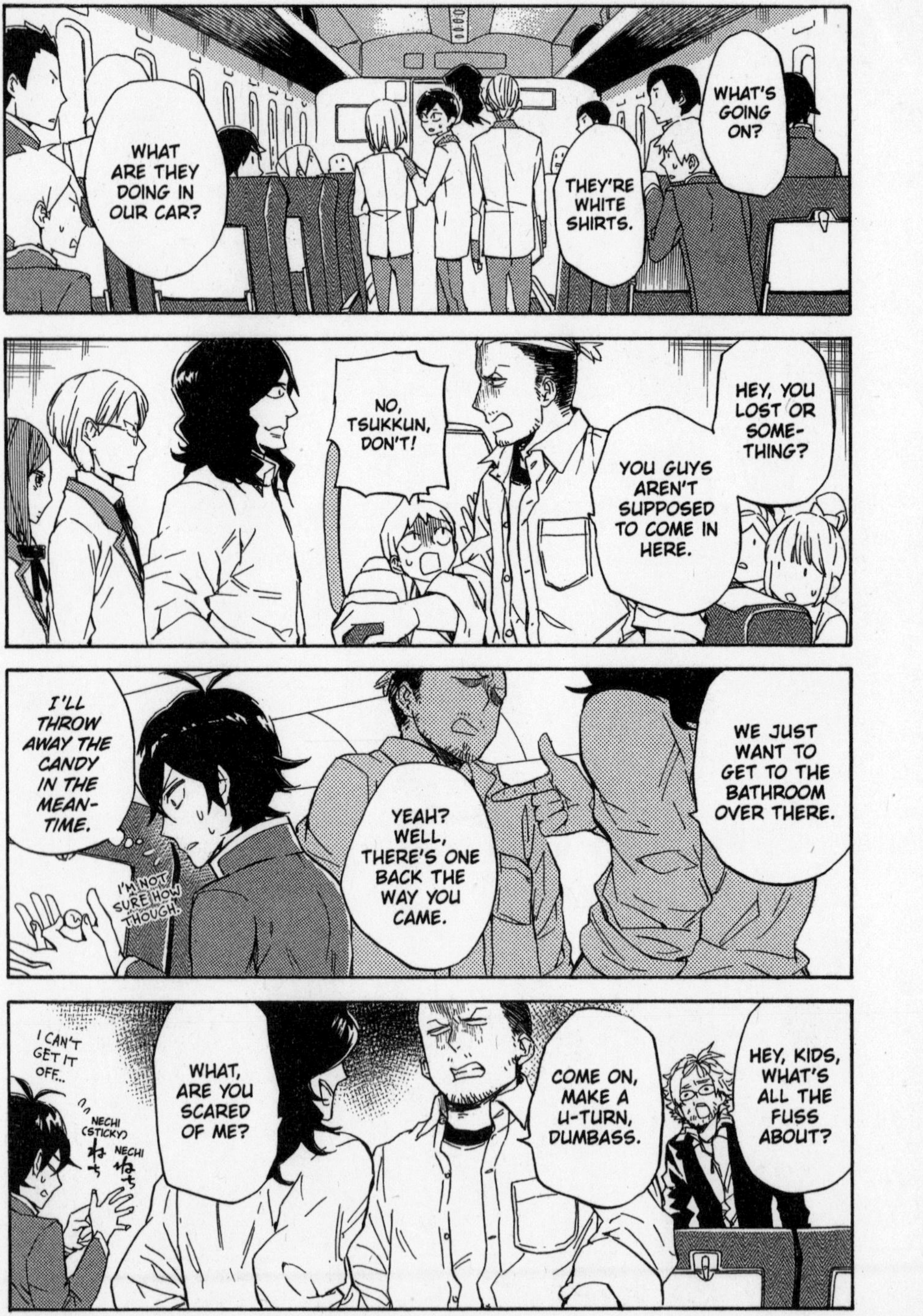
WHAT'S GOING ON?
THEY'RE WHITE SHIRTS.
WHAT ARE THEY DOING IN OUR CAR?
HEY, YOU LOST OR SOME-THING?
YOU GUYS AREN'T SUPPOSED TO COME IN HERE.
NO, TSUKKUN, DON'T!
WE JUST WANT TO GET TO THE BATHROOM OVER THERE.
YEAH? WELL, THERE'S ONE BACK THE WAY YOU CAME.
I'LL THROW AWAY THE CANDY IN THE MEAN-TIME.
I'M NOT SURE HOW THOUGH.
HEY, KIDS, WHAT'S ALL THE FUSS ABOUT?
COME ON, MAKE A U-TURN, DUMBASS.
WHAT, ARE YOU SCARED OF ME?
I CAN'T GET IT OFF...
NECHI (STICKY) ねち
NECHI ねち

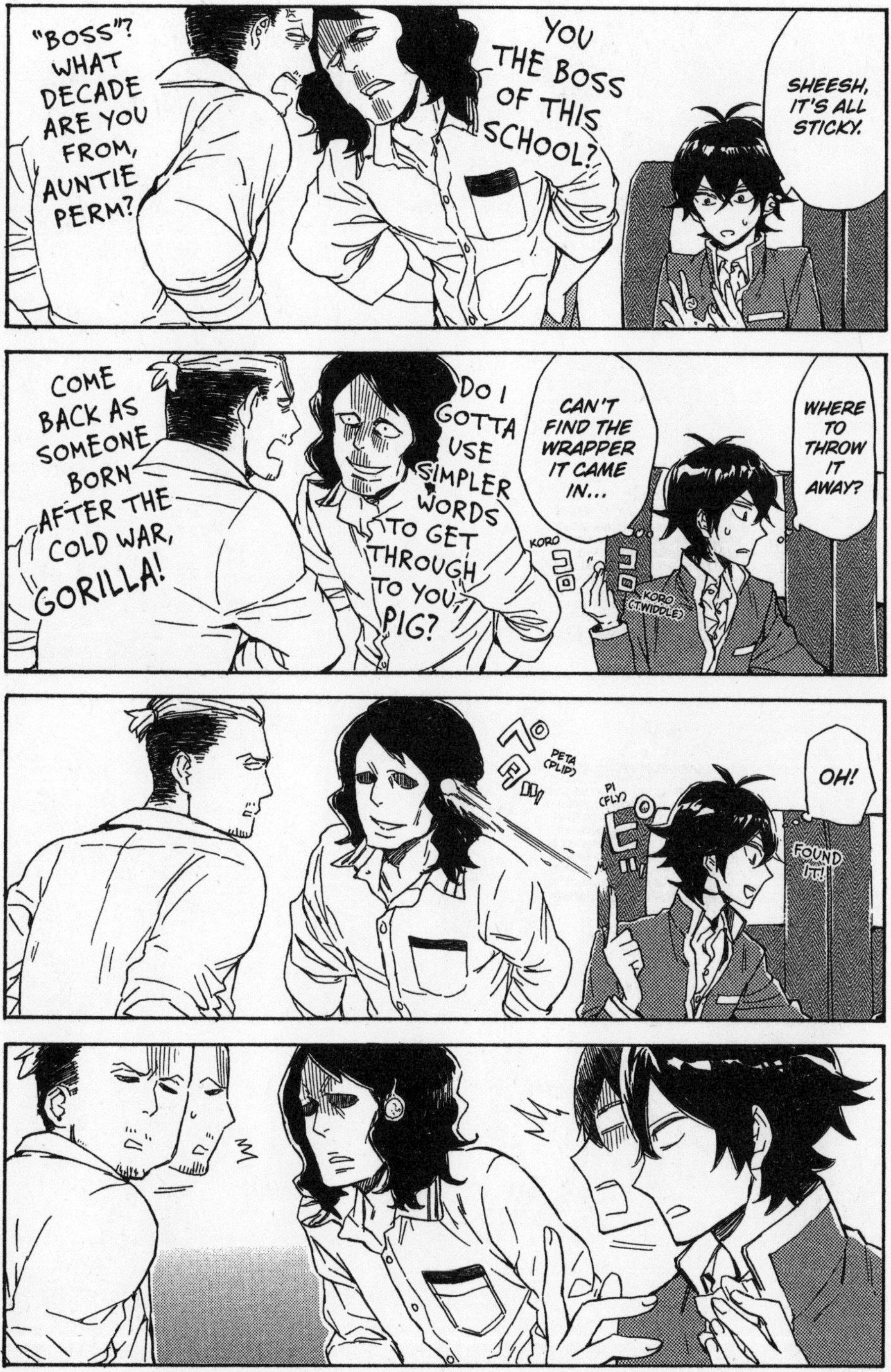
SHEESH, IT'S ALL STICKY.
YOU THE BOSS OF THIS SCHOOL?
"BOSS"? WHAT DECADE ARE YOU FROM, AUNTIE PERM?
WHERE TO THROW IT AWAY?
CAN'T FIND THE WRAPPER IT CAME IN...
KORO KORO (TWIDDLE)
DO I GOTTA USE SIMPLER WORDS TO GET THROUGH TO YOU, PIG?
COME BACK AS SOMEONE BORN AFTER THE COLD WAR, GORILLA!
OH!
FOUND IT!
PI (FLY)
PETA (PLIP)

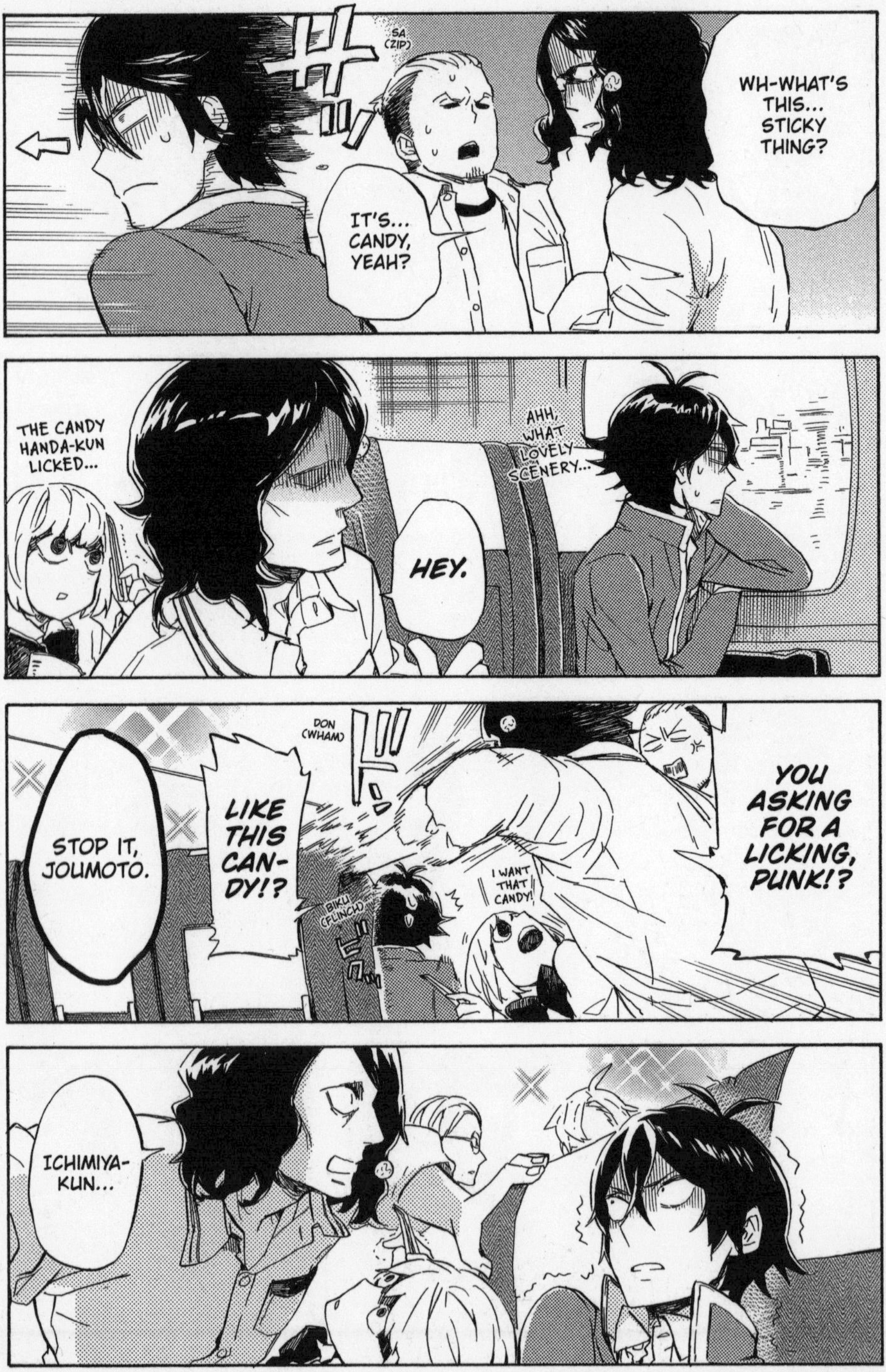
WH-WHAT'S THIS... STICKY THING?
SA (ZIP)
IT'S... CANDY, YEAH?
AHH, WHAT LOVELY SCENERY...
HEY.
THE CANDY HANDA-KUN LICKED...
YOU ASKING FOR A LICKING, PUNK!?
I WANT THAT CANDY!
DON (WHAM)
BIKU (FLINCH)
LIKE THIS CAN-DY!?
STOP IT, JOUMOTO.
ICHIMIYA-KUN...

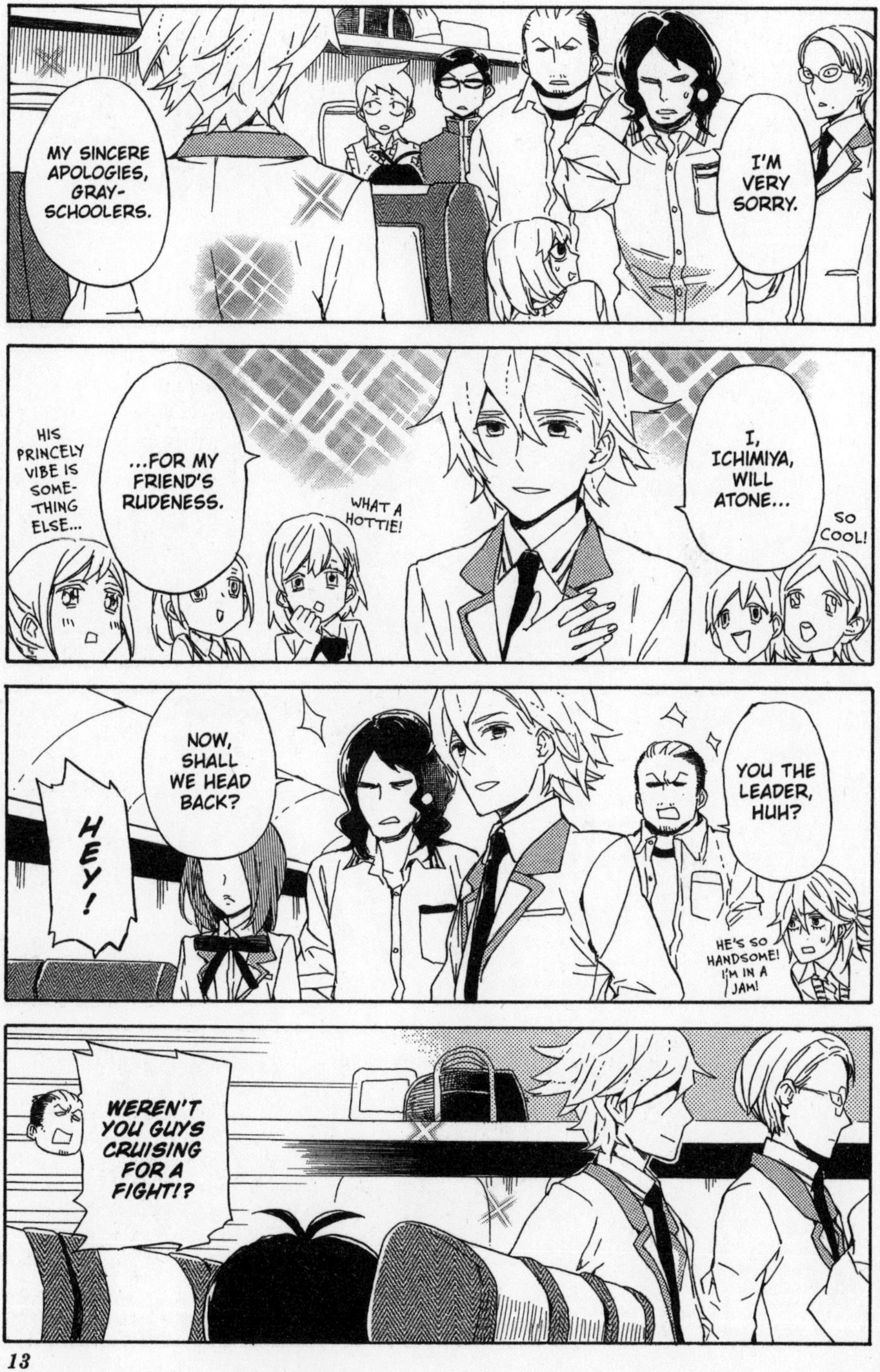

I'M VERY SORRY.
MY SINCERE APOLOGIES, GRAY-SCHOOLERS.
SO COOL!
I, ICHIMIYA, WILL ATONE...
WHAT A HOTTIE!
...FOR MY FRIEND'S RUDENESS.
HIS PRINCELY VIBE IS SOMETHING ELSE...
YOU THE LEADER, HUH?
HE'S SO HANDSOME! I'M IN A JAM!
NOW, SHALL WE HEAD BACK?
HEY!
WEREN'T YOU GUYS CRUISING FOR A FIGHT!?

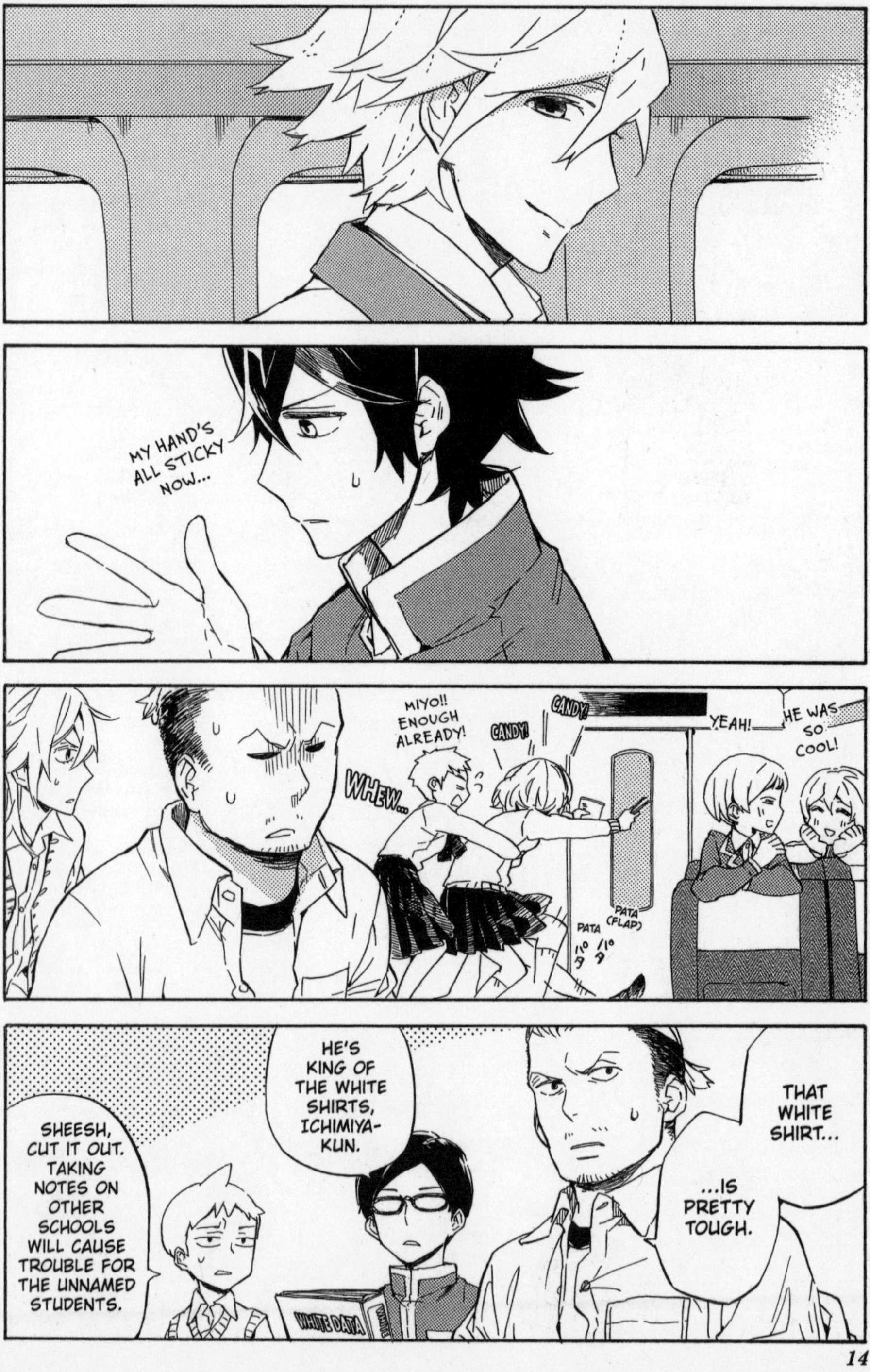
MY HAND'S ALL STICKY NOW...
HE WAS SO COOL!
YEAH!
CANDY!
CANDY!
MIYO!! ENOUGH ALREADY!
WHEW...
PATA (FLAP)
PATA
パタパタ
THAT WHITE SHIRT...
...IS PRETTY TOUGH.
HE'S KING OF THE WHITE SHIRTS, ICHIMIYA-KUN.
SHEESH, CUT IT OUT. TAKING NOTES ON OTHER SCHOOLS WILL CAUSE TROUBLE FOR THE UNNAMED STUDENTS.
WHITE DATA

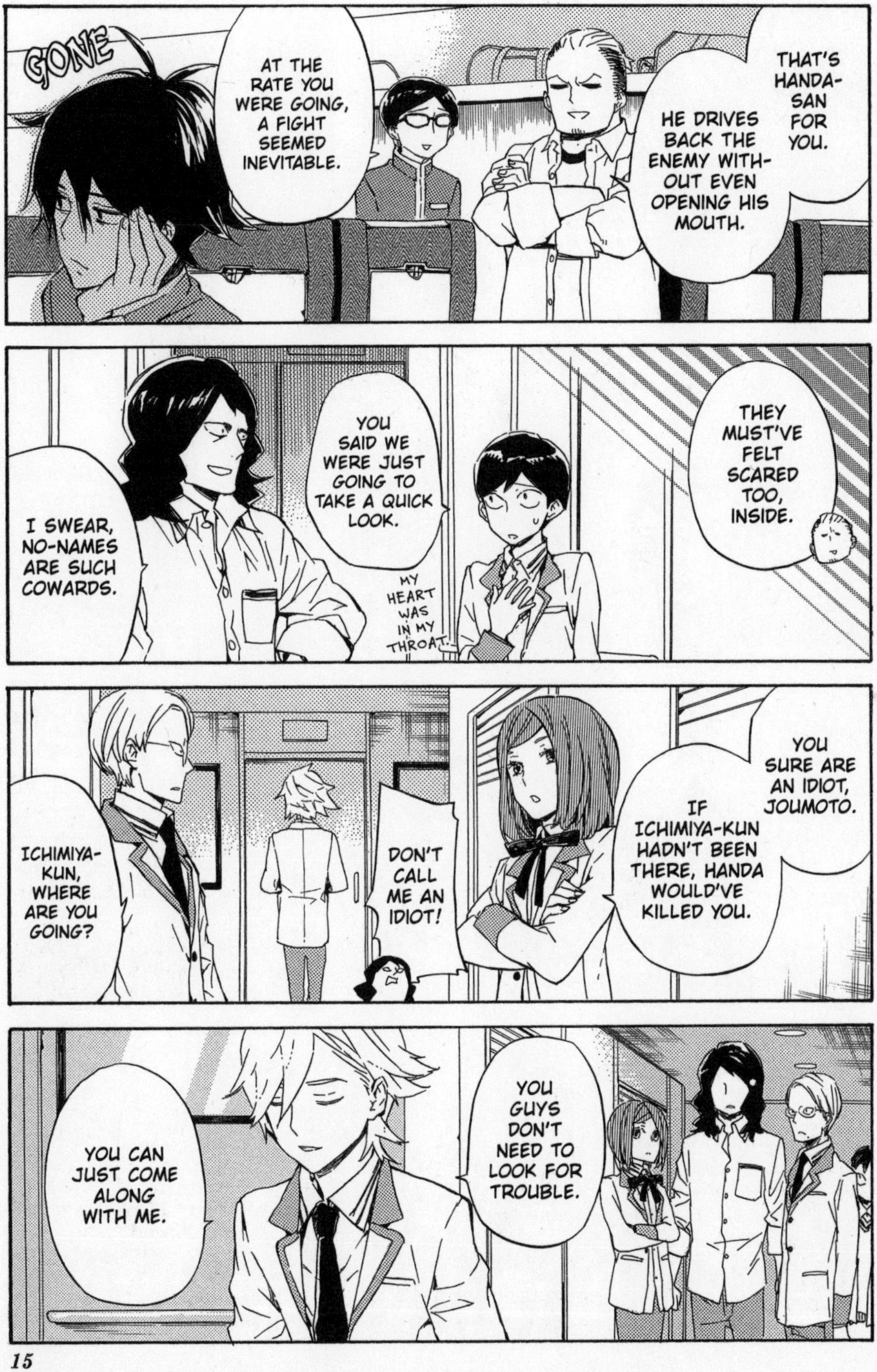
THAT'S HANDA-SAN FOR YOU.
HE DRIVES BACK THE ENEMY WITHOUT EVEN OPENING HIS MOUTH.
AT THE RATE YOU WERE GOING, A FIGHT SEEMED INEVITABLE.
GONE
THEY MUST'VE FELT SCARED TOO, INSIDE.
YOU SAID WE WERE JUST GOING TO TAKE A QUICK LOOK.
MY HEART WAS IN MY THROAT.
I SWEAR, NO-NAMES ARE SUCH COWARDS.
YOU SURE ARE AN IDIOT, JOUMOTO.
IF ICHIMIYA-KUN HADN'T BEEN THERE, HANDA WOULD'VE KILLED YOU.
DON'T CALL ME AN IDIOT!
ICHIMIYA-KUN, WHERE ARE YOU GOING?
YOU GUYS DON'T NEED TO LOOK FOR TROUBLE.
YOU CAN JUST COME ALONG WITH ME.

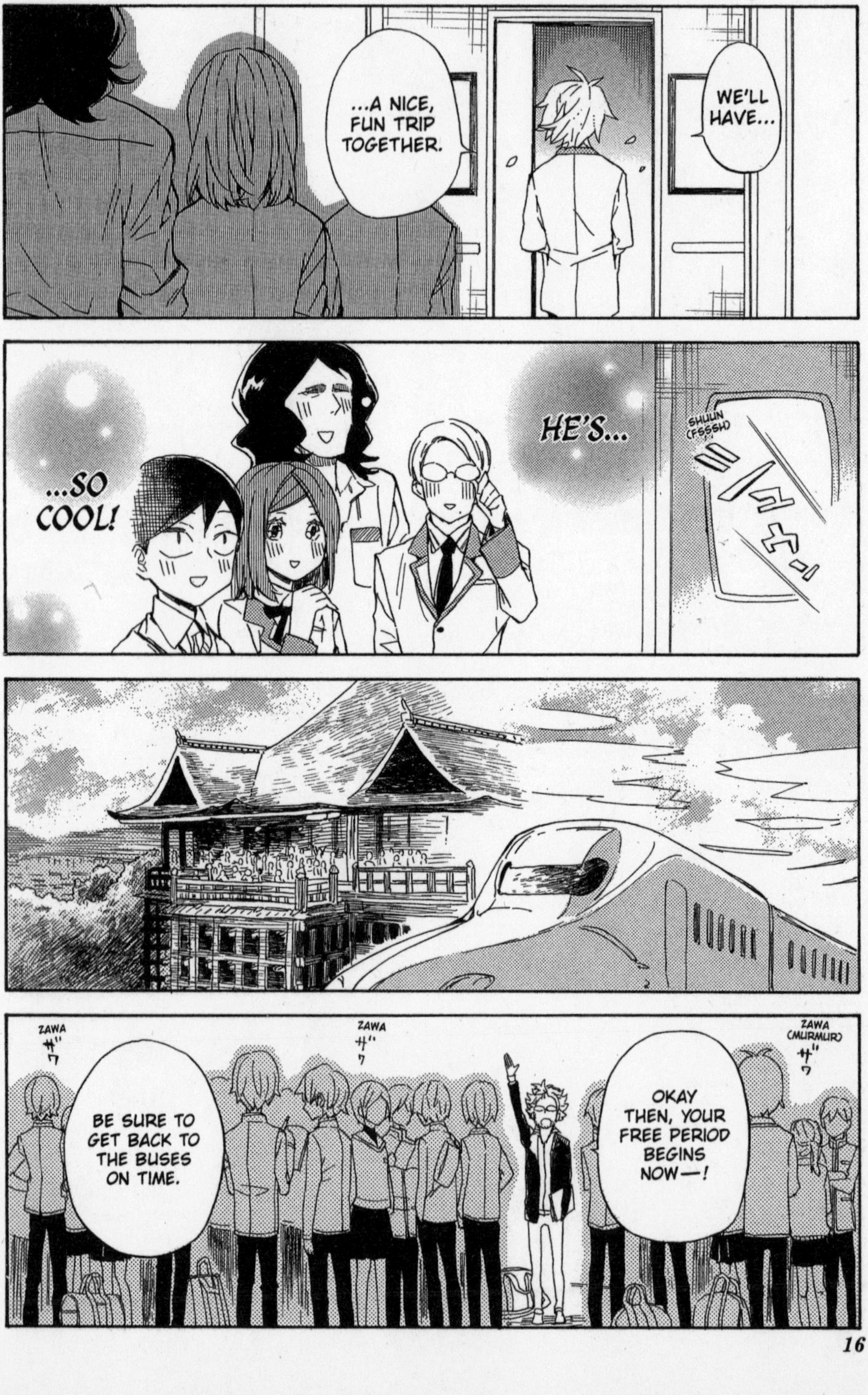
WE'LL HAVE...
...A NICE, FUN TRIP TOGETHER.
SHUUN (FSSSH)
HE'S...
...SO COOL!
ZAWA (MURMUR)
OKAY THEN, YOUR FREE PERIOD BEGINS NOW—!
ZAWA
BE SURE TO GET BACK TO THE BUSES ON TIME.
ZAWA

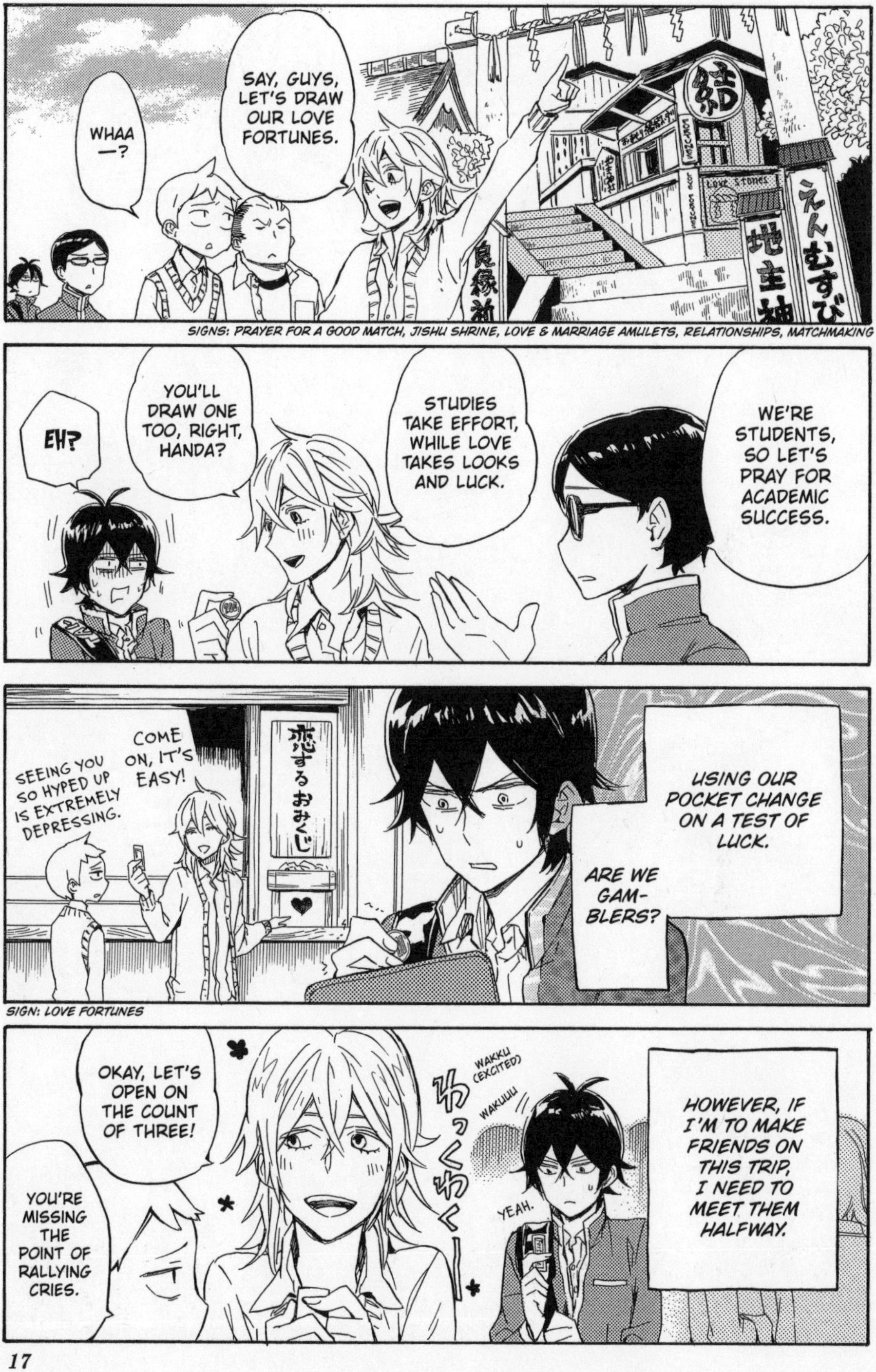
SAY, GUYS, LET'S DRAW OUR LOVE FORTUNES.
WHAA—?
えんむすび
地主神
SIGNS: PRAYER FOR A GOOD MATCH, JISHU SHRINE, LOVE & MARRIAGE AMULETS, RELATIONSHIPS, MATCHMAKING
WE'RE STUDENTS, SO LET'S PRAY FOR ACADEMIC SUCCESS.
STUDIES TAKE EFFORT, WHILE LOVE TAKES LOOKS AND LUCK.
YOU'LL DRAW ONE TOO, RIGHT, HANDA?
EH?
USING OUR POCKET CHANGE ON A TEST OF LUCK.
ARE WE GAMBLERS?
恋するおみくじ
COME ON, IT'S EASY!
SEEING YOU SO HYPED UP IS EXTREMELY DEPRESSING.
SIGN: LOVE FORTUNES
HOWEVER, IF I'M TO MAKE FRIENDS ON THIS TRIP, I NEED TO MEET THEM HALFWAY.
WAKKU (EXCITED)
WAKUUU
YEAH.
わっくわくー
OKAY, LET'S OPEN ON THE COUNT OF THREE!
YOU'RE MISSING THE POINT OF RALLYING CRIES.

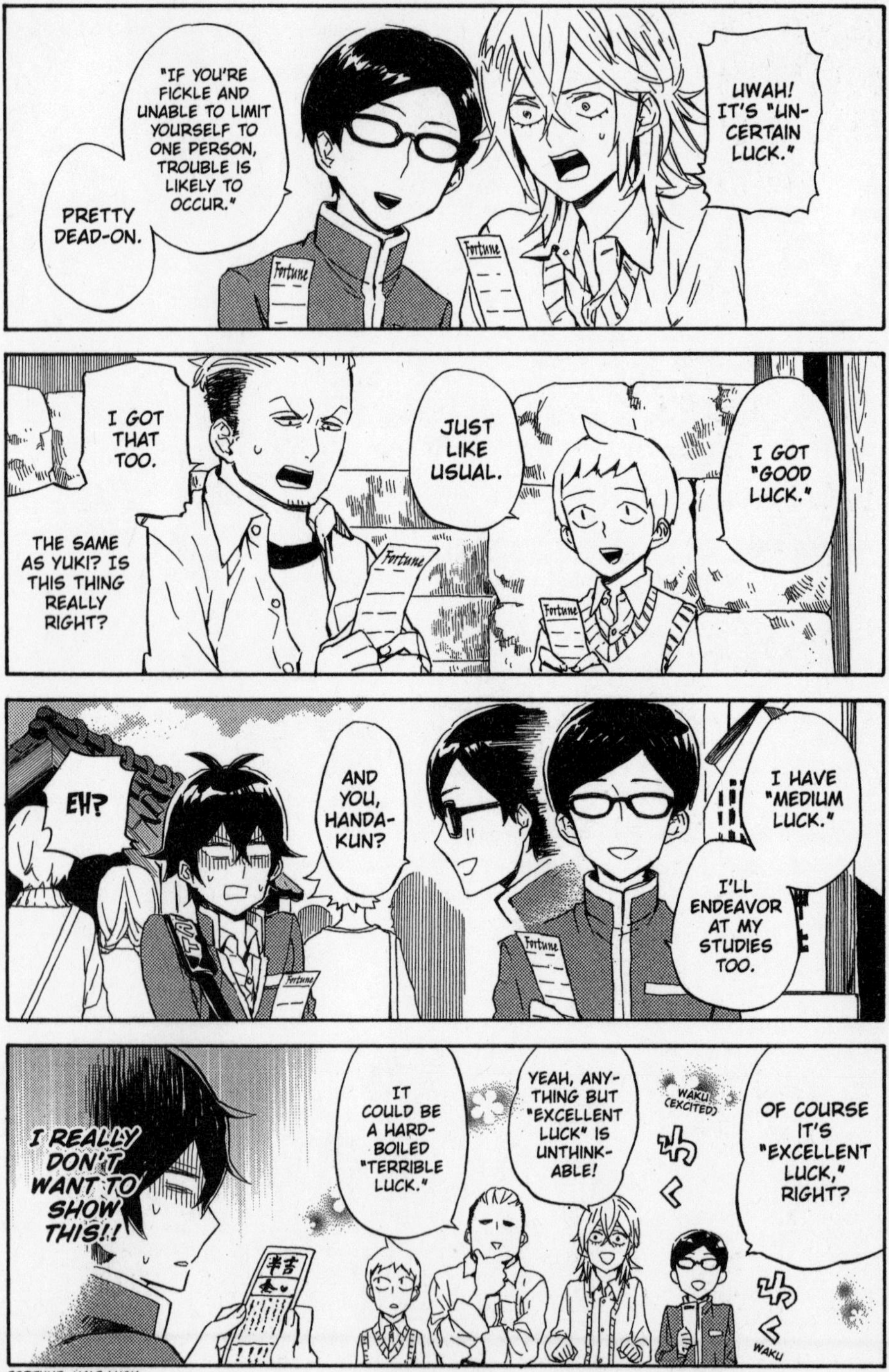
UWAH! IT'S "UN-CERTAIN LUCK."
"IF YOU'RE FICKLE AND UNABLE TO LIMIT YOURSELF TO ONE PERSON, TROUBLE IS LIKELY TO OCCUR."
PRETTY DEAD-ON.
Fortune
I GOT "GOOD LUCK."
JUST LIKE USUAL.
I GOT THAT TOO.
THE SAME AS YUKI? IS THIS THING REALLY RIGHT?
Fortune
I HAVE "MEDIUM LUCK."
I'LL ENDEAVOR AT MY STUDIES TOO.
AND YOU, HANDA-KUN?
EH?
Fortune
OF COURSE IT'S "EXCELLENT LUCK," RIGHT?
WAKU (EXCITED)
YEAH, ANY-THING BUT "EXCELLENT LUCK" IS UNTHINK-ABLE!
IT COULD BE A HARD-BOILED "TERRIBLE LUCK."
I REALLY DON'T WANT TO SHOW THIS!!
WAKU

FORTUNE: HALF LUCK

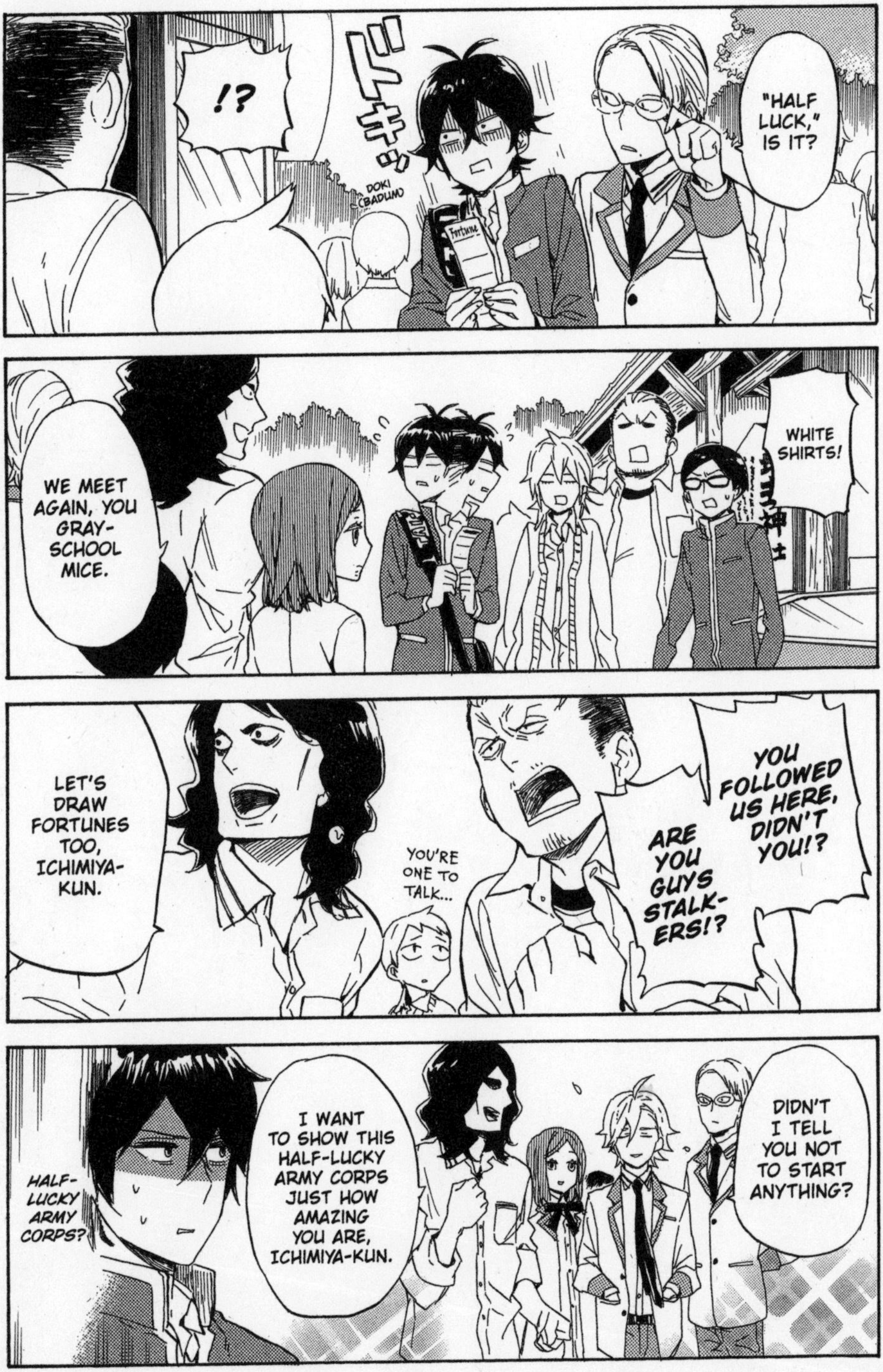
"HALF LUCK," IS IT?
ドキッ
DOKI (BADUM)
Fortune
!?
WHITE SHIRTS!
WE MEET AGAIN, YOU GRAY-SCHOOL MICE.
YOU FOLLOWED US HERE, DIDN'T YOU!?
ARE YOU GUYS STALKERS!?
YOU'RE ONE TO TALK...
LET'S DRAW FORTUNES TOO, ICHIMIYA-KUN.
DIDN'T I TELL YOU NOT TO START ANYTHING?
I WANT TO SHOW THIS HALF-LUCKY ARMY CORPS JUST HOW AMAZING YOU ARE, ICHIMIYA-KUN.
HALF-LUCKY ARMY CORPS?

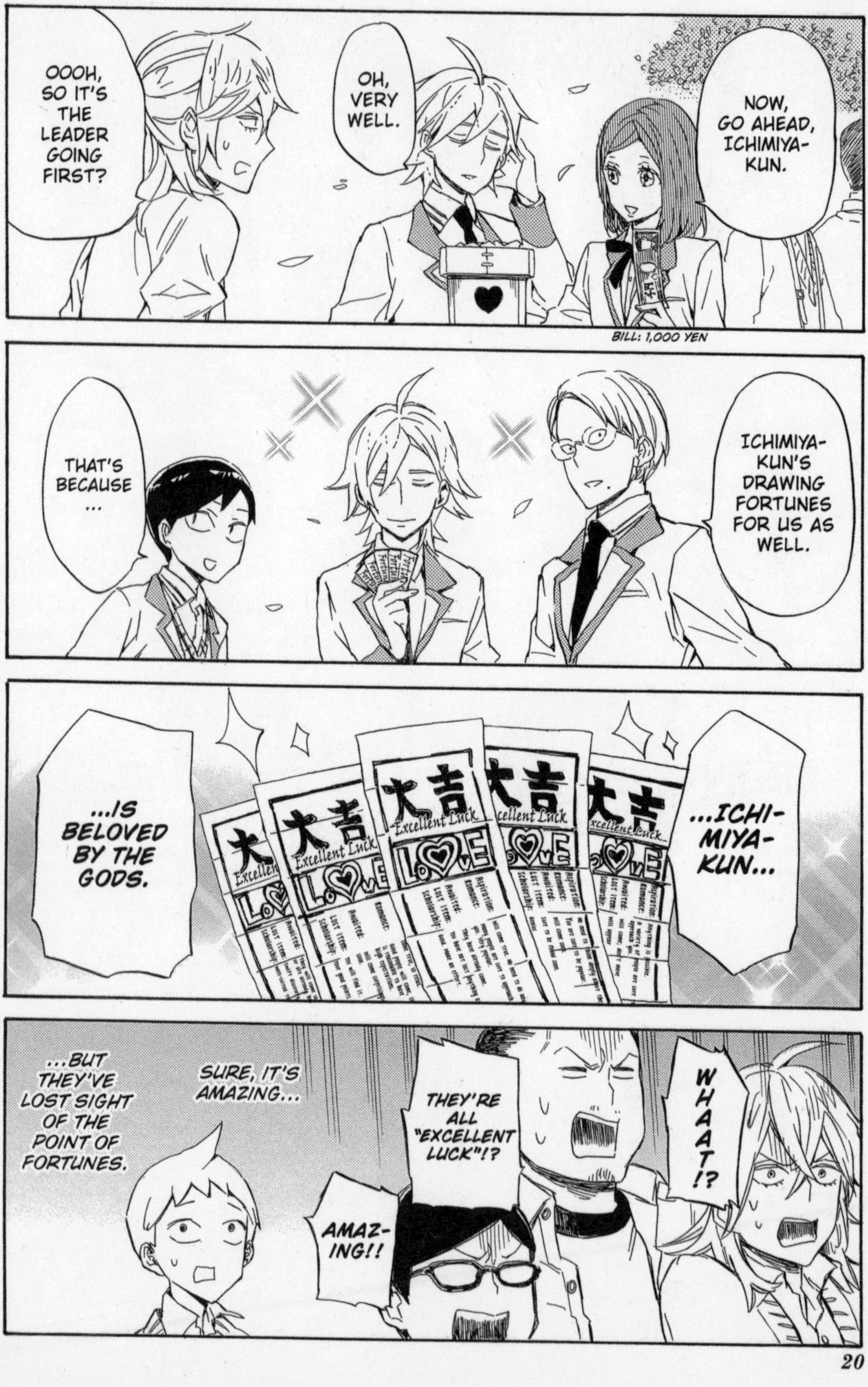
NOW, GO AHEAD, ICHIMIYA-KUN.
OH, VERY WELL.
OOOH, SO IT'S THE LEADER GOING FIRST?
BILL: 1,000 YEN
ICHIMIYA-KUN'S DRAWING FORTUNES FOR US AS WELL.
THAT'S BECAUSE...
...ICHI-MIYA-KUN...
...IS BELOVED BY THE GODS.
大吉
Excellent Luck
WHAAAT!?
THEY'RE ALL "EXCELLENT LUCK"!?
AMAZ-ING!!
SURE, IT'S AMAZING...
...BUT THEY'VE LOST SIGHT OF THE POINT OF FORTUNES.

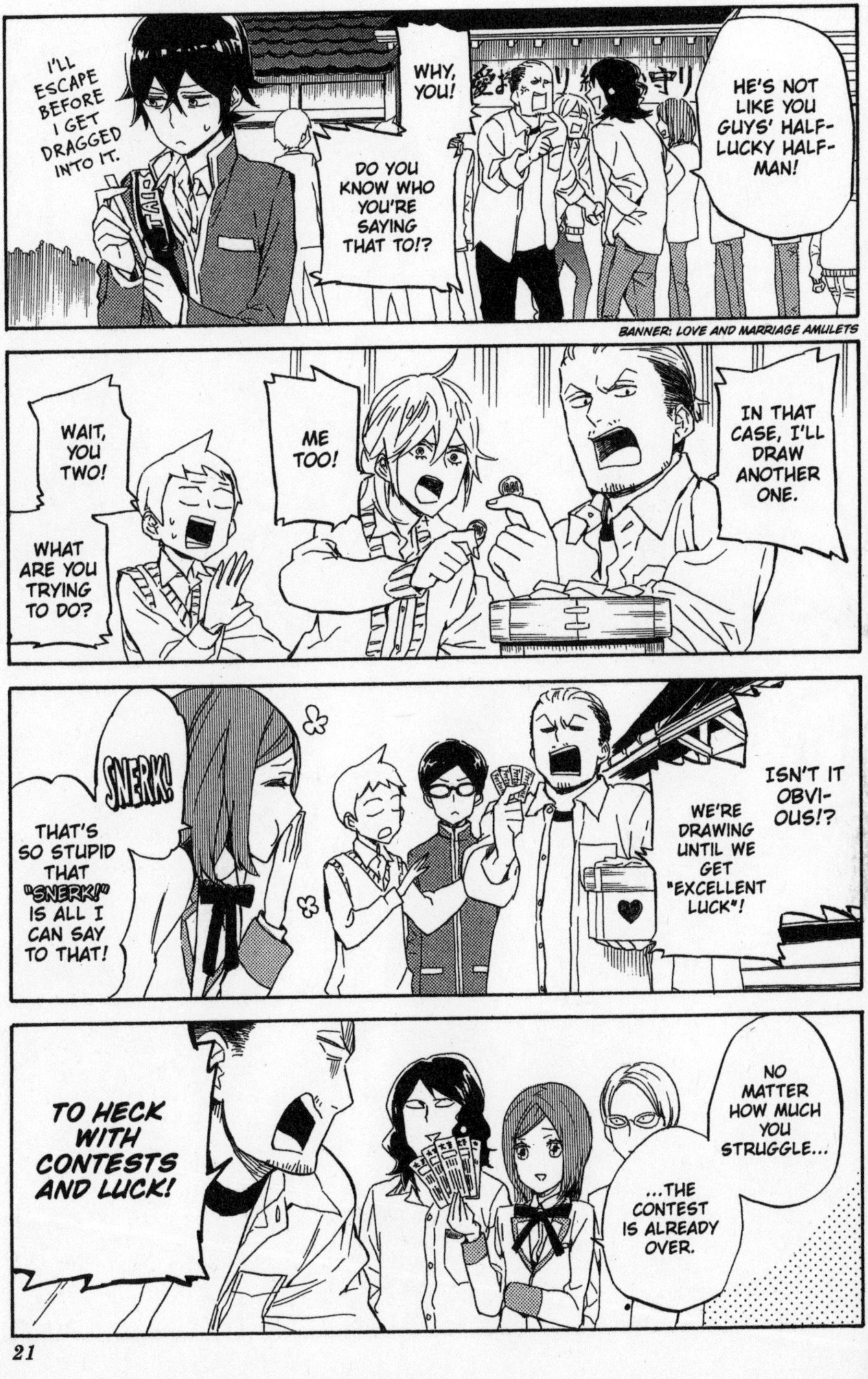
HE'S NOT LIKE YOU GUYS' HALF-LUCKY HALF-MAN!
WHY, YOU!
DO YOU KNOW WHO YOU'RE SAYING THAT TO!?
I'LL ESCAPE BEFORE I GET DRAGGED INTO IT.
BANNER: LOVE AND MARRIAGE AMULETS
IN THAT CASE, I'LL DRAW ANOTHER ONE.
ME TOO!
WAIT, YOU TWO!
WHAT ARE YOU TRYING TO DO?
ISN'T IT OBVIOUS!?
WE'RE DRAWING UNTIL WE GET "EXCELLENT LUCK"!
SNERK!
THAT'S SO STUPID THAT "SNERK!" IS ALL I CAN SAY TO THAT!
NO MATTER HOW MUCH YOU STRUGGLE...
...THE CONTEST IS ALREADY OVER.
TO HECK WITH CONTESTS AND LUCK!

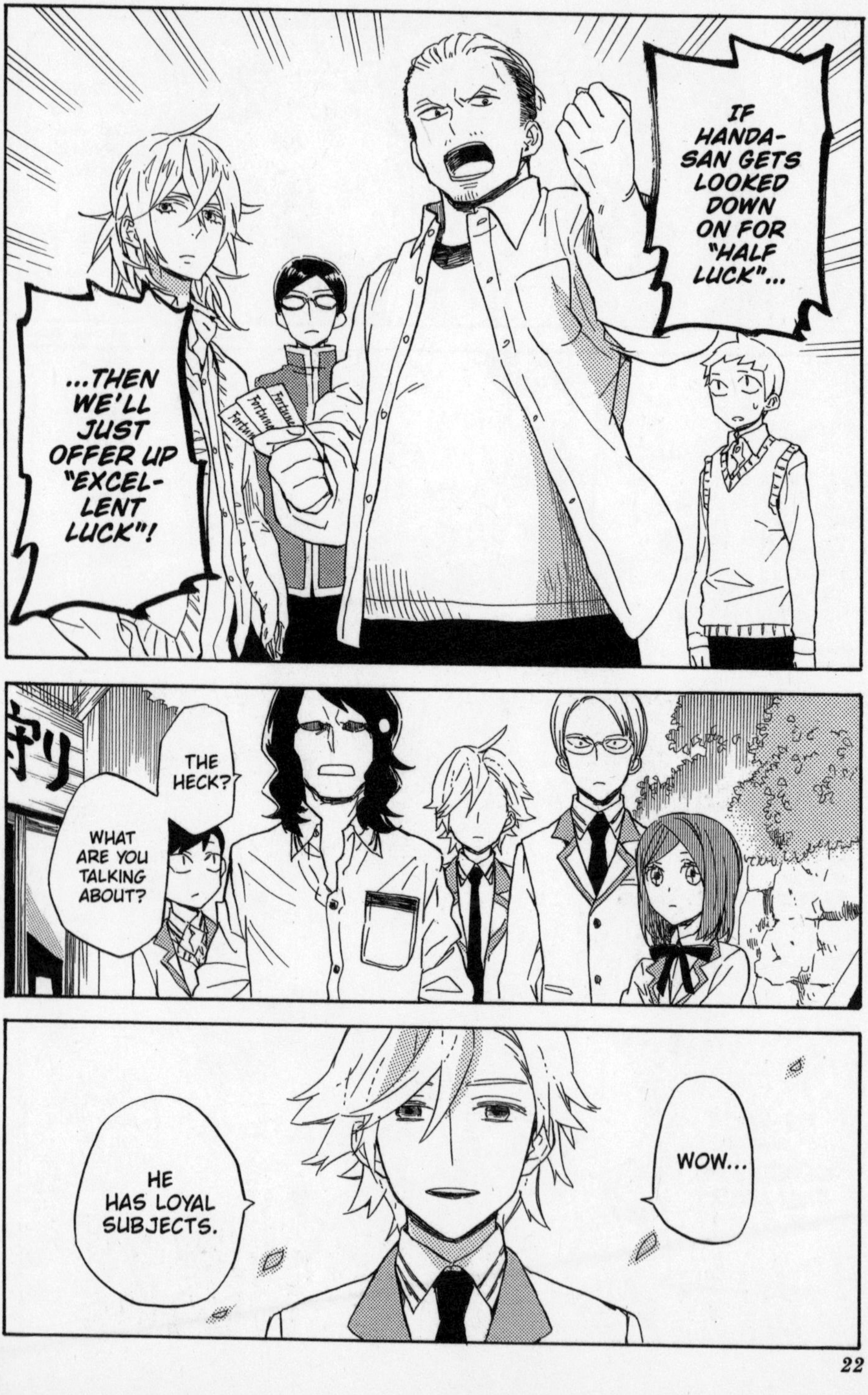
IF HANDA-SAN GETS LOOKED DOWN ON FOR "HALF LUCK"...
...THEN WE'LL JUST OFFER UP "EXCEL-LENT LUCK"!
THE HECK?
WHAT ARE YOU TALKING ABOUT?
WOW...
HE HAS LOYAL SUBJECTS.

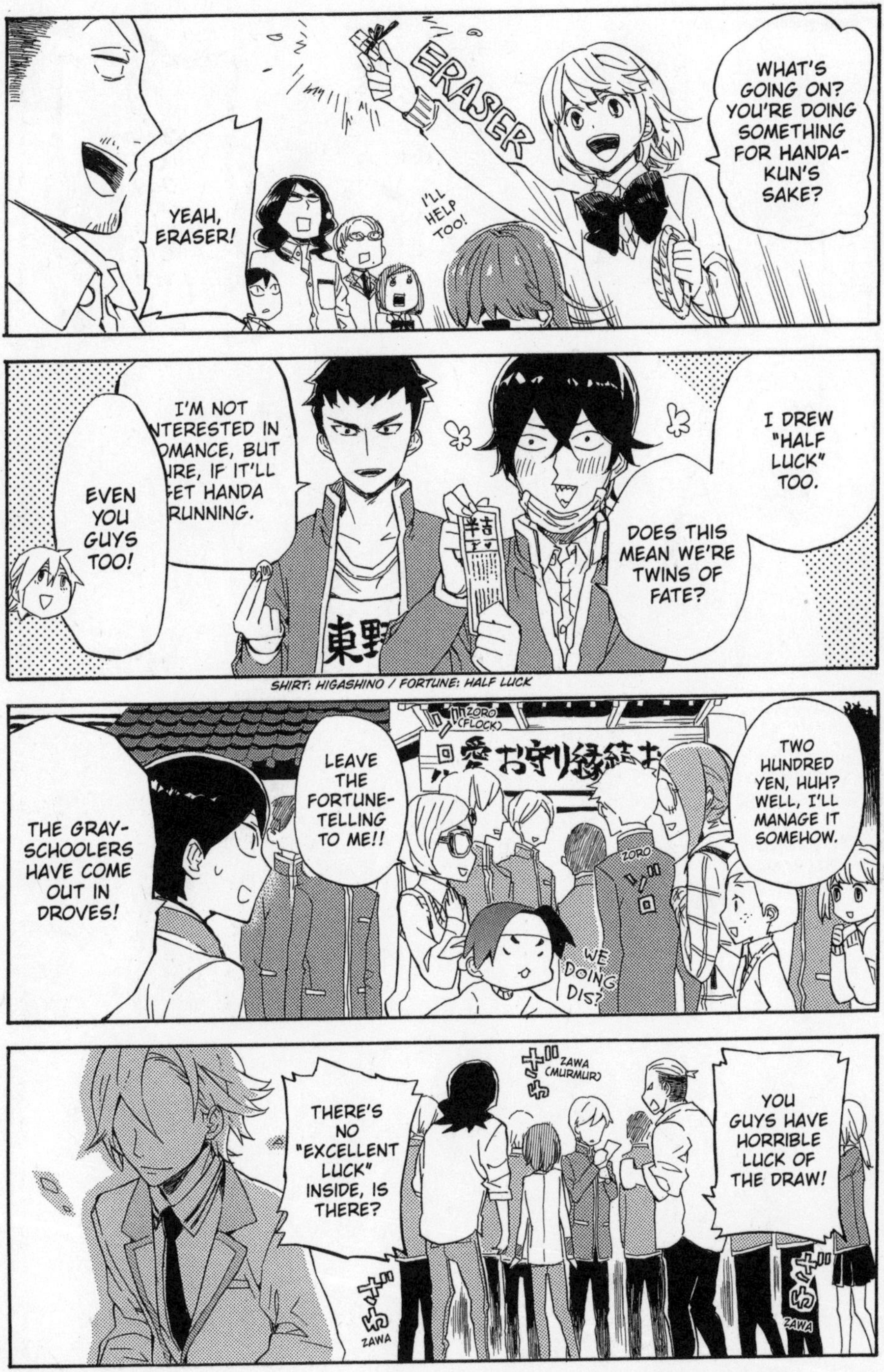
WHAT'S GOING ON? YOU'RE DOING SOMETHING FOR HANDA-KUN'S SAKE?
ERASER
I'LL HELP TOO!
YEAH, ERASER!
I DREW "HALF LUCK" TOO.
DOES THIS MEAN WE'RE TWINS OF FATE?
I'M NOT INTERESTED IN ROMANCE, BUT SURE, IF IT'LL GET HANDA RUNNING.
EVEN YOU GUYS TOO!
SHIRT: HIGASHINO / FORTUNE: HALF LUCK
TWO HUNDRED YEN, HUH? WELL, I'LL MANAGE IT SOMEHOW.
ZORO (FLOCK)
ZORO
WE DOING DIS?
LEAVE THE FORTUNE-TELLING TO ME!!
THE GRAY-SCHOOLERS HAVE COME OUT IN DROVES!
YOU GUYS HAVE HORRIBLE LUCK OF THE DRAW!
ZAWA (MURMUR)
ZAWA
THERE'S NO "EXCELLENT LUCK" INSIDE, IS THERE?
ZAWA

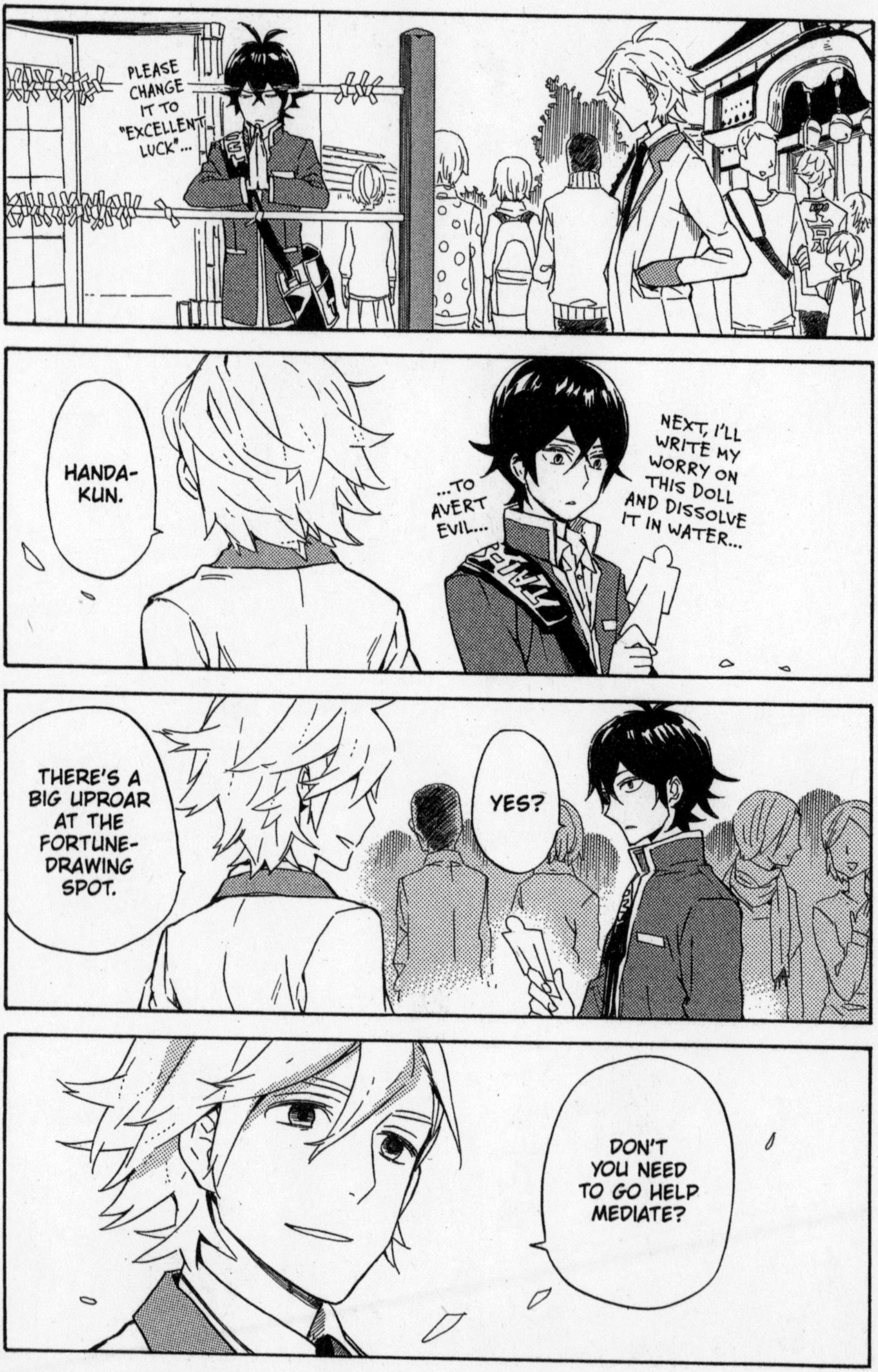
PLEASE CHANGE IT TO "EXCELLENT LUCK"...
NEXT, I'LL WRITE MY WORRY ON THIS DOLL AND DISSOLVE IT IN WATER...
...TO AVERT EVIL...
HANDA-KUN.
YES?
THERE'S A BIG UPROAR AT THE FORTUNE-DRAWING SPOT.
DON'T YOU NEED TO GO HELP MEDIATE?

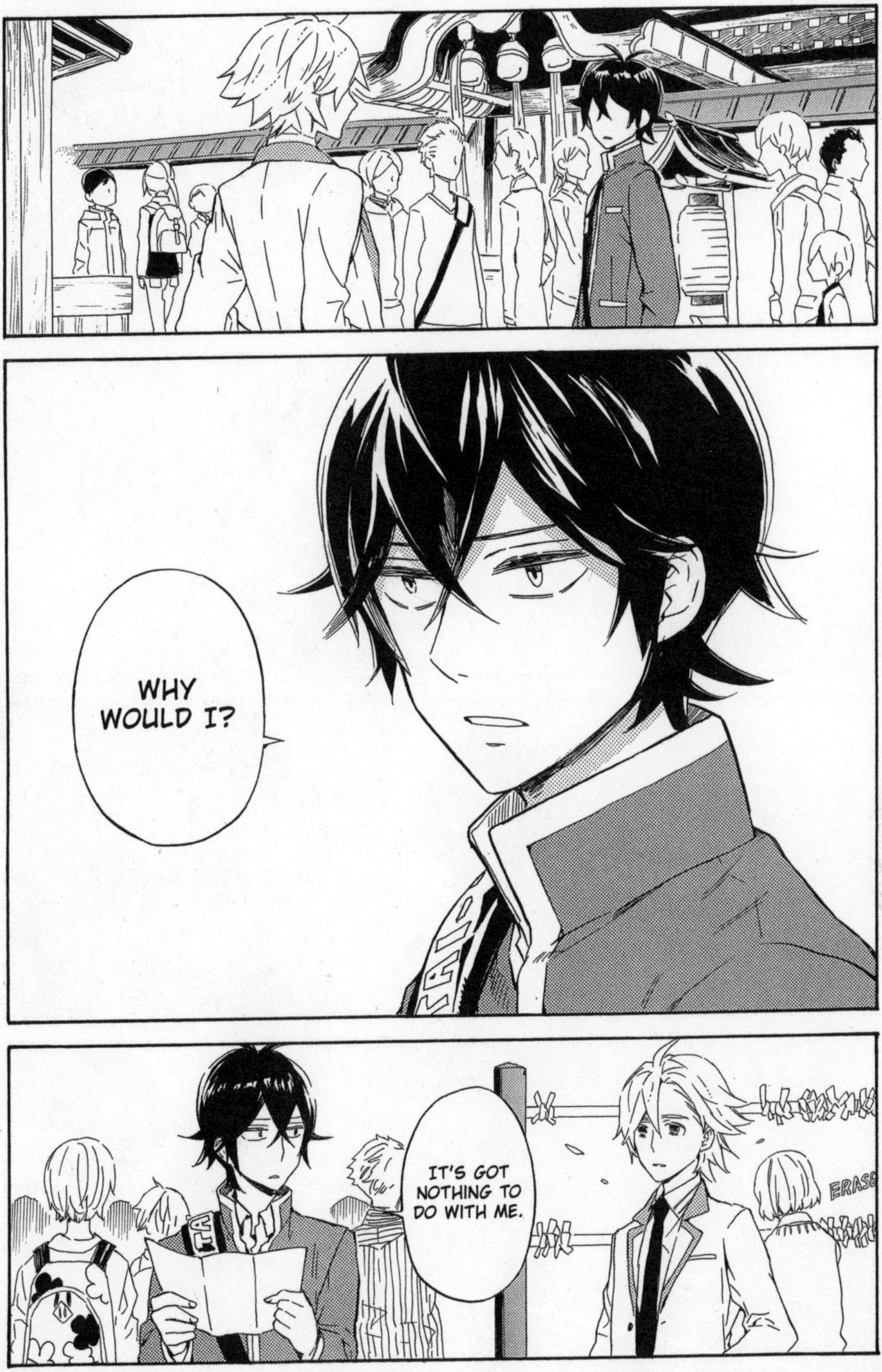
WHY WOULD I?
IT'S GOT NOTHING TO DO WITH ME.
ERASE

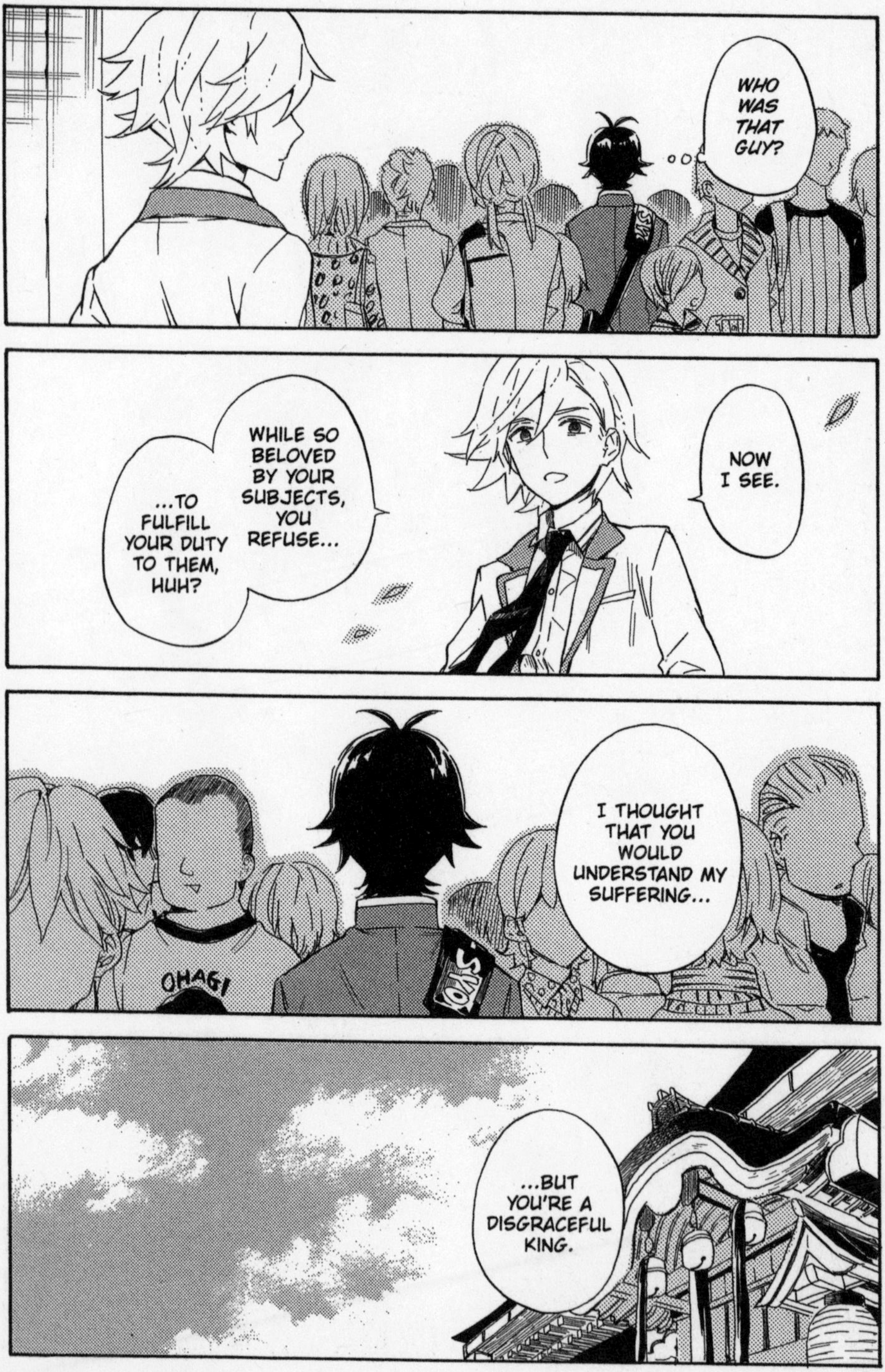
WHO WAS THAT GUY?
NOW I SEE.
WHILE SO BELOVED BY YOUR SUBJECTS, YOU REFUSE...
...TO FULFILL YOUR DUTY TO THEM, HUH?
I THOUGHT THAT YOU WOULD UNDERSTAND MY SUFFERING...
OHAGI
...BUT YOU'RE A DISGRACEFUL KING.

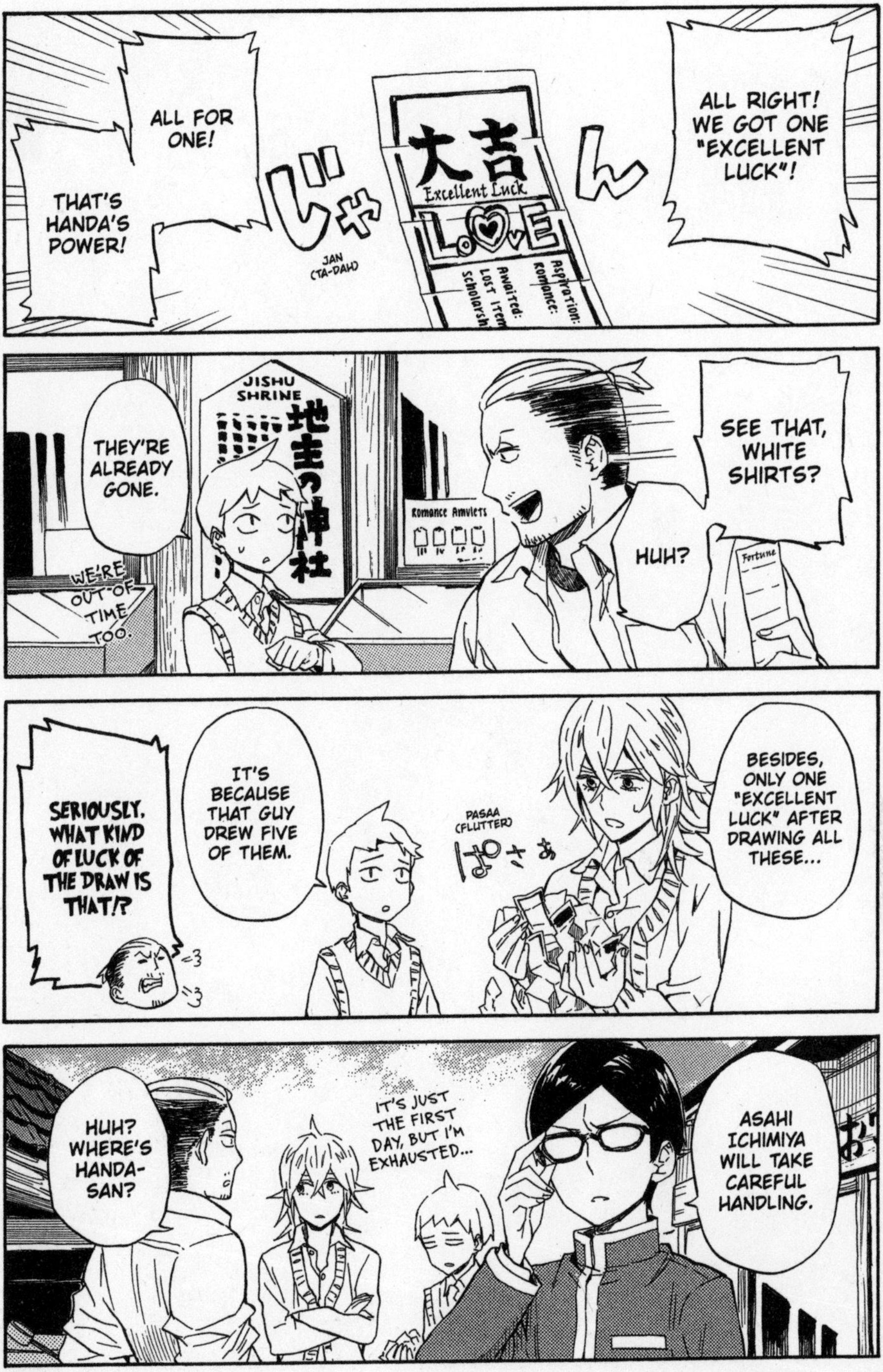
ALL RIGHT! WE GOT ONE "EXCELLENT LUCK"!
大吉
Excellent Luck
LOVE
Aspiration:
Romance:
Awaited:
じゃん
JAN (TA-DAH)
ALL FOR ONE!
THAT'S HANDA'S POWER!
SEE THAT, WHITE SHIRTS?
HUH?
Fortune
Romance Amulets
JISHU SHRINE
地主の神社
THEY'RE ALREADY GONE.
WE'RE OUT OF TIME TOO.
BESIDES, ONLY ONE "EXCELLENT LUCK" AFTER DRAWING ALL THESE...
ぱさぁ
PASAA (FLUTTER)
IT'S BECAUSE THAT GUY DREW FIVE OF THEM.
SERIOUSLY. WHAT KIND OF LUCK OF THE DRAW IS THAT!?
ASAHI ICHIMIYA WILL TAKE CAREFUL HANDLING.
IT'S JUST THE FIRST DAY, BUT I'M EXHAUSTED...
HUH? WHERE'S HANDA-SAN?

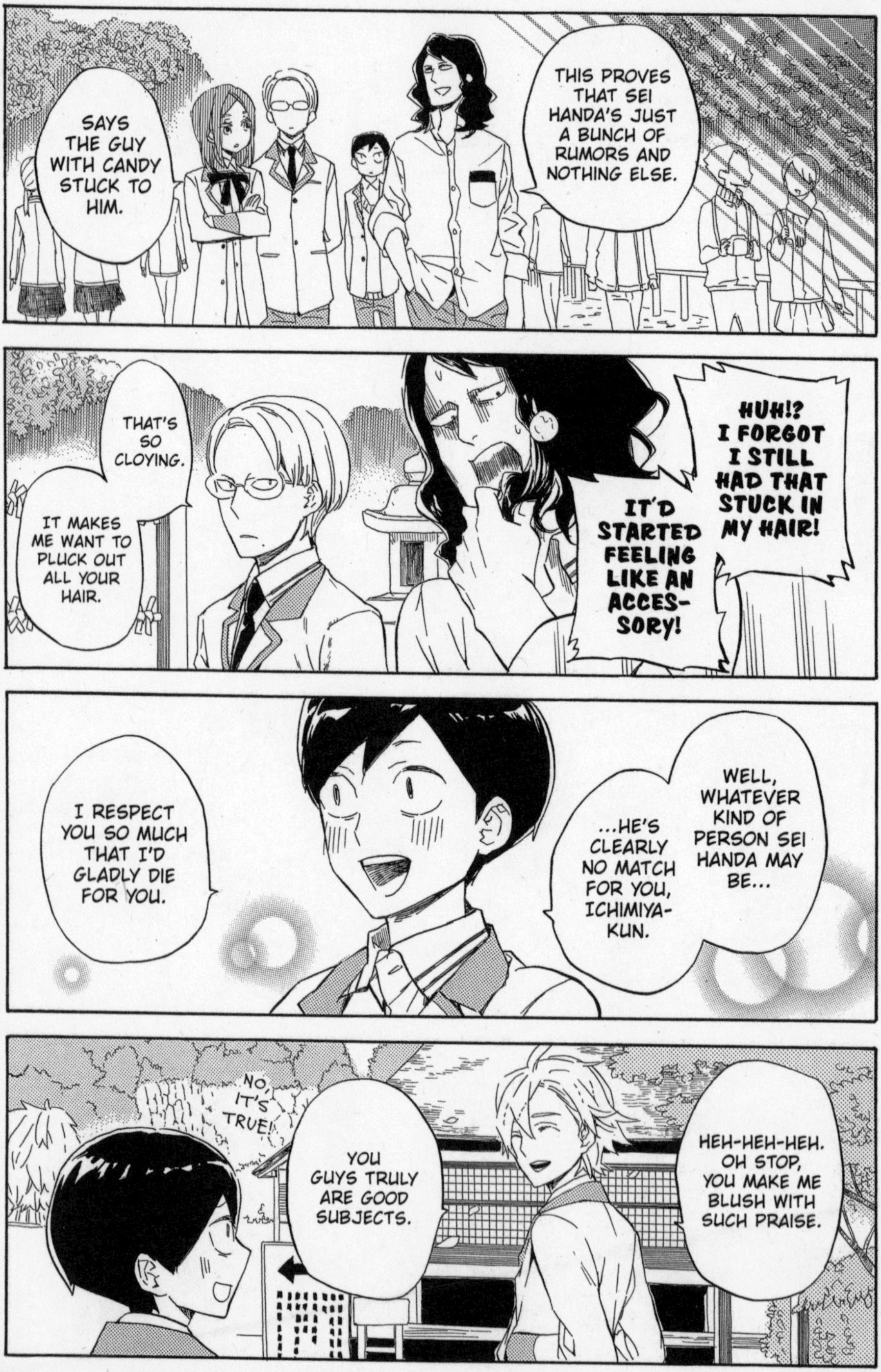
THIS PROVES THAT SEI HANDA'S JUST A BUNCH OF RUMORS AND NOTHING ELSE.
SAYS THE GUY WITH CANDY STUCK TO HIM.
HUH!? I FORGOT I STILL HAD THAT STUCK IN MY HAIR!
IT'D STARTED FEELING LIKE AN ACCES-SORY!
THAT'S SO CLOYING.
IT MAKES ME WANT TO PLUCK OUT ALL YOUR HAIR.
WELL, WHATEVER KIND OF PERSON SEI HANDA MAY BE...
...HE'S CLEARLY NO MATCH FOR YOU, ICHIMIYA-KUN.
I RESPECT YOU SO MUCH THAT I'D GLADLY DIE FOR YOU.
HEH-HEH-HEH. OH STOP, YOU MAKE ME BLUSH WITH SUCH PRAISE.
YOU GUYS TRULY ARE GOOD SUBJECTS.
NO, IT'S TRUE!

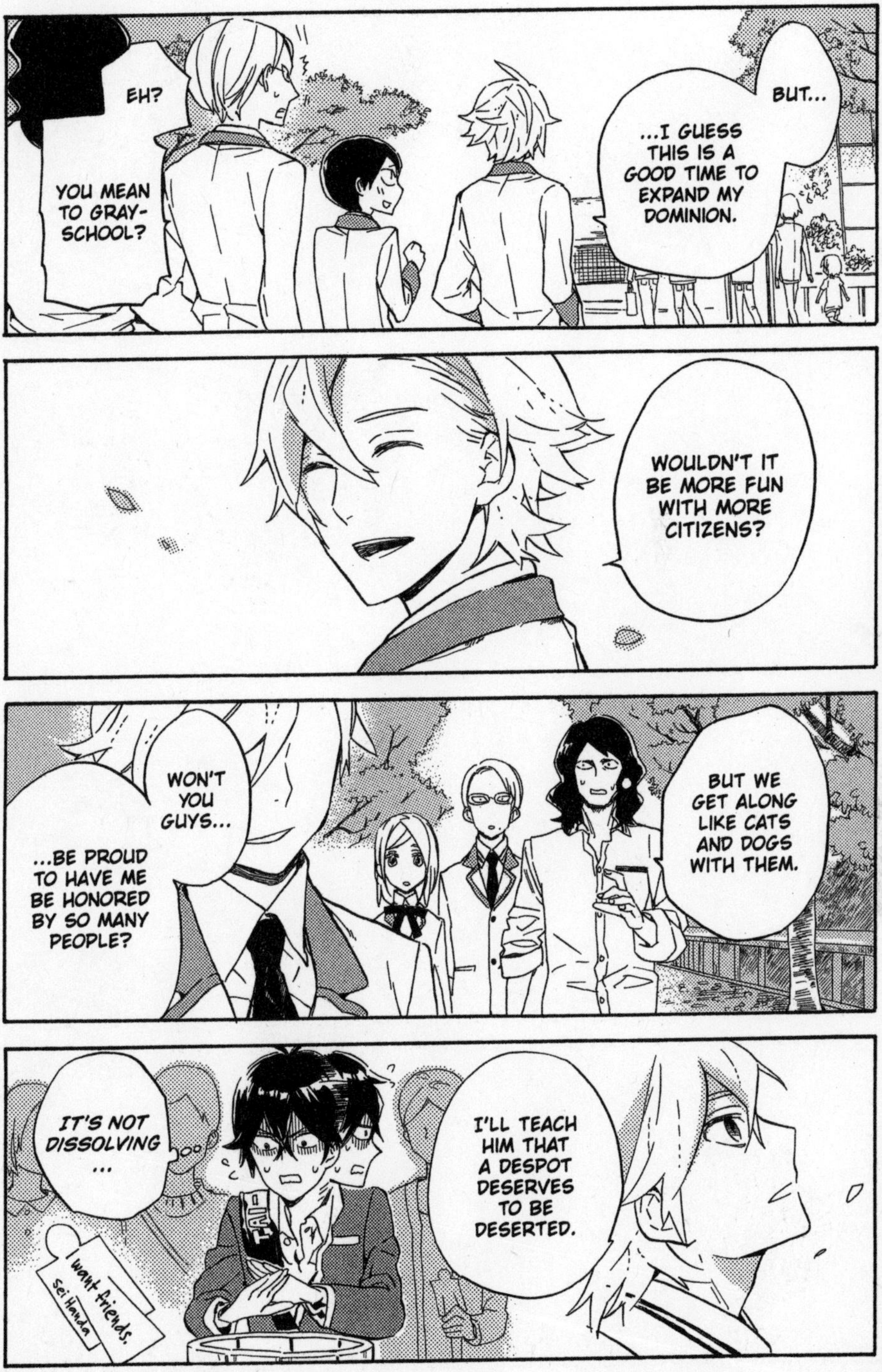
BUT...
...I GUESS THIS IS A GOOD TIME TO EXPAND MY DOMINION.
EH?
YOU MEAN TO GRAY-SCHOOL?
WOULDN'T IT BE MORE FUN WITH MORE CITIZENS?
BUT WE GET ALONG LIKE CATS AND DOGS WITH THEM.
WON'T YOU GUYS...
...BE PROUD TO HAVE ME BE HONORED BY SO MANY PEOPLE?
I'LL TEACH HIM THAT A DESPOT DESERVES TO BE DESERTED.
IT'S NOT DISSOLVING ...
I want friends.
Sei Handa

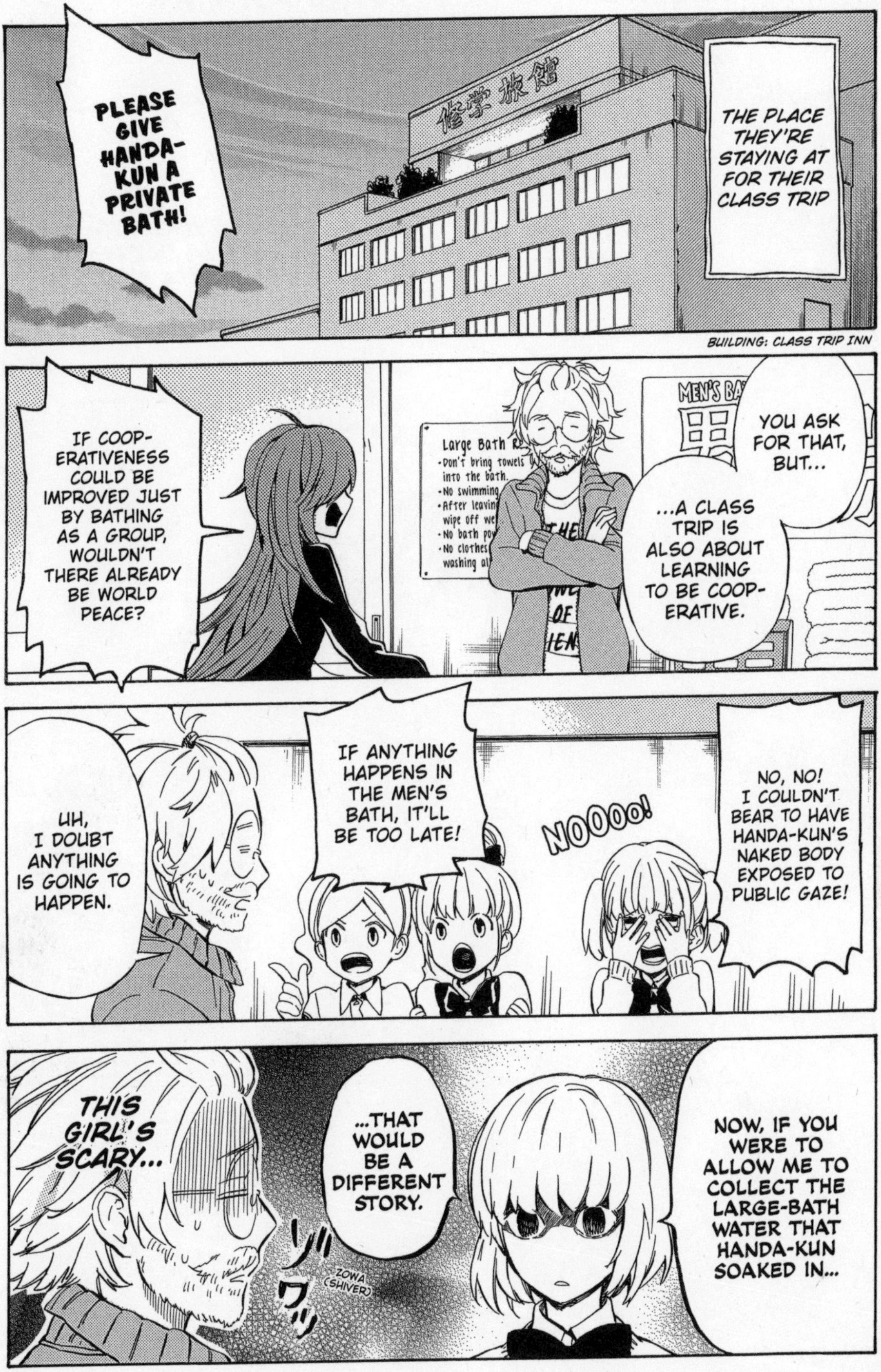
THE PLACE THEY'RE STAYING AT FOR THEIR CLASS TRIP
PLEASE GIVE HANDA-KUN A PRIVATE BATH!
修学旅館
BUILDING: CLASS TRIP INN
YOU ASK FOR THAT, BUT...
...A CLASS TRIP IS ALSO ABOUT LEARNING TO BE COOP-ERATIVE.
IF COOP-ERATIVENESS COULD BE IMPROVED JUST BY BATHING AS A GROUP, WOULDN'T THERE ALREADY BE WORLD PEACE?
NO, NO! I COULDN'T BEAR TO HAVE HANDA-KUN'S NAKED BODY EXPOSED TO PUBLIC GAZE!
NOOOo!
IF ANYTHING HAPPENS IN THE MEN'S BATH, IT'LL BE TOO LATE!
UH, I DOUBT ANYTHING IS GOING TO HAPPEN.
NOW, IF YOU WERE TO ALLOW ME TO COLLECT THE LARGE-BATH WATER THAT HANDA-KUN SOAKED IN...
...THAT WOULD BE A DIFFERENT STORY.
ZOWA (SHIVER)
THIS GIRL'S SCARY...

Chapter 22: Handa-kun & the Class Trip, Night 1

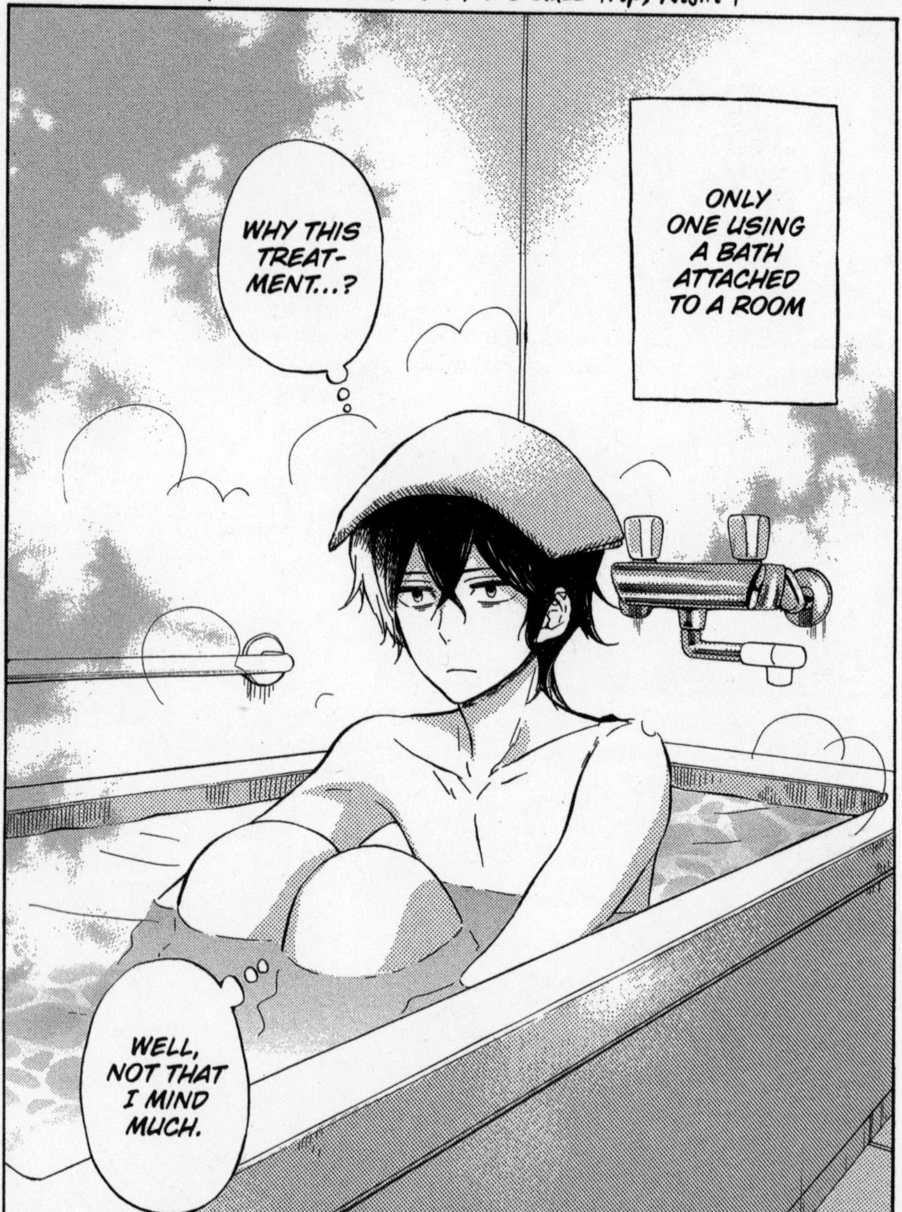
ONLY ONE USING A BATH ATTACHED TO A ROOM
WHY THIS TREAT-MENT...?
WELL, NOT THAT I MIND MUCH.

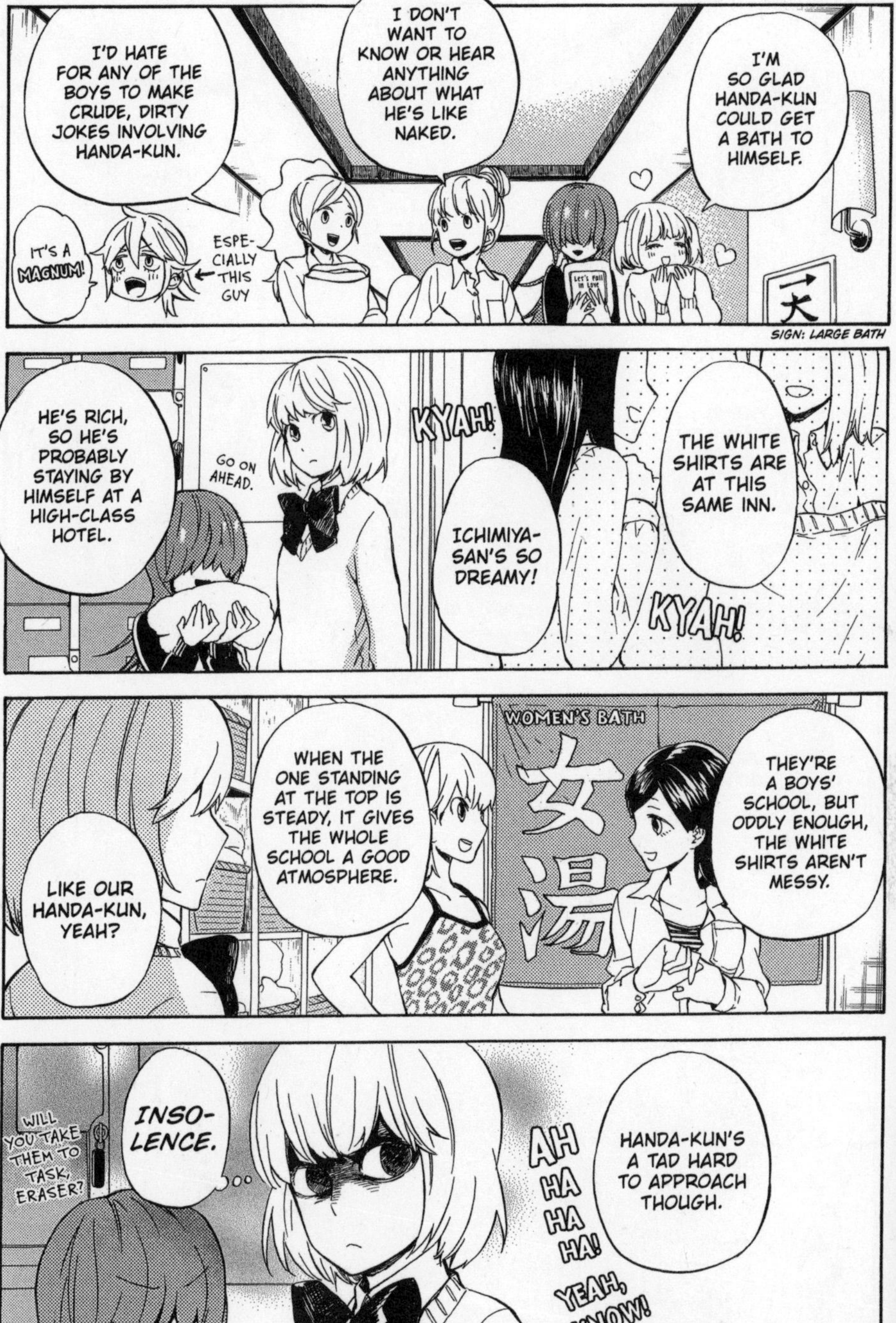
I'M SO GLAD HANDA-KUN COULD GET A BATH TO HIMSELF.
大
SIGN: LARGE BATH
I DON'T WANT TO KNOW OR HEAR ANYTHING ABOUT WHAT HE'S LIKE NAKED.
I'D HATE FOR ANY OF THE BOYS TO MAKE CRUDE, DIRTY JOKES INVOLVING HANDA-KUN.
ESPECIALLY THIS GUY
IT'S A MAGNUM!
THE WHITE SHIRTS ARE AT THIS SAME INN.
KYAH!
ICHIMIYA-SAN'S SO DREAMY!
KYAH!
GO ON AHEAD.
HE'S RICH, SO HE'S PROBABLY STAYING BY HIMSELF AT A HIGH-CLASS HOTEL.
THEY'RE A BOYS' SCHOOL, BUT ODDLY ENOUGH, THE WHITE SHIRTS AREN'T MESSY.
WOMEN'S BATH
女湯
WHEN THE ONE STANDING AT THE TOP IS STEADY, IT GIVES THE WHOLE SCHOOL A GOOD ATMOSPHERE.
LIKE OUR HANDA-KUN, YEAH?
HANDA-KUN'S A TAD HARD TO APPROACH THOUGH.
AH HA HA HA!
YEAH, I KNOW!
INSOLENCE.
WILL YOU TAKE THEM TO TASK, ERASER?

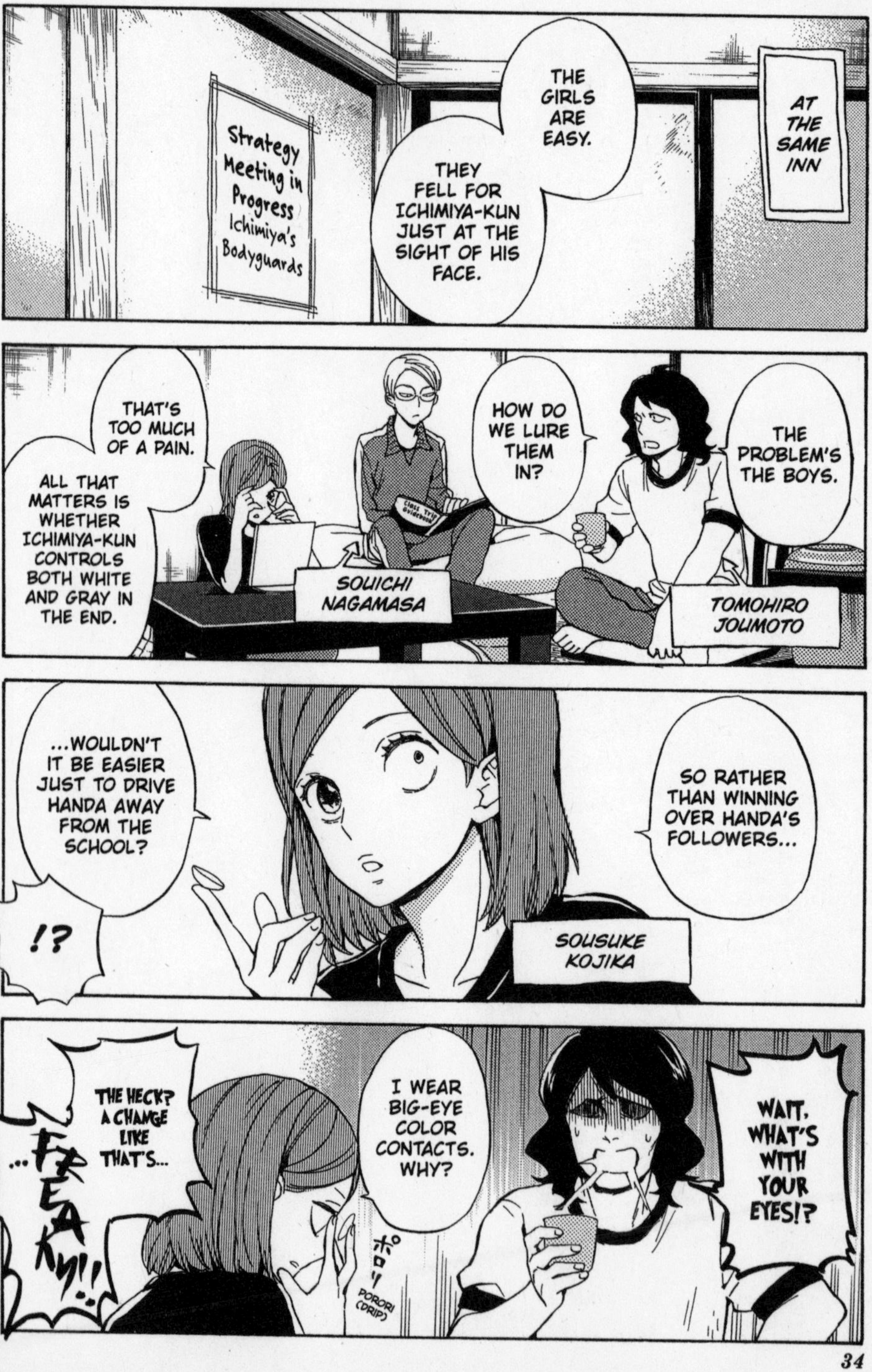
AT THE SAME INN
THE GIRLS ARE EASY.
THEY FELL FOR ICHIMIYA-KUN JUST AT THE SIGHT OF HIS FACE.
Strategy Meeting in Progress Ichimiya's Bodyguards
THE PROBLEM'S THE BOYS.
TOMOHIRO JOUMOTO
HOW DO WE LURE THEM IN?
SOUICHI NAGAMASA
Class Trip Guidebook
THAT'S TOO MUCH OF A PAIN.
ALL THAT MATTERS IS WHETHER ICHIMIYA-KUN CONTROLS BOTH WHITE AND GRAY IN THE END.
SO RATHER THAN WINNING OVER HANDA'S FOLLOWERS...
SOUSUKE KOJIKA
...WOULDN'T IT BE EASIER JUST TO DRIVE HANDA AWAY FROM THE SCHOOL?
!?
WAIT. WHAT'S WITH YOUR EYES!?
I WEAR BIG-EYE COLOR CONTACTS. WHY?
ポロリ
PORORI (DRIP)
THE HECK? A CHANGE LIKE THAT'S...
...FREAKY!!

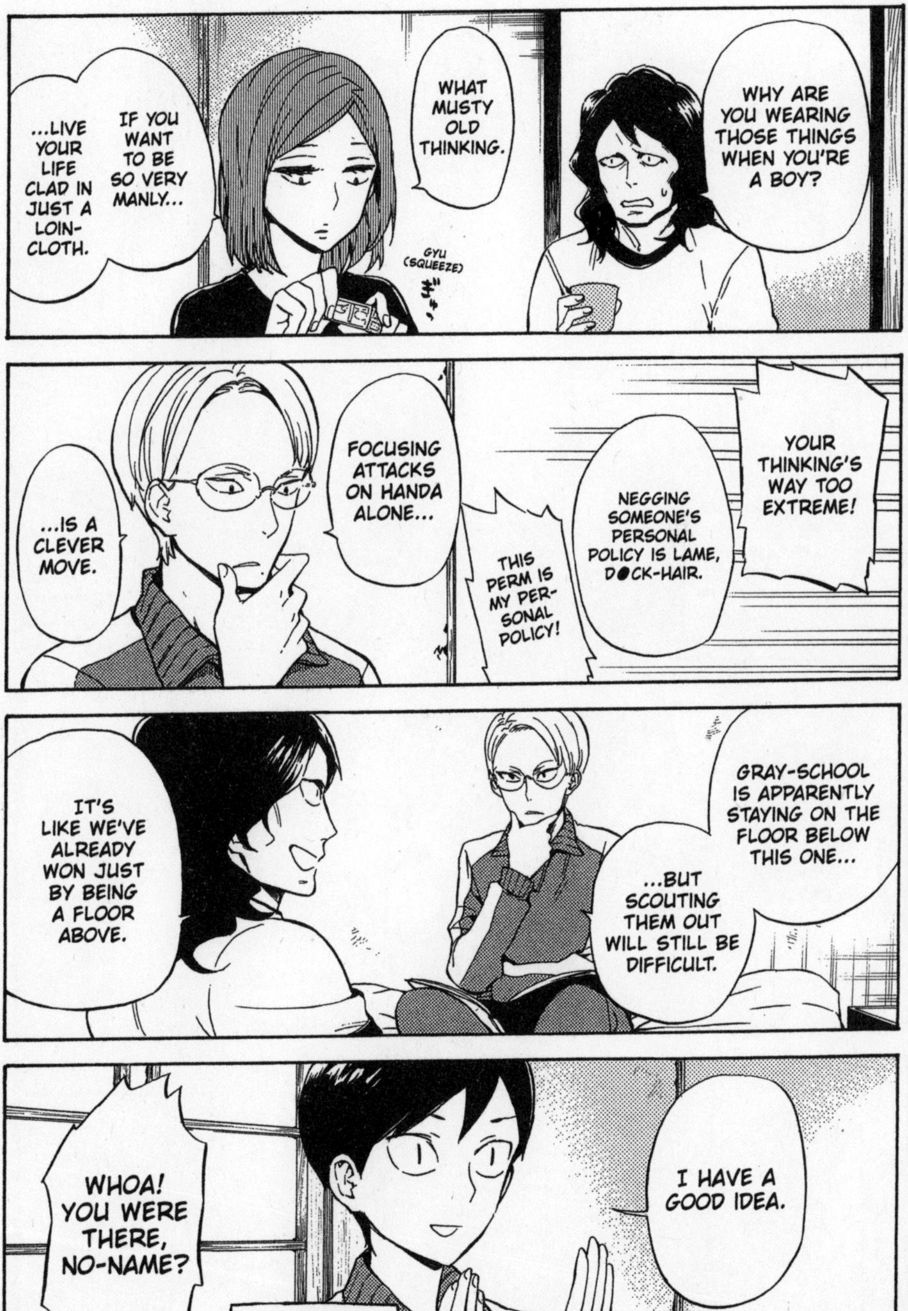
WHY ARE YOU WEARING THOSE THINGS WHEN YOU'RE A BOY?
WHAT MUSTY OLD THINKING.
IF YOU WANT TO BE SO VERY MANLY...
...LIVE YOUR LIFE CLAD IN JUST A LOIN-CLOTH.
GYU (SQUEEZE)
ぎゅ
YOUR THINKING'S WAY TOO EXTREME!
NEGGING SOMEONE'S PERSONAL POLICY IS LAME, D●CK-HAIR.
THIS PERM IS MY PER-SONAL POLICY!
FOCUSING ATTACKS ON HANDA ALONE...
...IS A CLEVER MOVE.
GRAY-SCHOOL IS APPARENTLY STAYING ON THE FLOOR BELOW THIS ONE...
...BUT SCOUTING THEM OUT WILL STILL BE DIFFICULT.
IT'S LIKE WE'VE ALREADY WON JUST BY BEING A FLOOR ABOVE.
I HAVE A GOOD IDEA.
WHOA! YOU WERE THERE, NO-NAME?
TSUKASA KOMICHI

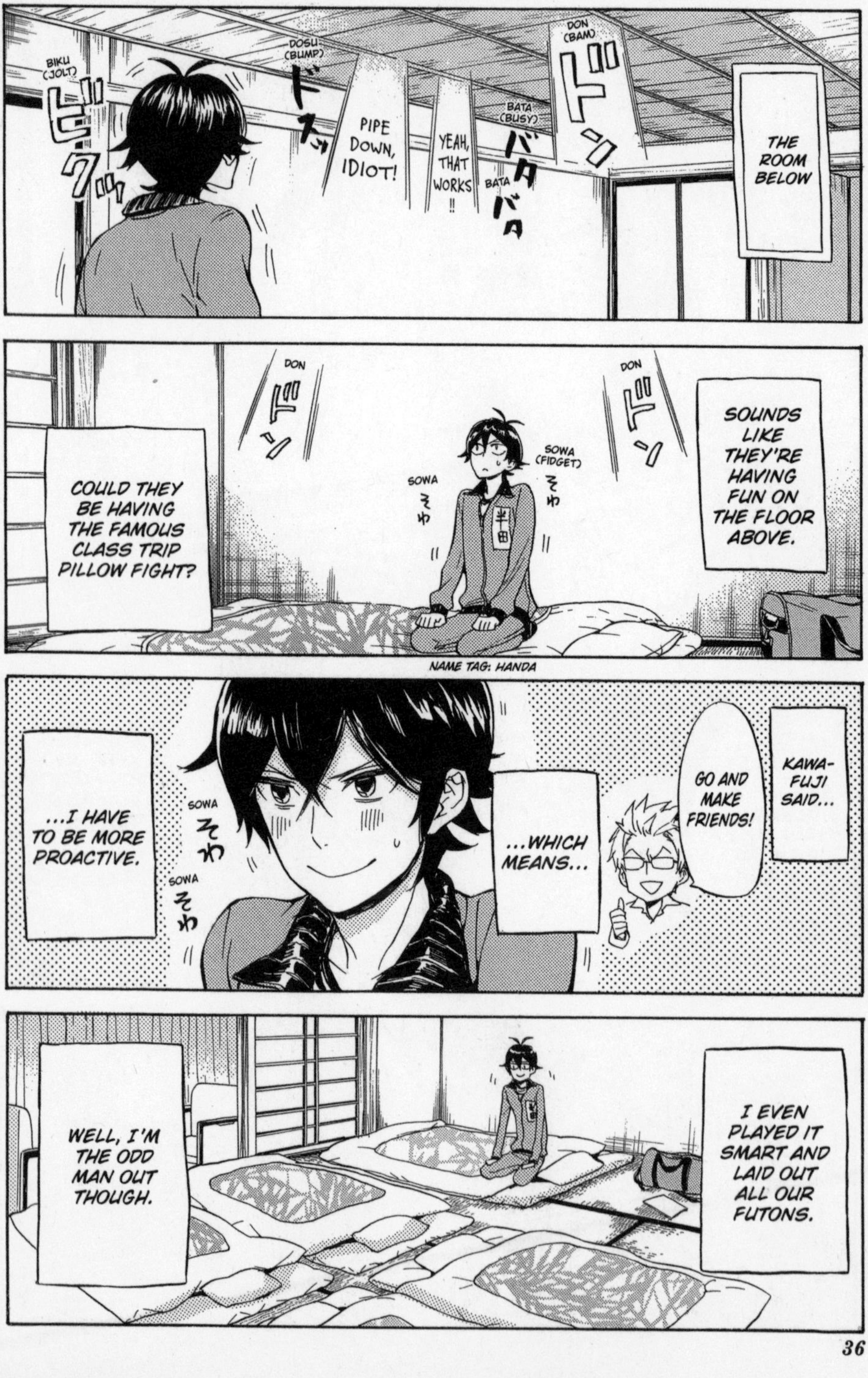
THE ROOM BELOW
DON (BAM)
BATA (BUSY)
BATA
YEAH, THAT WORKS!!
PIPE DOWN, IDIOT!
DOSU (BUMP)
BIKU (JOLT)
SOUNDS LIKE THEY'RE HAVING FUN ON THE FLOOR ABOVE.
DON
SOWA (FIDGET)
DON
SOWA
COULD THEY BE HAVING THE FAMOUS CLASS TRIP PILLOW FIGHT?
NAME TAG: HANDA
KAWA-FUJI SAID...
GO AND MAKE FRIENDS!
...WHICH MEANS...
SOWA
SOWA
...I HAVE TO BE MORE PROACTIVE.
I EVEN PLAYED IT SMART AND LAID OUT ALL OUR FUTONS.
WELL, I'M THE ODD MAN OUT THOUGH.

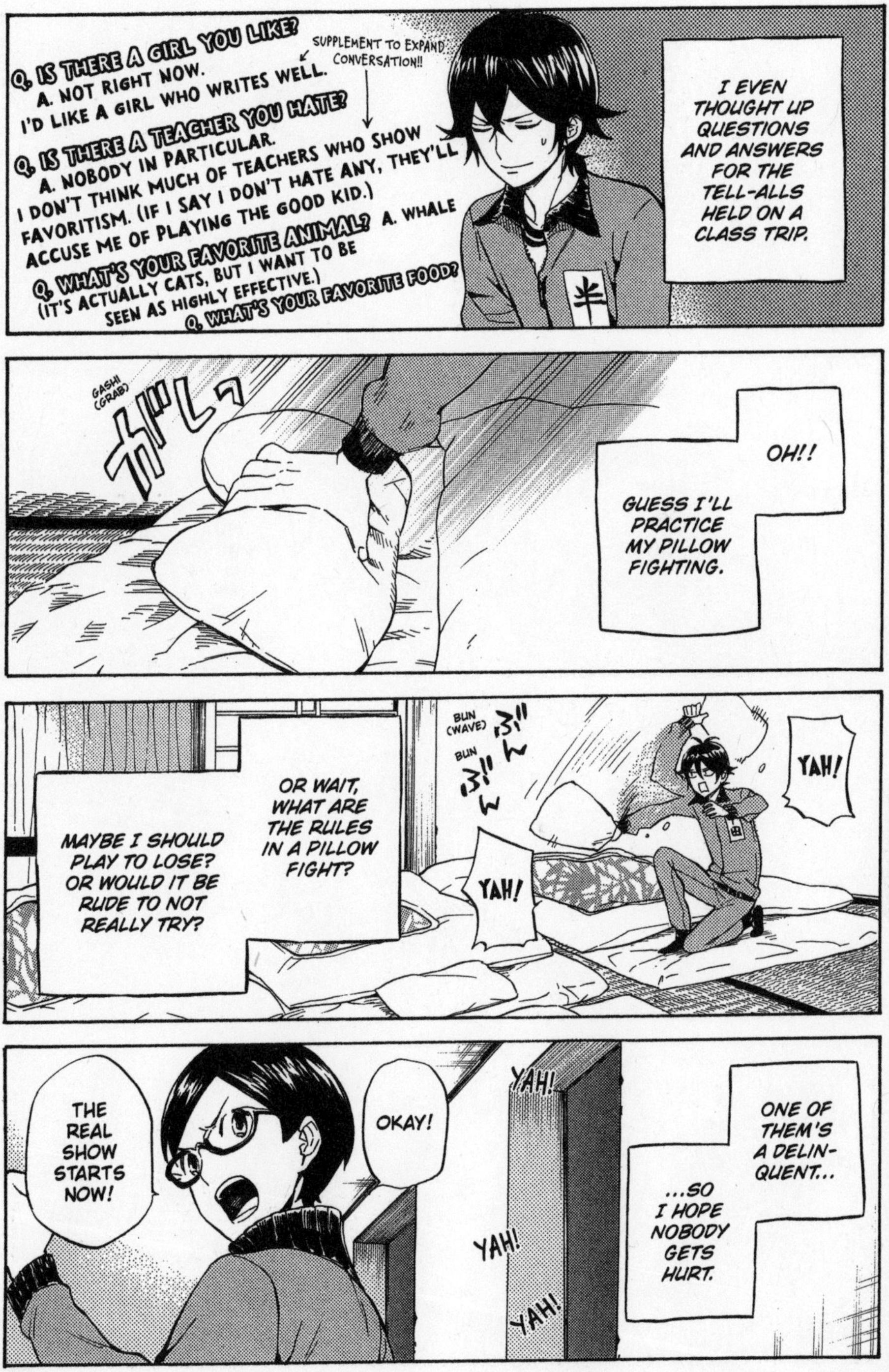
I EVEN THOUGHT UP QUESTIONS AND ANSWERS FOR THE TELL-ALLS HELD ON A CLASS TRIP.
SUPPLEMENT TO EXPAND CONVERSATION!!
Q. IS THERE A GIRL YOU LIKE?
A. NOT RIGHT NOW.
I'D LIKE A GIRL WHO WRITES WELL.
Q. IS THERE A TEACHER YOU HATE?
A. NOBODY IN PARTICULAR.
I DON'T THINK MUCH OF TEACHERS WHO SHOW FAVORITISM. (IF I SAY I DON'T HATE ANY, THEY'LL ACCUSE ME OF PLAYING THE GOOD KID.)
Q. WHAT'S YOUR FAVORITE ANIMAL? A. WHALE
(IT'S ACTUALLY CATS, BUT I WANT TO BE SEEN AS HIGHLY EFFECTIVE.)
Q. WHAT'S YOUR FAVORITE FOOD?
OH!!
GUESS I'LL PRACTICE MY PILLOW FIGHTING.
GASHI (GRAB)
YAH!
BUN (WAVE)
BUN
YAH!
OR WAIT, WHAT ARE THE RULES IN A PILLOW FIGHT?
MAYBE I SHOULD PLAY TO LOSE? OR WOULD IT BE RUDE TO NOT REALLY TRY?
ONE OF THEM'S A DELIN-QUENT...
...SO I HOPE NOBODY GETS HURT.
YAH!
YAH!
YAH!
OKAY!
THE REAL SHOW STARTS NOW!

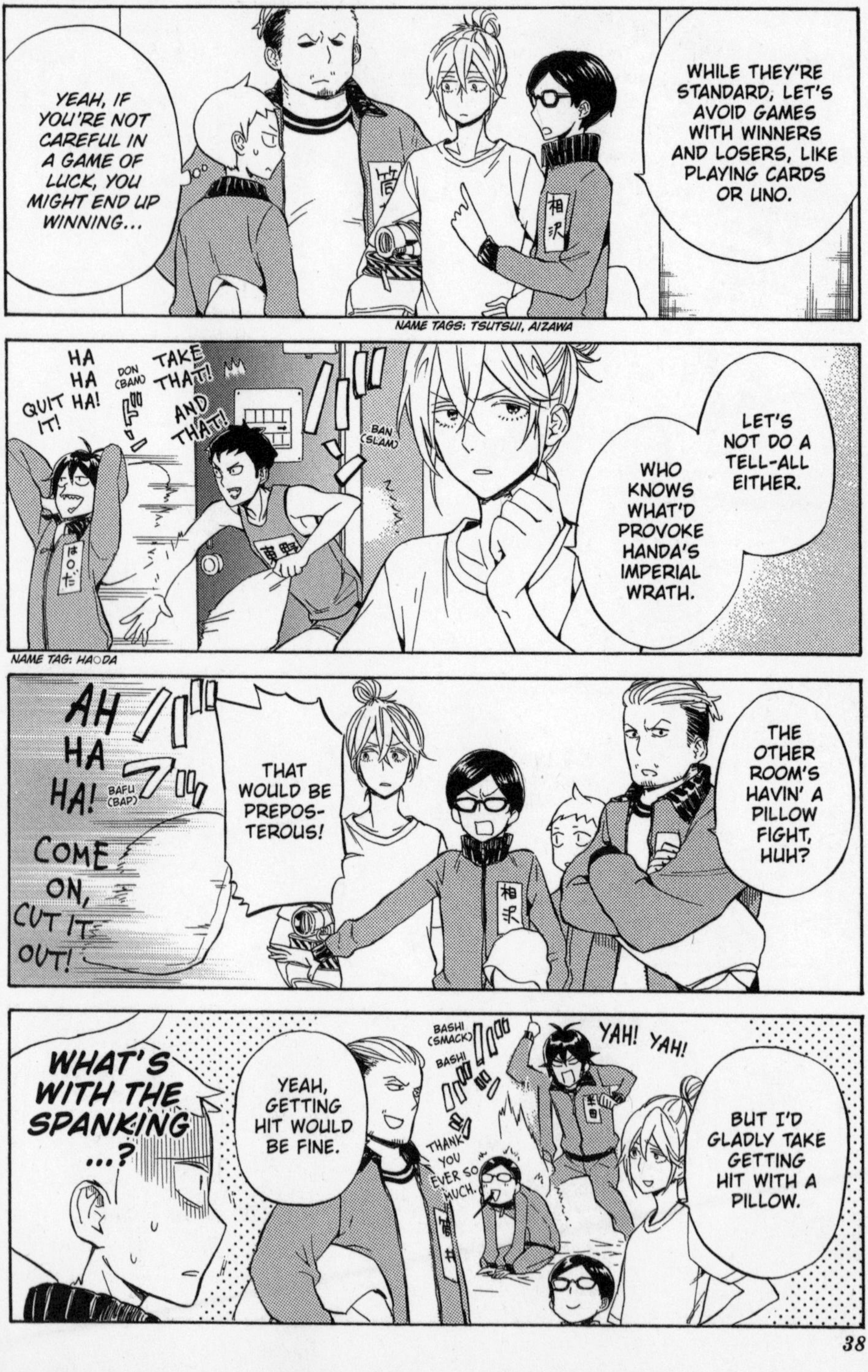

WHILE THEY'RE STANDARD, LET'S AVOID GAMES WITH WINNERS AND LOSERS, LIKE PLAYING CARDS OR UNO.
YEAH, IF YOU'RE NOT CAREFUL IN A GAME OF LUCK, YOU MIGHT END UP WINNING...
NAME TAGS: TSUTSUI, AIZAWA
LET'S NOT DO A TELL-ALL EITHER.
WHO KNOWS WHAT'D PROVOKE HANDA'S IMPERIAL WRATH.
BAN (SLAM)
TAKE THAT!
AND THAT!
DON (BAM)
HA HA HA!
QUIT IT!
NAME TAG: HA○DA
THE OTHER ROOM'S HAVIN' A PILLOW FIGHT, HUH?
THAT WOULD BE PREPOSTEROUS!
BAFU (BAP)
AH HA HA!
COME ON, CUT IT OUT!
BUT I'D GLADLY TAKE GETTING HIT WITH A PILLOW.
YAH! YAH!
BASHI (SMACK)
BASHI
THANK YOU EVER SO MUCH.
YEAH, GETTING HIT WOULD BE FINE.
WHAT'S WITH THE SPANKING...?

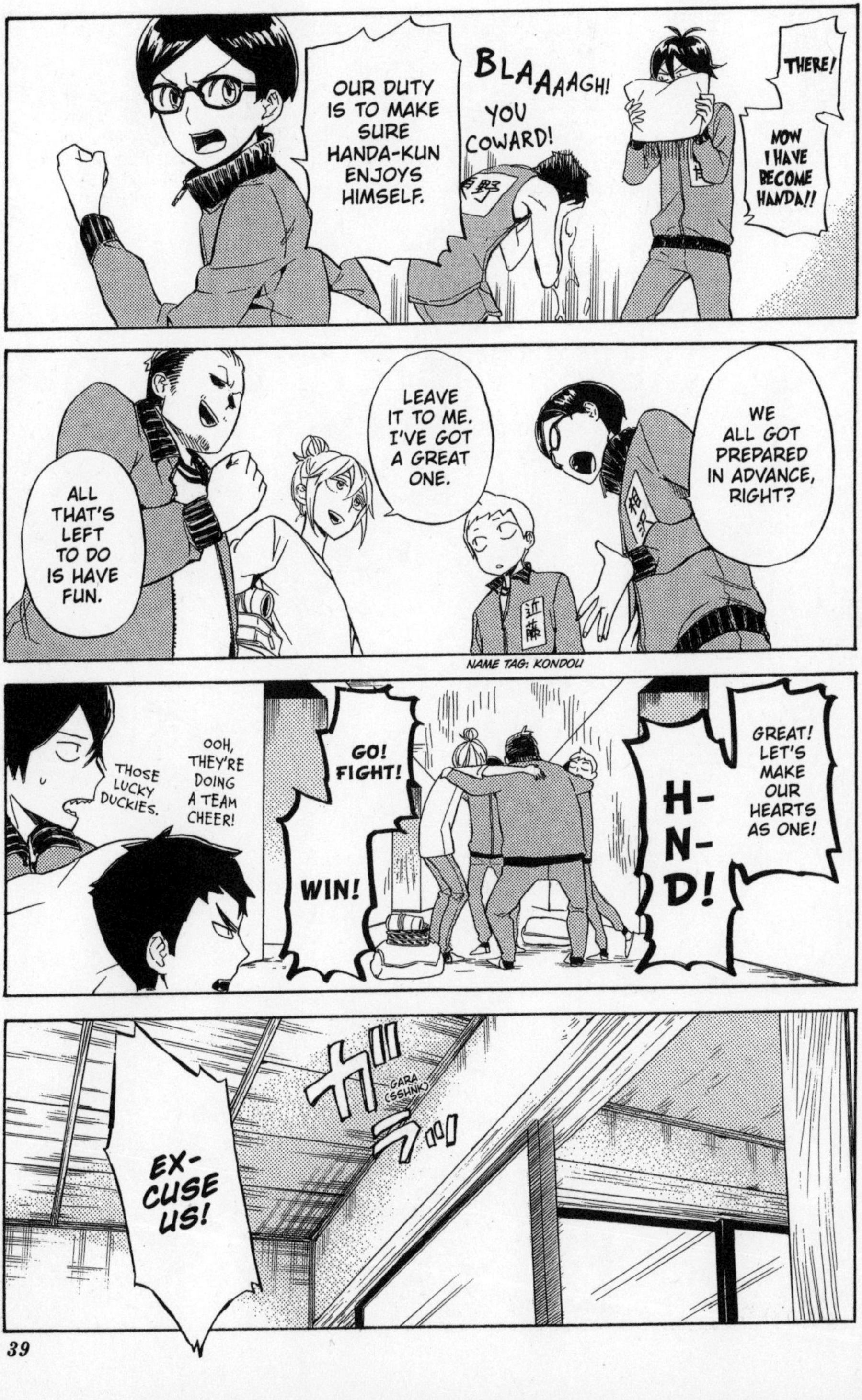
THERE!
NOW I HAVE BECOME HANDA!!
BLAAAAGH!
YOU COWARD!
OUR DUTY IS TO MAKE SURE HANDA-KUN ENJOYS HIMSELF.
WE ALL GOT PREPARED IN ADVANCE, RIGHT?
LEAVE IT TO ME. I'VE GOT A GREAT ONE.
ALL THAT'S LEFT TO DO IS HAVE FUN.
NAME TAG: KONDOU
GREAT! LET'S MAKE OUR HEARTS AS ONE!
H-N-D!
GO! FIGHT!
WIN!
OOH, THEY'RE DOING A TEAM CHEER!
THOSE LUCKY DUCKIES.
GARA (SSHNK)
EX-CUSE US!

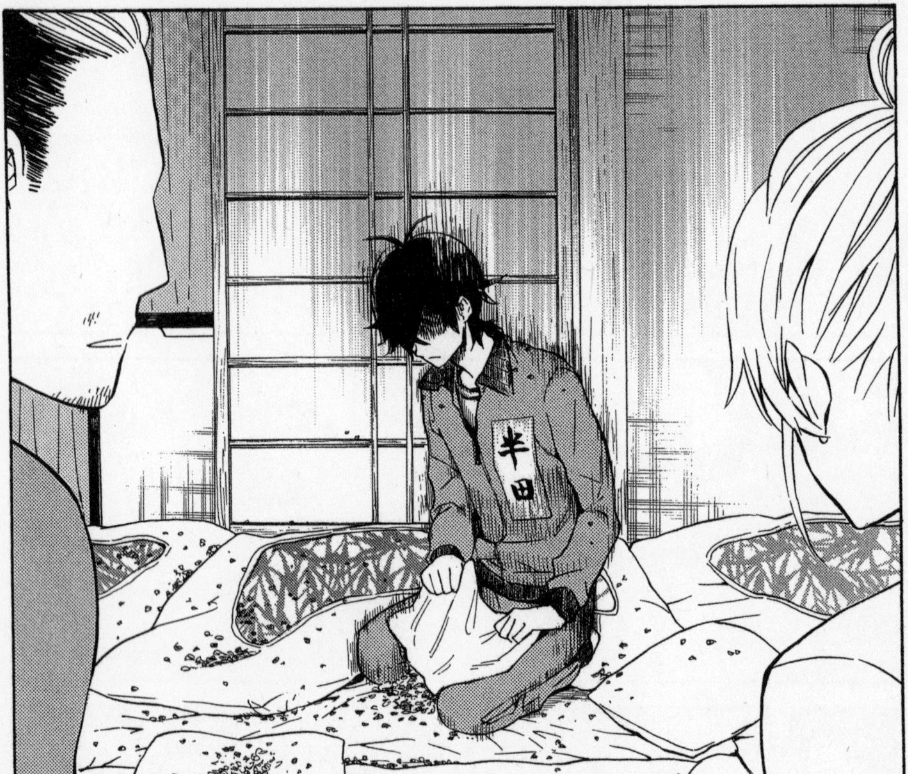
半田

NAME TAG: HANDA

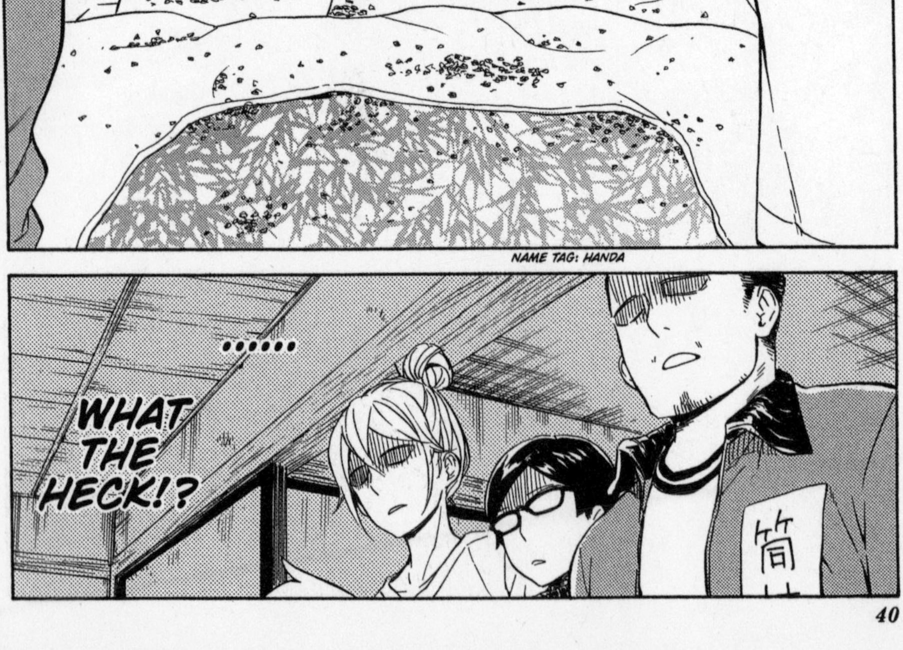
......
WHAT THE HECK!?

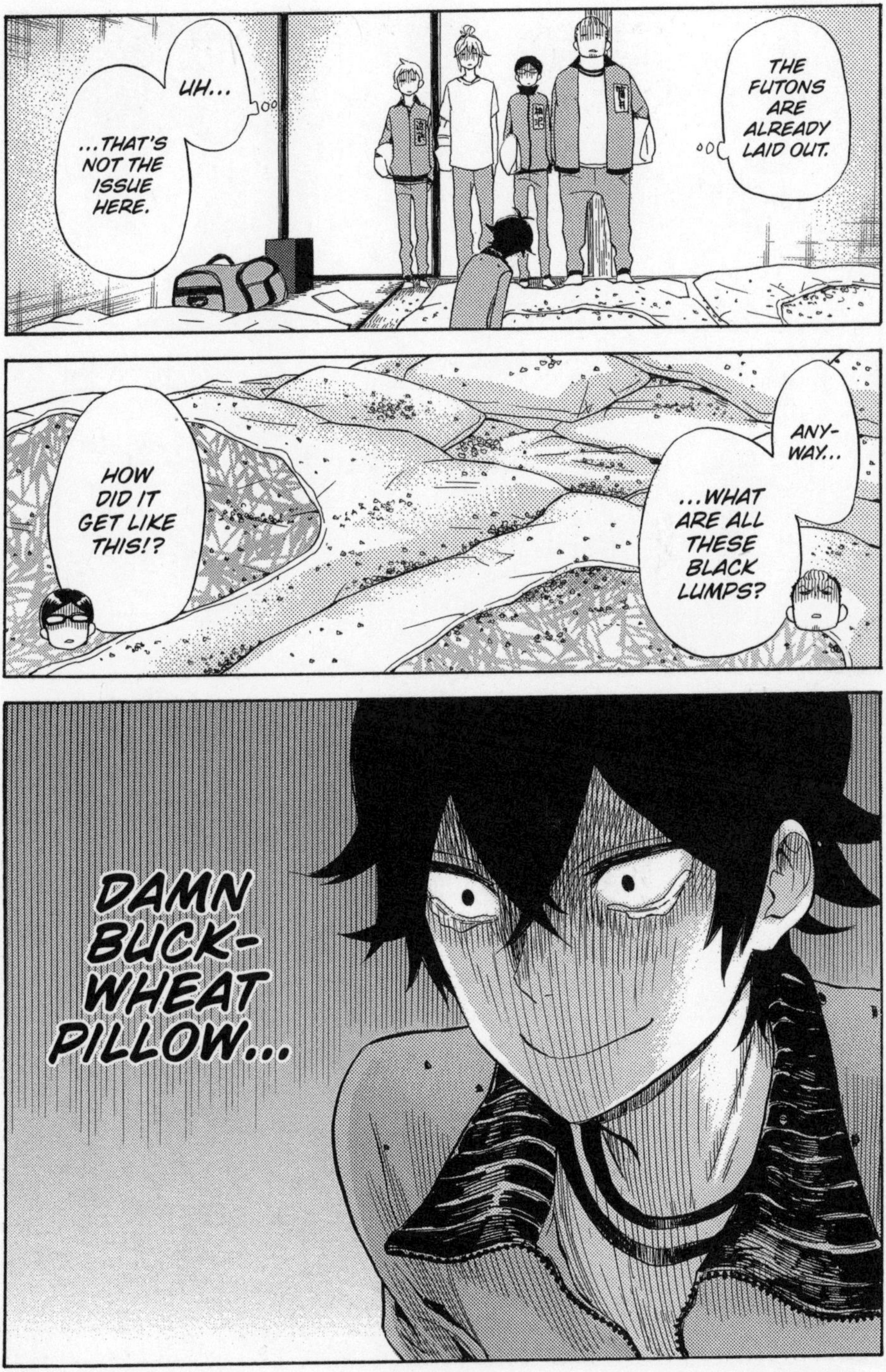
THE FUTONS ARE ALREADY LAID OUT.
UH...
...THAT'S NOT THE ISSUE HERE.
ANY-WAY...
...WHAT ARE ALL THESE BLACK LUMPS?
HOW DID IT GET LIKE THIS!?
DAMN BUCK-WHEAT PILLOW...

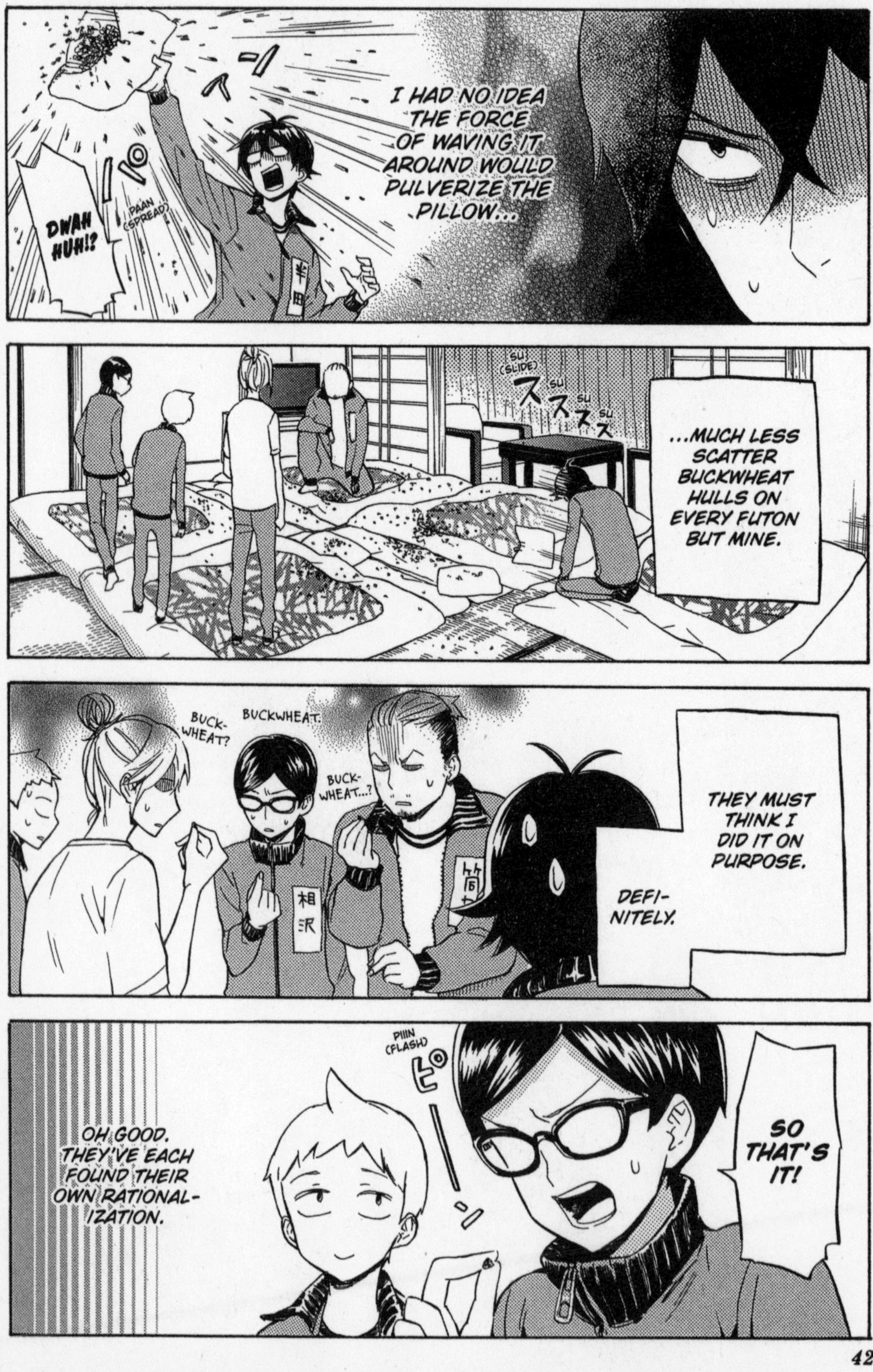
I HAD NO IDEA THE FORCE OF WAVING IT AROUND WOULD PULVERIZE THE PILLOW...
PAAN (SPREAD)
DWAH HUH!?
SU (SLIDE)
SU
SU
SU
...MUCH LESS SCATTER BUCKWHEAT HULLS ON EVERY FUTON BUT MINE.
THEY MUST THINK I DID IT ON PURPOSE.
DEFI-NITELY.
BUCK-WHEAT...?
BUCKWHEAT.
BUCK-WHEAT?
SO THAT'S IT!
PIIIN (FLASH)
OH GOOD. THEY'VE EACH FOUND THEIR OWN RATIONAL-IZATION.

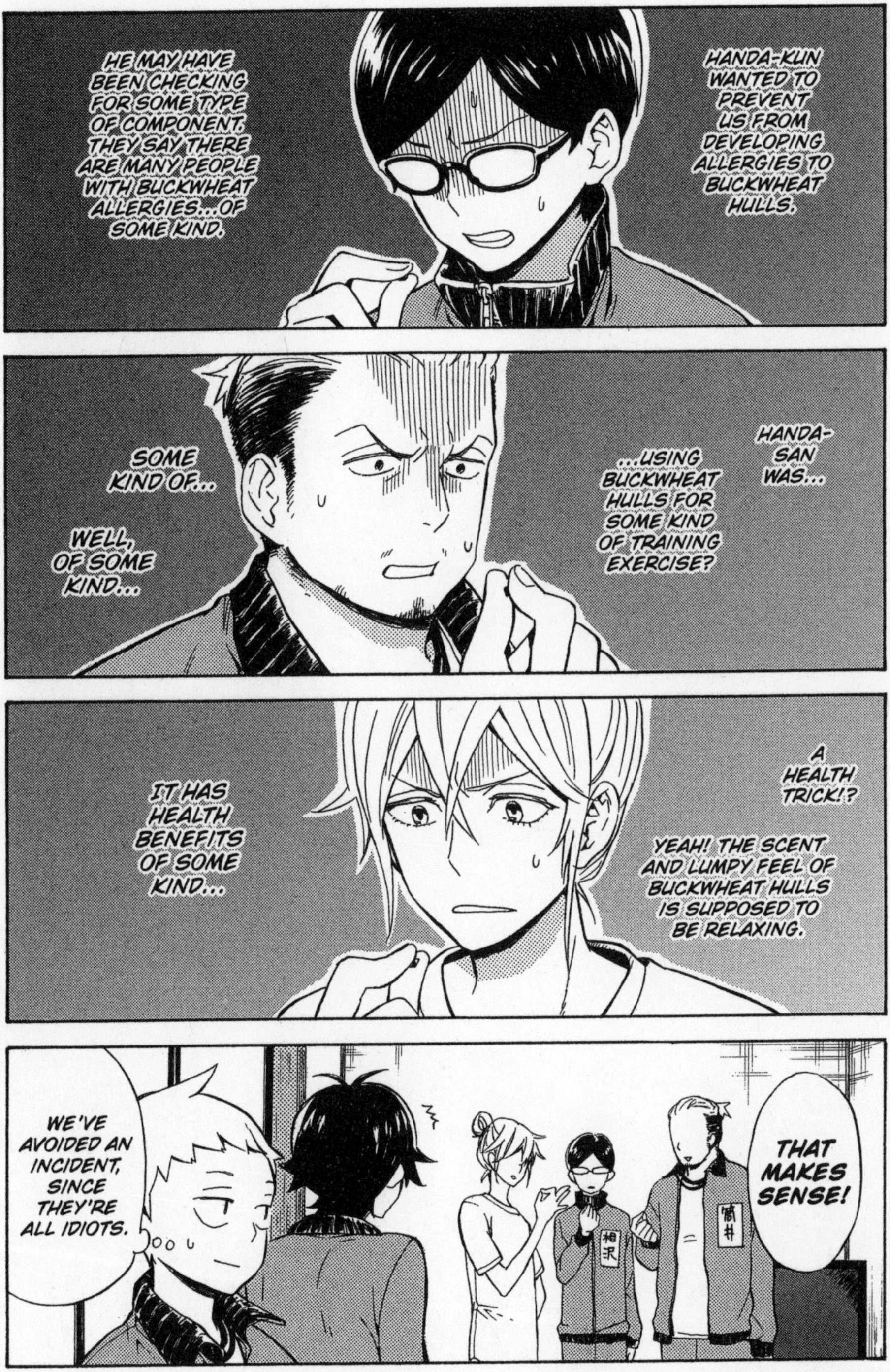
HANDA-KUN WANTED TO PREVENT US FROM DEVELOPING ALLERGIES TO BUCKWHEAT HULLS.
HE MAY HAVE BEEN CHECKING FOR SOME TYPE OF COMPONENT. THEY SAY THERE ARE MANY PEOPLE WITH BUCKWHEAT ALLERGIES...OF SOME KIND.
HANDA-SAN WAS...
...USING BUCKWHEAT HULLS FOR SOME KIND OF TRAINING EXERCISE?
SOME KIND OF...
WELL, OF SOME KIND...
A HEALTH TRICK!?
YEAH! THE SCENT AND LUMPY FEEL OF BUCKWHEAT HULLS IS SUPPOSED TO BE RELAXING.
IT HAS HEALTH BENEFITS OF SOME KIND...
THAT MAKES SENSE!
富井
相沢
WE'VE AVOIDED AN INCIDENT, SINCE THEY'RE ALL IDIOTS.

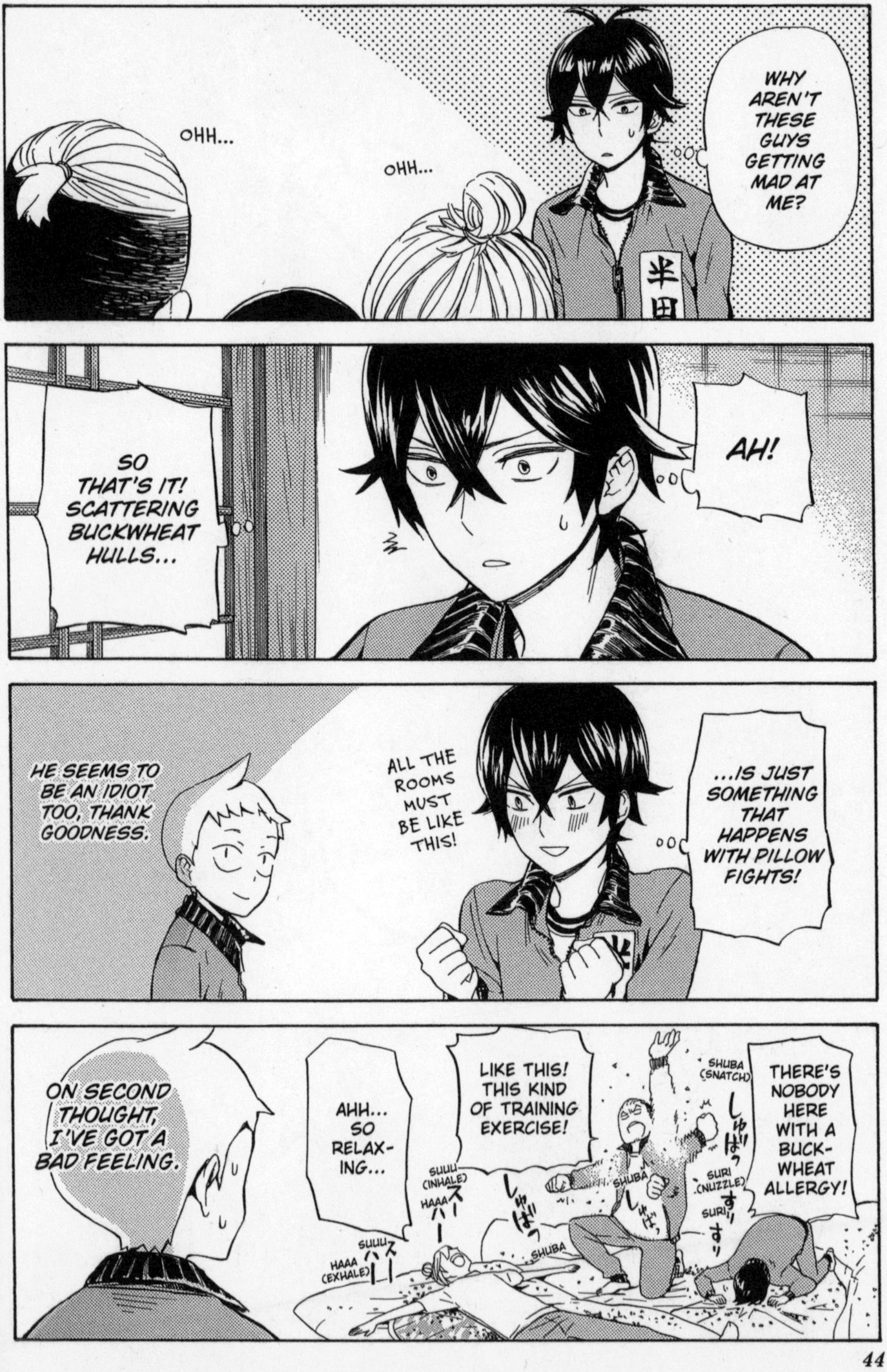
WHY AREN'T THESE GUYS GETTING MAD AT ME?
OHH...
OHH...
AH!
SO THAT'S IT! SCATTERING BUCKWHEAT HULLS...
...IS JUST SOMETHING THAT HAPPENS WITH PILLOW FIGHTS!
ALL THE ROOMS MUST BE LIKE THIS!
HE SEEMS TO BE AN IDIOT TOO, THANK GOODNESS.
THERE'S NOBODY HERE WITH A BUCK-WHEAT ALLERGY!
SHUBA (SNATCH)
しゅばっ
SURI (NUZZLE)
すりっ
SURI
すりっ
SHUBA
しゅばっ
しゅばっ
SHUBA
LIKE THIS! THIS KIND OF TRAINING EXERCISE!
SUUU (INHALE)
スー
HAAA
ハー
AHH... SO RELAX-ING...
SUUU
スー
HAAA (EXHALE)
ハー
ON SECOND THOUGHT, I'VE GOT A BAD FEELING.

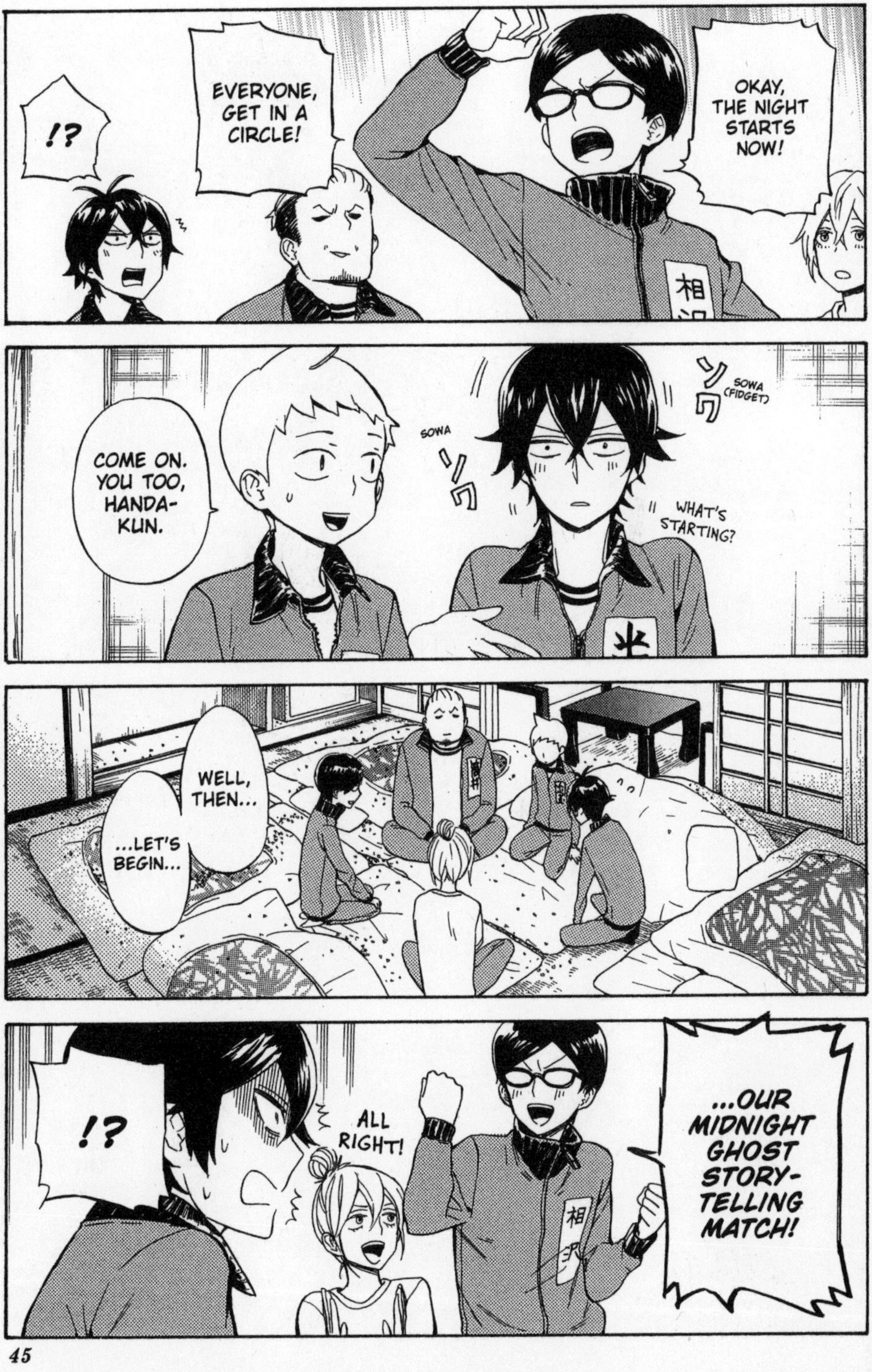
OKAY, THE NIGHT STARTS NOW!
EVERYONE, GET IN A CIRCLE!
!?
ソワ
SOWA (FIDGET)
WHAT'S STARTING?
SOWA
ソワ
COME ON. YOU TOO, HANDA-KUN.
WELL, THEN...
...LET'S BEGIN...
...OUR MIDNIGHT GHOST STORY-TELLING MATCH!
ALL RIGHT!
!?

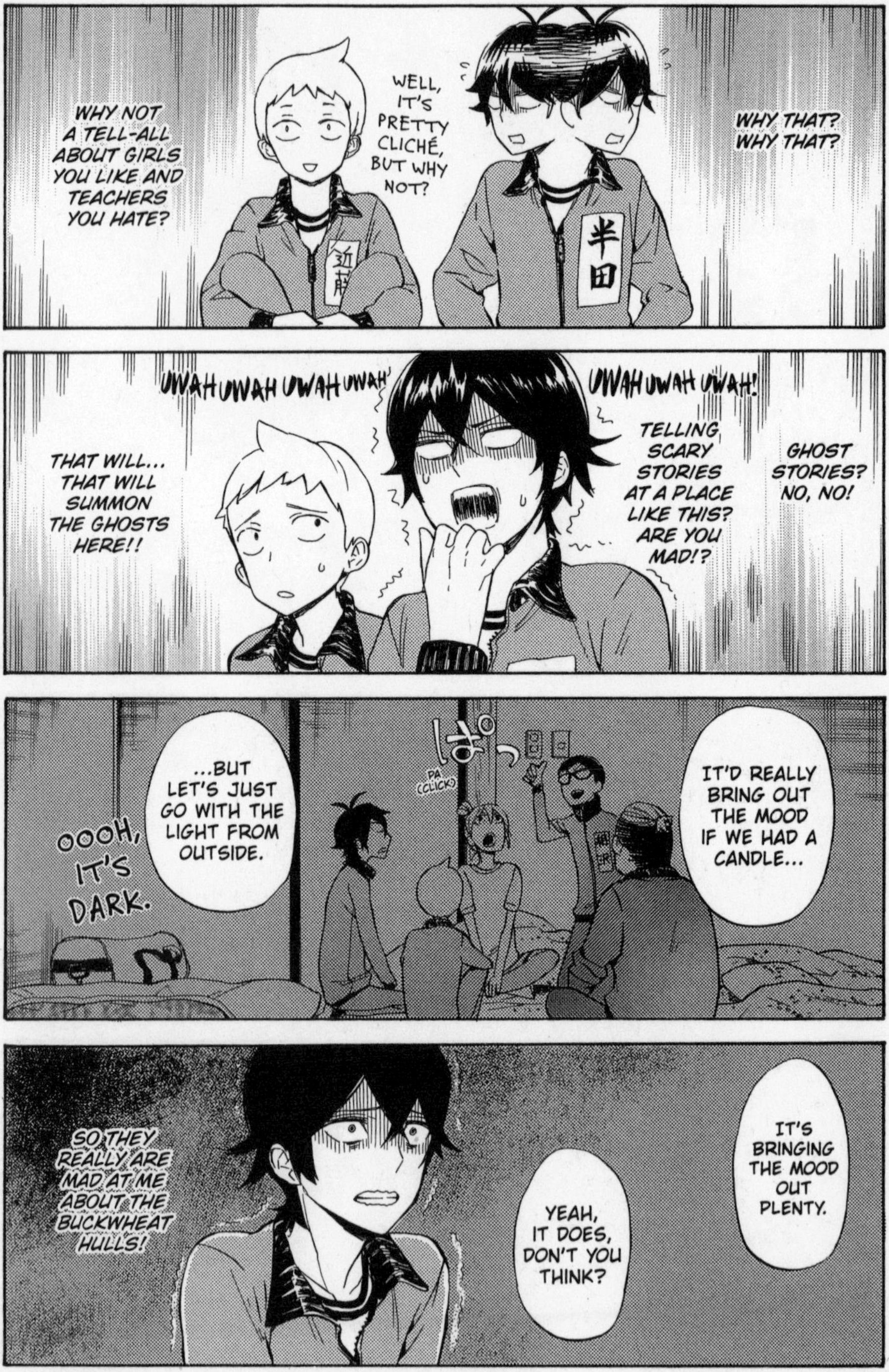
WHY THAT? WHY THAT?
半田
WELL, IT'S PRETTY CLICHÉ, BUT WHY NOT?
WHY NOT A TELL-ALL ABOUT GIRLS YOU LIKE AND TEACHERS YOU HATE?
UWAH UWAH UWAH!
GHOST STORIES? NO, NO!
TELLING SCARY STORIES AT A PLACE LIKE THIS? ARE YOU MAD!?
UWAH UWAH UWAH UWAH
THAT WILL... THAT WILL SUMMON THE GHOSTS HERE!!
IT'D REALLY BRING OUT THE MOOD IF WE HAD A CANDLE...
ぱっ
PA (CLICK)
...BUT LET'S JUST GO WITH THE LIGHT FROM OUTSIDE.
OOOH, IT'S DARK.
IT'S BRINGING THE MOOD OUT PLENTY.
YEAH, IT DOES, DON'T YOU THINK?
SO THEY REALLY ARE MAD AT ME ABOUT THE BUCKWHEAT HULLS!

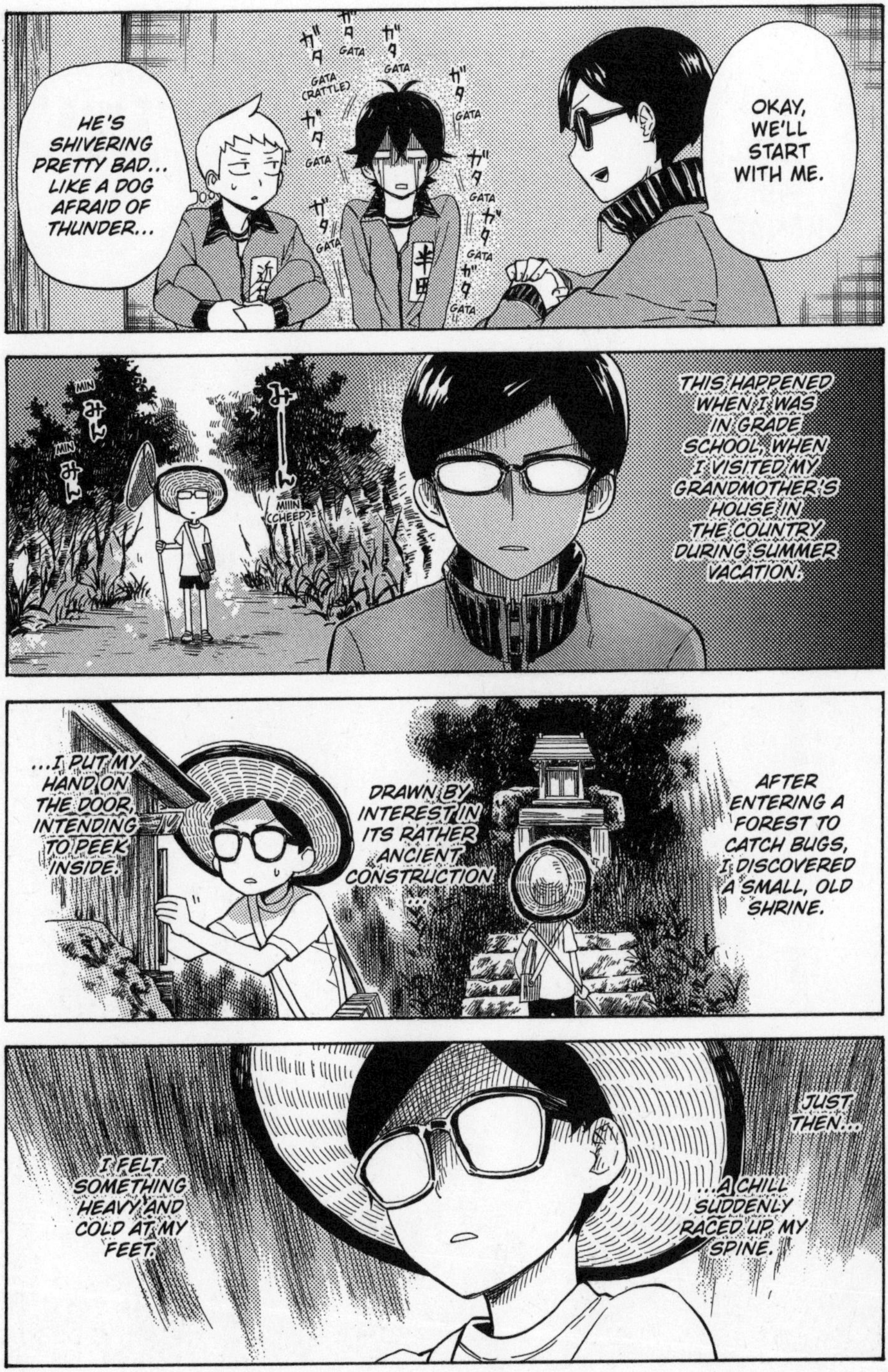
OKAY, WE'LL START WITH ME.
ガタ GATA
ガタ GATA
GATA (RATTLE)
ガタ GATA
ガタ GATA
ガタ GATA
ガタ GATA
ガタ GATA
HE'S SHIVERING PRETTY BAD... LIKE A DOG AFRAID OF THUNDER...
THIS HAPPENED WHEN I WAS IN GRADE SCHOOL, WHEN I VISITED MY GRANDMOTHER'S HOUSE IN THE COUNTRY DURING SUMMER VACATION.
みーん MIIN (CHEEP)
みん MIN
みん MIN
AFTER ENTERING A FOREST TO CATCH BUGS, I DISCOVERED A SMALL, OLD SHRINE.
DRAWN BY INTEREST IN ITS RATHER ANCIENT CONSTRUCTION...
...I PUT MY HAND ON THE DOOR, INTENDING TO PEEK INSIDE.
JUST THEN...
...A CHILL SUDDENLY RACED UP MY SPINE.
I FELT SOMETHING HEAVY AND COLD AT MY FEET.

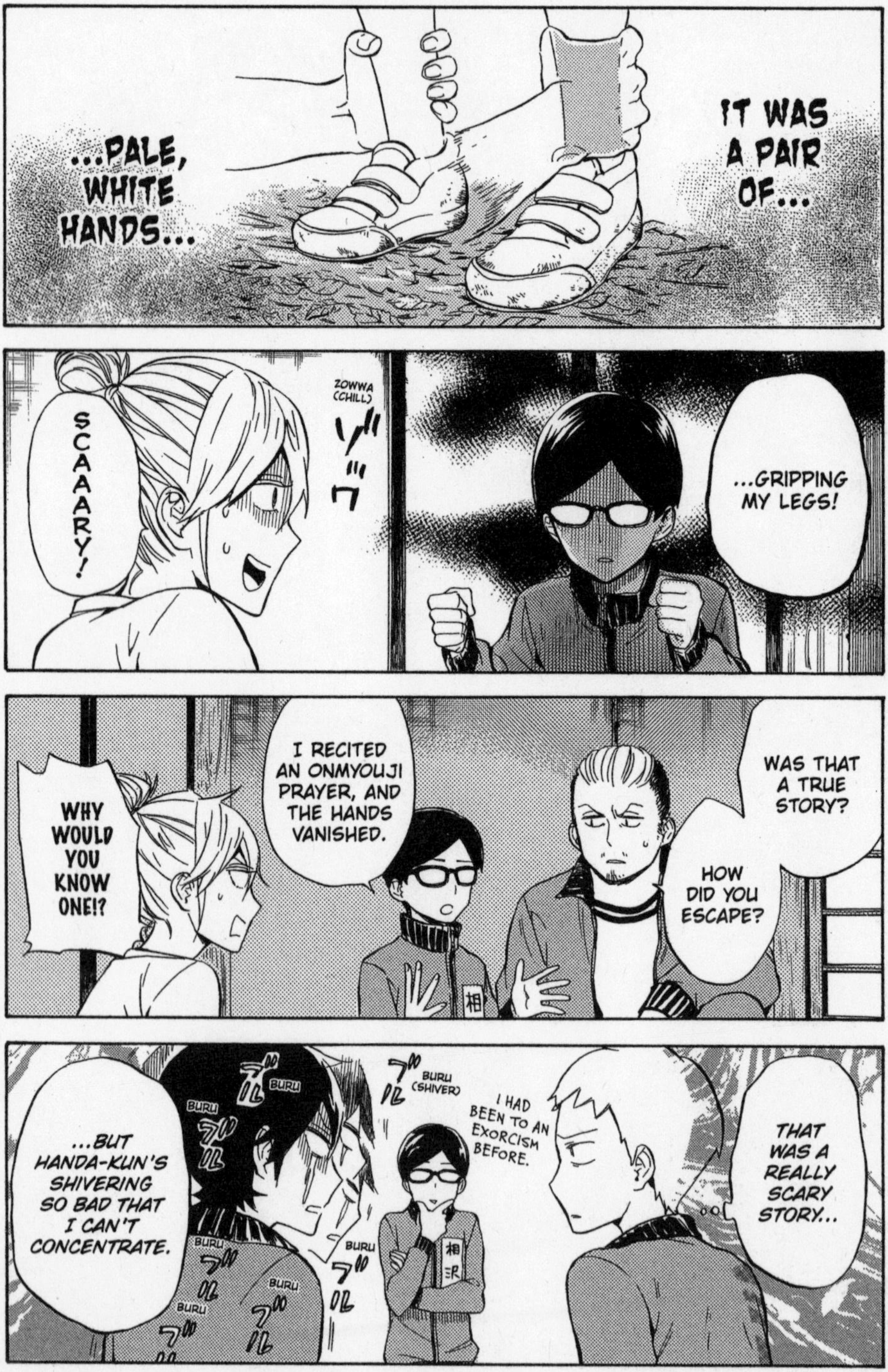
IT WAS A PAIR OF...
...PALE, WHITE HANDS...
...GRIPPING MY LEGS!
ZOWWA (CHILL)
SCAAARY!
WAS THAT A TRUE STORY?
HOW DID YOU ESCAPE?
I RECITED AN ONMYOUJI PRAYER, AND THE HANDS VANISHED.
WHY WOULD YOU KNOW ONE!?
THAT WAS A REALLY SCARY STORY...
I HAD BEEN TO AN EXORCISM BEFORE.
BURU (SHIVER)
BURU
BURU
...BUT HANDA-KUN'S SHIVERING SO BAD THAT I CAN'T CONCENTRATE.
BURU
BURU
BURU
BURU

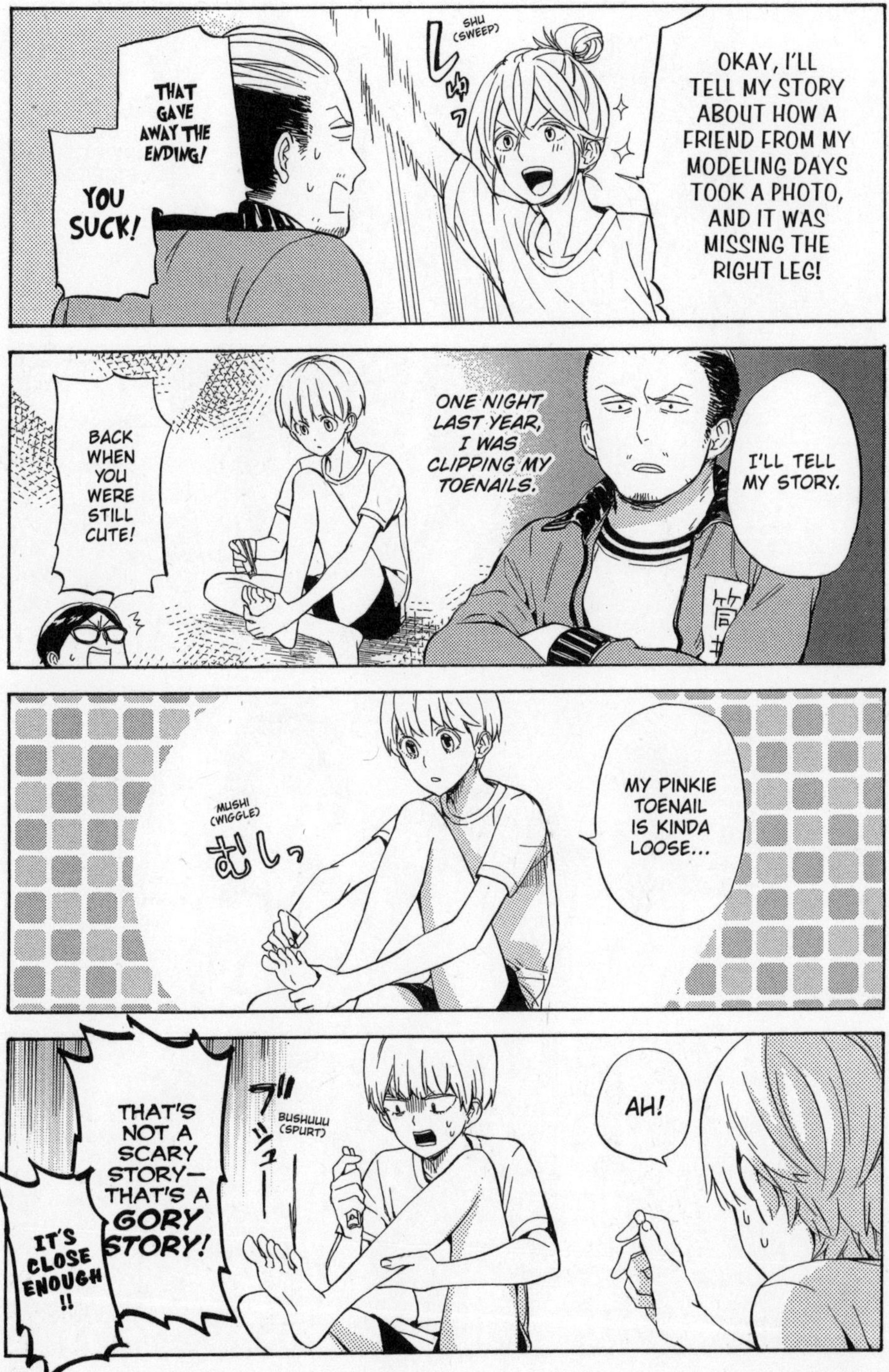
OKAY, I'LL TELL MY STORY ABOUT HOW A FRIEND FROM MY MODELING DAYS TOOK A PHOTO, AND IT WAS MISSING THE RIGHT LEG!
SHU (SWEEP)
しゅっ
THAT GAVE AWAY THE ENDING!
YOU SUCK!
I'LL TELL MY STORY.
ONE NIGHT LAST YEAR, I WAS CLIPPING MY TOENAILS.
BACK WHEN YOU WERE STILL CUTE!
MY PINKIE TOENAIL IS KINDA LOOSE...
MUSHI (WIGGLE)
むしっ
AH!
BUSHUUU (SPURT)
ブシュー
THAT'S NOT A SCARY STORY—THAT'S A GORY STORY!
IT'S CLOSE ENOUGH!!

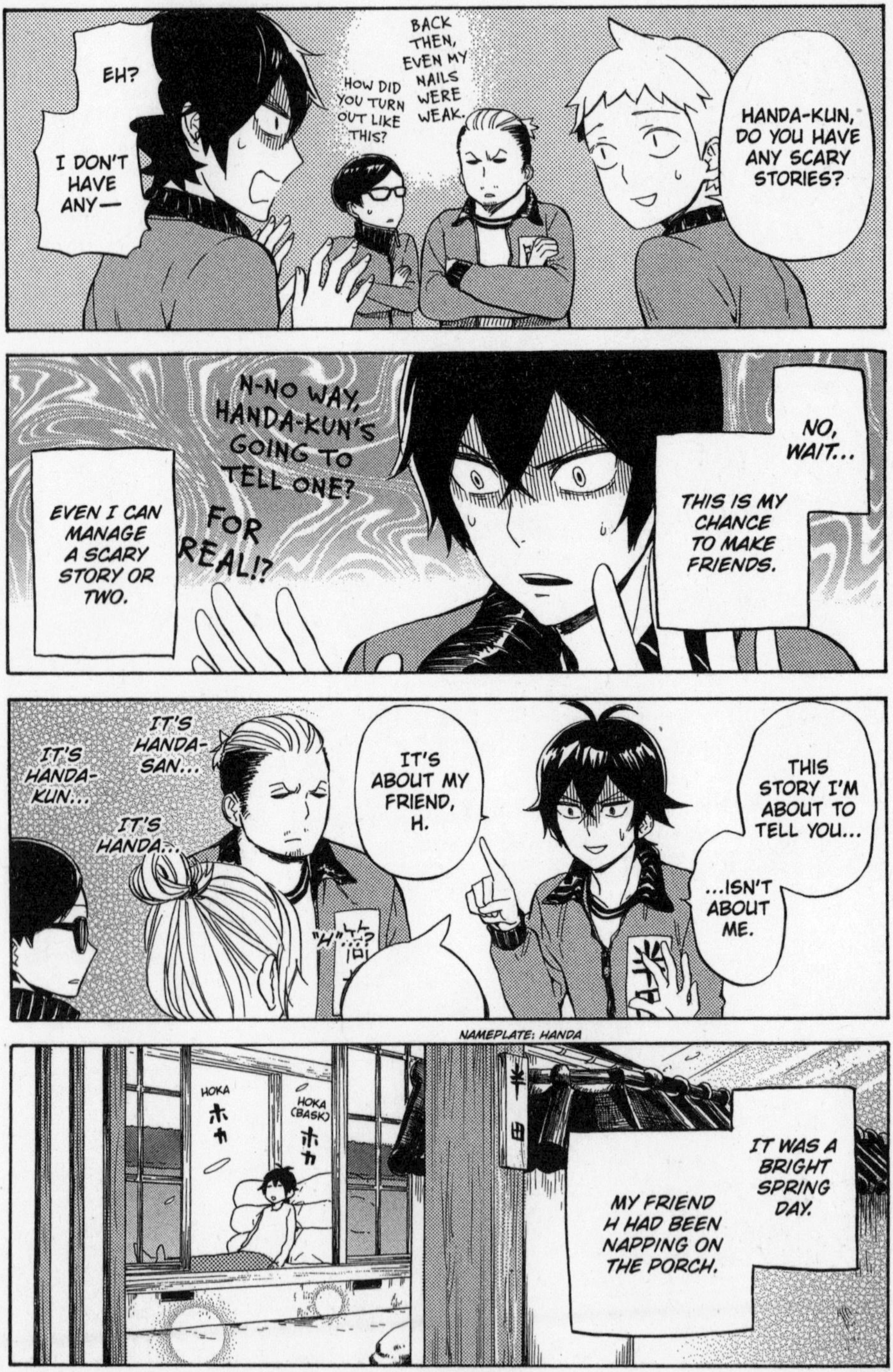
HANDA-KUN, DO YOU HAVE ANY SCARY STORIES?
BACK THEN, EVEN MY NAILS WERE WEAK.
HOW DID YOU TURN OUT LIKE THIS?
EH?
I DON'T HAVE ANY—
NO, WAIT...
THIS IS MY CHANCE TO MAKE FRIENDS.
N-NO WAY, HANDA-KUN'S GOING TO TELL ONE?
FOR REAL!?
EVEN I CAN MANAGE A SCARY STORY OR TWO.
THIS STORY I'M ABOUT TO TELL YOU...
...ISN'T ABOUT ME.
IT'S ABOUT MY FRIEND, H.
IT'S HANDA-SAN...
IT'S HANDA-KUN...
IT'S HANDA...
"H"...?
NAMEPLATE: HANDA
IT WAS A BRIGHT SPRING DAY.
MY FRIEND H HAD BEEN NAPPING ON THE PORCH.
HOKA (BASK)
ホカ
HOKA
ホカ

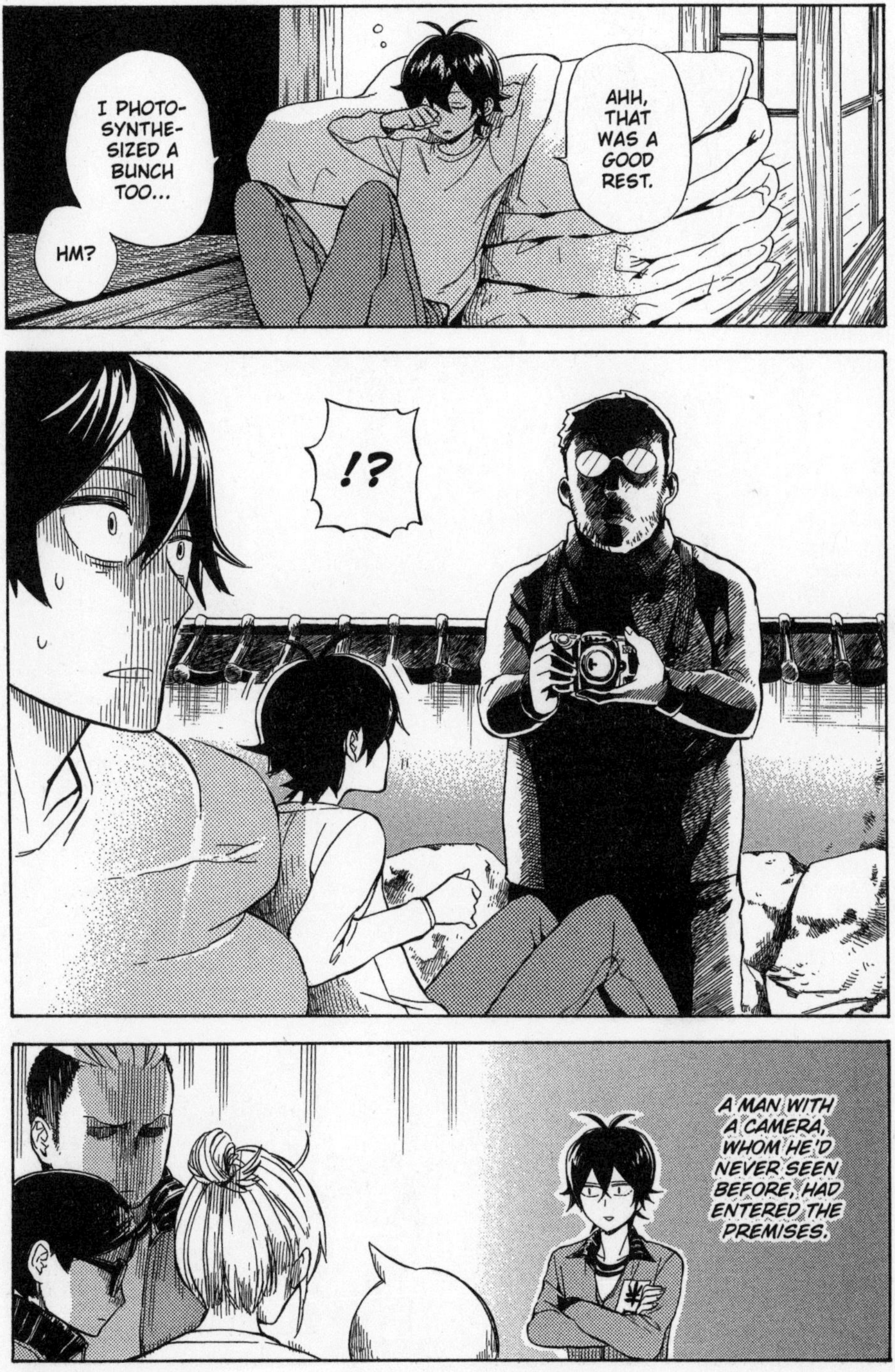
AHH, THAT WAS A GOOD REST.
I PHOTO-SYNTHE-SIZED A BUNCH TOO...
HM?
!?
A MAN WITH A CAMERA, WHOM HE'D NEVER SEEN BEFORE, HAD ENTERED THE PREMISES.

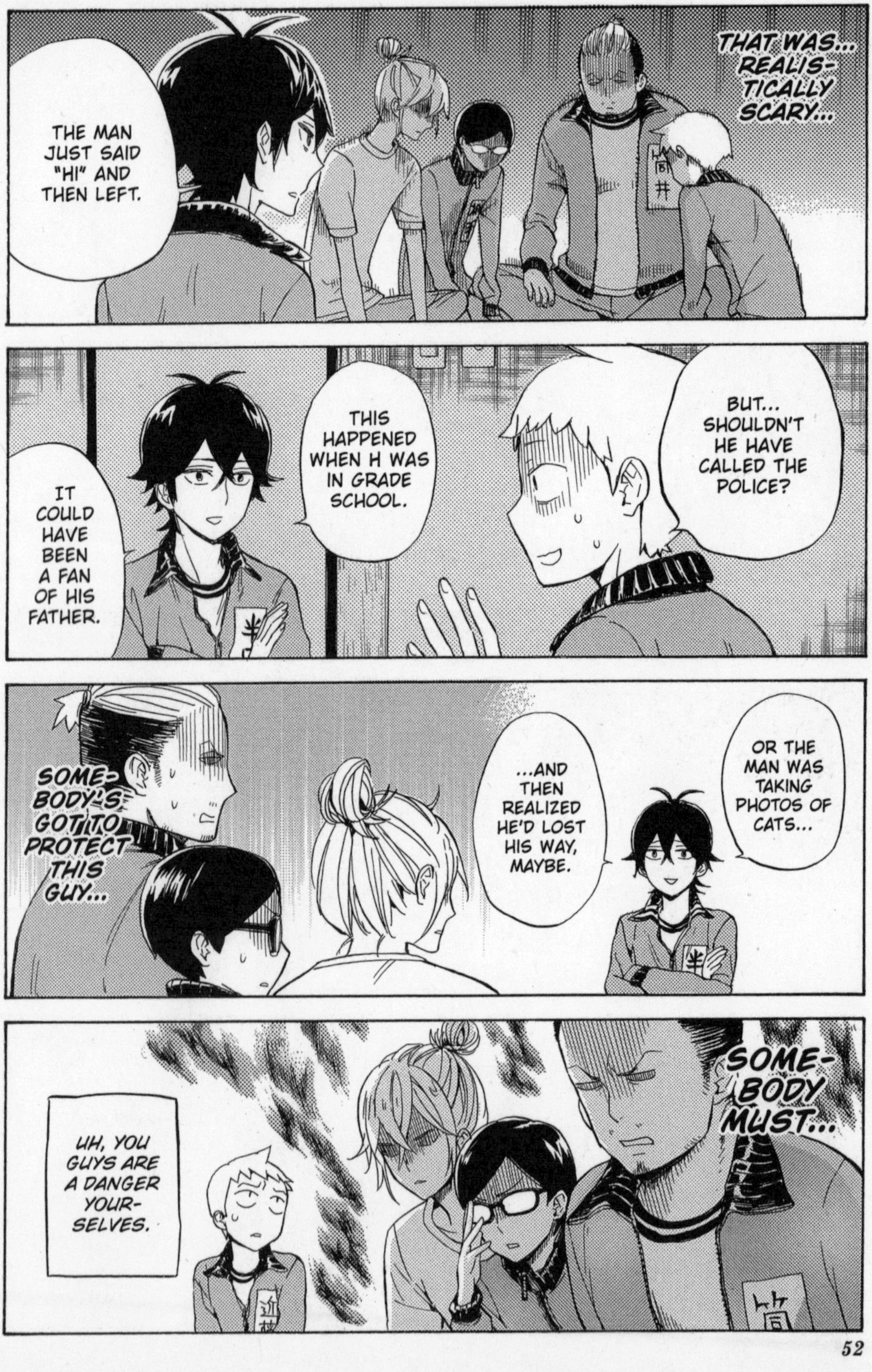
THAT WAS... REALIS-TICALLY SCARY...
THE MAN JUST SAID "HI" AND THEN LEFT.
BUT... SHOULDN'T HE HAVE CALLED THE POLICE?
THIS HAPPENED WHEN H WAS IN GRADE SCHOOL.
IT COULD HAVE BEEN A FAN OF HIS FATHER.
OR THE MAN WAS TAKING PHOTOS OF CATS...
...AND THEN REALIZED HE'D LOST HIS WAY, MAYBE.
SOME-BODY'S GOT TO PROTECT THIS GUY...
SOME-BODY MUST...
UH, YOU GUYS ARE A DANGER YOUR-SELVES.

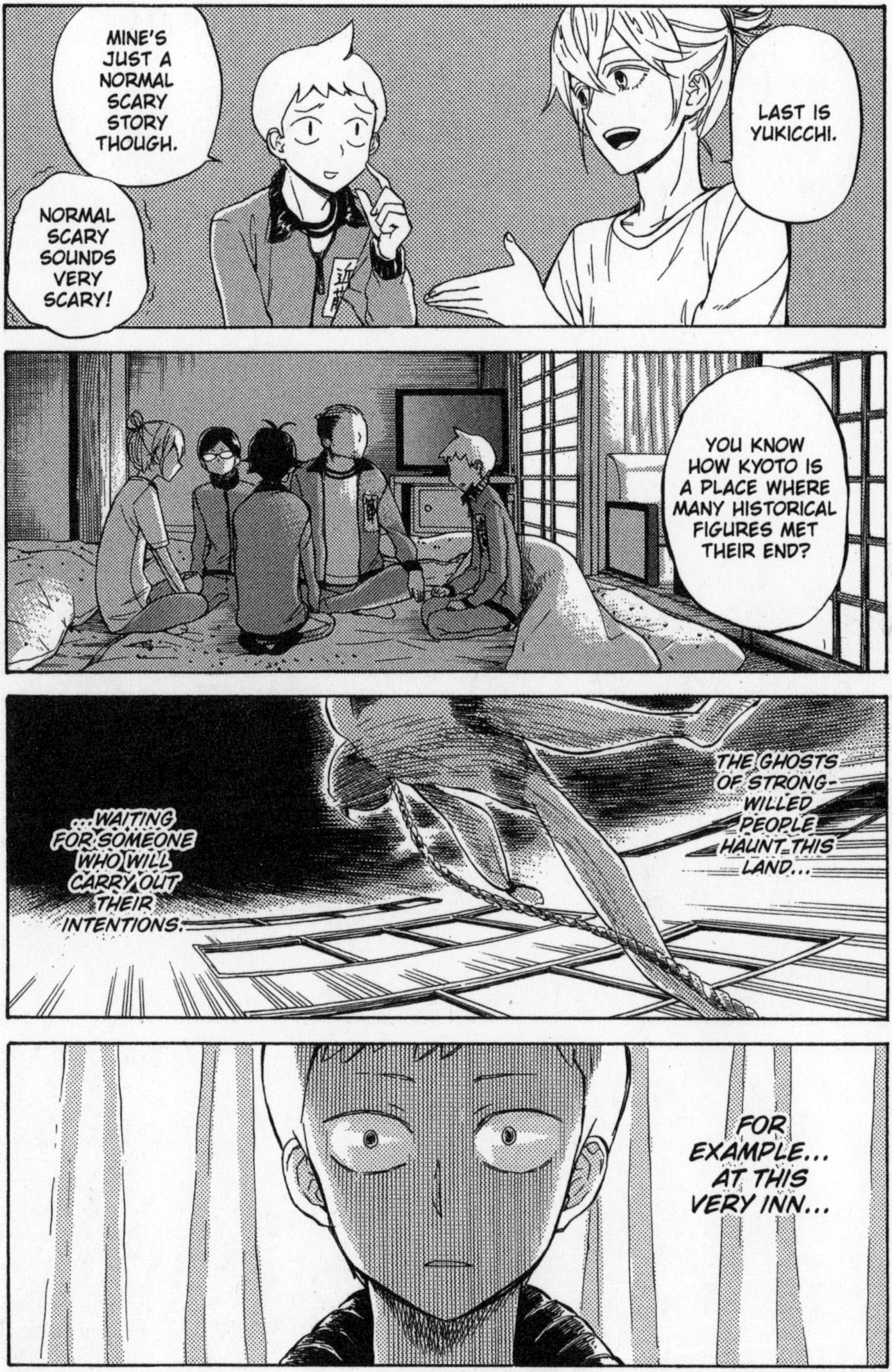
LAST IS YUKICCHI.
MINE'S JUST A NORMAL SCARY STORY THOUGH.
NORMAL SCARY SOUNDS VERY SCARY!
YOU KNOW HOW KYOTO IS A PLACE WHERE MANY HISTORICAL FIGURES MET THEIR END?
THE GHOSTS OF STRONG-WILLED PEOPLE HAUNT THIS LAND...
...WAITING FOR SOMEONE WHO WILL CARRY OUT THEIR INTENTIONS.
FOR EXAMPLE... AT THIS VERY INN...

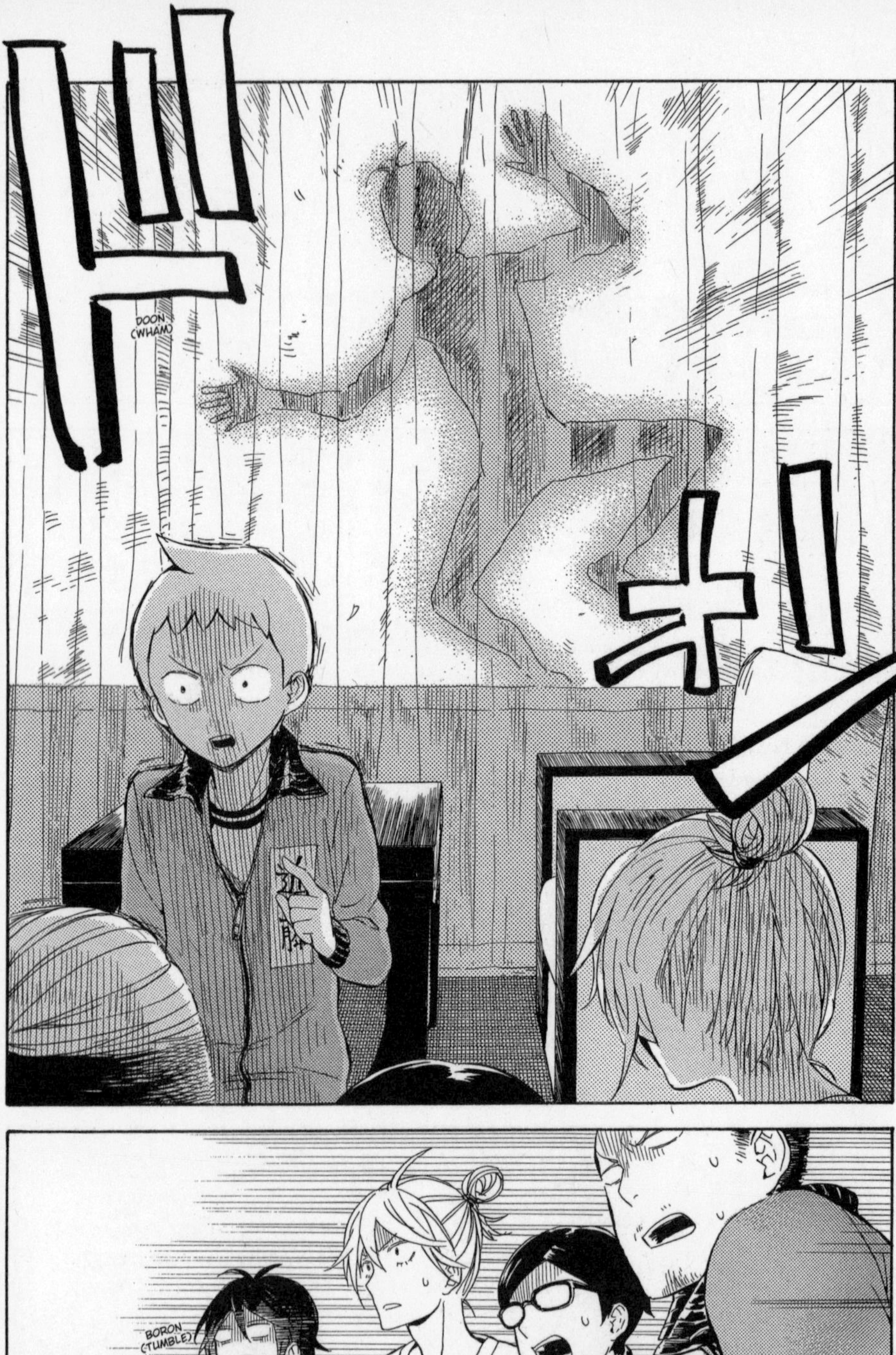
DOON
(WHAM)
BORON
(TUMBLE)

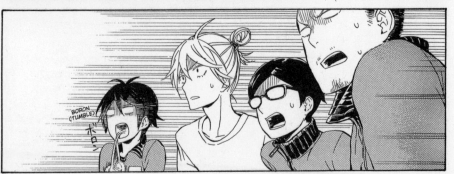

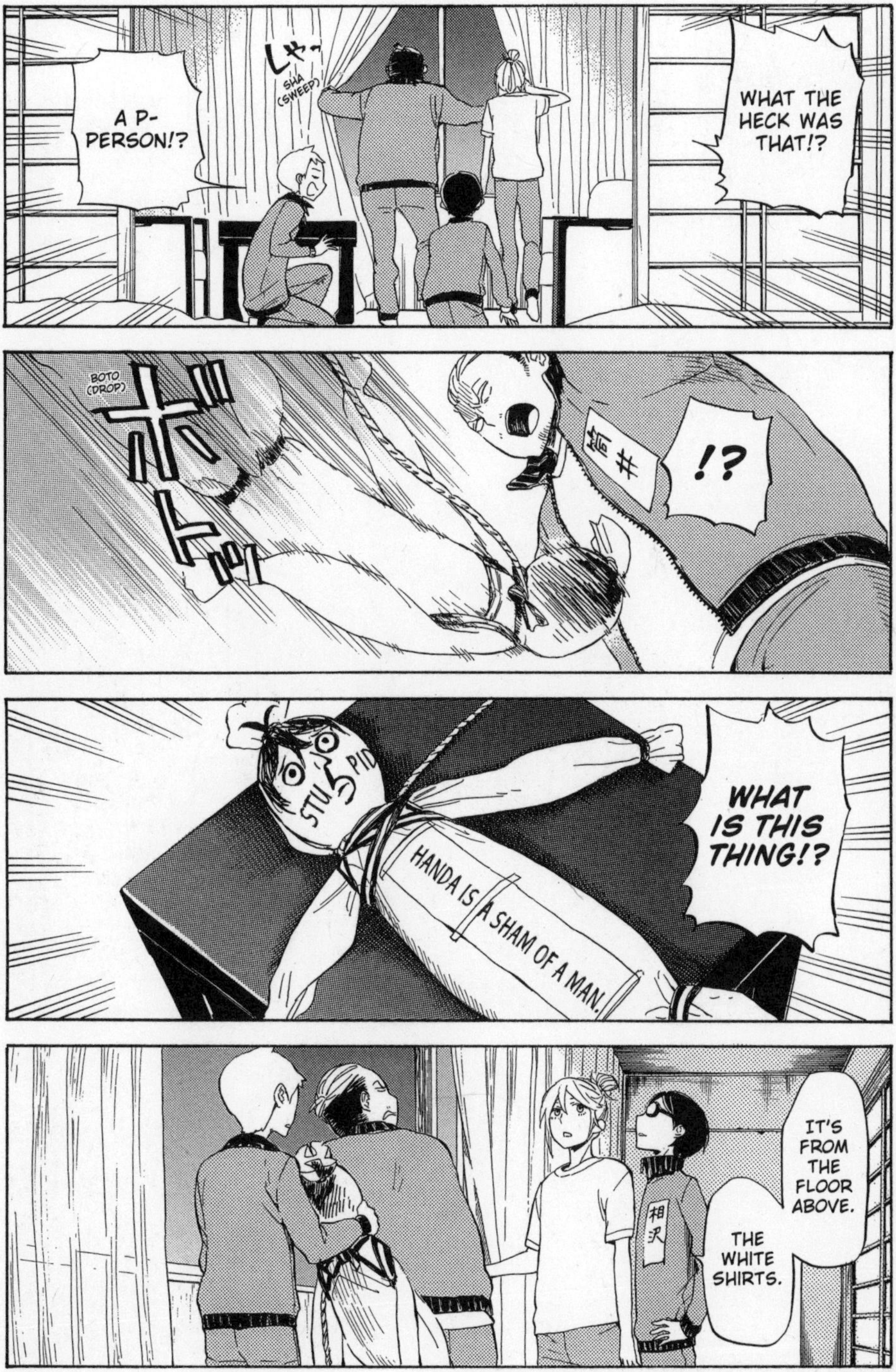
WHAT THE HECK WAS THAT!?
しゃっ
SHA (SWEEP)
A P-PERSON!?
!?
ボトッ
BOTO (DROP)
WHAT IS THIS THING!?
STUPID
HANDA IS A SHAM OF A MAN.
IT'S FROM THE FLOOR ABOVE.
THE WHITE SHIRTS.
相沢

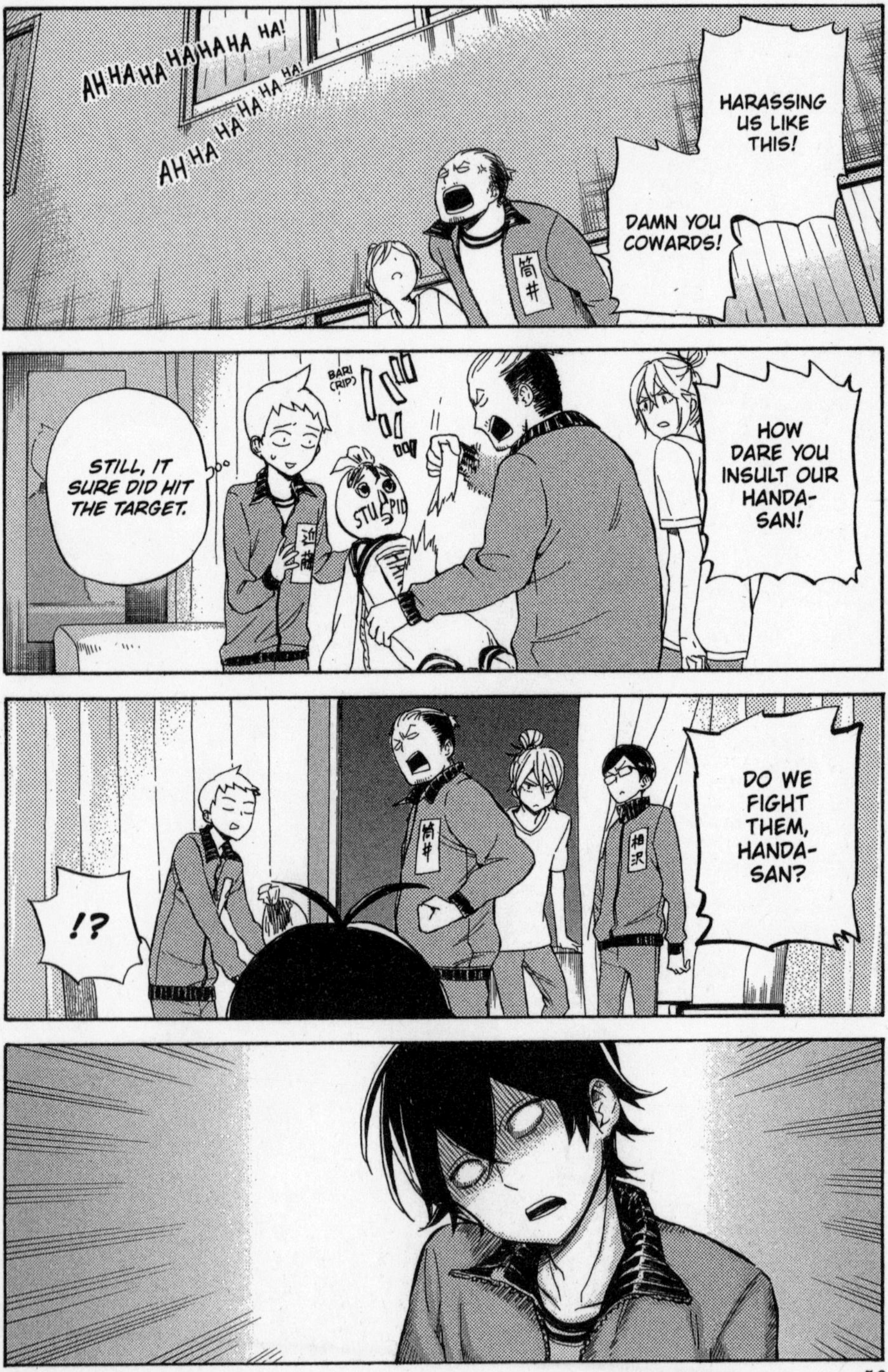
HARASSING US LIKE THIS!
DAMN YOU COWARDS!
筒井
AH HA HA HA HA HA HA!
AH HA HA HA HA HA!
HOW DARE YOU INSULT OUR HANDA-SAN!
BARI (RIP)
STUPID
近藤
STILL, IT SURE DID HIT THE TARGET.
DO WE FIGHT THEM, HANDA-SAN?
相沢
筒井
!?

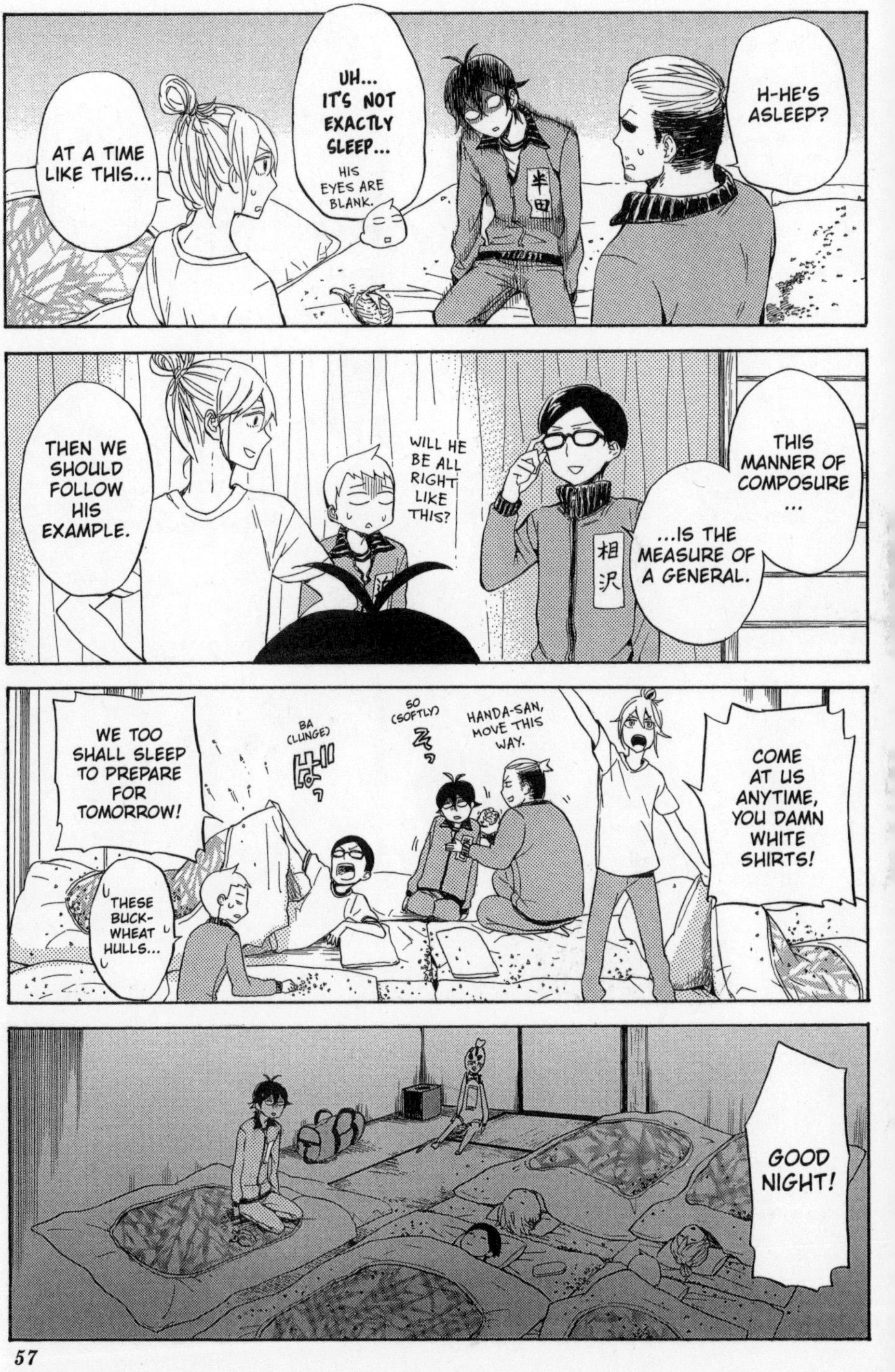
H-HE'S ASLEEP?
UH... IT'S NOT EXACTLY SLEEP...
HIS EYES ARE BLANK.
AT A TIME LIKE THIS...
THIS MANNER OF COMPOSURE ...
...IS THE MEASURE OF A GENERAL.
WILL HE BE ALL RIGHT LIKE THIS?
THEN WE SHOULD FOLLOW HIS EXAMPLE.
COME AT US ANYTIME, YOU DAMN WHITE SHIRTS!
HANDA-SAN, MOVE THIS WAY.
SO (SOFTLY)
BA (LUNGE)
WE TOO SHALL SLEEP TO PREPARE FOR TOMORROW!
THESE BUCK-WHEAT HULLS...
GOOD NIGHT!

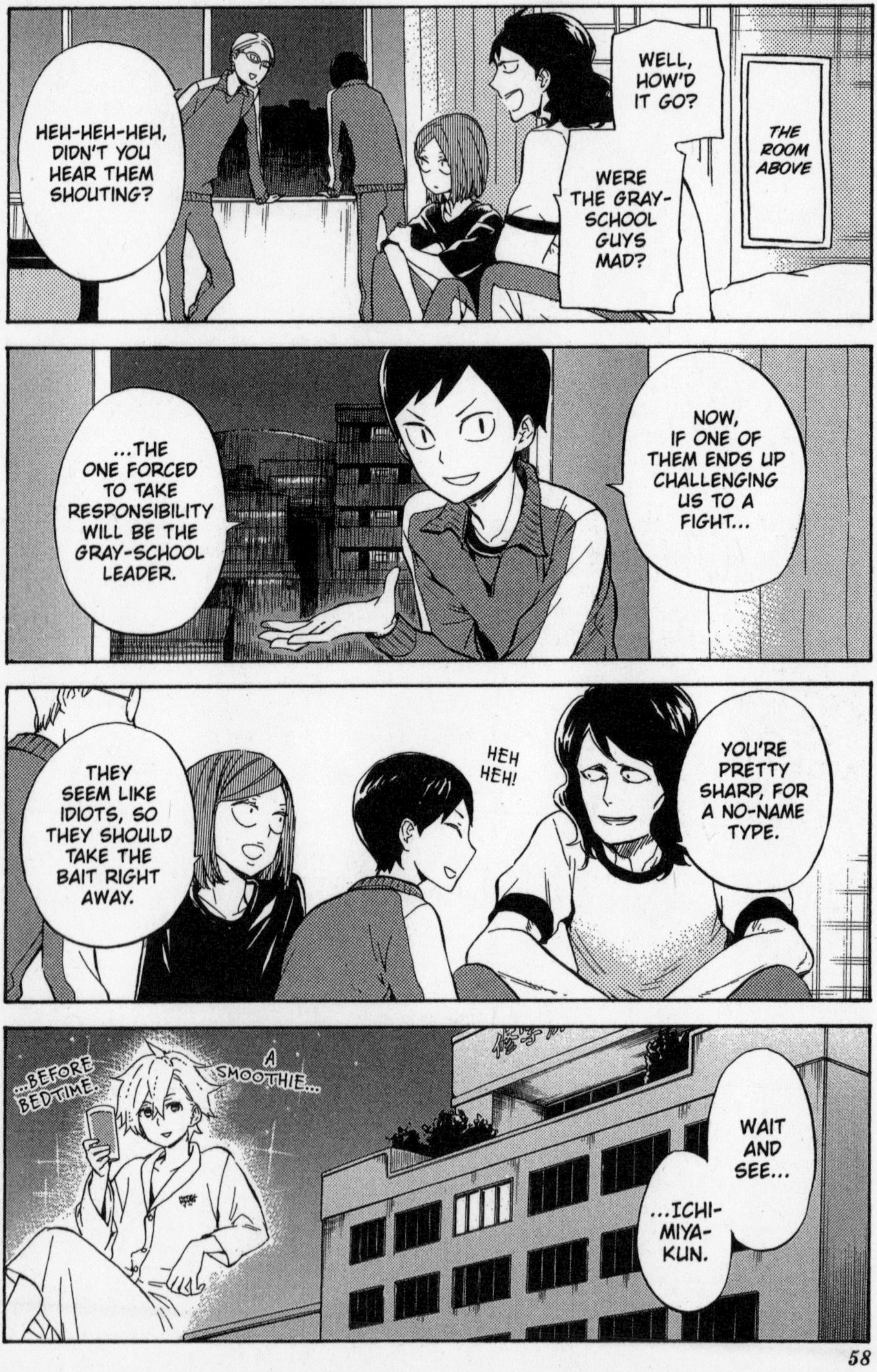
THE ROOM ABOVE
WELL, HOW'D IT GO?
WERE THE GRAY-SCHOOL GUYS MAD?
HEH-HEH-HEH, DIDN'T YOU HEAR THEM SHOUTING?
NOW, IF ONE OF THEM ENDS UP CHALLENGING US TO A FIGHT...
...THE ONE FORCED TO TAKE RESPONSIBILITY WILL BE THE GRAY-SCHOOL LEADER.
YOU'RE PRETTY SHARP, FOR A NO-NAME TYPE.
HEH HEH!
THEY SEEM LIKE IDIOTS, SO THEY SHOULD TAKE THE BAIT RIGHT AWAY.
WAIT AND SEE...
...ICHI-MIYA-KUN.
A SMOOTHIE...
...BEFORE BEDTIME.

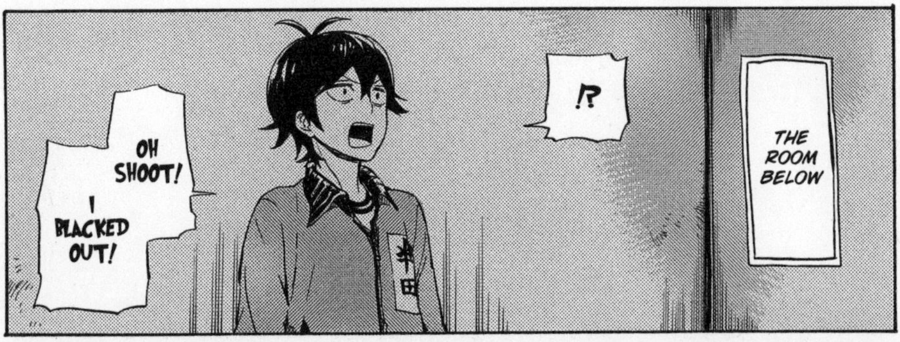
THE ROOM BELOW
!?
OH SHOOT!
I BLACKED OUT!

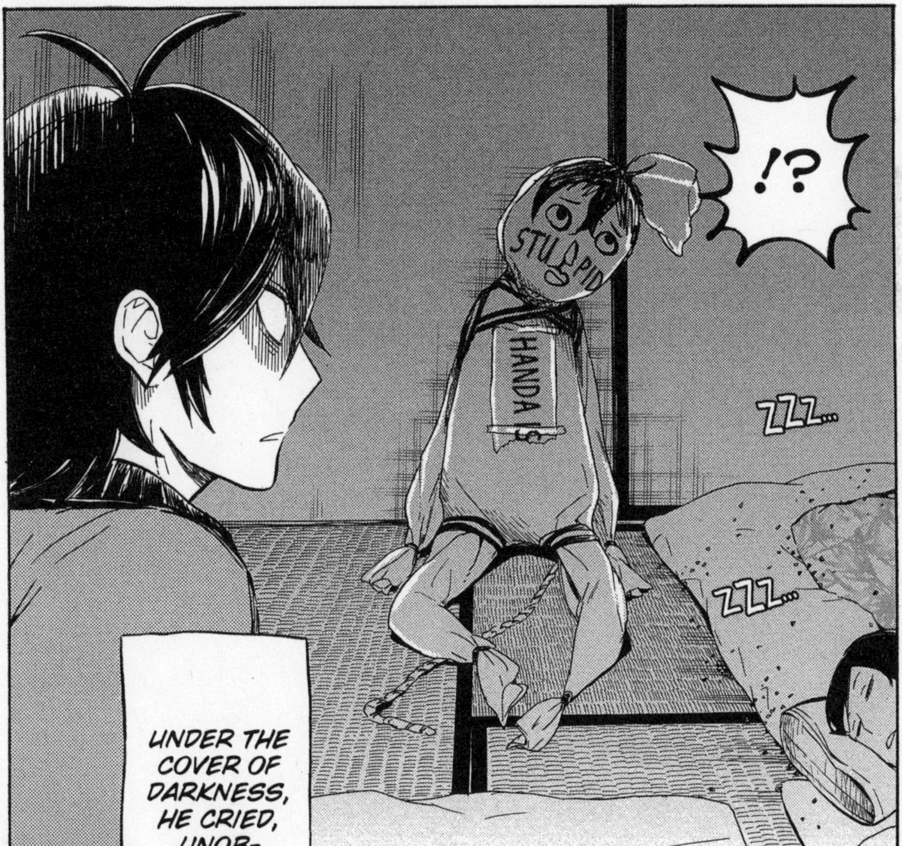
!?
STUPID
HANDA
ZZZ...
ZZZ...
UNDER THE COVER OF DARKNESS, HE CRIED, UNOB-SERVED.

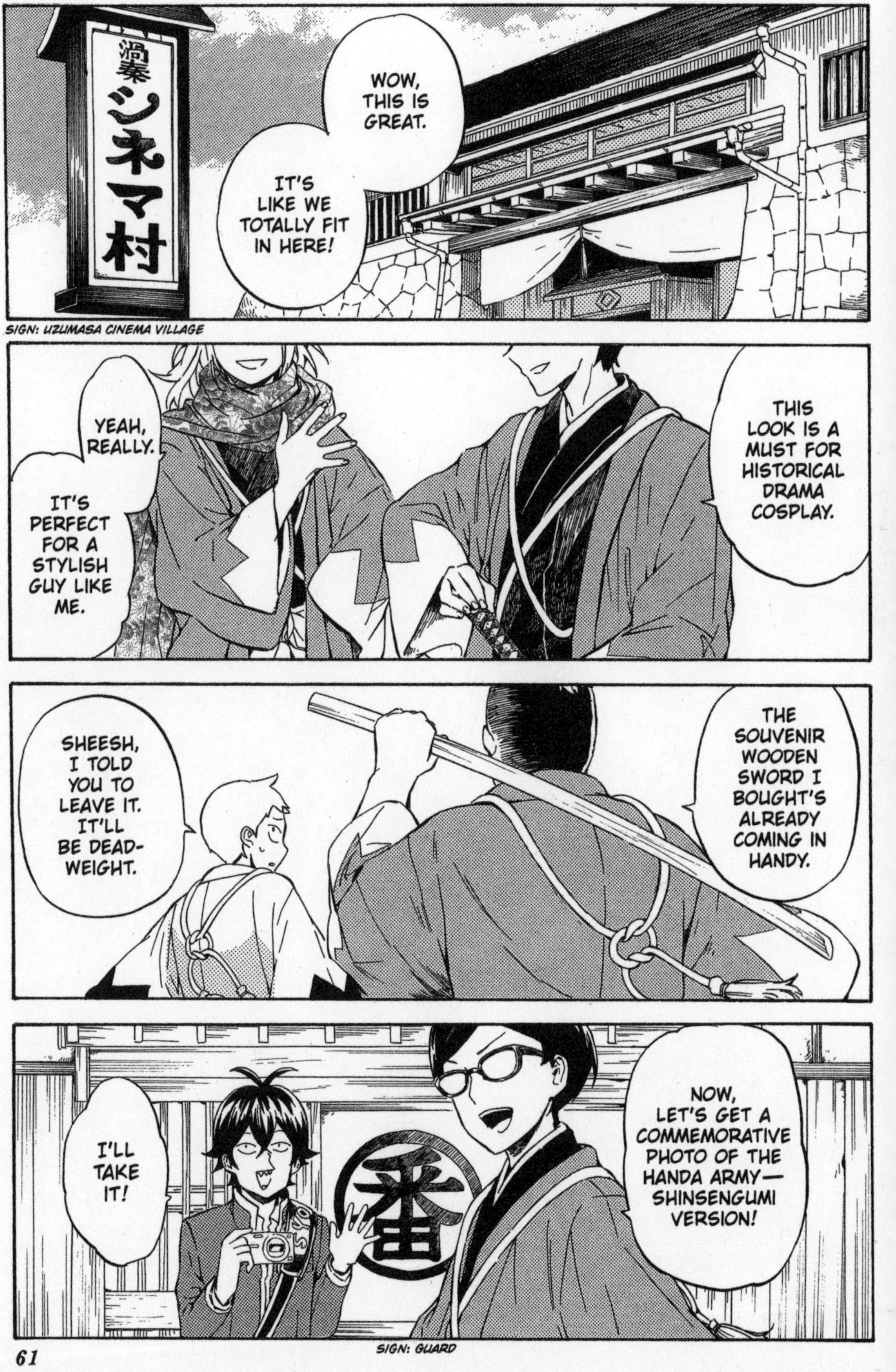
渦秦シネマ村
WOW, THIS IS GREAT.
IT'S LIKE WE TOTALLY FIT IN HERE!
SIGN: UZUMASA CINEMA VILLAGE
THIS LOOK IS A MUST FOR HISTORICAL DRAMA COSPLAY.
YEAH, REALLY.
IT'S PERFECT FOR A STYLISH GUY LIKE ME.
THE SOUVENIR WOODEN SWORD I BOUGHT'S ALREADY COMING IN HANDY.
SHEESH, I TOLD YOU TO LEAVE IT. IT'LL BE DEAD-WEIGHT.
NOW, LET'S GET A COMMEMORATIVE PHOTO OF THE HANDA ARMY—SHINSENGUMI VERSION!
I'LL TAKE IT!
SIGN: GUARD

Chapter 23: Handa-kun & the Class Trip, Day 2

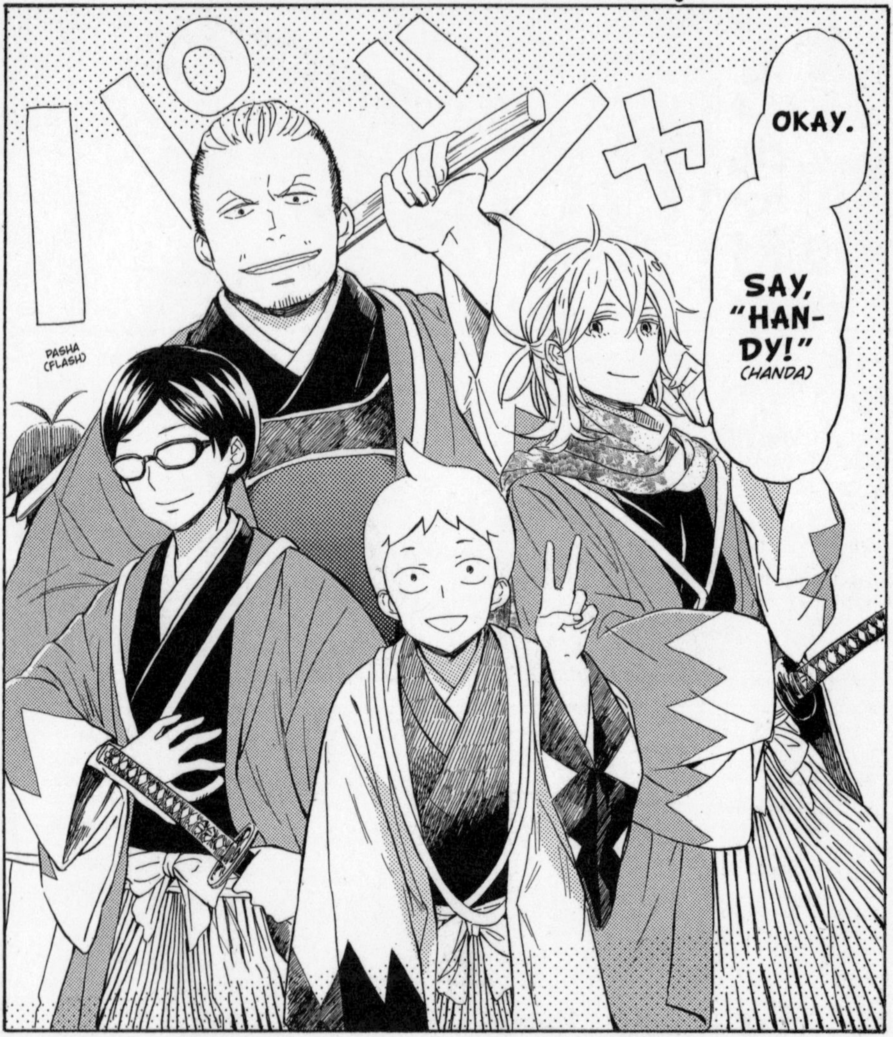
OKAY.
SAY, "HAN-DY!" (HANDA)
PASHA (FLASH)

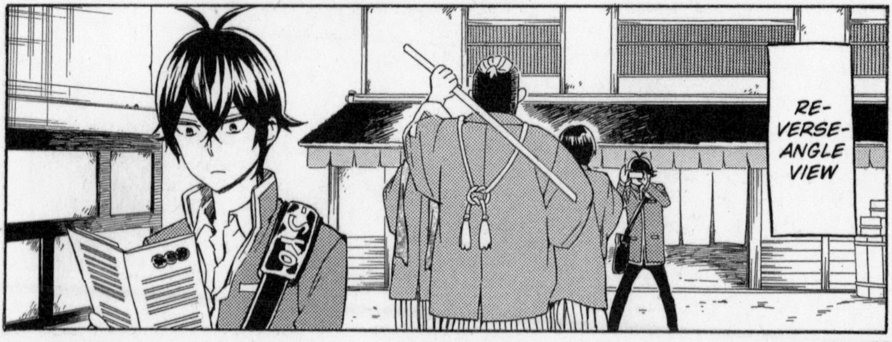
RE-VERSE-ANGLE VIEW

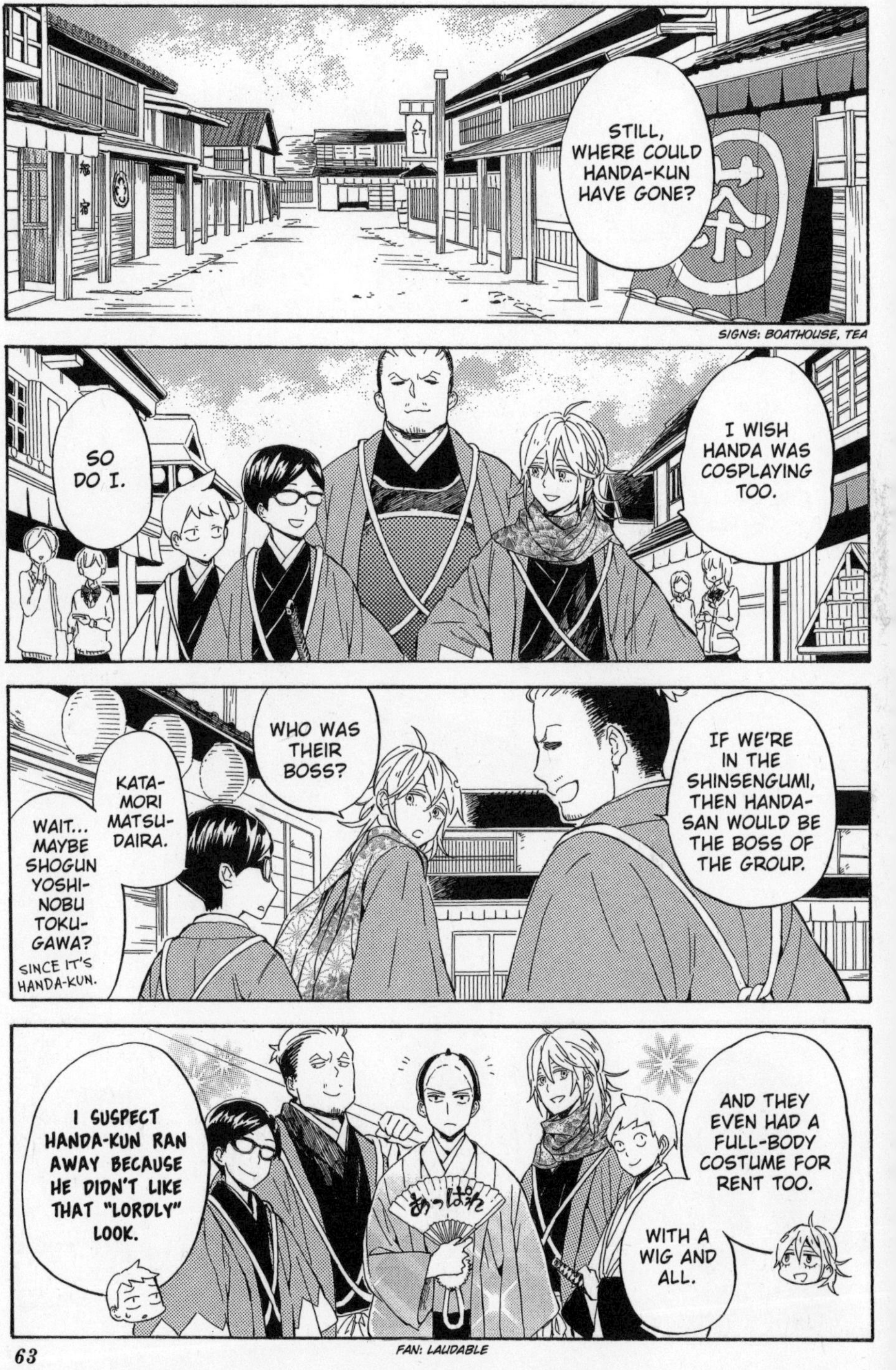
STILL, WHERE COULD HANDA-KUN HAVE GONE?
茶
I WISH HANDA WAS COSPLAYING TOO.
SO DO I.
IF WE'RE IN THE SHINSENGUMI, THEN HANDA-SAN WOULD BE THE BOSS OF THE GROUP.
WHO WAS THEIR BOSS?
KATA-MORI MATSU-DAIRA.
WAIT... MAYBE SHOGUN YOSHI-NOBU TOKU-GAWA?
SINCE IT'S HANDA-KUN.
AND THEY EVEN HAD A FULL-BODY COSTUME FOR RENT TOO.
WITH A WIG AND ALL.
あっぱれ
I SUSPECT HANDA-KUN RAN AWAY BECAUSE HE DIDN'T LIKE THAT "LORDLY" LOOK.

SIGNS: BOATHOUSE, TEA

FAN: LAUDABLE

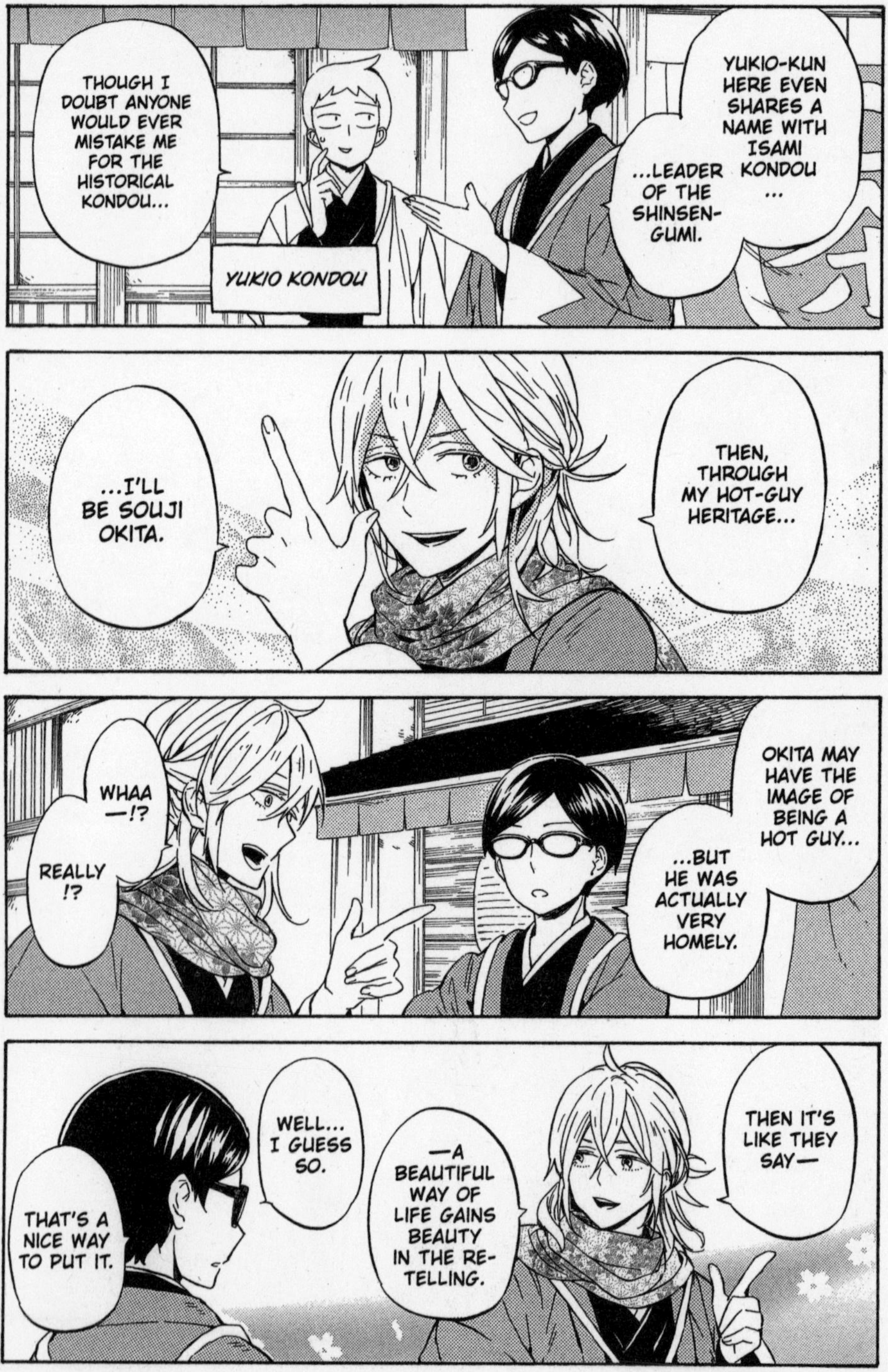
YUKIO-KUN HERE EVEN SHARES A NAME WITH ISAMI KONDOU ...
...LEADER OF THE SHINSEN-GUMI.
THOUGH I DOUBT ANYONE WOULD EVER MISTAKE ME FOR THE HISTORICAL KONDOU...
YUKIO KONDOU
THEN, THROUGH MY HOT-GUY HERITAGE...
...I'LL BE SOUJI OKITA.
OKITA MAY HAVE THE IMAGE OF BEING A HOT GUY...
...BUT HE WAS ACTUALLY VERY HOMELY.
WHAA—!?
REALLY!?
THEN IT'S LIKE THEY SAY—
—A BEAUTIFUL WAY OF LIFE GAINS BEAUTY IN THE RE-TELLING.
WELL... I GUESS SO.
THAT'S A NICE WAY TO PUT IT.

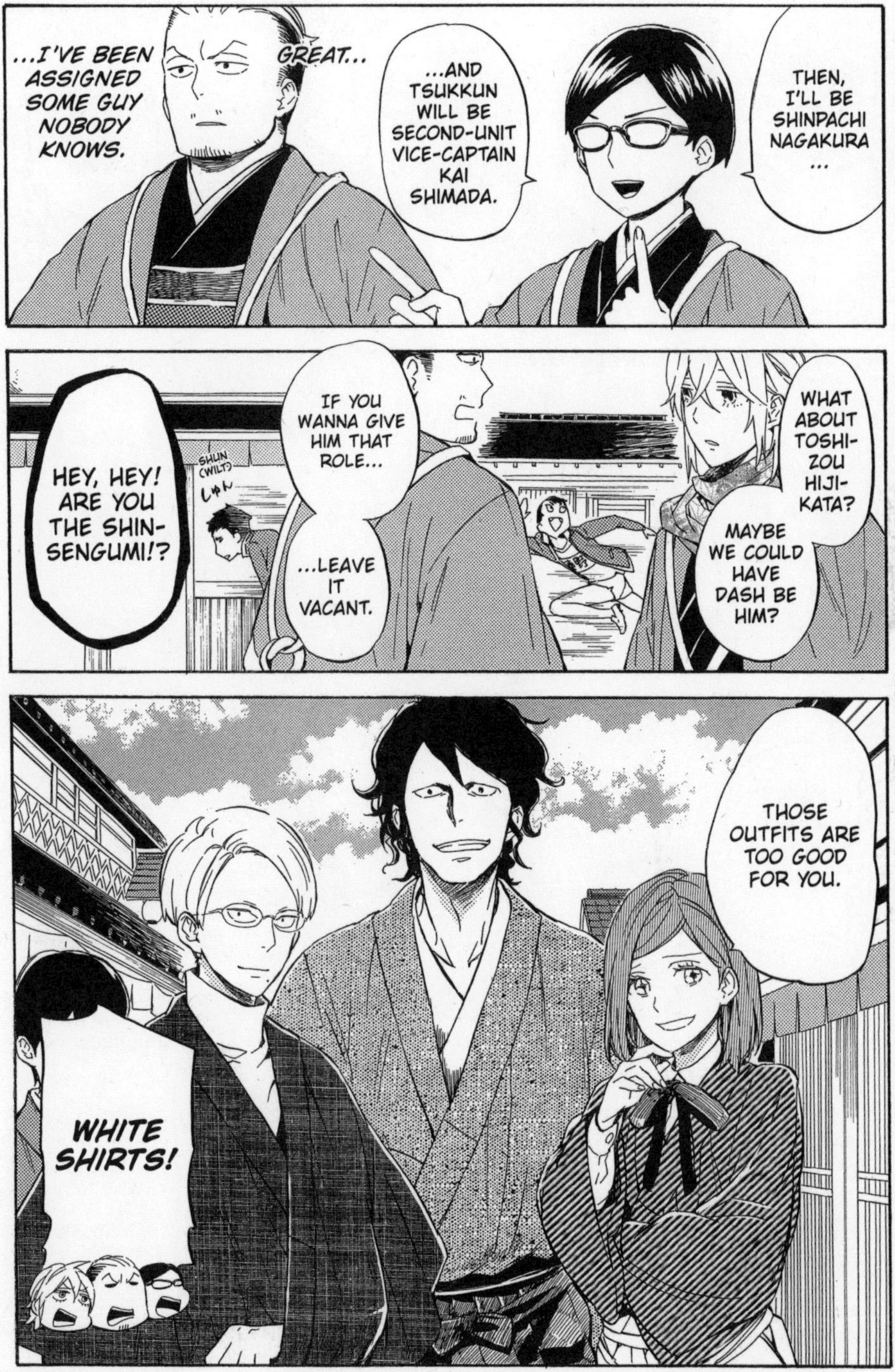
THEN, I'LL BE SHINPACHI NAGAKURA...
...AND TSUKKUN WILL BE SECOND-UNIT VICE-CAPTAIN KAI SHIMADA.
GREAT...
...I'VE BEEN ASSIGNED SOME GUY NOBODY KNOWS.
WHAT ABOUT TOSHI-ZOU HIJI-KATA?
MAYBE WE COULD HAVE DASH BE HIM?
IF YOU WANNA GIVE HIM THAT ROLE...
...LEAVE IT VACANT.
SHUN (WILT) しゅん
HEY, HEY! ARE YOU THE SHIN-SENGUMI!?
THOSE OUTFITS ARE TOO GOOD FOR YOU.
WHITE SHIRTS!

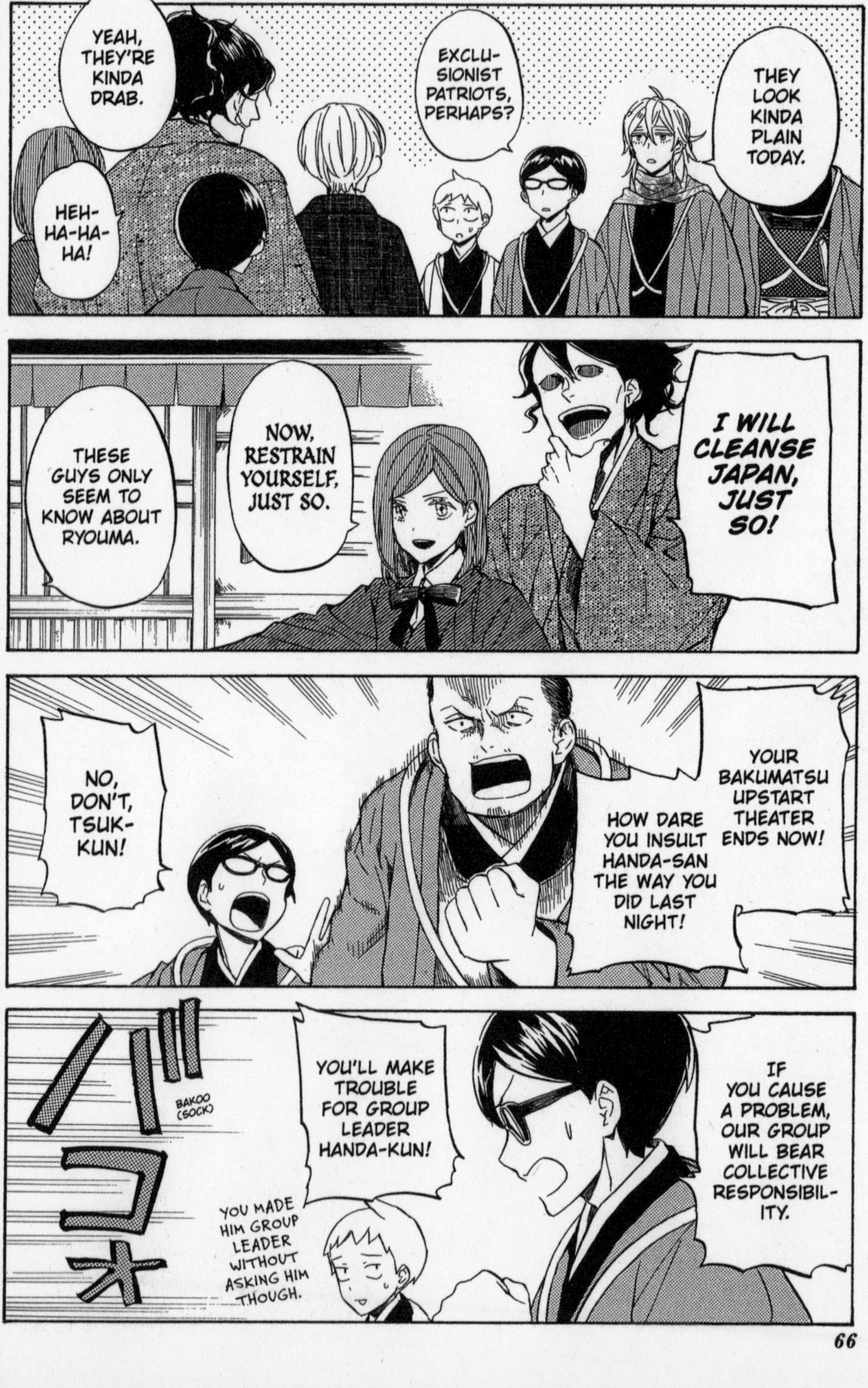
THEY LOOK KINDA PLAIN TODAY.
EXCLUSIONIST PATRIOTS, PERHAPS?
YEAH, THEY'RE KINDA DRAB.
HEH-HA-HA-HA!
I WILL CLEANSE JAPAN, JUST SO!
NOW, RESTRAIN YOURSELF, JUST SO.
THESE GUYS ONLY SEEM TO KNOW ABOUT RYOUMA.
YOUR BAKUMATSU UPSTART THEATER ENDS NOW!
HOW DARE YOU INSULT HANDA-SAN THE WAY YOU DID LAST NIGHT!
NO, DON'T, TSUK-KUN!
IF YOU CAUSE A PROBLEM, OUR GROUP WILL BEAR COLLECTIVE RESPONSIBILITY.
YOU'LL MAKE TROUBLE FOR GROUP LEADER HANDA-KUN!
バコォ
BAKOO (SOCK)
YOU MADE HIM GROUP LEADER WITHOUT ASKING HIM THOUGH.

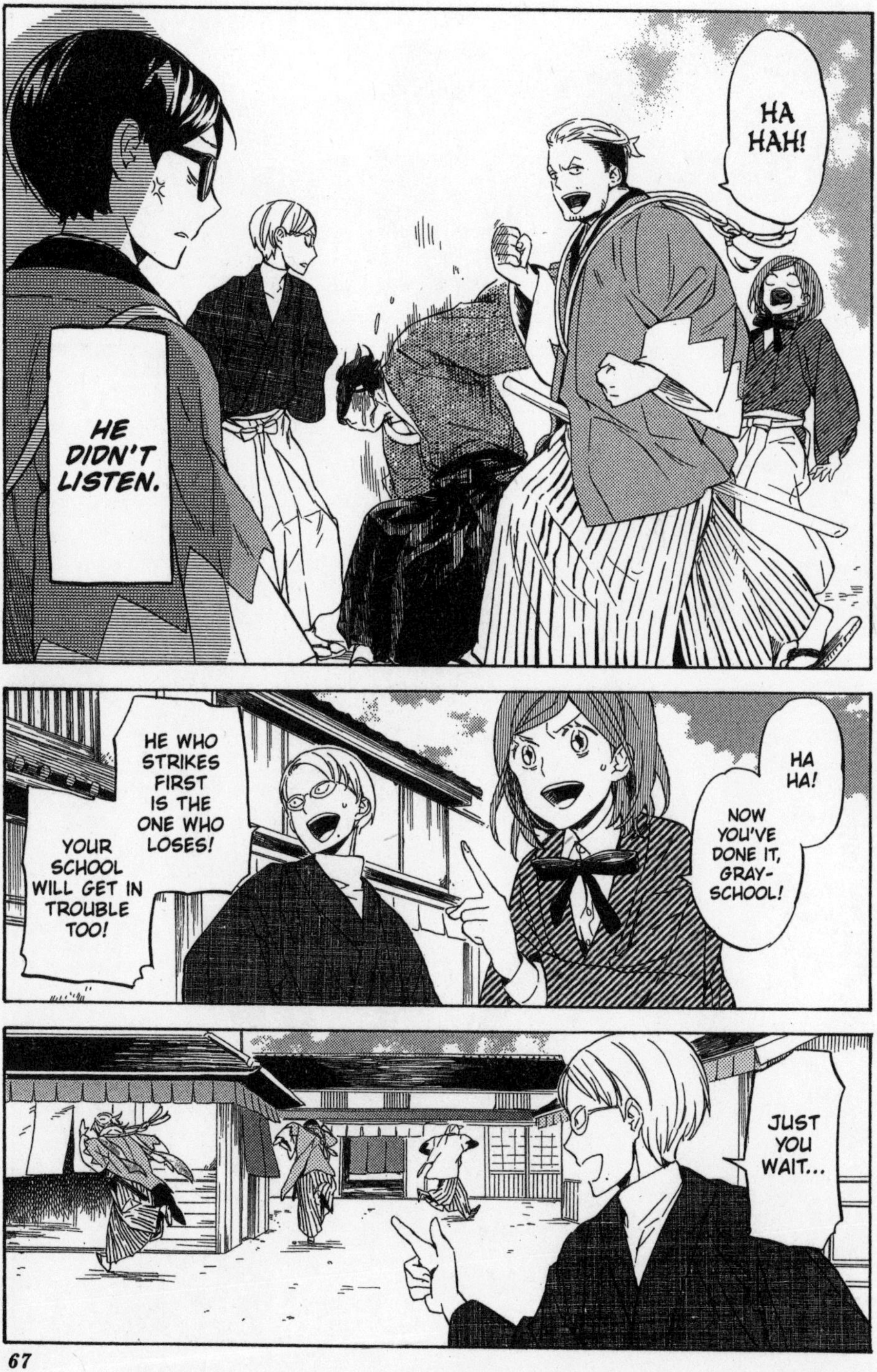
HA HAH!
HE DIDN'T LISTEN.
HA HA! NOW YOU'VE DONE IT, GRAY-SCHOOL!
HE WHO STRIKES FIRST IS THE ONE WHO LOSES!
YOUR SCHOOL WILL GET IN TROUBLE TOO!
JUST YOU WAIT...

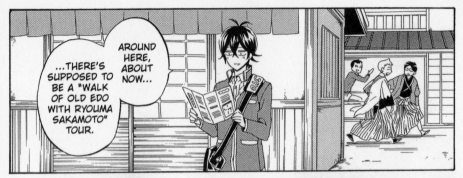

AROUND HERE, ABOUT NOW...
...THERE'S SUPPOSED TO BE A "WALK OF OLD EDO WITH RYOUMA SAKAMOTO" TOUR.
SEE, OVER THERE IS THE BRUSH SELLER.
LOVELY!!
WELL-VERSED!
HE'S A GENIUS!!
SUCH CHARISMA!
OH, GIRLS ARE GATHERING THERE.
THAT MUST BE IT.
SIGN: SNACKS
I'LL FOLLOW ALONG WITH THE TOUR.
AT A BIT OF A DISTANCE, SINCE GIRLS ARE SCARY.
KYAH!
NOW, TOWN GIRLS...
KYAH! KYAH!
...ON TO THE NEXT POINT OF INTEREST.
KYAH!

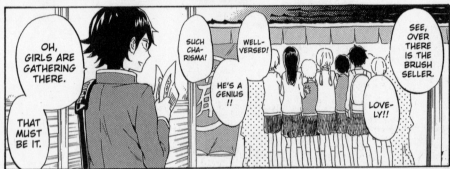

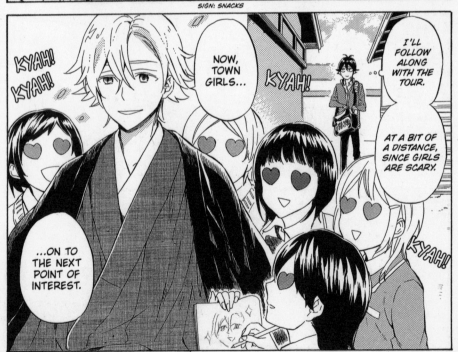

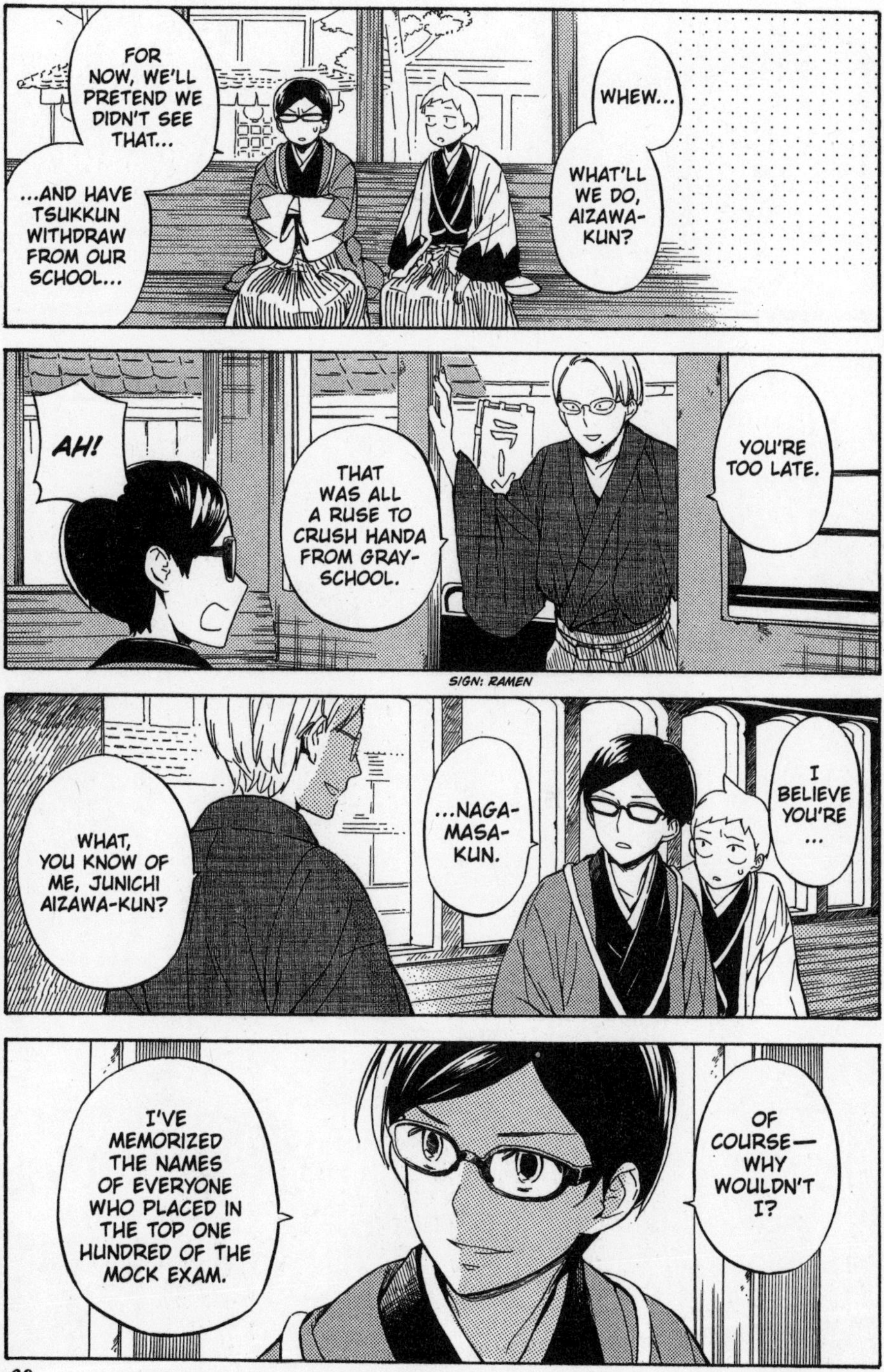
WHEW...
WHAT'LL WE DO, AIZAWA-KUN?
FOR NOW, WE'LL PRETEND WE DIDN'T SEE THAT...
...AND HAVE TSUKKUN WITHDRAW FROM OUR SCHOOL...
YOU'RE TOO LATE.
THAT WAS ALL A RUSE TO CRUSH HANDA FROM GRAY-SCHOOL.
AH!
SIGN: RAMEN
I BELIEVE YOU'RE ...
...NAGA-MASA-KUN.
WHAT, YOU KNOW OF ME, JUNICHI AIZAWA-KUN?
OF COURSE—WHY WOULDN'T I?
I'VE MEMORIZED THE NAMES OF EVERYONE WHO PLACED IN THE TOP ONE HUNDRED OF THE MOCK EXAM.

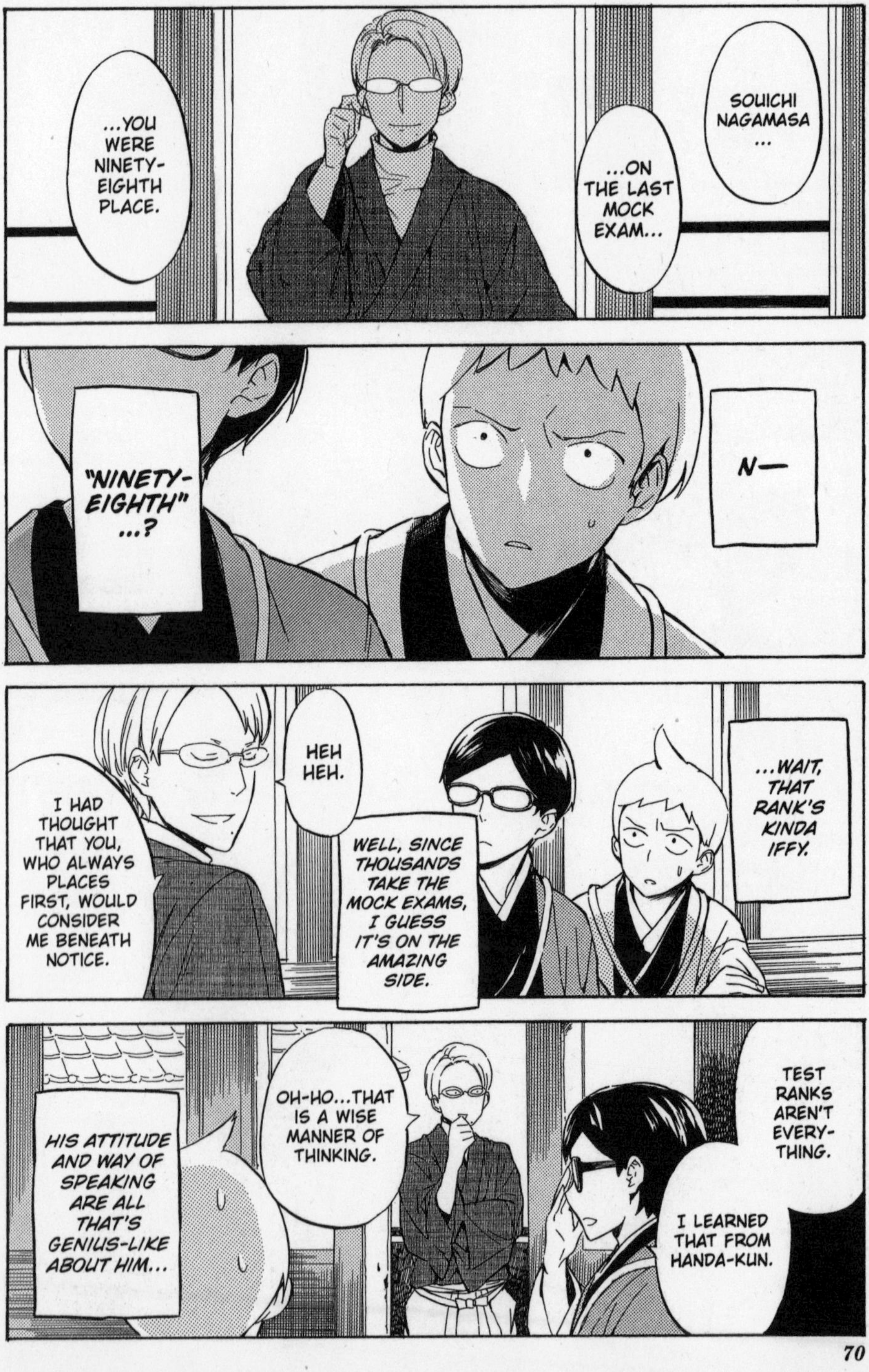
SOUICHI NAGAMASA ...
...ON THE LAST MOCK EXAM...
...YOU WERE NINETY-EIGHTH PLACE.
N—
"NINETY-EIGHTH" ...?
...WAIT, THAT RANK'S KINDA IFFY.
WELL, SINCE THOUSANDS TAKE THE MOCK EXAMS, I GUESS IT'S ON THE AMAZING SIDE.
HEH HEH.
I HAD THOUGHT THAT YOU, WHO ALWAYS PLACES FIRST, WOULD CONSIDER ME BENEATH NOTICE.
TEST RANKS AREN'T EVERY-THING.
I LEARNED THAT FROM HANDA-KUN.
OH-HO...THAT IS A WISE MANNER OF THINKING.
HIS ATTITUDE AND WAY OF SPEAKING ARE ALL THAT'S GENIUS-LIKE ABOUT HIM...

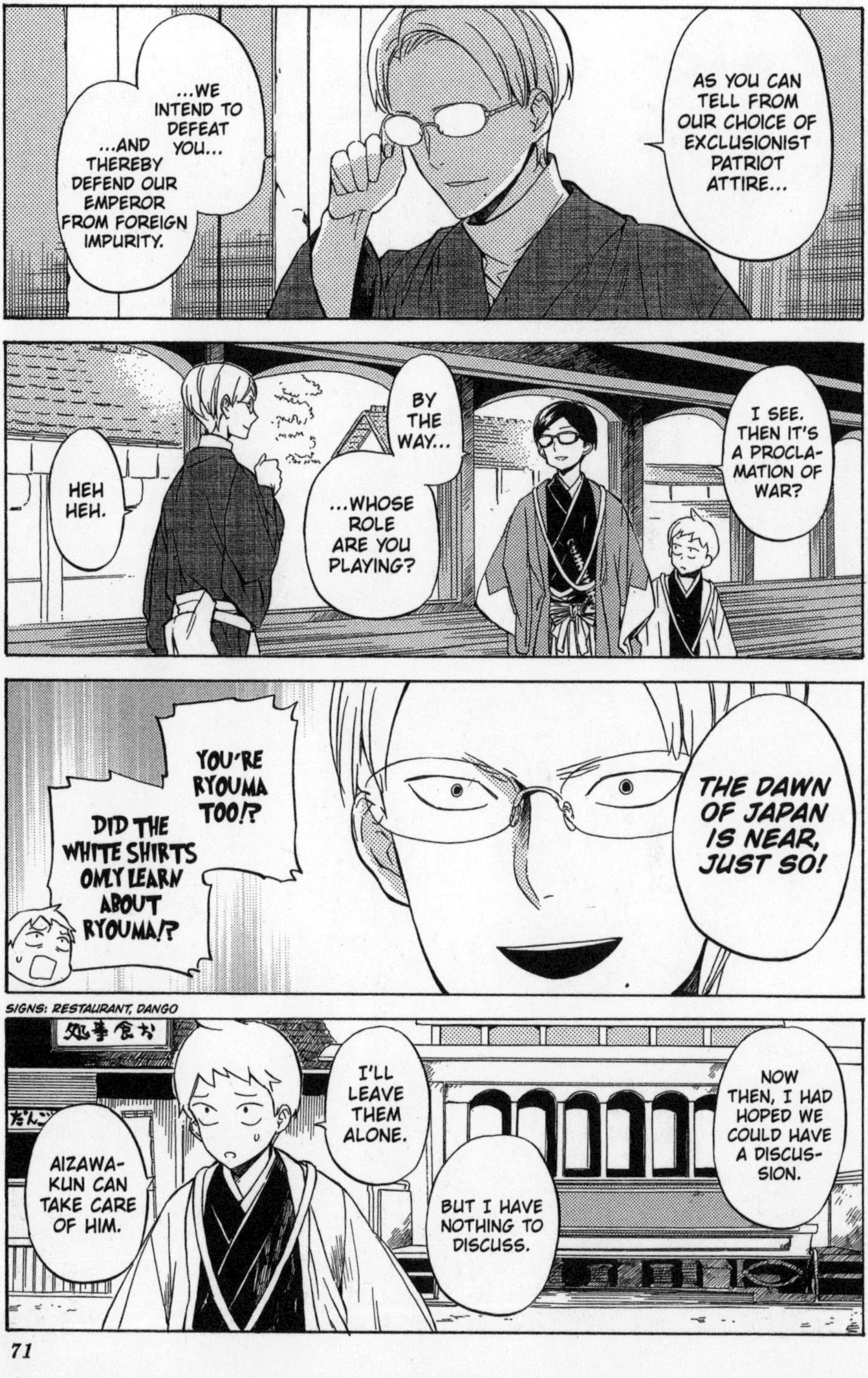
AS YOU CAN TELL FROM OUR CHOICE OF EXCLUSIONIST PATRIOT ATTIRE...
...WE INTEND TO DEFEAT YOU...
...AND THEREBY DEFEND OUR EMPEROR FROM FOREIGN IMPURITY.
I SEE. THEN IT'S A PROCLAMATION OF WAR?
BY THE WAY...
...WHOSE ROLE ARE YOU PLAYING?
HEH HEH.
THE DAWN OF JAPAN IS NEAR, JUST SO!
YOU'RE RYOUMA TOO!?
DID THE WHITE SHIRTS ONLY LEARN ABOUT RYOUMA!?
SIGNS: RESTAURANT, DANGO
お食事処
だんご
NOW THEN, I HAD HOPED WE COULD HAVE A DISCUSSION.
BUT I HAVE NOTHING TO DISCUSS.
I'LL LEAVE THEM ALONE.
AIZAWA-KUN CAN TAKE CARE OF HIM.

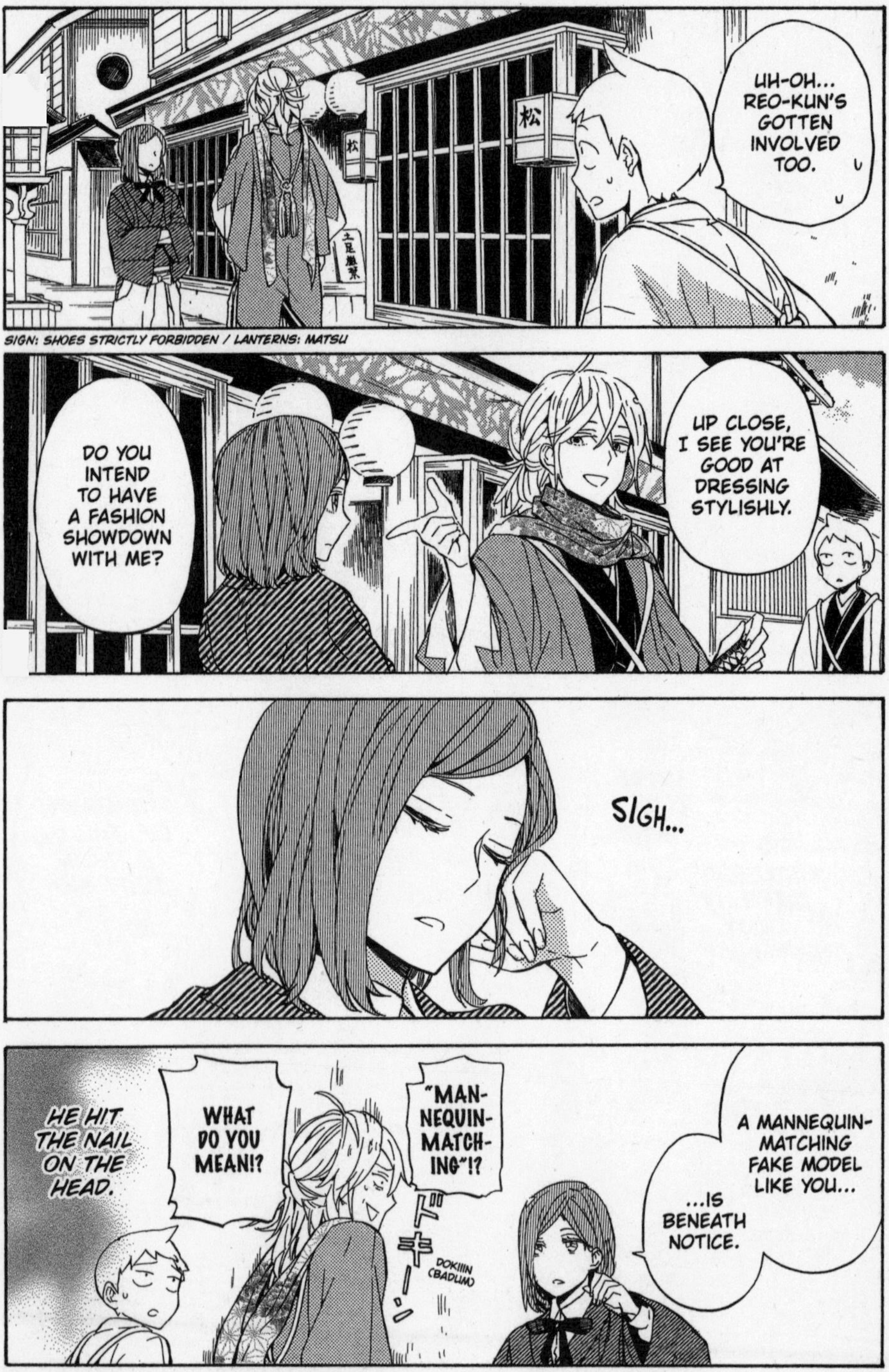
UH-OH... REO-KUN'S GOTTEN INVOLVED TOO.
SIGN: SHOES STRICTLY FORBIDDEN / LANTERNS: MATSU
UP CLOSE, I SEE YOU'RE GOOD AT DRESSING STYLISHLY.
DO YOU INTEND TO HAVE A FASHION SHOWDOWN WITH ME?
SIGH...
A MANNEQUIN-MATCHING FAKE MODEL LIKE YOU...
...IS BENEATH NOTICE.
DOKIIIN (BADUM)
"MANNEQUIN-MATCHING"!?
WHAT DO YOU MEAN!?
HE HIT THE NAIL ON THE HEAD.

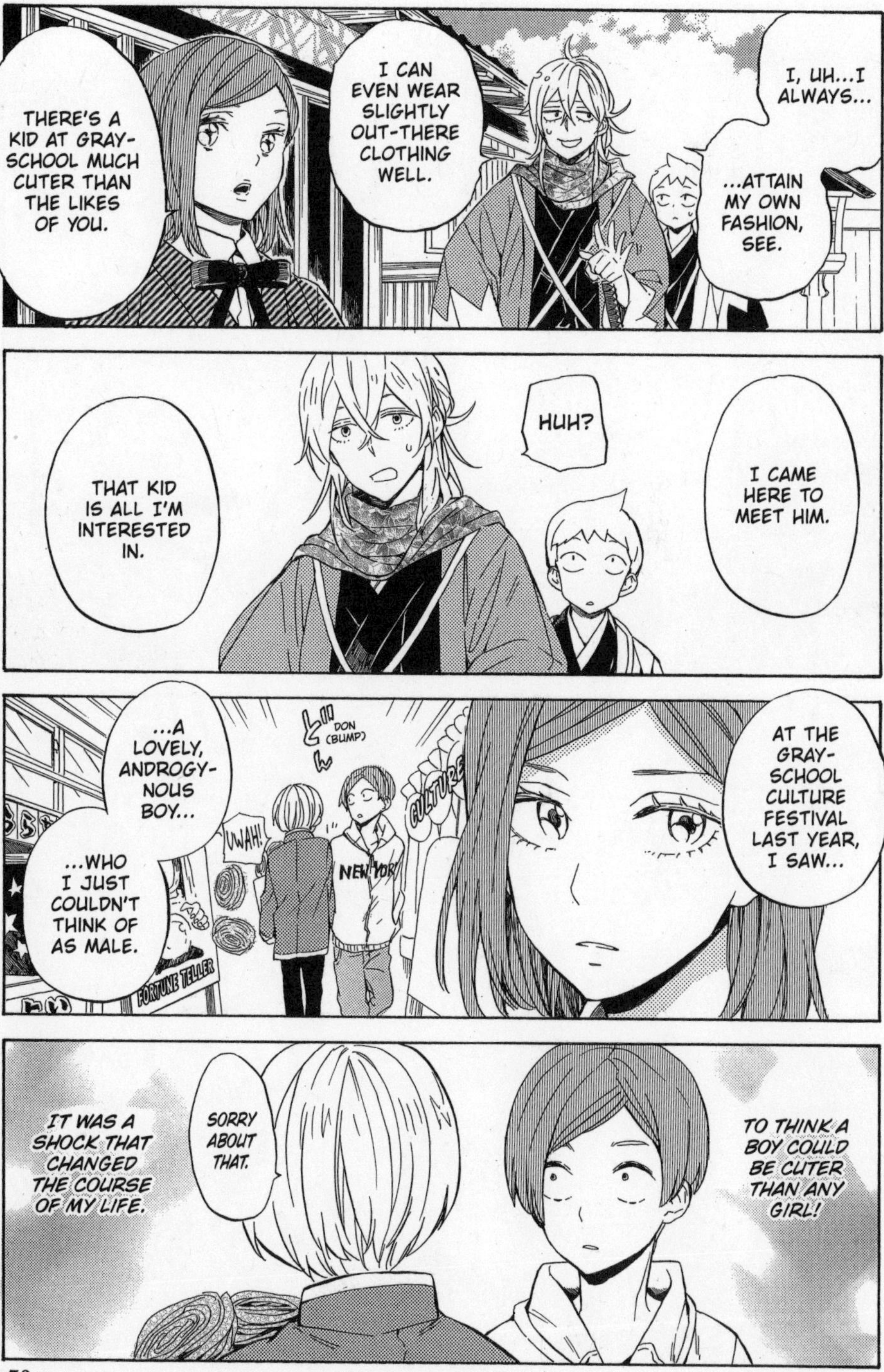
I, UH...I ALWAYS...
...ATTAIN MY OWN FASHION, SEE.
I CAN EVEN WEAR SLIGHTLY OUT-THERE CLOTHING WELL.
THERE'S A KID AT GRAY-SCHOOL MUCH CUTER THAN THE LIKES OF YOU.
I CAME HERE TO MEET HIM.
HUH?
THAT KID IS ALL I'M INTERESTED IN.
AT THE GRAY-SCHOOL CULTURE FESTIVAL LAST YEAR, I SAW...
CULTURE
DON (BUMP)
...A LOVELY, ANDROGYNOUS BOY...
UWAH!
NEW YOR
...WHO I JUST COULDN'T THINK OF AS MALE.
FORTUNE TELLER
TO THINK A BOY COULD BE CUTER THAN ANY GIRL!
SORRY ABOUT THAT.
IT WAS A SHOCK THAT CHANGED THE COURSE OF MY LIFE.

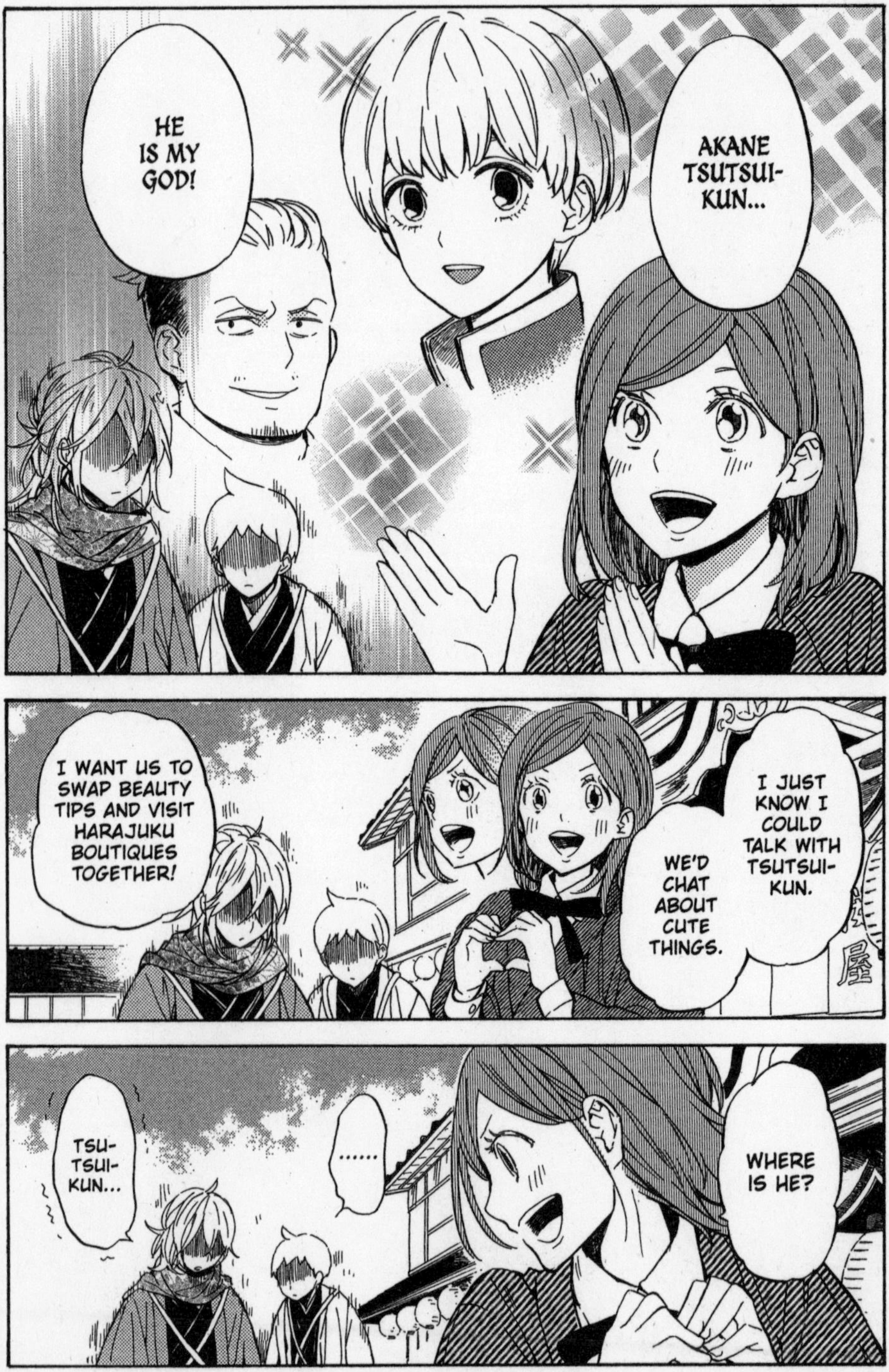
AKANE TSUTSUI-KUN...
HE IS MY GOD!
I JUST KNOW I COULD TALK WITH TSUTSUI-KUN.
WE'D CHAT ABOUT CUTE THINGS.
I WANT US TO SWAP BEAUTY TIPS AND VISIT HARAJUKU BOUTIQUES TOGETHER!
WHERE IS HE?
......
TSU-TSUI-KUN...

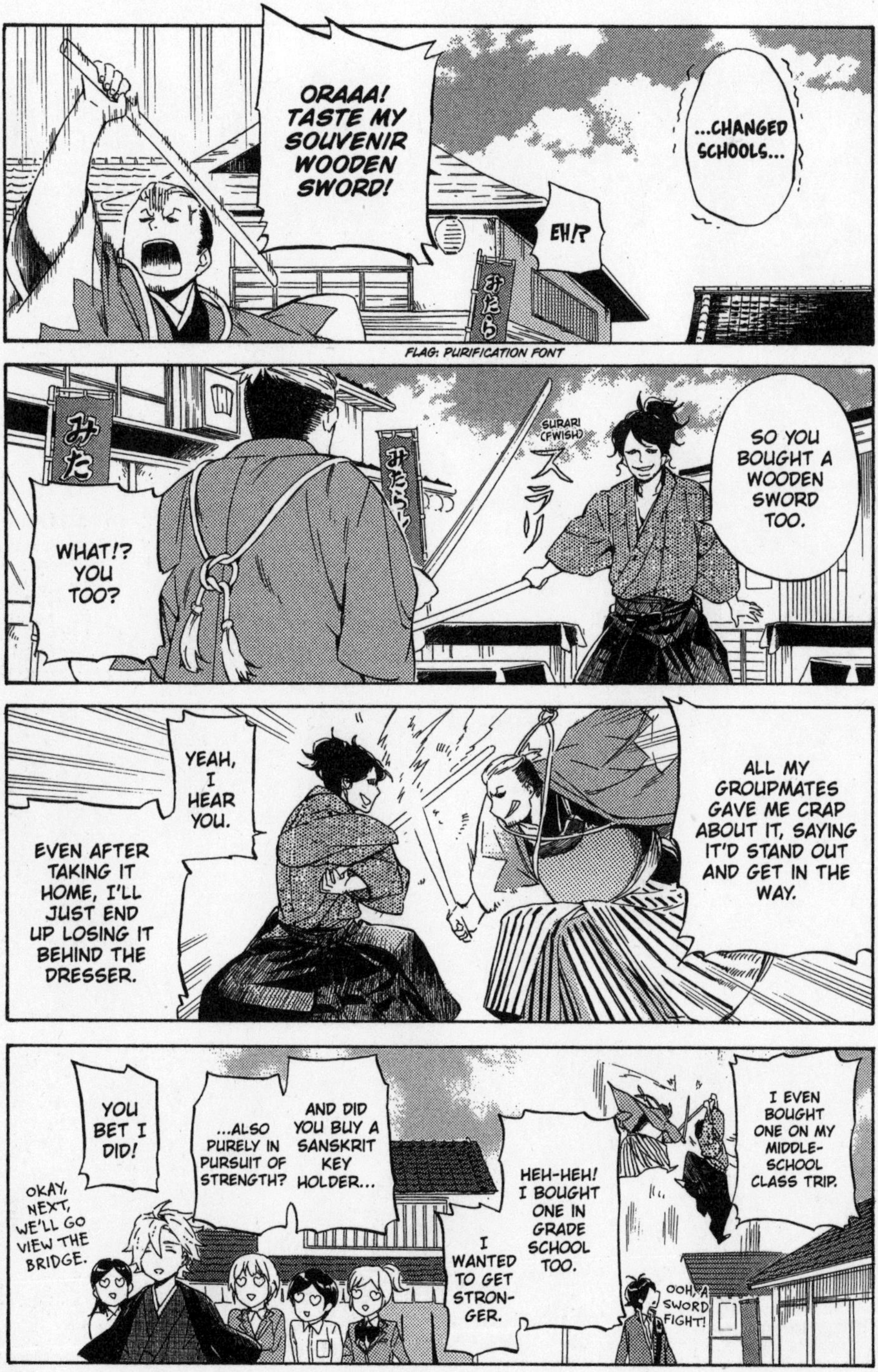
...CHANGED SCHOOLS...
EH!?
ORAAA! TASTE MY SOUVENIR WOODEN SWORD!
FLAG: PURIFICATION FONT
SO YOU BOUGHT A WOODEN SWORD TOO.
SURARI (FWISH)
スラリ
WHAT!? YOU TOO?
ALL MY GROUPMATES GAVE ME CRAP ABOUT IT, SAYING IT'D STAND OUT AND GET IN THE WAY.
YEAH, I HEAR YOU.
EVEN AFTER TAKING IT HOME, I'LL JUST END UP LOSING IT BEHIND THE DRESSER.
I EVEN BOUGHT ONE ON MY MIDDLE-SCHOOL CLASS TRIP.
OOH, A SWORD FIGHT!
HEH-HEH! I BOUGHT ONE IN GRADE SCHOOL TOO.
I WANTED TO GET STRON-GER.
AND DID YOU BUY A SANSKRIT KEY HOLDER...
...ALSO PURELY IN PURSUIT OF STRENGTH?
YOU BET I DID!
OKAY, NEXT, WE'LL GO VIEW THE BRIDGE.

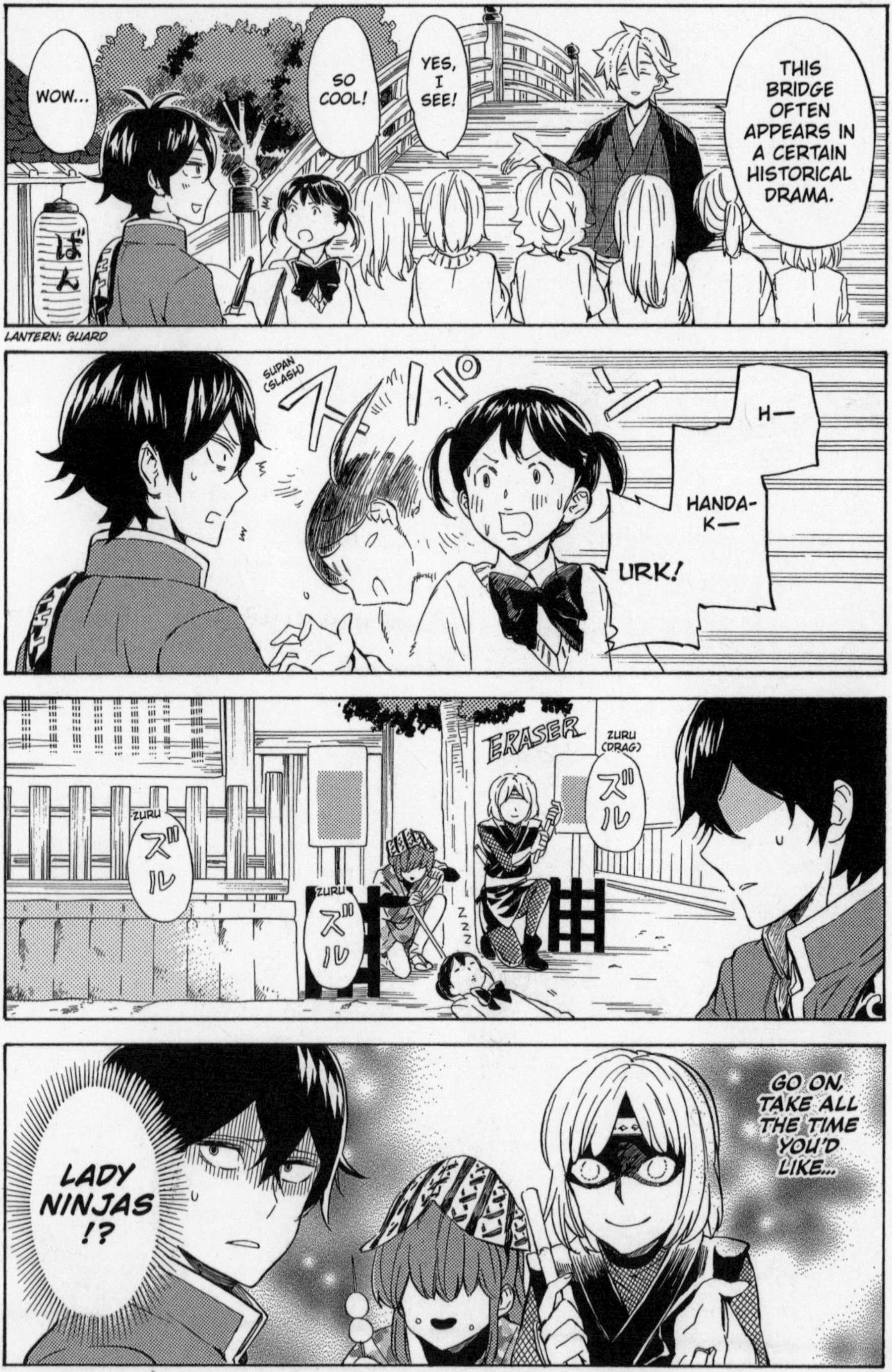
THIS BRIDGE OFTEN APPEARS IN A CERTAIN HISTORICAL DRAMA.
YES, I SEE!
SO COOL!
WOW...
ばん
LANTERN: GUARD
H—
HANDA-K—
URK!
SUPAN (SLASH)
ZURU (DRAG)
ズル
ERASER
ZZZ
ZURU
ズル
ZURU
ズル
GO ON, TAKE ALL THE TIME YOU'D LIKE...
LADY NINJAS!?

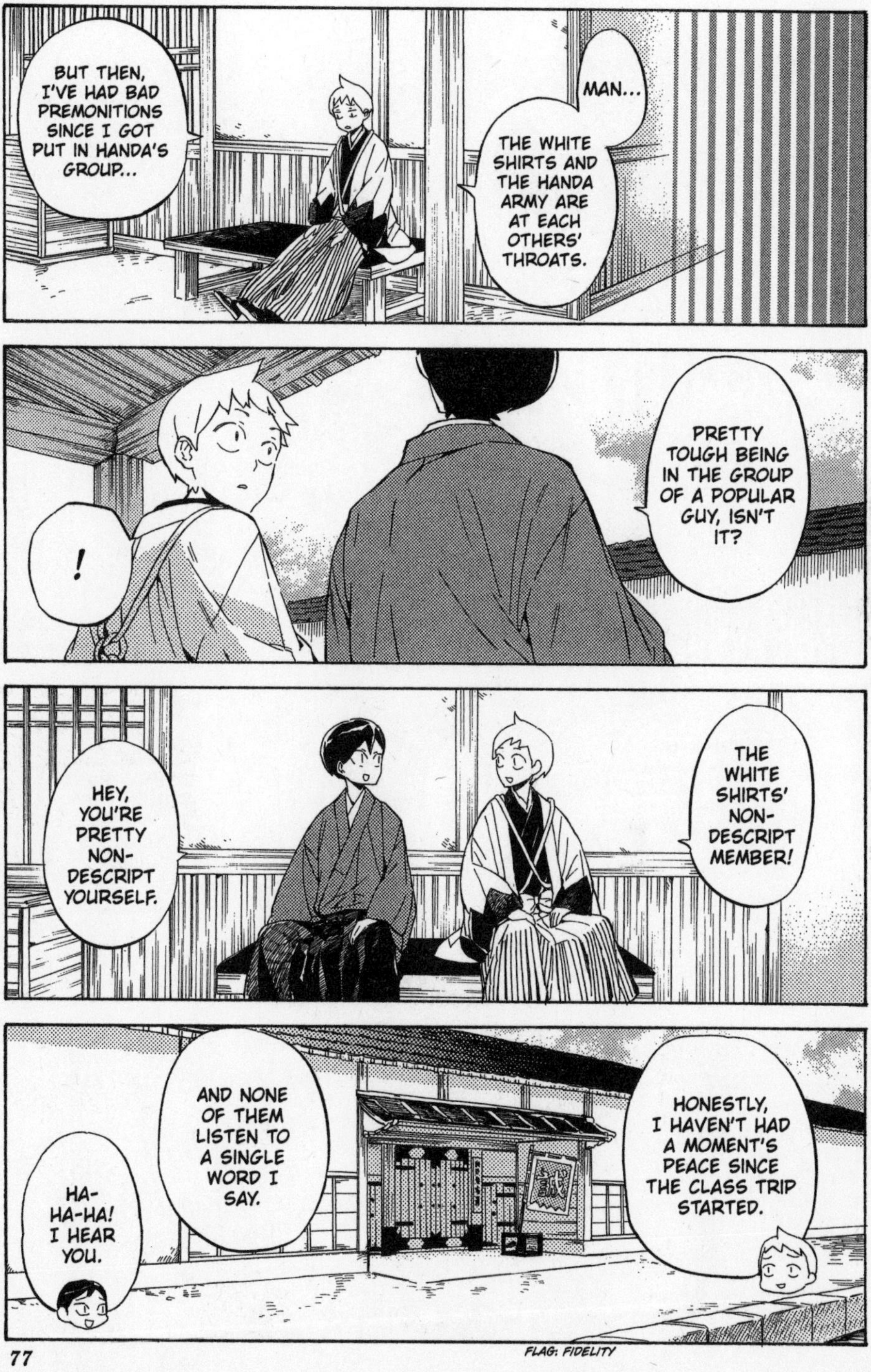
MAN...
THE WHITE SHIRTS AND THE HANDA ARMY ARE AT EACH OTHERS' THROATS.
BUT THEN, I'VE HAD BAD PREMONITIONS SINCE I GOT PUT IN HANDA'S GROUP...
PRETTY TOUGH BEING IN THE GROUP OF A POPULAR GUY, ISN'T IT?
!
THE WHITE SHIRTS' NON-DESCRIPT MEMBER!
HEY, YOU'RE PRETTY NON-DESCRIPT YOURSELF.
HONESTLY, I HAVEN'T HAD A MOMENT'S PEACE SINCE THE CLASS TRIP STARTED.
AND NONE OF THEM LISTEN TO A SINGLE WORD I SAY.
HA-HA-HA! I HEAR YOU.

FLAG: FIDELITY

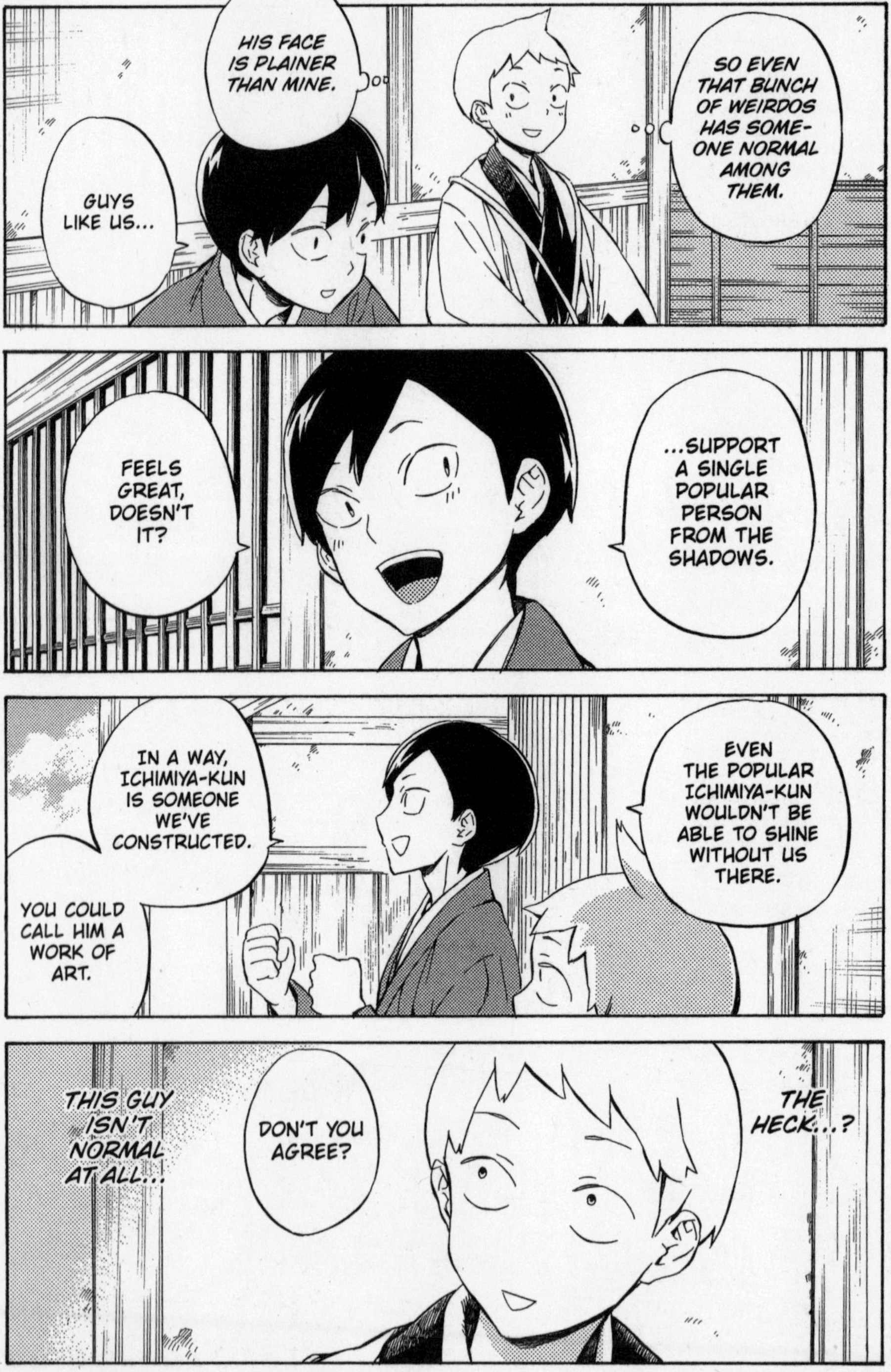
SO EVEN THAT BUNCH OF WEIRDOS HAS SOME-ONE NORMAL AMONG THEM.
HIS FACE IS PLAINER THAN MINE.
GUYS LIKE US...
...SUPPORT A SINGLE POPULAR PERSON FROM THE SHADOWS.
FEELS GREAT, DOESN'T IT?
EVEN THE POPULAR ICHIMIYA-KUN WOULDN'T BE ABLE TO SHINE WITHOUT US THERE.
IN A WAY, ICHIMIYA-KUN IS SOMEONE WE'VE CONSTRUCTED.
YOU COULD CALL HIM A WORK OF ART.
THE HECK...?
DON'T YOU AGREE?
THIS GUY ISN'T NORMAL AT ALL...

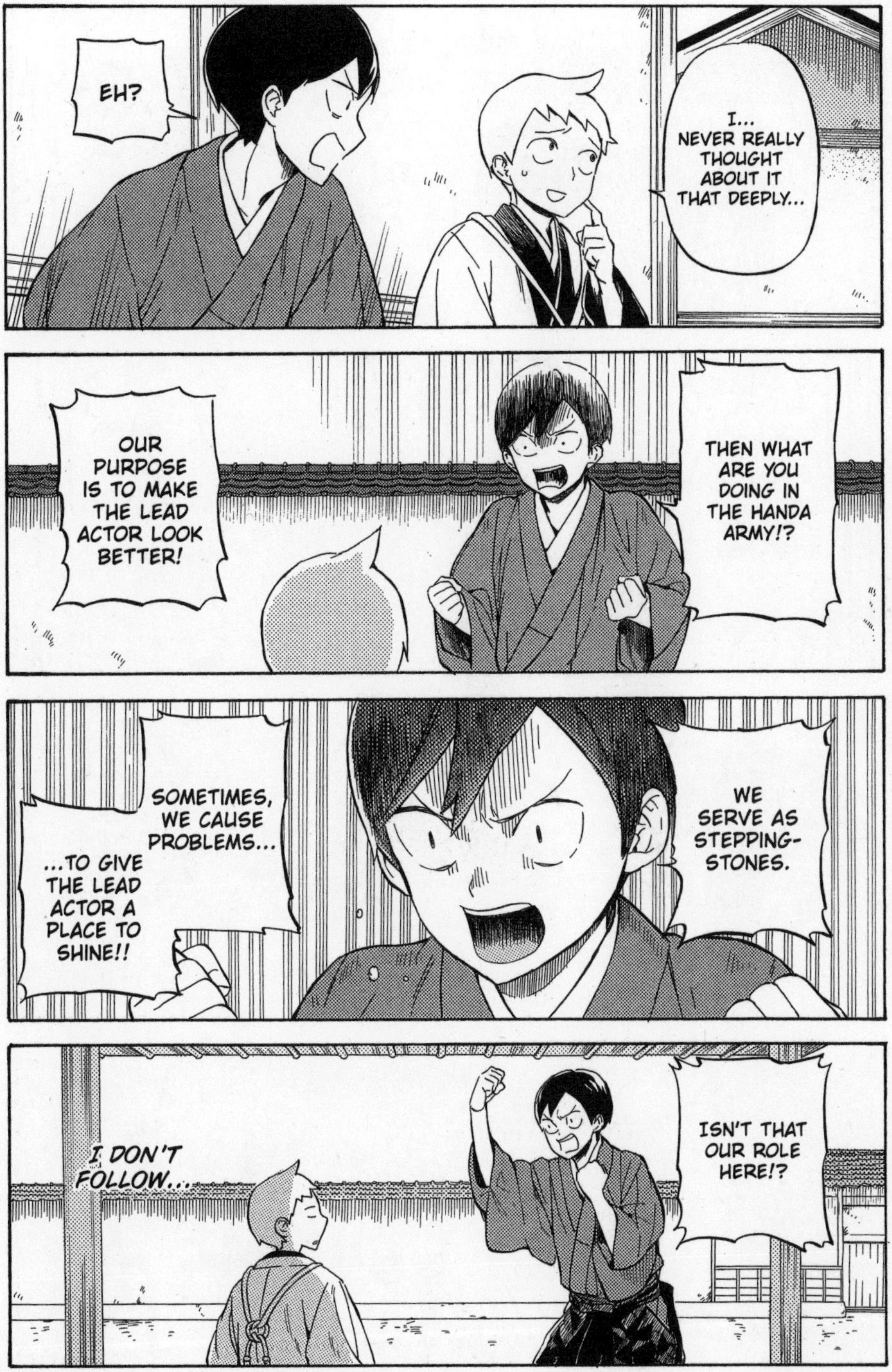
I... NEVER REALLY THOUGHT ABOUT IT THAT DEEPLY...
EH?
THEN WHAT ARE YOU DOING IN THE HANDA ARMY!?
OUR PURPOSE IS TO MAKE THE LEAD ACTOR LOOK BETTER!
WE SERVE AS STEPPING-STONES.
SOMETIMES, WE CAUSE PROBLEMS...
...TO GIVE THE LEAD ACTOR A PLACE TO SHINE!!
ISN'T THAT OUR ROLE HERE!?
I DON'T FOLLOW...

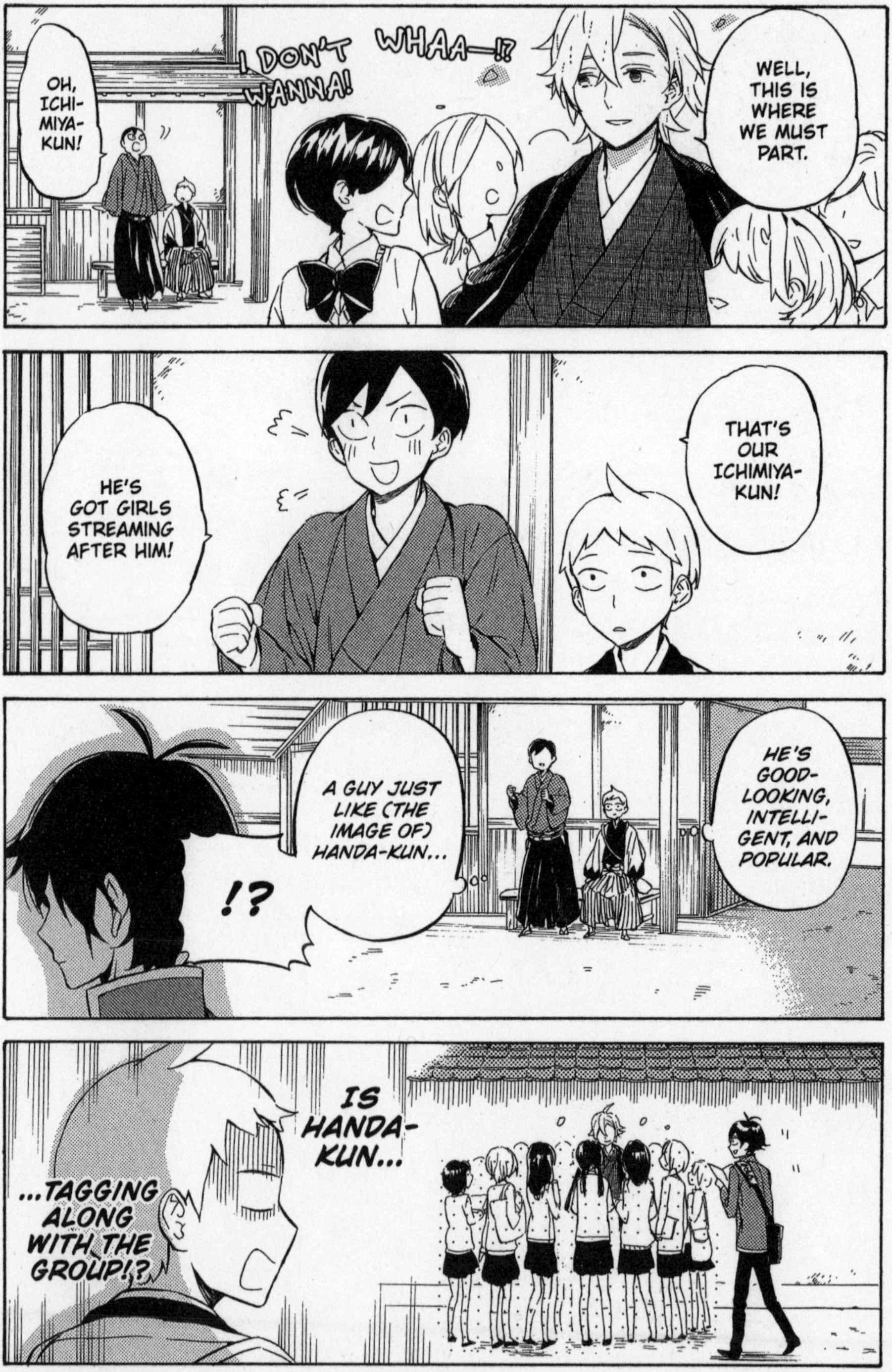
WELL, THIS IS WHERE WE MUST PART.
WHAA—!?
I DON'T WANNA!
OH, ICHIMIYA-KUN!
THAT'S OUR ICHIMIYA-KUN!
HE'S GOT GIRLS STREAMING AFTER HIM!
HE'S GOOD-LOOKING, INTELLIGENT, AND POPULAR.
A GUY JUST LIKE (THE IMAGE OF) HANDA-KUN...
!?
IS HANDA-KUN...
...TAGGING ALONG WITH THE GROUP!?

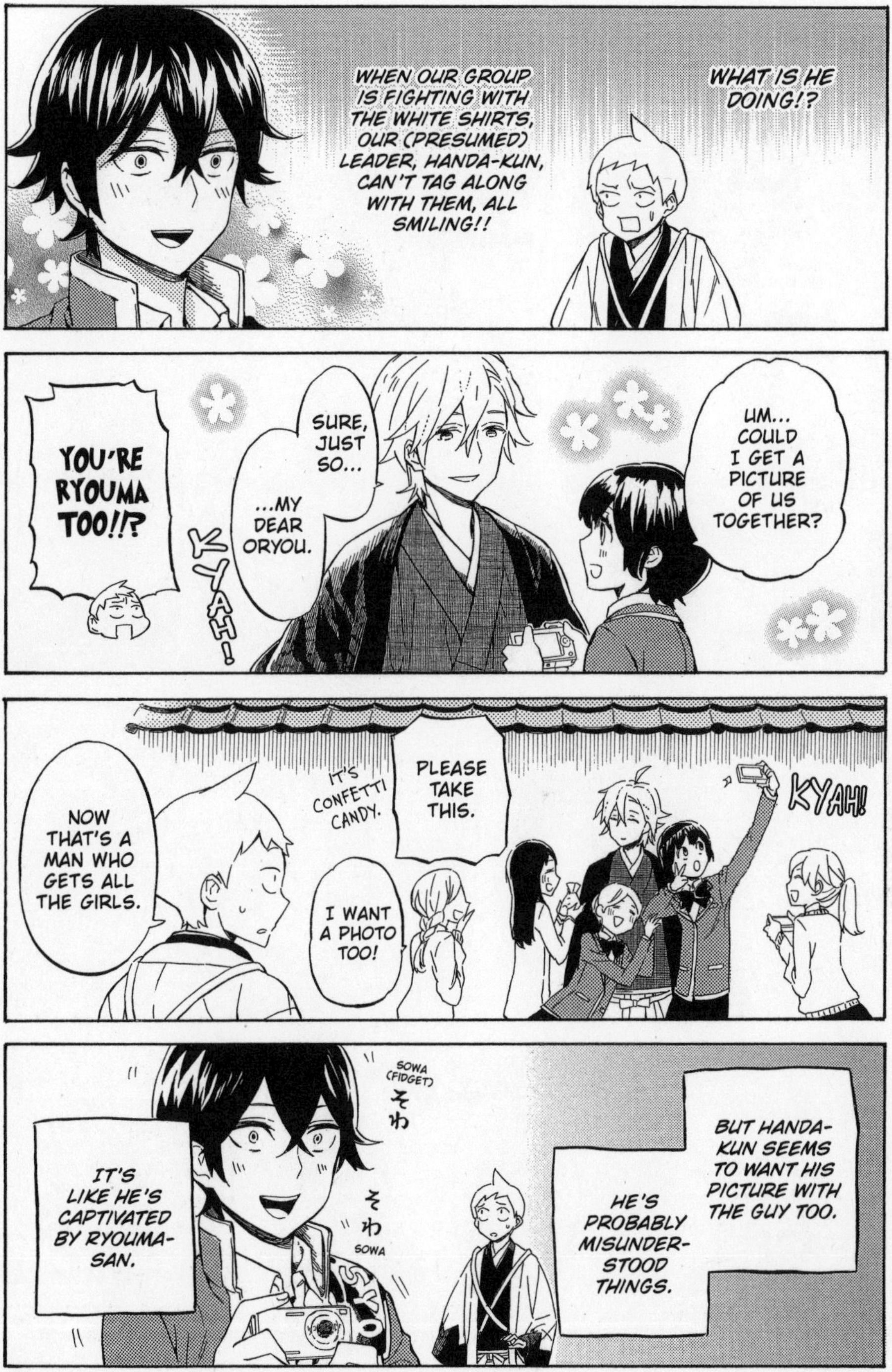
WHAT IS HE DOING!?
WHEN OUR GROUP IS FIGHTING WITH THE WHITE SHIRTS, OUR (PRESUMED) LEADER, HANDA-KUN, CAN'T TAG ALONG WITH THEM, ALL SMILING!!
UM... COULD I GET A PICTURE OF US TOGETHER?
SURE, JUST SO...
...MY DEAR ORYOU.
KYAH!
YOU'RE RYOUMA TOO!!?
KYAH!
PLEASE TAKE THIS.
IT'S CONFETTI CANDY.
I WANT A PHOTO TOO!
NOW THAT'S A MAN WHO GETS ALL THE GIRLS.
BUT HANDA-KUN SEEMS TO WANT HIS PICTURE WITH THE GUY TOO.
HE'S PROBABLY MISUNDERSTOOD THINGS.
SOWA (FIDGET)
そわ
そわ
SOWA
IT'S LIKE HE'S CAPTIVATED BY RYOUMA-SAN.

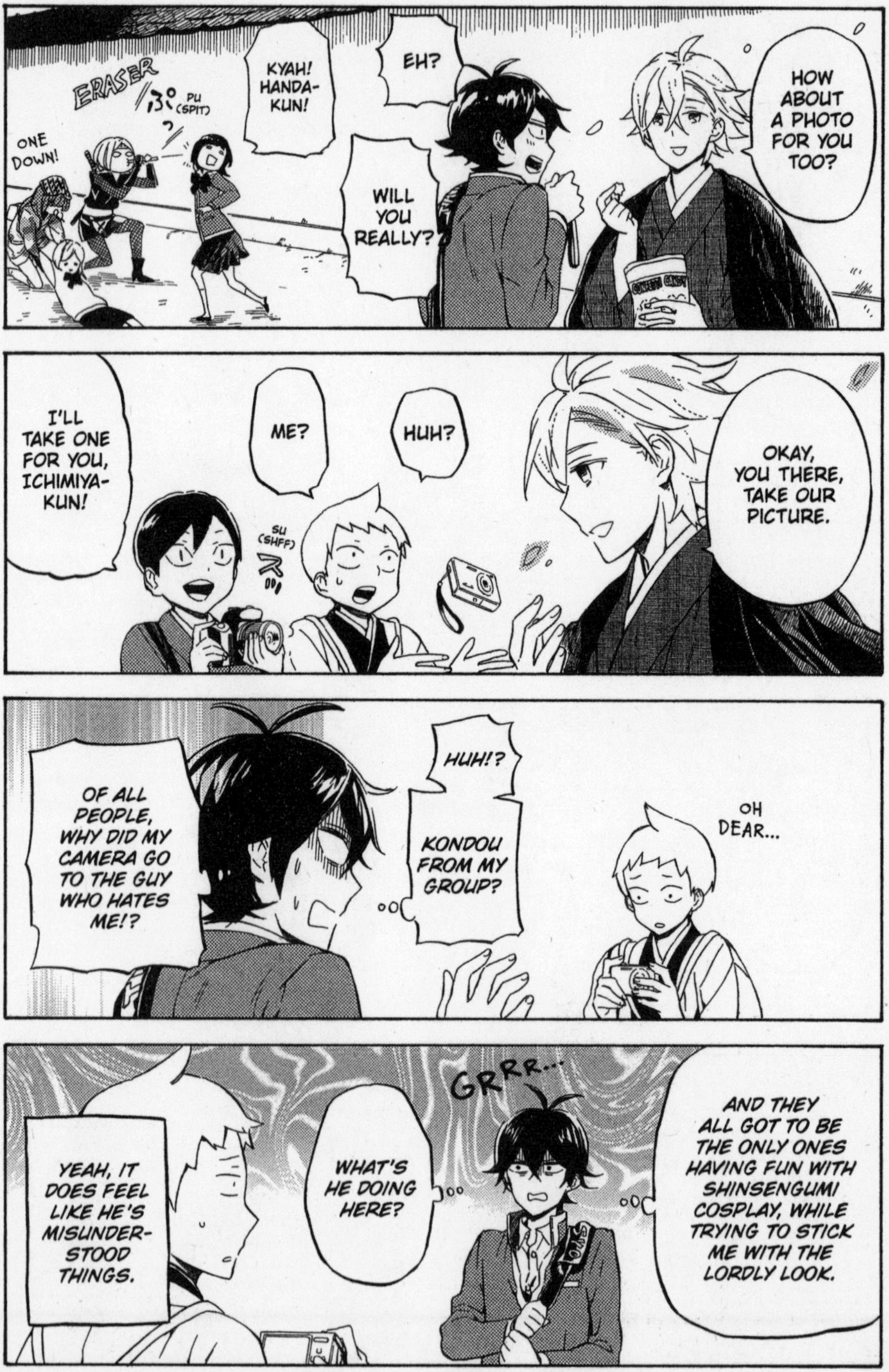
HOW ABOUT A PHOTO FOR YOU TOO?
EH?
WILL YOU REALLY?
KYAH! HANDA-KUN!
ERASER
ぷ PU (SPIT)
ONE DOWN!
OKAY, YOU THERE, TAKE OUR PICTURE.
HUH?
ME?
ス SU (SHFF)
I'LL TAKE ONE FOR YOU, ICHIMIYA-KUN!
OH DEAR...
HUH!?
KONDOU FROM MY GROUP?
OF ALL PEOPLE, WHY DID MY CAMERA GO TO THE GUY WHO HATES ME!?
AND THEY ALL GOT TO BE THE ONLY ONES HAVING FUN WITH SHINSENGUMI COSPLAY, WHILE TRYING TO STICK ME WITH THE LORDLY LOOK.
GRRR...
WHAT'S HE DOING HERE?
YEAH, IT DOES FEEL LIKE HE'S MISUNDER-STOOD THINGS.

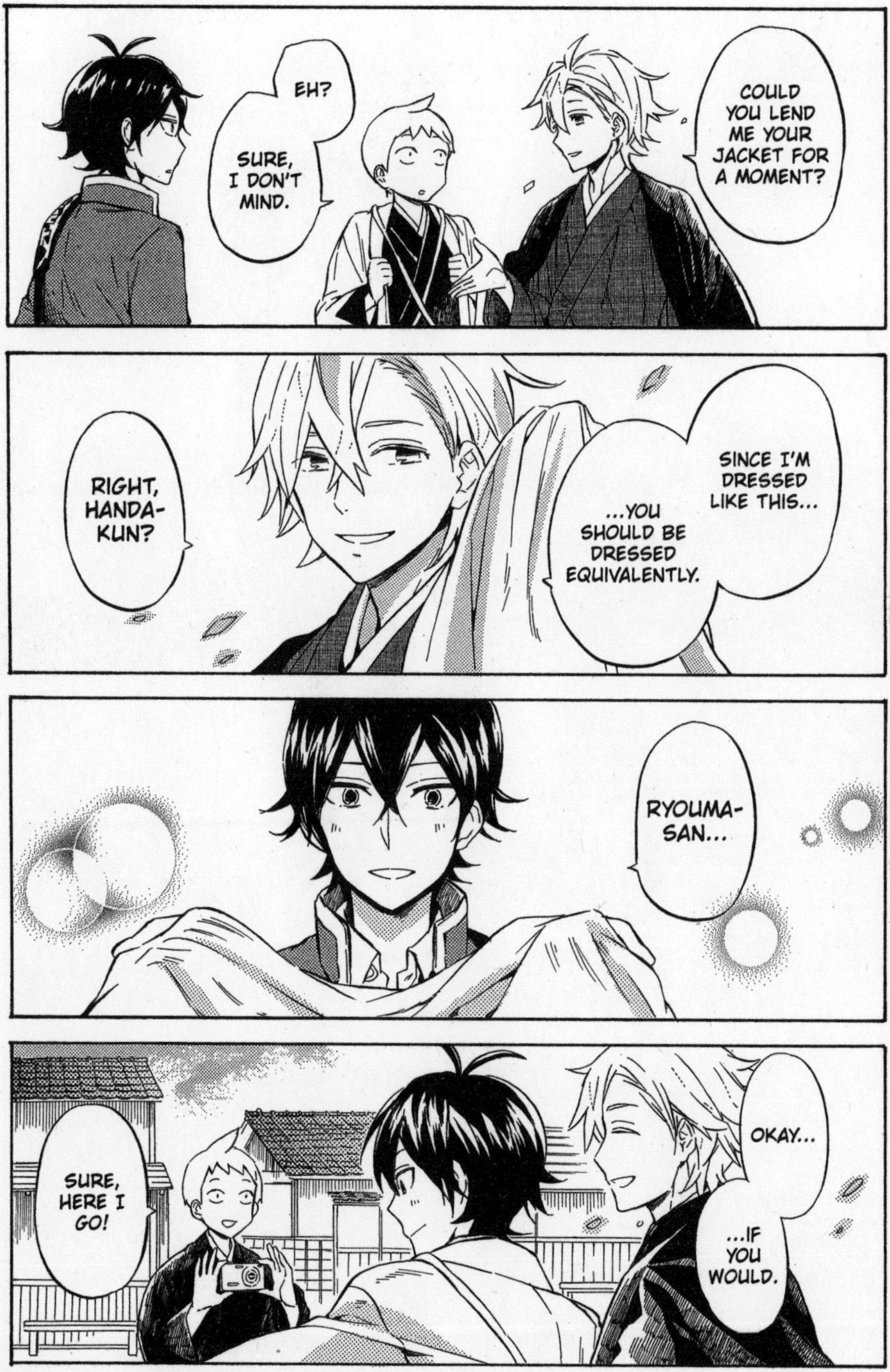
COULD YOU LEND ME YOUR JACKET FOR A MOMENT?
EH?
SURE, I DON'T MIND.
SINCE I'M DRESSED LIKE THIS...
...YOU SHOULD BE DRESSED EQUIVALENTLY.
RIGHT, HANDA-KUN?
RYOUMA-SAN...
OKAY...
...IF YOU WOULD.
SURE, HERE I GO!

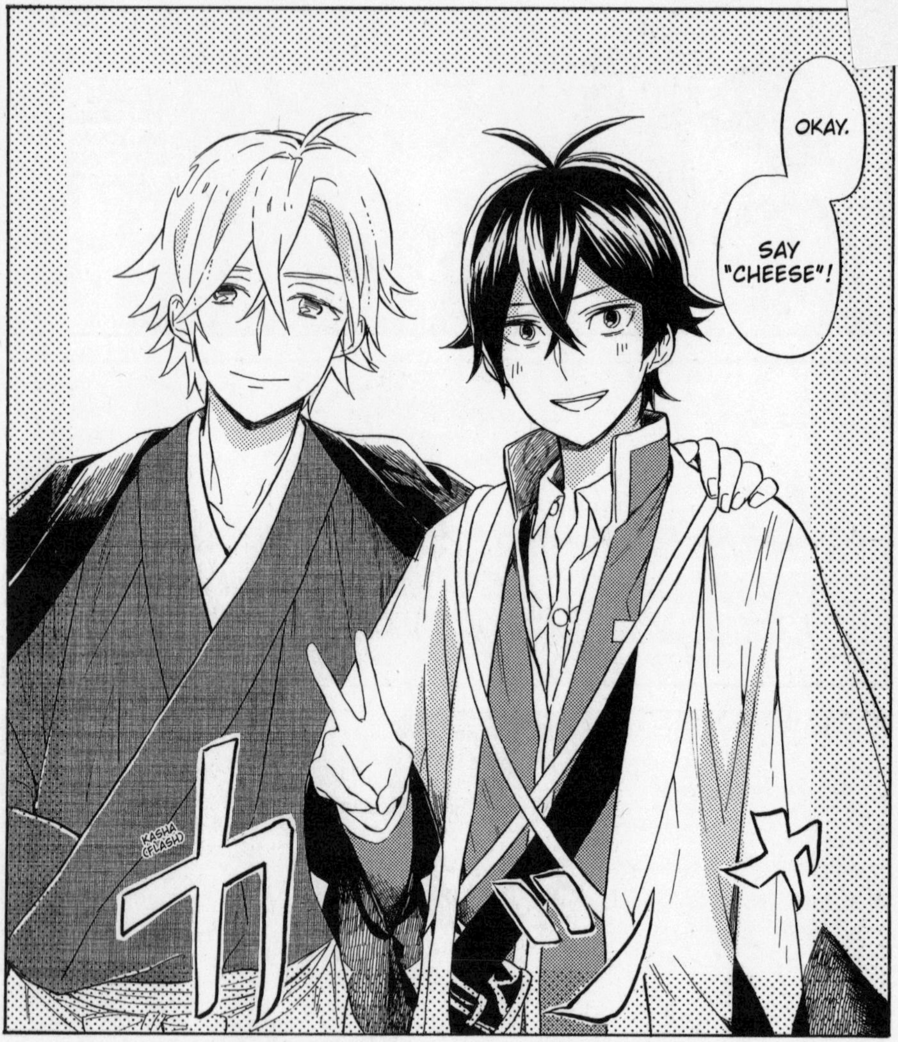
OKAY.
SAY "CHEESE"!
KASHA (FLASH)

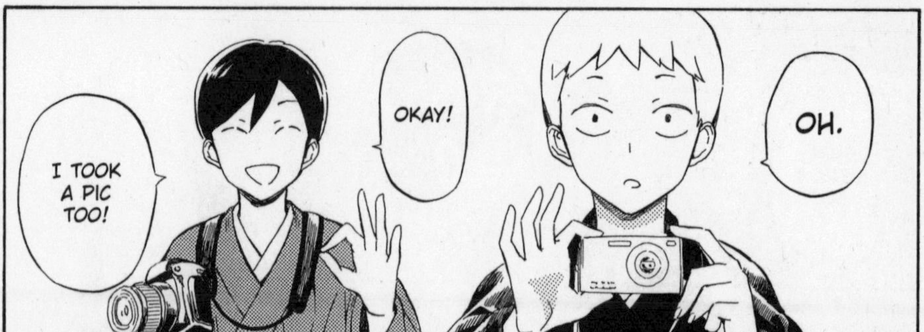
OH.
OKAY!
I TOOK A PIC TOO!

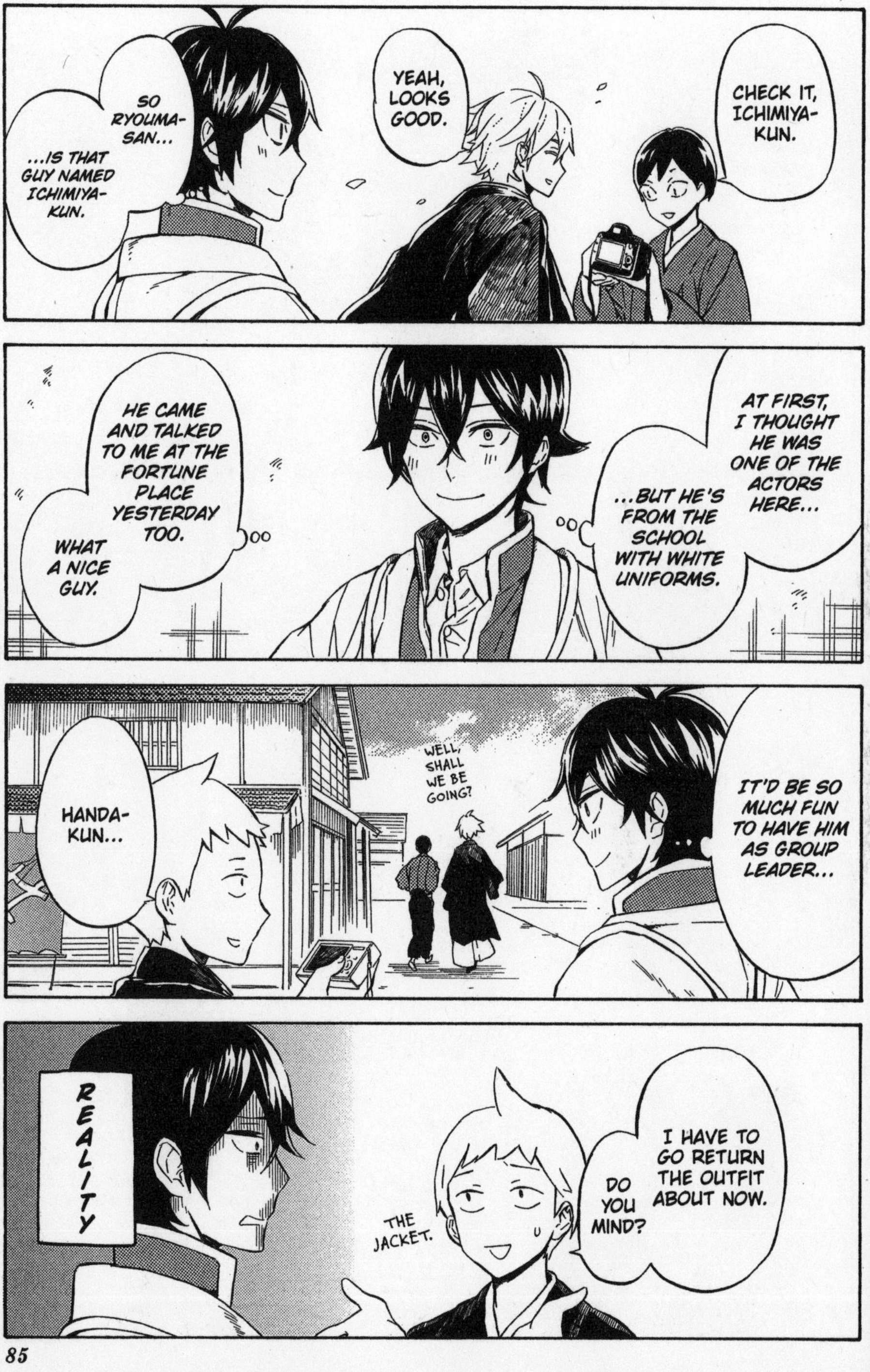
CHECK IT, ICHIMIYA-KUN.
YEAH, LOOKS GOOD.
SO RYOUMA-SAN...
...IS THAT GUY NAMED ICHIMIYA-KUN.
AT FIRST, I THOUGHT HE WAS ONE OF THE ACTORS HERE...
...BUT HE'S FROM THE SCHOOL WITH WHITE UNIFORMS.
HE CAME AND TALKED TO ME AT THE FORTUNE PLACE YESTERDAY TOO.
WHAT A NICE GUY.
IT'D BE SO MUCH FUN TO HAVE HIM AS GROUP LEADER...
WELL, SHALL WE BE GOING?
HANDA-KUN...
I HAVE TO GO RETURN THE OUTFIT ABOUT NOW.
DO YOU MIND?
THE JACKET.
REALITY

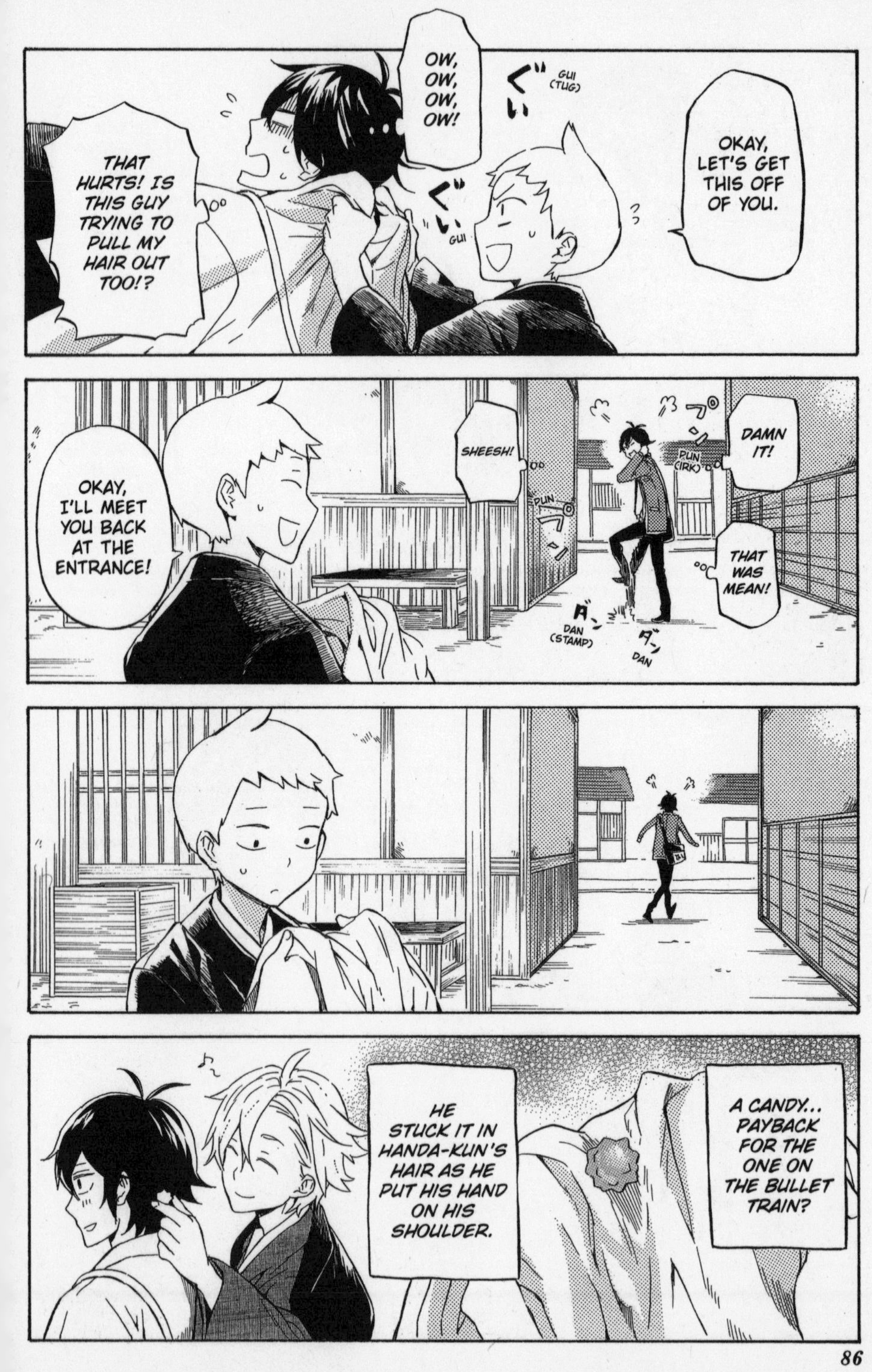
OKAY, LET'S GET THIS OFF OF YOU.
GUI (TUG)
OW, OW, OW, OW!
GUI
THAT HURTS! IS THIS GUY TRYING TO PULL MY HAIR OUT TOO!?
DAMN IT!
PUN (IRK)
THAT WAS MEAN!
SHEESH!
PUN
DAN (STAMP)
DAN
OKAY, I'LL MEET YOU BACK AT THE ENTRANCE!
A CANDY... PAYBACK FOR THE ONE ON THE BULLET TRAIN?
HE STUCK IT IN HANDA-KUN'S HAIR AS HE PUT HIS HAND ON HIS SHOULDER.

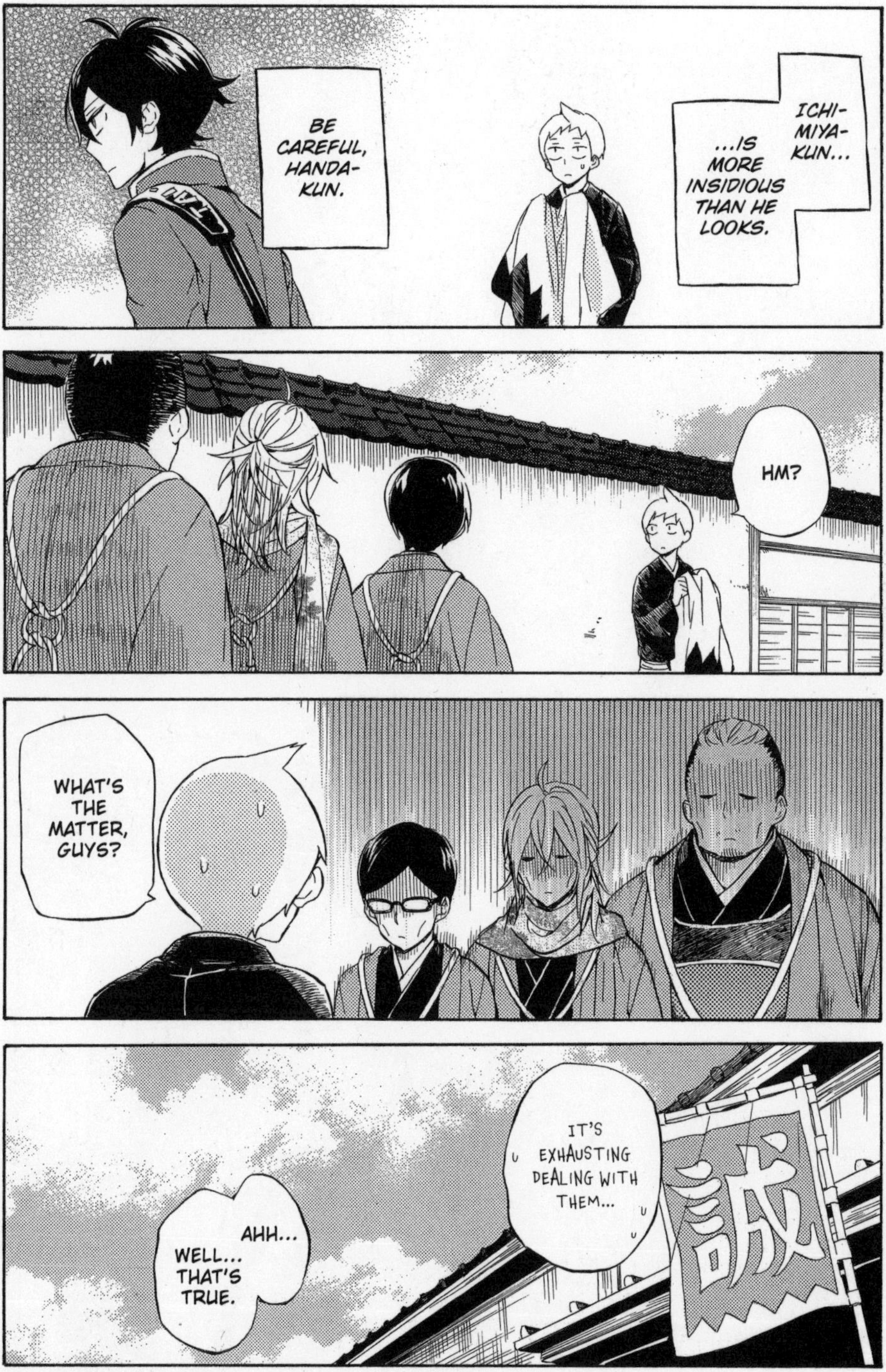
ICHI-MIYA-KUN...
...IS MORE INSIDIOUS THAN HE LOOKS.
BE CAREFUL, HANDA-KUN.
HM?
WHAT'S THE MATTER, GUYS?
IT'S EXHAUSTING DEALING WITH THEM...
誠
AHH... WELL... THAT'S TRUE.

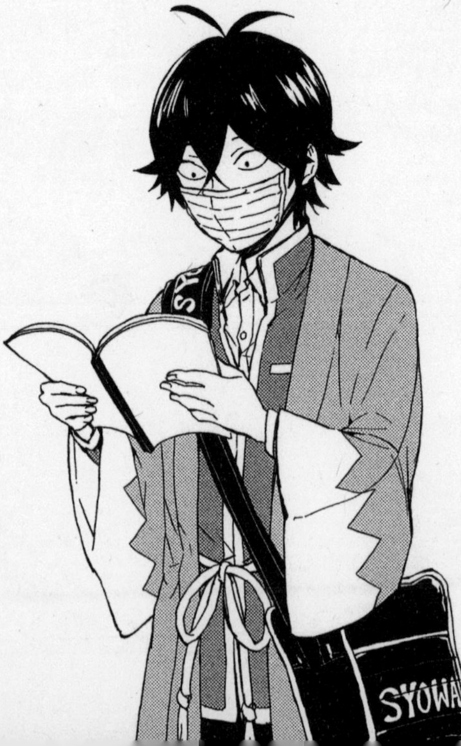
SYOWA

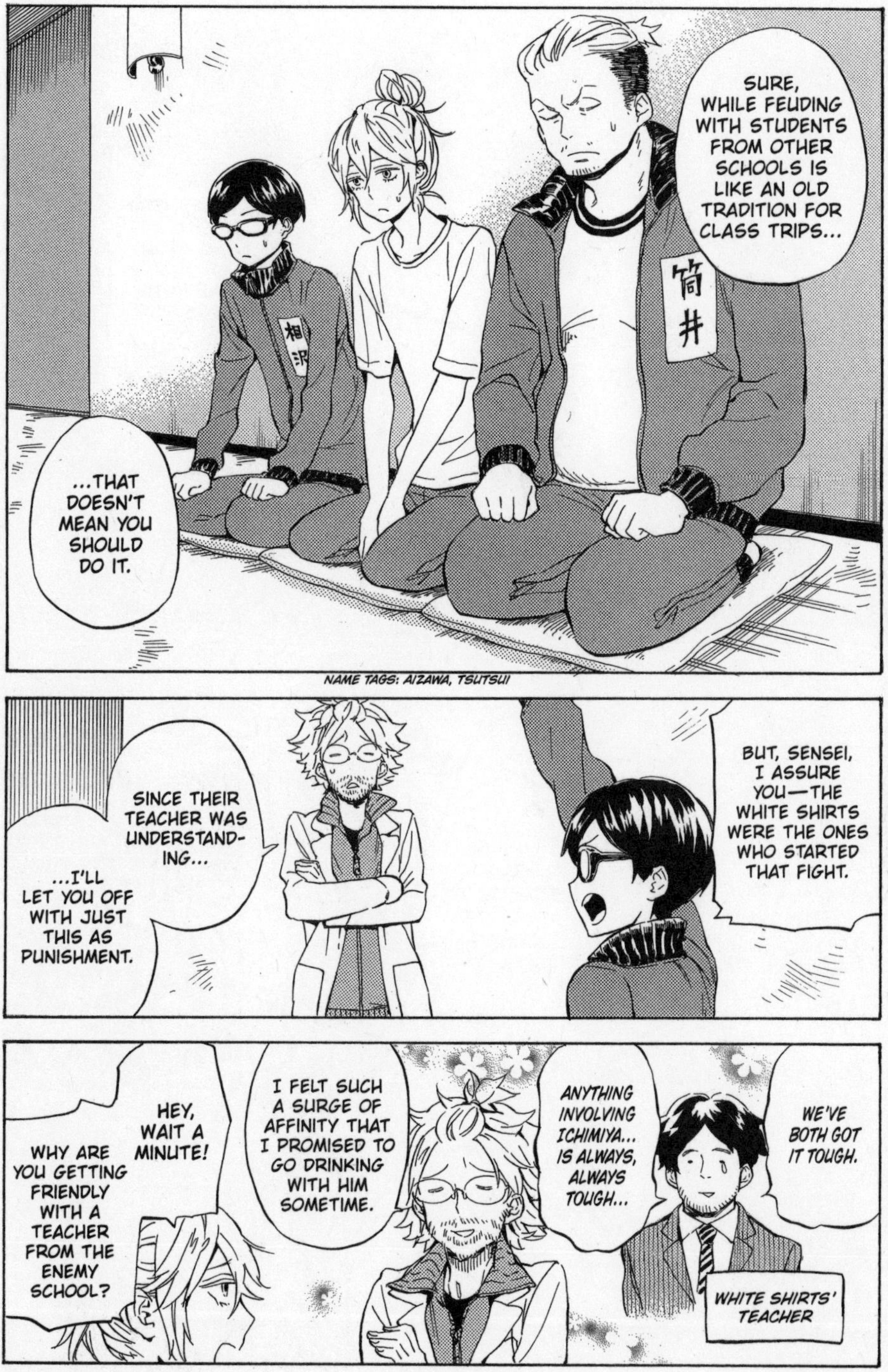

SURE, WHILE FEUDING WITH STUDENTS FROM OTHER SCHOOLS IS LIKE AN OLD TRADITION FOR CLASS TRIPS...
筒井
相沢
...THAT DOESN'T MEAN YOU SHOULD DO IT.
NAME TAGS: AIZAWA, TSUTSUI
BUT, SENSEI, I ASSURE YOU—THE WHITE SHIRTS WERE THE ONES WHO STARTED THAT FIGHT.
SINCE THEIR TEACHER WAS UNDERSTAND-ING...
...I'LL LET YOU OFF WITH JUST THIS AS PUNISHMENT.
WE'VE BOTH GOT IT TOUGH.
WHITE SHIRTS' TEACHER
ANYTHING INVOLVING ICHIMIYA... IS ALWAYS, ALWAYS TOUGH...
I FELT SUCH A SURGE OF AFFINITY THAT I PROMISED TO GO DRINKING WITH HIM SOMETIME.
HEY, WAIT A MINUTE!
WHY ARE YOU GETTING FRIENDLY WITH A TEACHER FROM THE ENEMY SCHOOL?

Chapter 24: Handa-kun & the Class Trip, Night 2

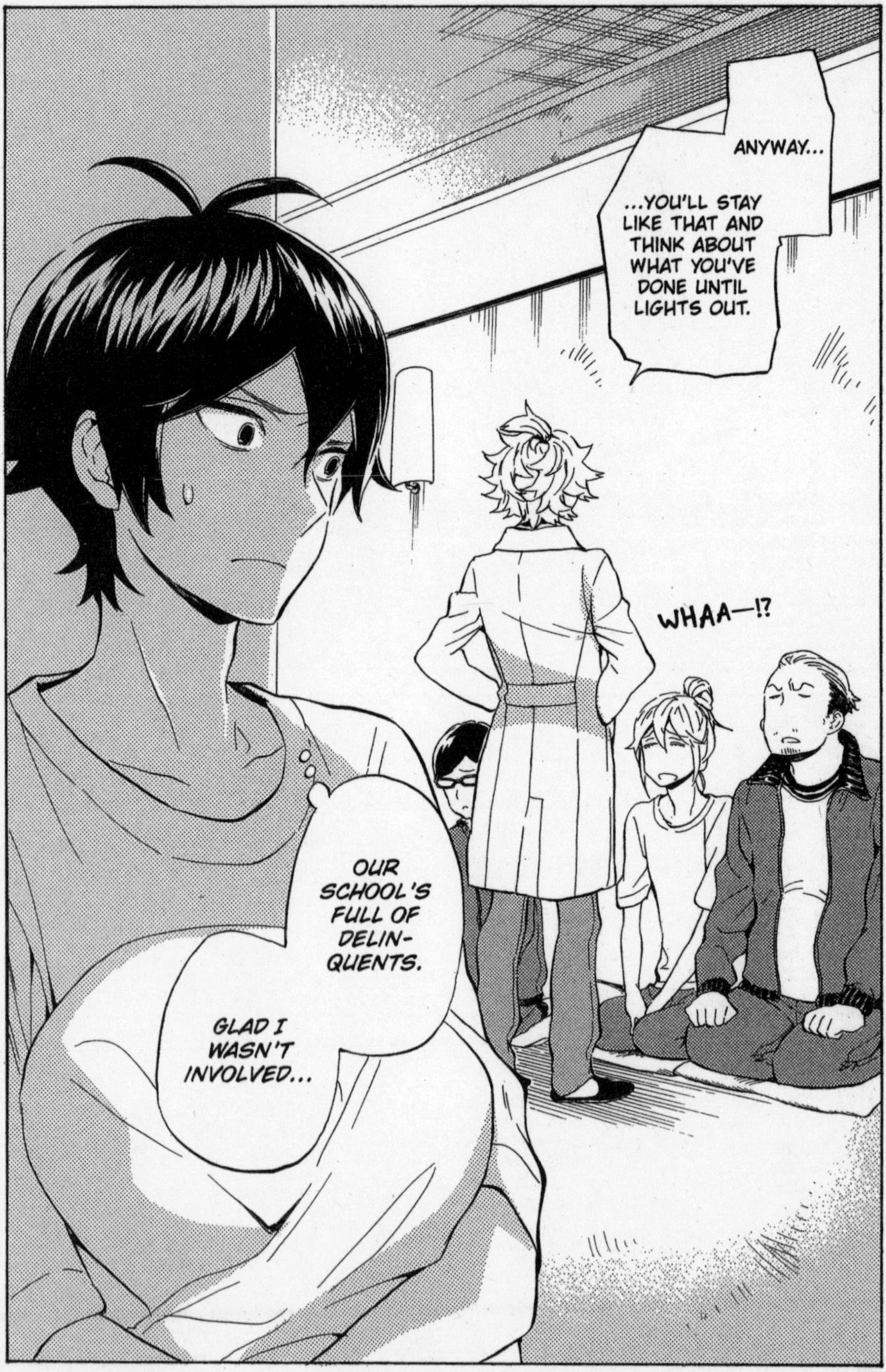
ANYWAY...
...YOU'LL STAY LIKE THAT AND THINK ABOUT WHAT YOU'VE DONE UNTIL LIGHTS OUT.
WHAA—!?
OUR SCHOOL'S FULL OF DELIN-QUENTS.
GLAD I WASN'T INVOLVED...

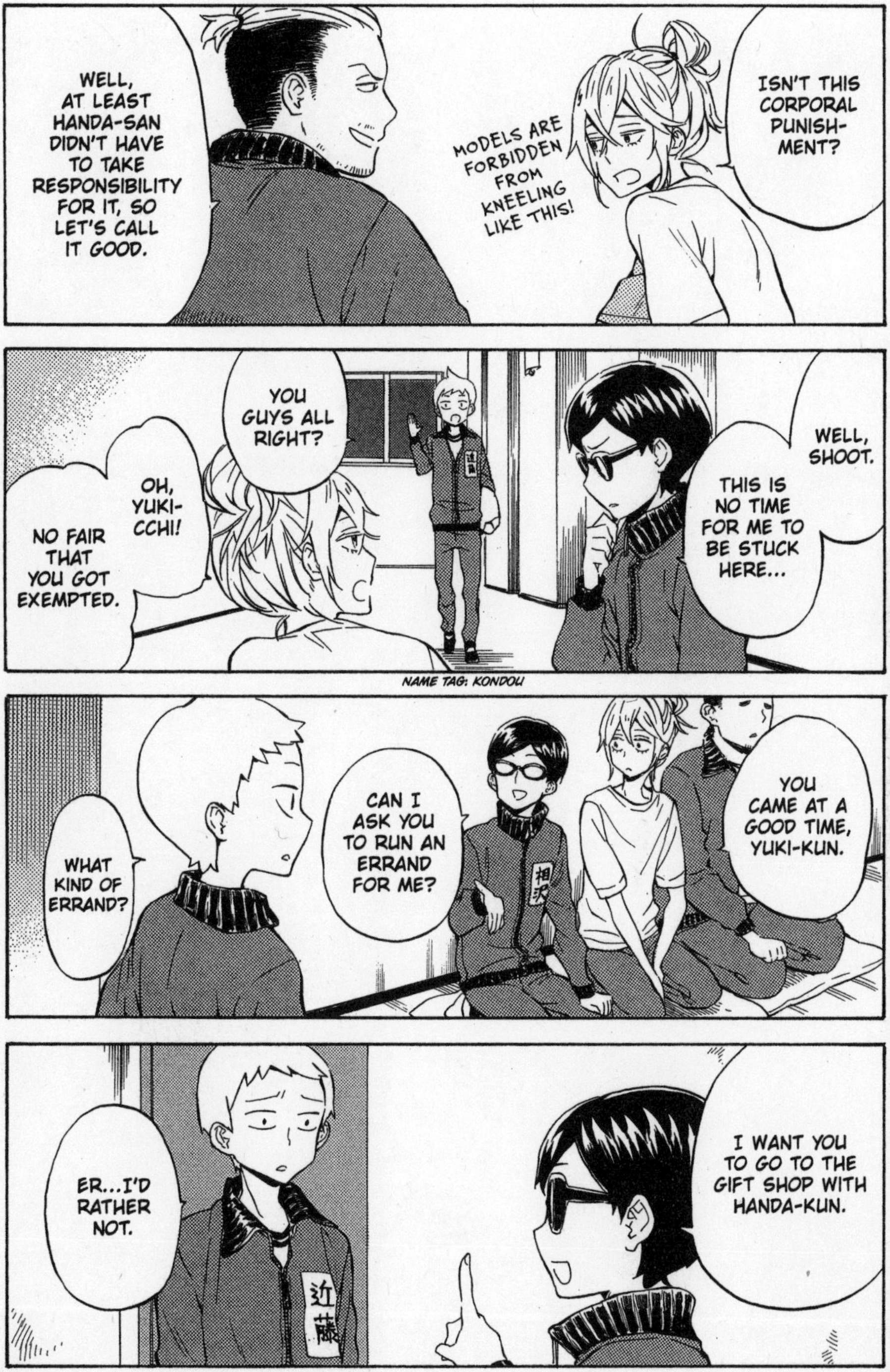

ISN'T THIS CORPORAL PUNISHMENT?
MODELS ARE FORBIDDEN FROM KNEELING LIKE THIS!
WELL, AT LEAST HANDA-SAN DIDN'T HAVE TO TAKE RESPONSIBILITY FOR IT, SO LET'S CALL IT GOOD.
WELL, SHOOT.
THIS IS NO TIME FOR ME TO BE STUCK HERE...
YOU GUYS ALL RIGHT?
OH, YUKI-CCHI!
NO FAIR THAT YOU GOT EXEMPTED.
NAME TAG: KONDOU
YOU CAME AT A GOOD TIME, YUKI-KUN.
CAN I ASK YOU TO RUN AN ERRAND FOR ME?
WHAT KIND OF ERRAND?
I WANT YOU TO GO TO THE GIFT SHOP WITH HANDA-KUN.
ER...I'D RATHER NOT.
近藤

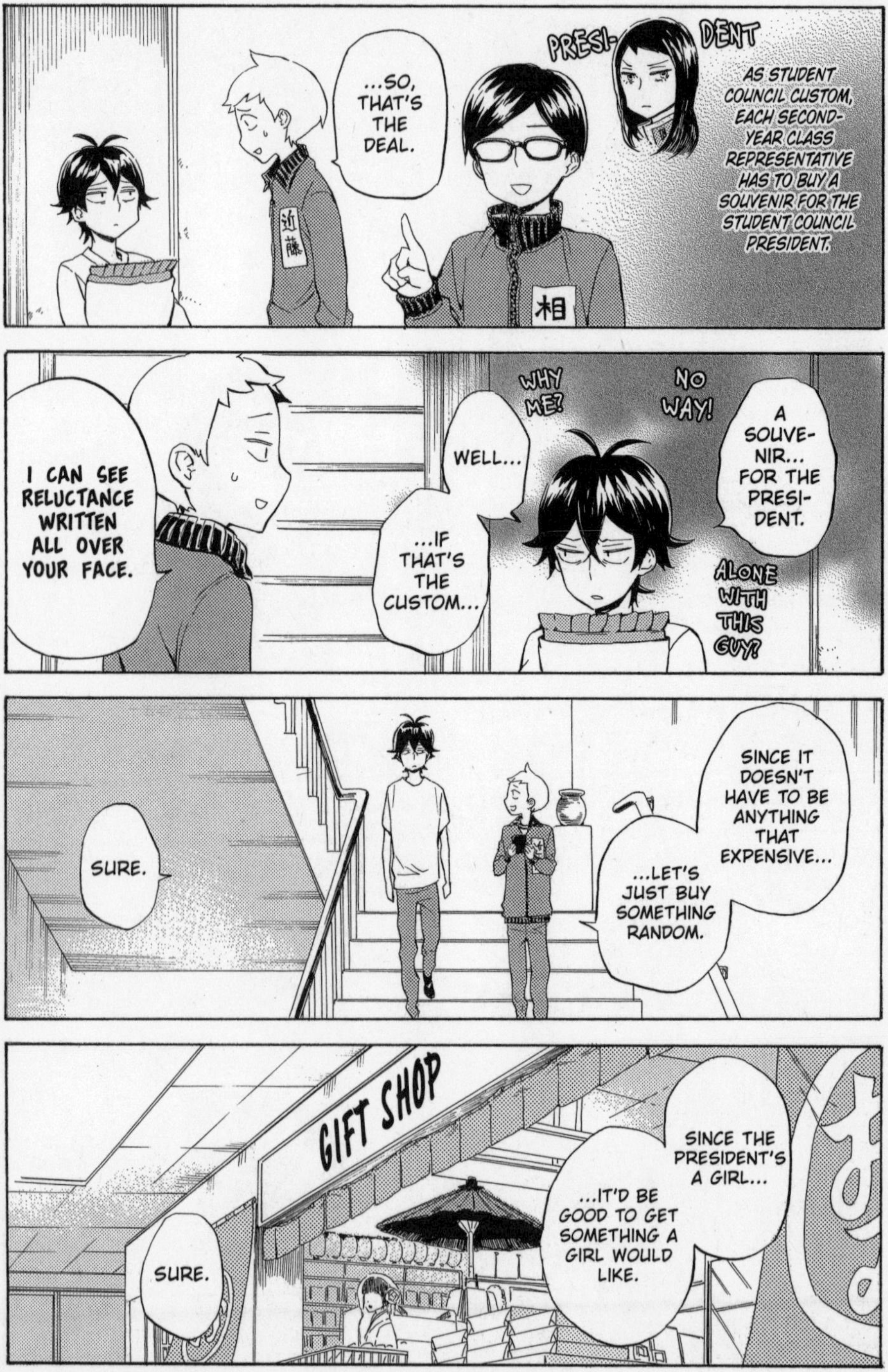
PRESI- DENT
AS STUDENT COUNCIL CUSTOM, EACH SECOND-YEAR CLASS REPRESENTATIVE HAS TO BUY A SOUVENIR FOR THE STUDENT COUNCIL PRESIDENT.
相
...SO, THAT'S THE DEAL.
近藤
A SOUVE-NIR... FOR THE PRESI-DENT.
NO WAY!
WHY ME?
ALONE WITH THIS GUY?
WELL...
...IF THAT'S THE CUSTOM...
I CAN SEE RELUCTANCE WRITTEN ALL OVER YOUR FACE.
SINCE IT DOESN'T HAVE TO BE ANYTHING THAT EXPENSIVE...
...LET'S JUST BUY SOMETHING RANDOM.
SURE.
GIFT SHOP
SINCE THE PRESIDENT'S A GIRL...
...IT'D BE GOOD TO GET SOMETHING A GIRL WOULD LIKE.
SURE.

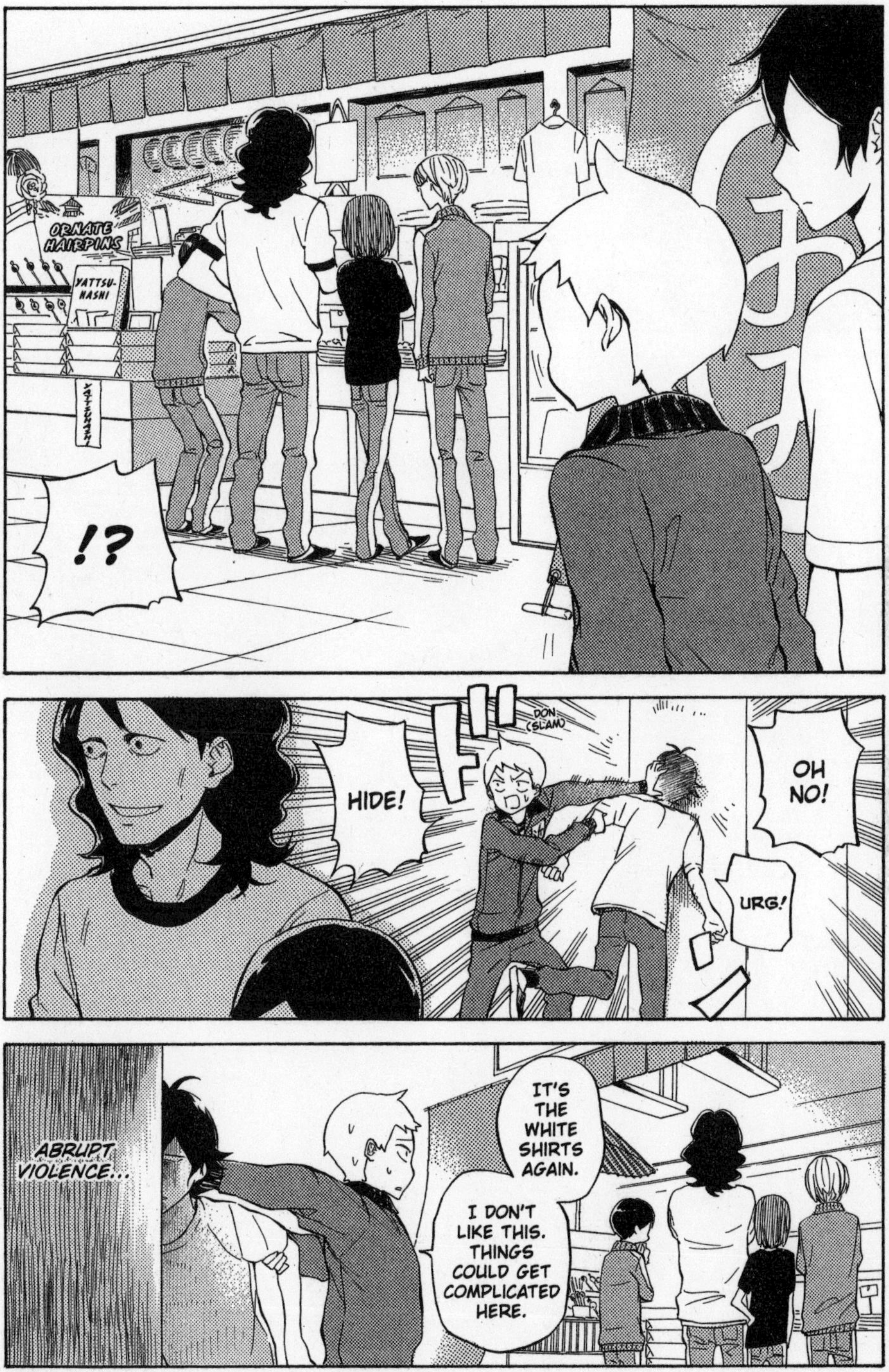
ORNATE HAIRPINS
YATTSU-HASHI
!?
OH NO!
DON (SLAM)
HIDE!
URG!
IT'S THE WHITE SHIRTS AGAIN.
I DON'T LIKE THIS. THINGS COULD GET COMPLICATED HERE.
ABRUPT VIOLENCE...

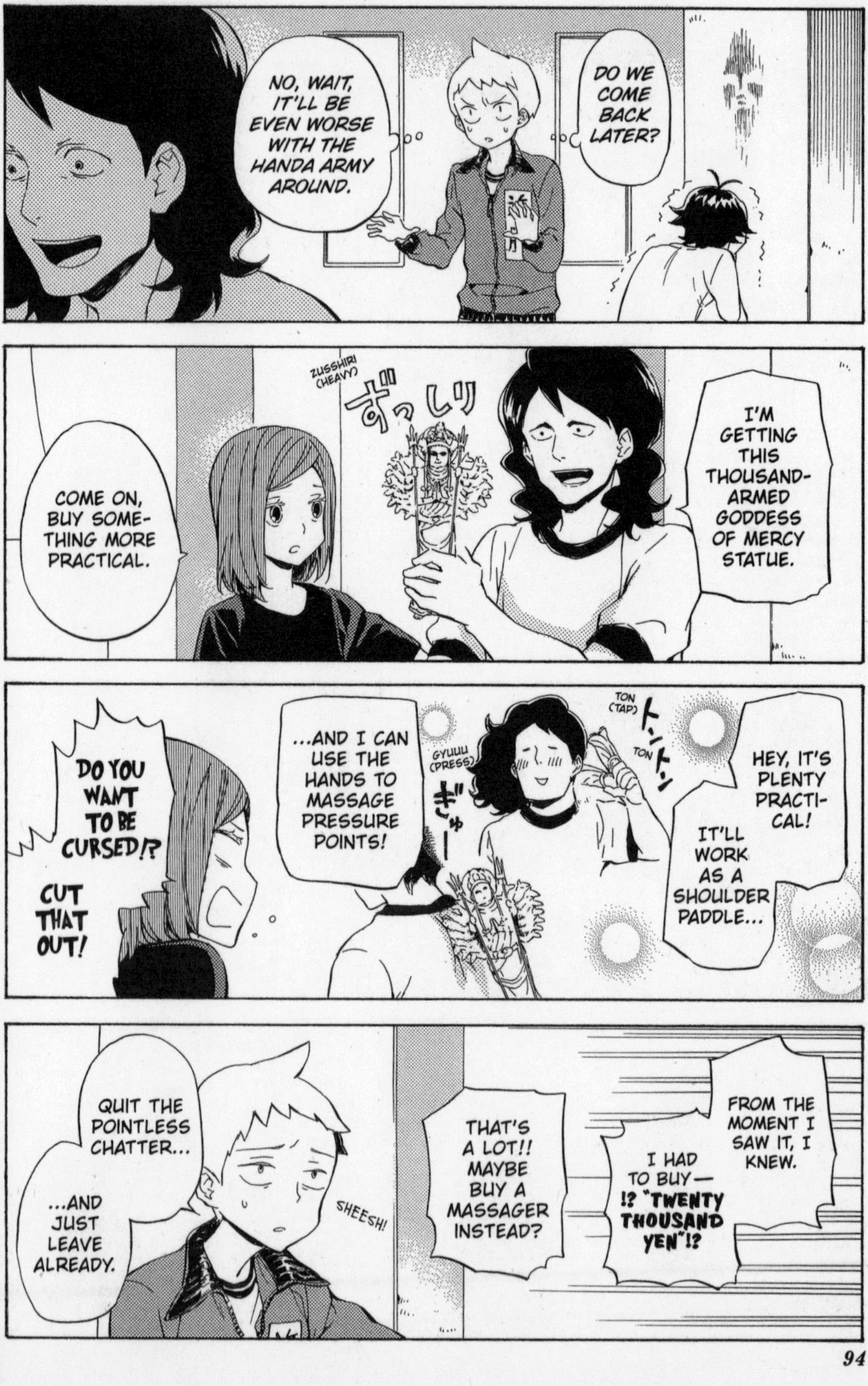
DO WE COME BACK LATER?
NO, WAIT, IT'LL BE EVEN WORSE WITH THE HANDA ARMY AROUND.
I'M GETTING THIS THOUSAND-ARMED GODDESS OF MERCY STATUE.
ZUSSHIRI (HEAVY)
ずっしり
COME ON, BUY SOME-THING MORE PRACTICAL.
HEY, IT'S PLENTY PRACTI-CAL!
IT'LL WORK AS A SHOULDER PADDLE...
TON (TAP)
TON
トントン
GYUUU (PRESS)
ぎゅー
...AND I CAN USE THE HANDS TO MASSAGE PRESSURE POINTS!
DO YOU WANT TO BE CURSED!?
CUT THAT OUT!
FROM THE MOMENT I SAW IT, I KNEW.
I HAD TO BUY—
!? "TWENTY THOUSAND YEN"!?
THAT'S A LOT!! MAYBE BUY A MASSAGER INSTEAD?
SHEESH!
QUIT THE POINTLESS CHATTER...
...AND JUST LEAVE ALREADY.

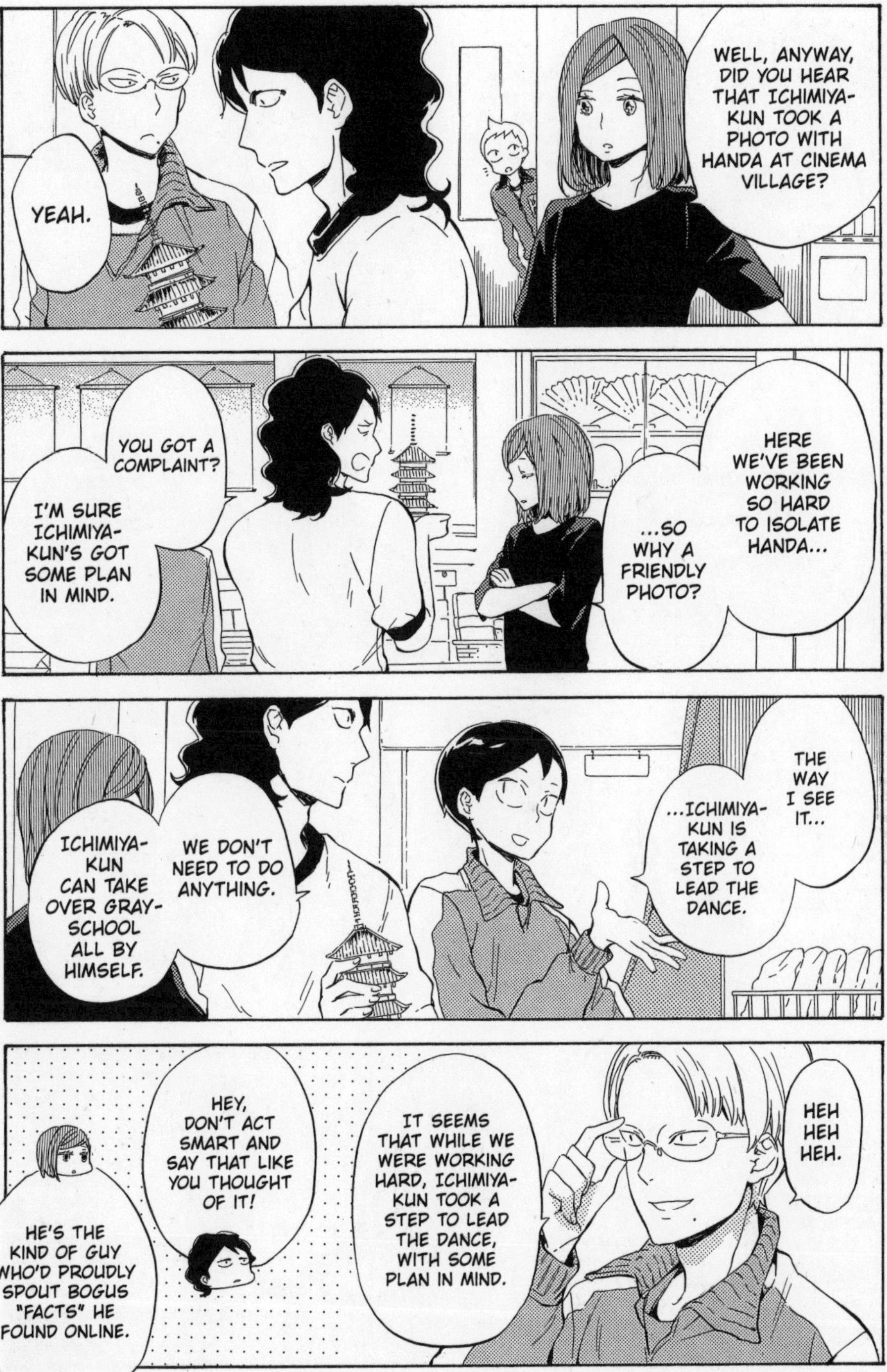
WELL, ANYWAY, DID YOU HEAR THAT ICHIMIYA-KUN TOOK A PHOTO WITH HANDA AT CINEMA VILLAGE?
YEAH.
HERE WE'VE BEEN WORKING SO HARD TO ISOLATE HANDA...
...SO WHY A FRIENDLY PHOTO?
YOU GOT A COMPLAINT?
I'M SURE ICHIMIYA-KUN'S GOT SOME PLAN IN MIND.
THE WAY I SEE IT...
...ICHIMIYA-KUN IS TAKING A STEP TO LEAD THE DANCE.
WE DON'T NEED TO DO ANYTHING.
ICHIMIYA-KUN CAN TAKE OVER GRAY-SCHOOL ALL BY HIMSELF.
HEH HEH HEH.
IT SEEMS THAT WHILE WE WERE WORKING HARD, ICHIMIYA-KUN TOOK A STEP TO LEAD THE DANCE, WITH SOME PLAN IN MIND.
HEY, DON'T ACT SMART AND SAY THAT LIKE YOU THOUGHT OF IT!
HE'S THE KIND OF GUY WHO'D PROUDLY SPOUT BOGUS "FACTS" HE FOUND ONLINE.

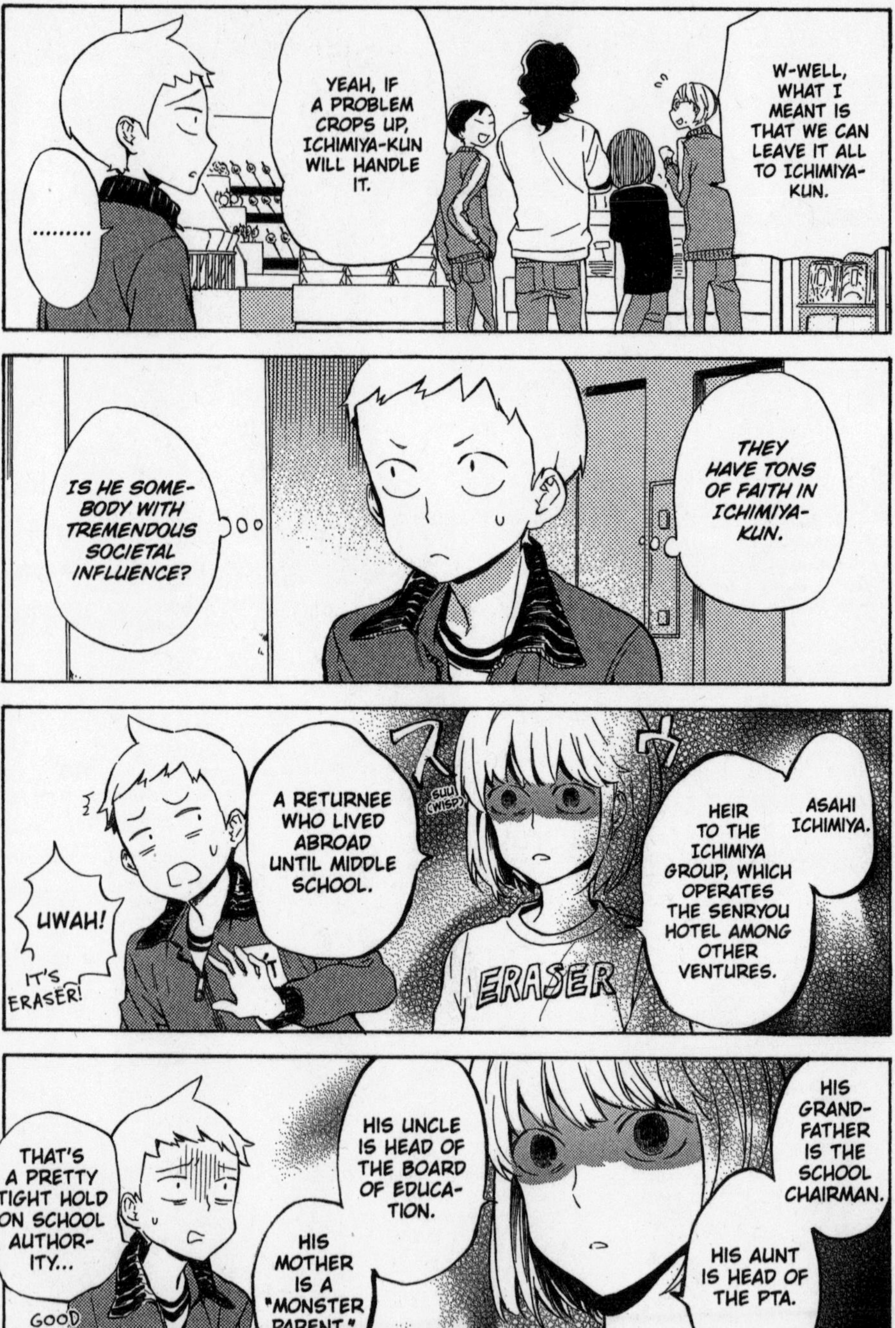
W-WELL, WHAT I MEANT IS THAT WE CAN LEAVE IT ALL TO ICHIMIYA-KUN.
YEAH, IF A PROBLEM CROPS UP, ICHIMIYA-KUN WILL HANDLE IT.
....
THEY HAVE TONS OF FAITH IN ICHIMIYA-KUN.
IS HE SOMEBODY WITH TREMENDOUS SOCIETAL INFLUENCE?
ASAHI ICHIMIYA.
HEIR TO THE ICHIMIYA GROUP, WHICH OPERATES THE SENRYOU HOTEL AMONG OTHER VENTURES.
SUU (WISP)
A RETURNEE WHO LIVED ABROAD UNTIL MIDDLE SCHOOL.
ERASER
UWAH!
IT'S ERASER!
HIS GRANDFATHER IS THE SCHOOL CHAIRMAN.
HIS AUNT IS HEAD OF THE PTA.
HIS UNCLE IS HEAD OF THE BOARD OF EDUCATION.
HIS MOTHER IS A "MONSTER PARENT."
THAT'S A PRETTY TIGHT HOLD ON SCHOOL AUTHORITY...
GOOD RESEARCH THERE.

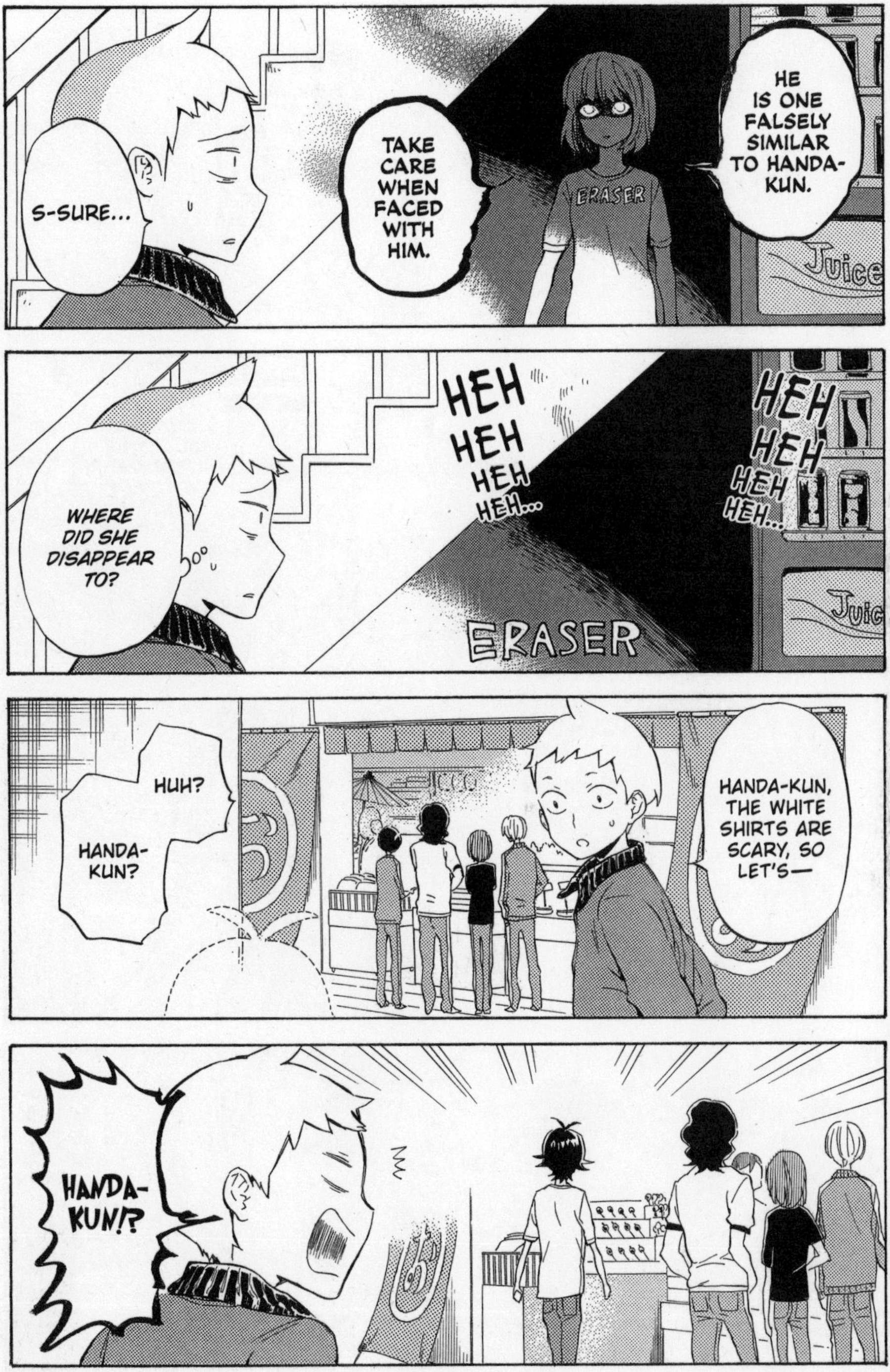
HE IS ONE FALSELY SIMILAR TO HANDA-KUN.
ERASER
TAKE CARE WHEN FACED WITH HIM.
S-SURE...
HEH HEH HEH HEH...
ERASER
HEH HEH HEH HEH...
WHERE DID SHE DISAPPEAR TO?
HANDA-KUN, THE WHITE SHIRTS ARE SCARY, SO LET'S—
HUH?
HANDA-KUN?
HANDA-KUN!?

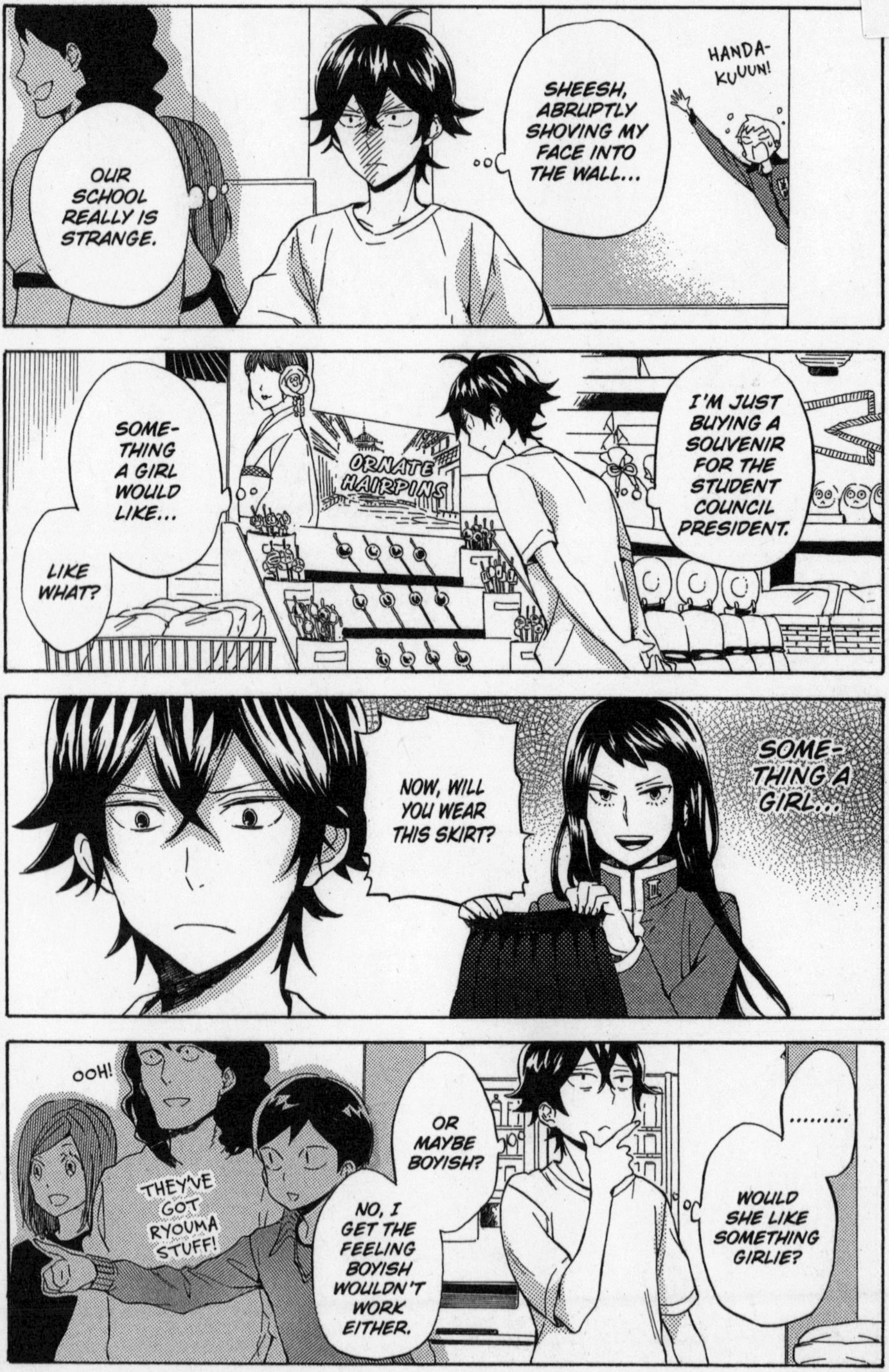
HANDA-KUUUN!
SHEESH, ABRUPTLY SHOVING MY FACE INTO THE WALL...
OUR SCHOOL REALLY IS STRANGE.
I'M JUST BUYING A SOUVENIR FOR THE STUDENT COUNCIL PRESIDENT.
ORNATE HAIRPINS
SOME-THING A GIRL WOULD LIKE...
LIKE WHAT?
SOME-THING A GIRL...
NOW, WILL YOU WEAR THIS SKIRT?
....
WOULD SHE LIKE SOMETHING GIRLIE?
OR MAYBE BOYISH?
NO, I GET THE FEELING BOYISH WOULDN'T WORK EITHER.
OOH!
THEY'VE GOT RYOUMA STUFF!

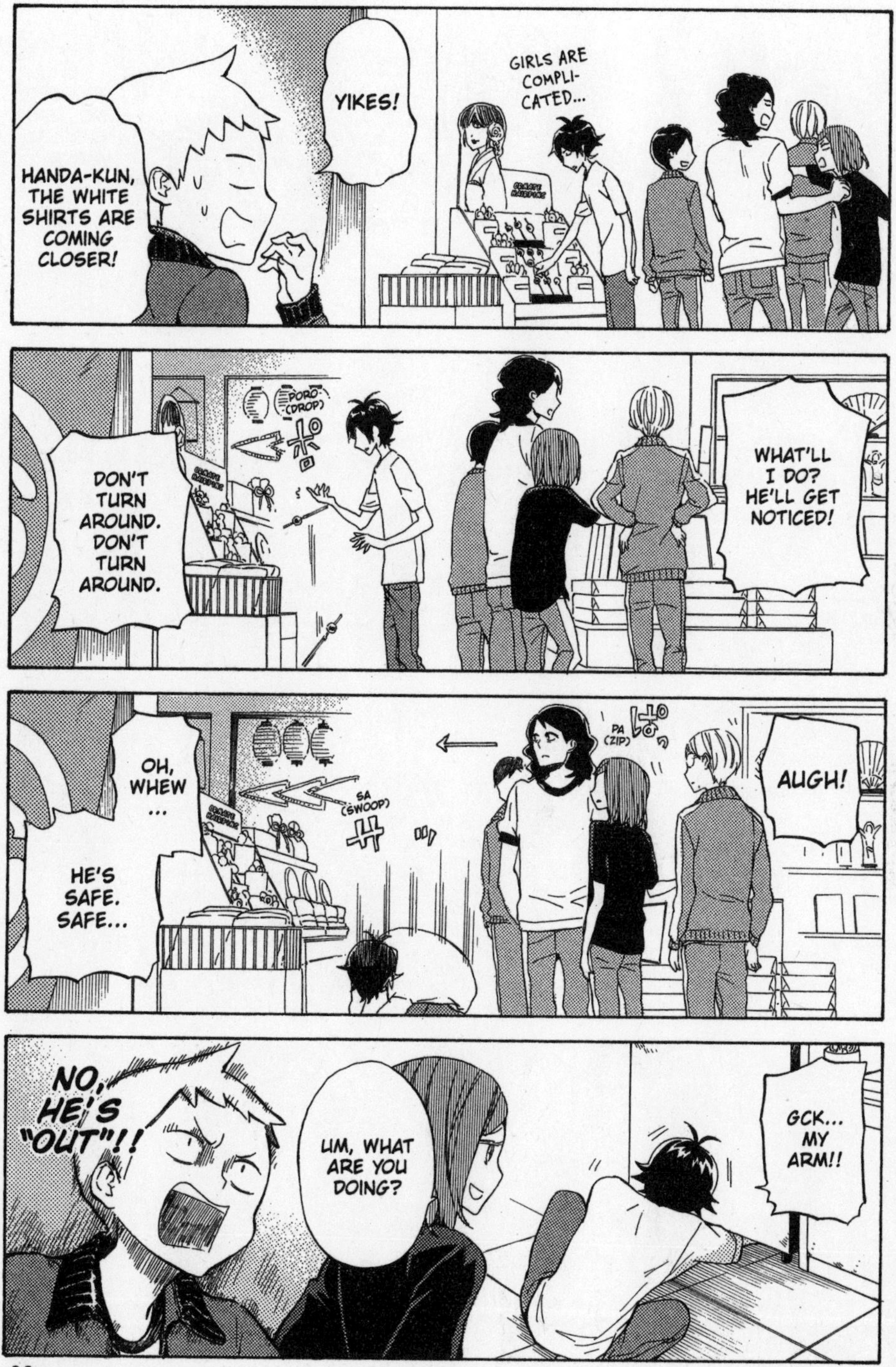
GIRLS ARE COMPLI-CATED...
YIKES!
HANDA-KUN, THE WHITE SHIRTS ARE COMING CLOSER!
WHAT'LL I DO? HE'LL GET NOTICED!
PORO (DROP)
DON'T TURN AROUND. DON'T TURN AROUND.
AUGH!
PA (ZIP)
SA (SWOOP)
OH, WHEW ...
HE'S SAFE. SAFE...
GCK... MY ARM!!
UM, WHAT ARE YOU DOING?
NO, HE'S "OUT"!!

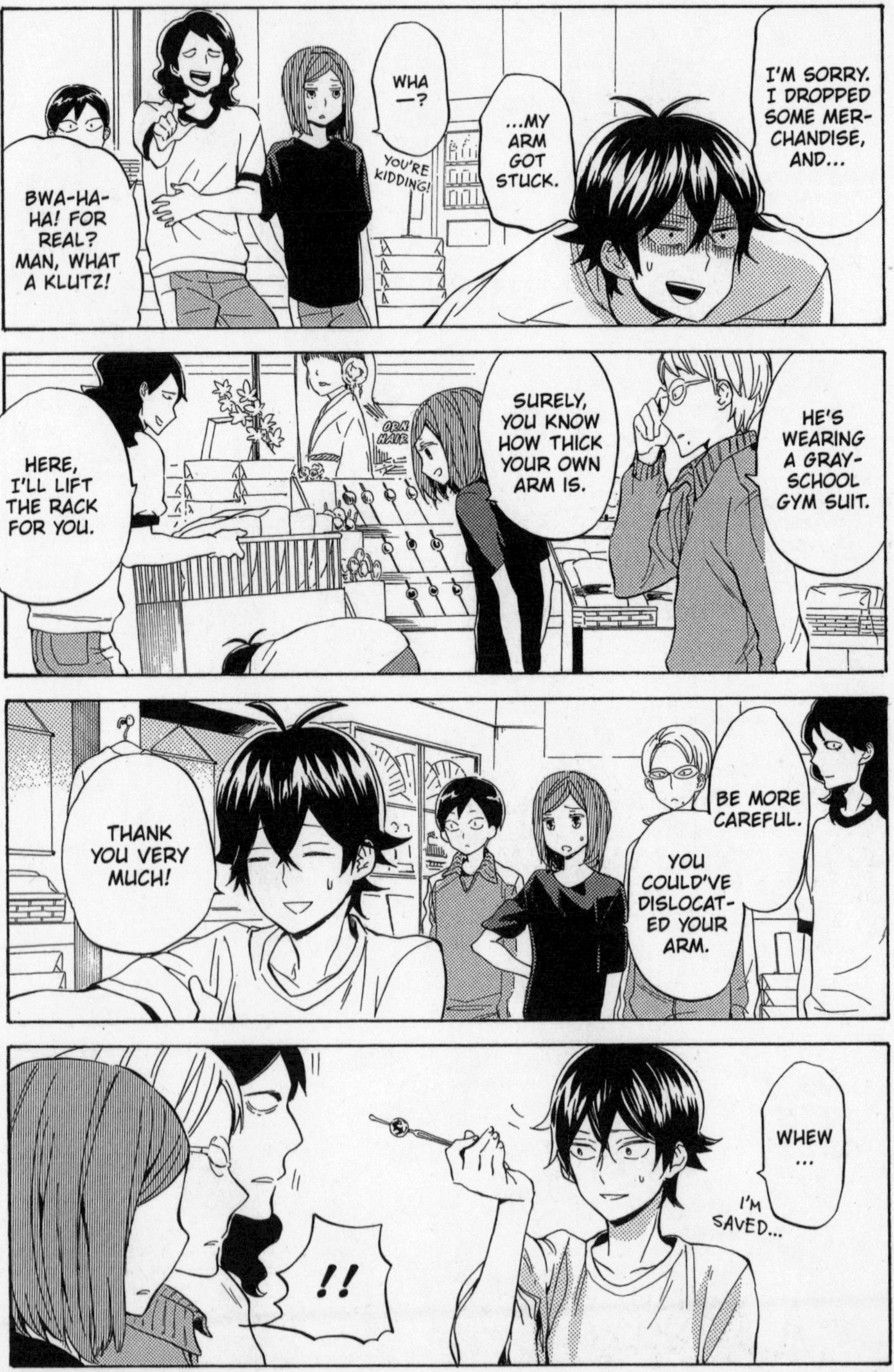
I'M SORRY. I DROPPED SOME MERCHANDISE, AND...
...MY ARM GOT STUCK.
WHA —?
YOU'RE KIDDING!
BWA-HA-HA! FOR REAL? MAN, WHAT A KLUTZ!
HE'S WEARING A GRAY-SCHOOL GYM SUIT.
SURELY, YOU KNOW HOW THICK YOUR OWN ARM IS.
ORN HAIR
HERE, I'LL LIFT THE RACK FOR YOU.
BE MORE CAREFUL.
YOU COULD'VE DISLOCATED YOUR ARM.
THANK YOU VERY MUCH!
WHEW ...
I'M SAVED...
!!

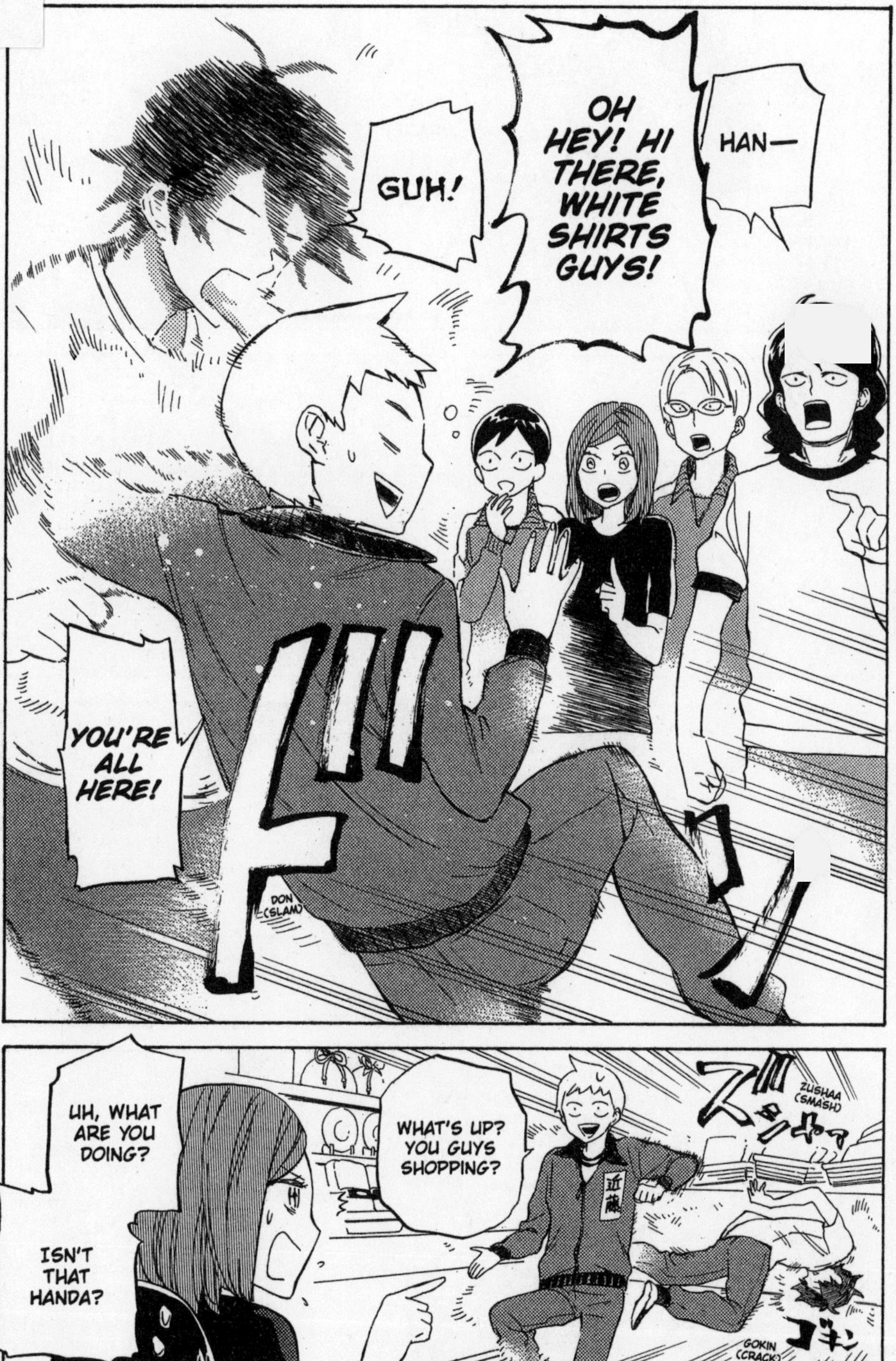
HAN—
OH HEY! HI THERE, WHITE SHIRTS GUYS!
GUH!
YOU'RE ALL HERE!
DON (SLAM)
ZUSHAA (SMASH)
WHAT'S UP? YOU GUYS SHOPPING?
UH, WHAT ARE YOU DOING?
GOKIN (CRACK)
ISN'T THAT HANDA?

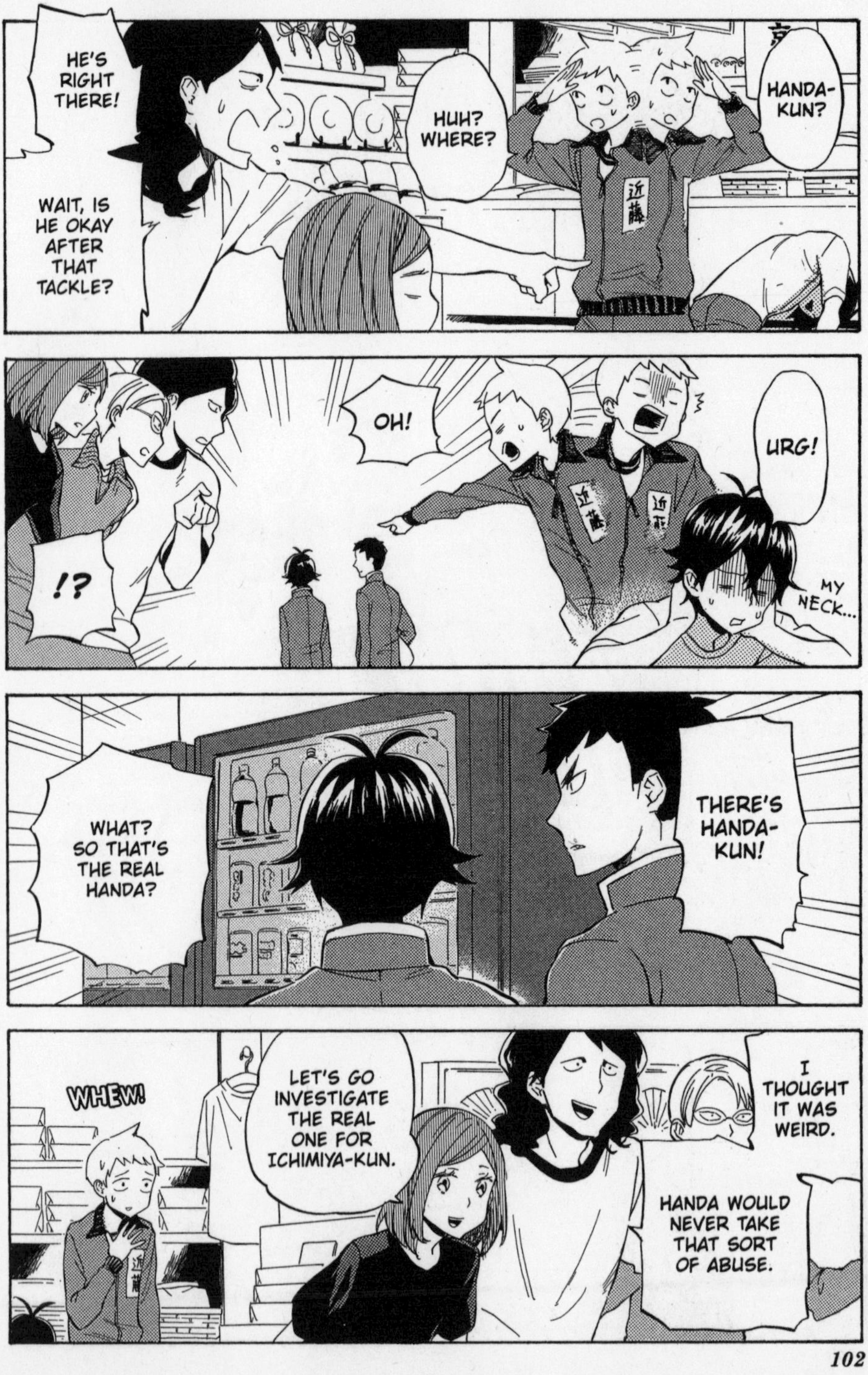
HANDA-KUN?
HUH? WHERE?
HE'S RIGHT THERE!
WAIT, IS HE OKAY AFTER THAT TACKLE?
URG!
MY NECK...
OH!
!?
THERE'S HANDA-KUN!
WHAT? SO THAT'S THE REAL HANDA?
I THOUGHT IT WAS WEIRD.
HANDA WOULD NEVER TAKE THAT SORT OF ABUSE.
LET'S GO INVESTIGATE THE REAL ONE FOR ICHIMIYA-KUN.
WHEW!

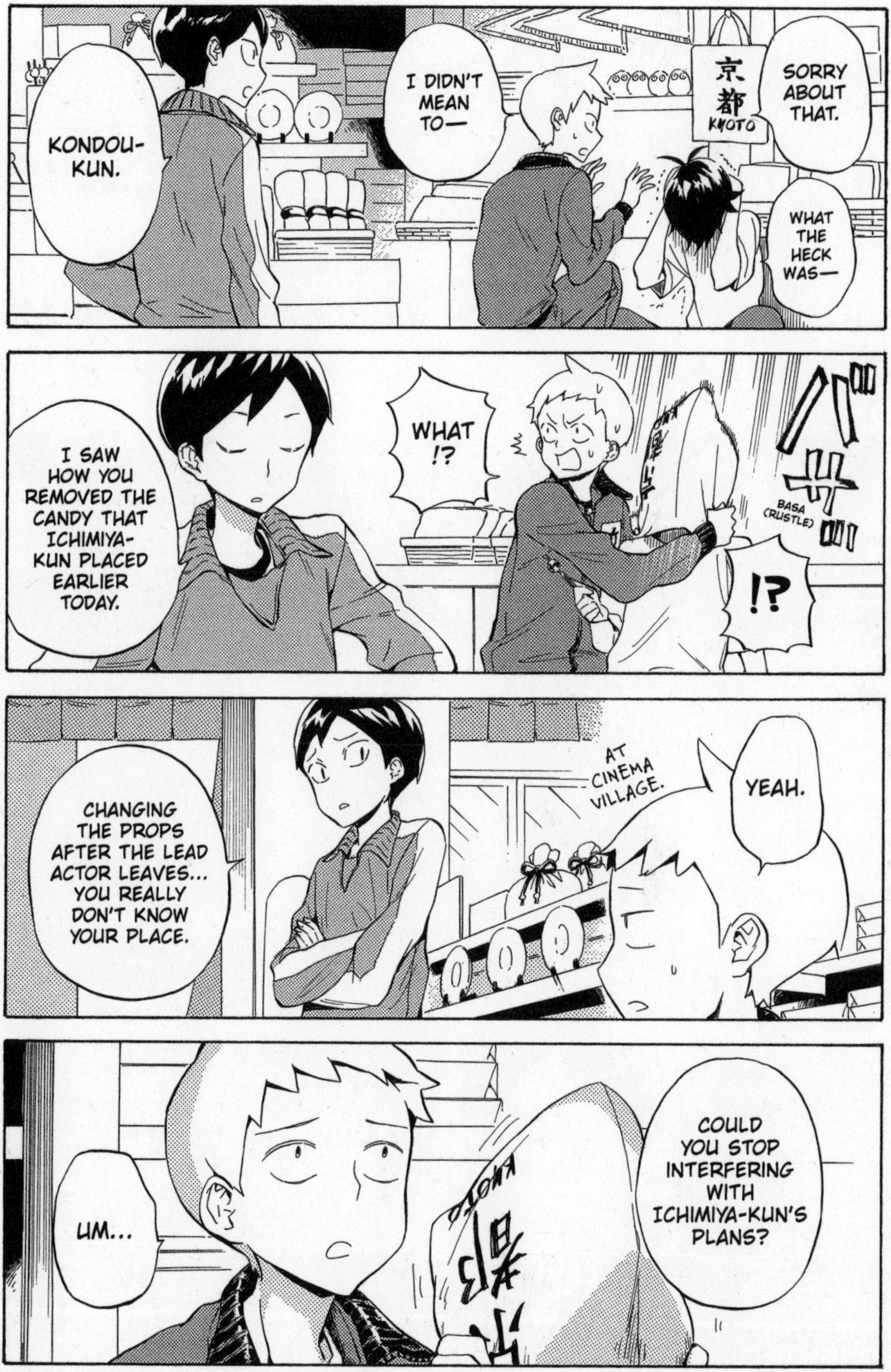
SORRY ABOUT THAT.
京都 KYOTO
WHAT THE HECK WAS—
I DIDN'T MEAN TO—
KONDOU-KUN.
BASA (RUSTLE)
!?
WHAT !?
I SAW HOW YOU REMOVED THE CANDY THAT ICHIMIYA-KUN PLACED EARLIER TODAY.
YEAH.
AT CINEMA VILLAGE.
CHANGING THE PROPS AFTER THE LEAD ACTOR LEAVES... YOU REALLY DON'T KNOW YOUR PLACE.
COULD YOU STOP INTERFERING WITH ICHIMIYA-KUN'S PLANS?
UM...

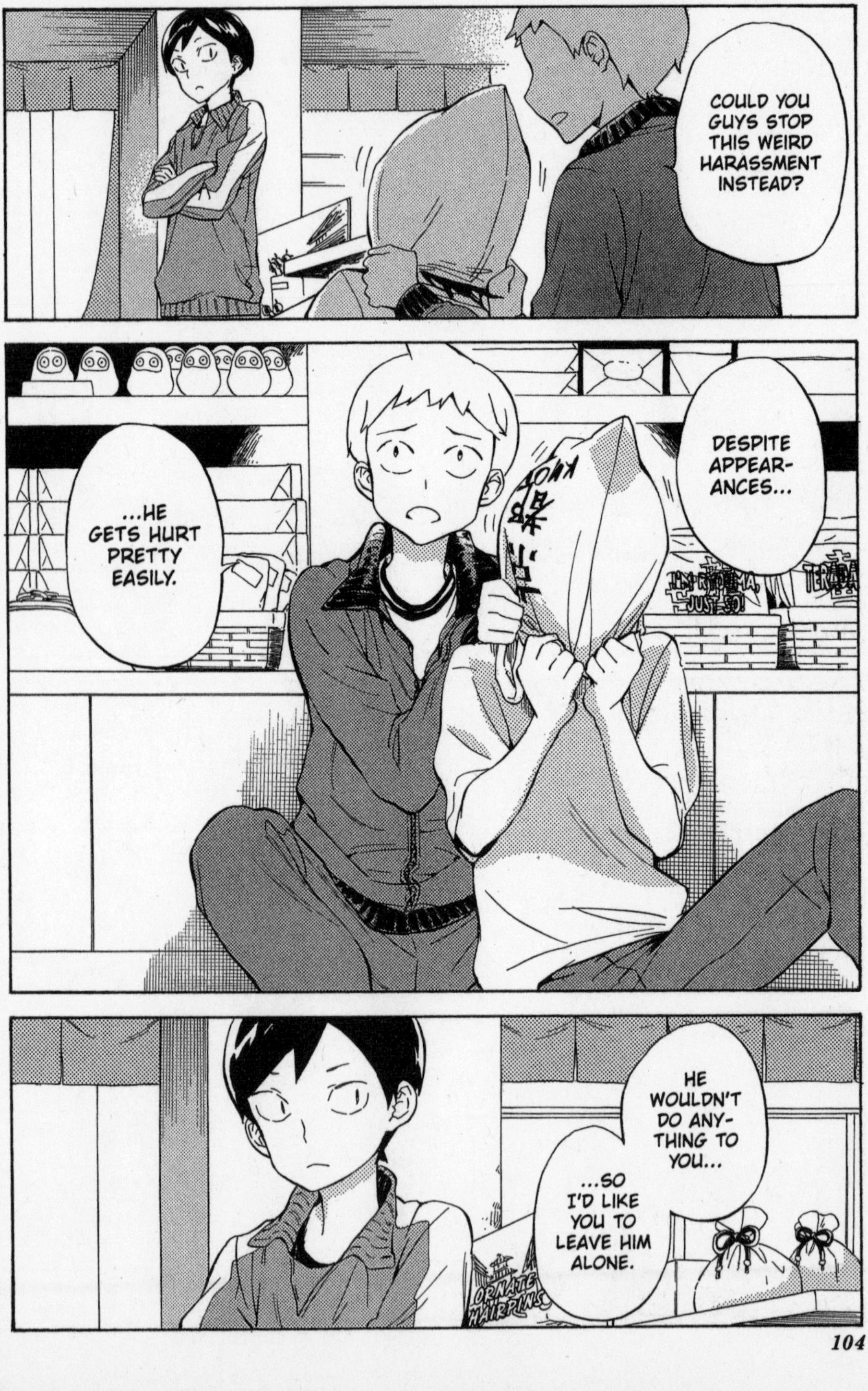
COULD YOU GUYS STOP THIS WEIRD HARASSMENT INSTEAD?
DESPITE APPEARANCES...
...HE GETS HURT PRETTY EASILY.
HE WOULDN'T DO ANYTHING TO YOU...
...SO I'D LIKE YOU TO LEAVE HIM ALONE.
ORNATE HAIRPINS

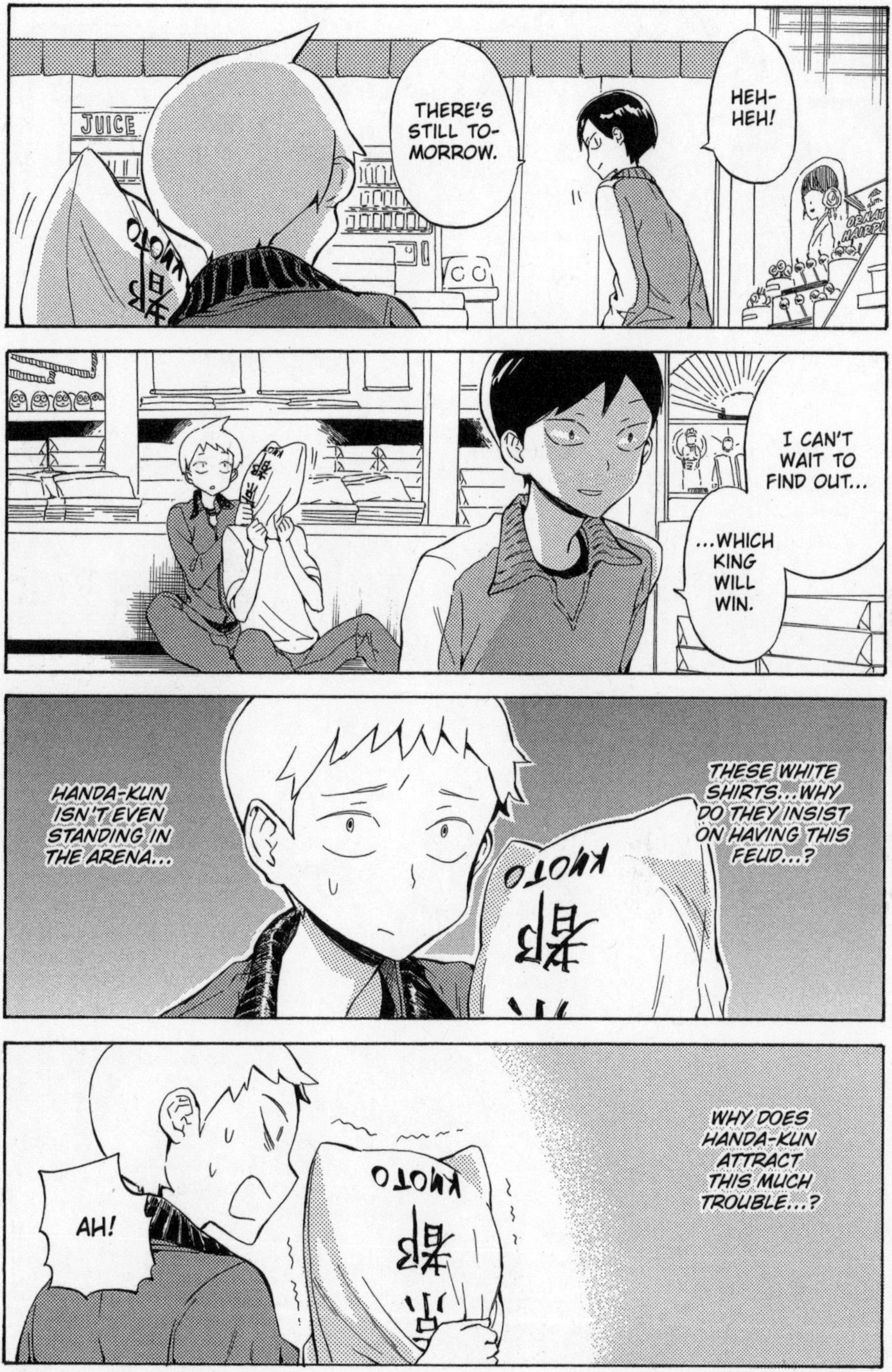
HEH-HEH!
THERE'S STILL TO-MORROW.
JUICE
I CAN'T WAIT TO FIND OUT...
...WHICH KING WILL WIN.
THESE WHITE SHIRTS...WHY DO THEY INSIST ON HAVING THIS FEUD...?
HANDA-KUN ISN'T EVEN STANDING IN THE ARENA...
WHY DOES HANDA-KUN ATTRACT THIS MUCH TROUBLE...?
AH!

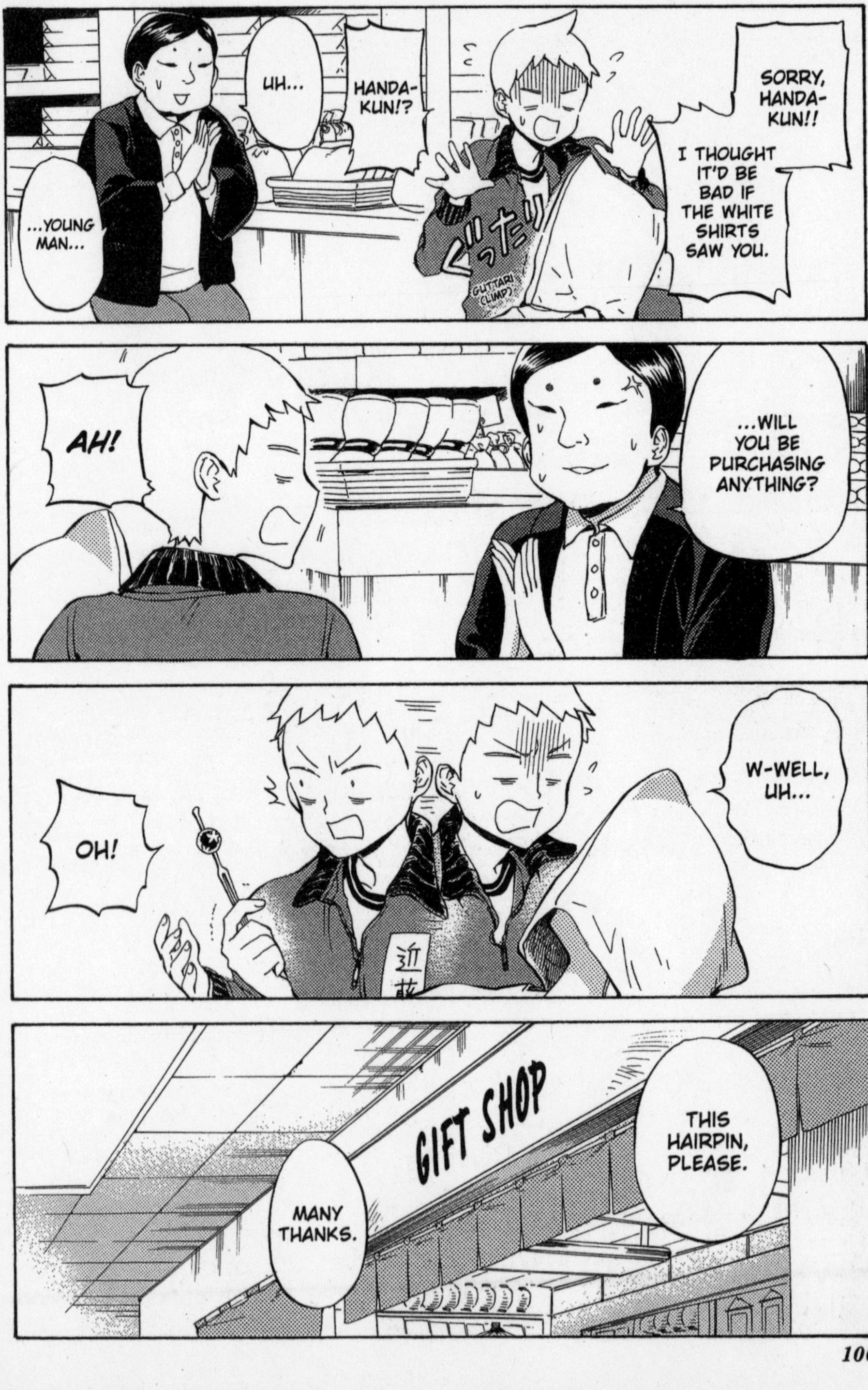

SORRY, HANDA-KUN!!
I THOUGHT IT'D BE BAD IF THE WHITE SHIRTS SAW YOU.
ぐったり
GUTTARI (LIMP)
HANDA-KUN!?
UH...
...YOUNG MAN...
...WILL YOU BE PURCHASING ANYTHING?
AH!
W-WELL, UH...
OH!
GIFT SHOP
THIS HAIRPIN, PLEASE.
MANY THANKS.

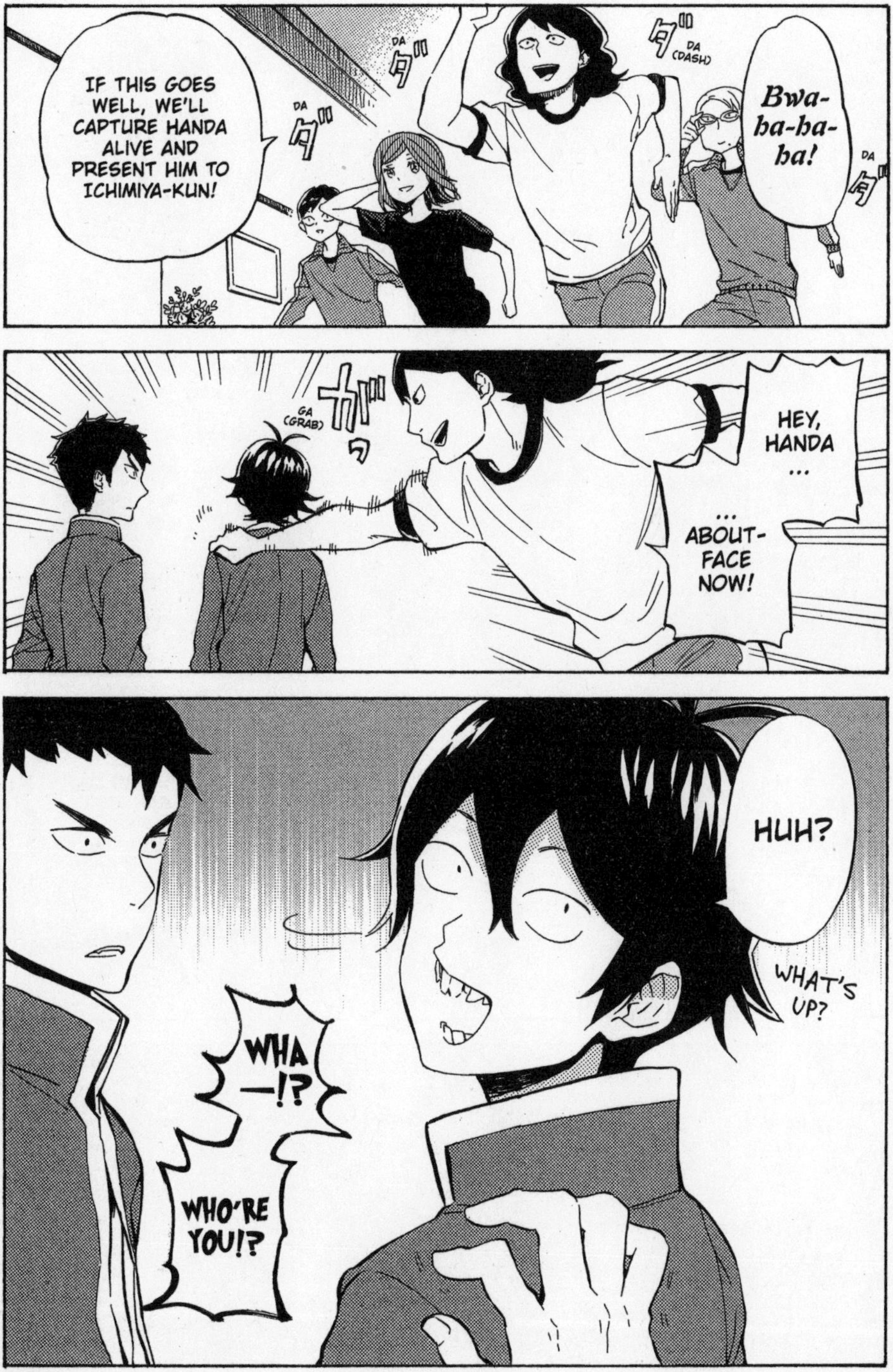
DA
Bwa-ha-ha-ha!
DA (DASH)
DA
DA
IF THIS GOES WELL, WE'LL CAPTURE HANDA ALIVE AND PRESENT HIM TO ICHIMIYA-KUN!
HEY, HANDA ...
... ABOUT-FACE NOW!
GA (GRAB)
HUH?
WHAT'S UP?
WHA—!?
WHO'RE YOU!?

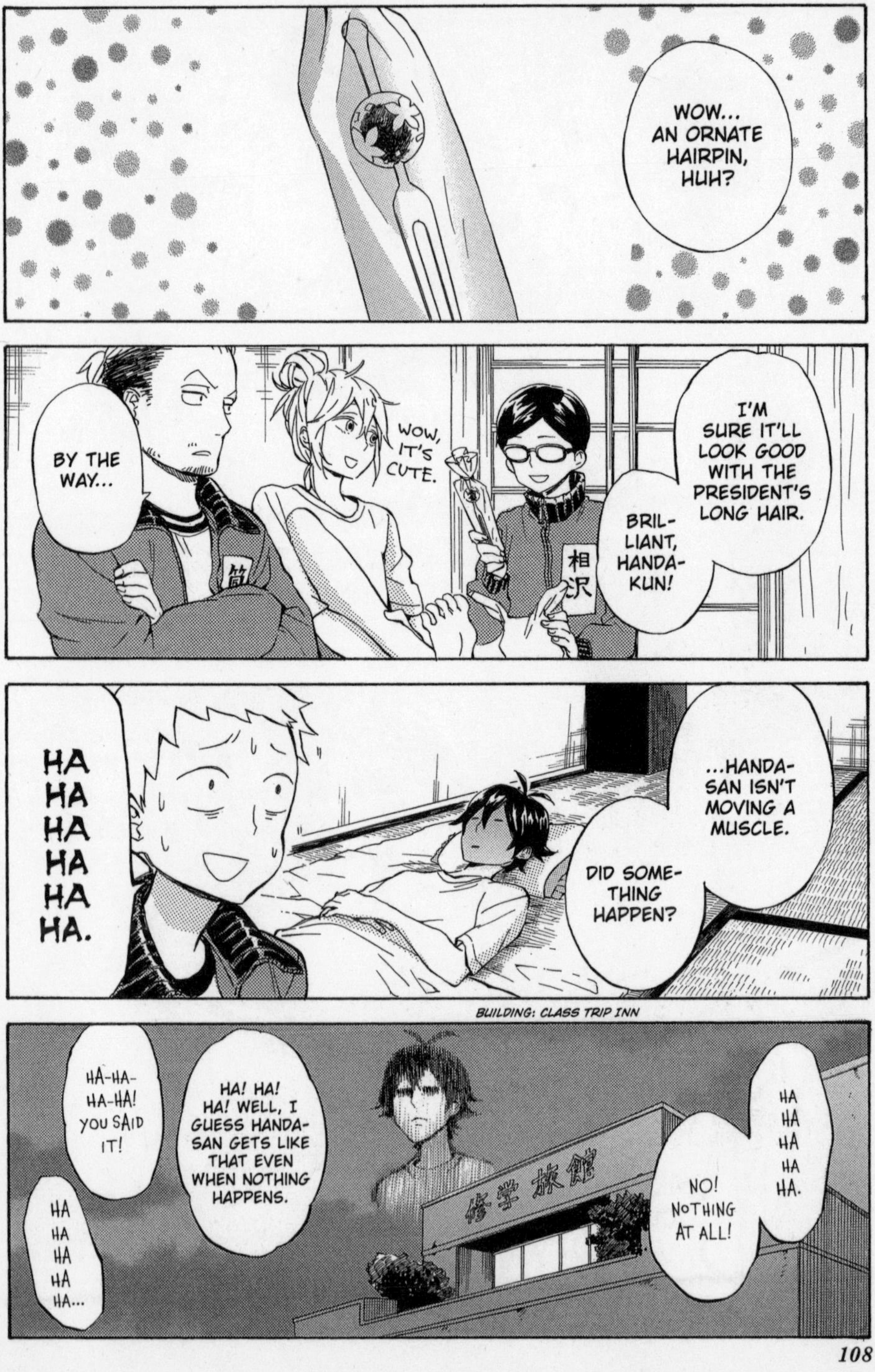
WOW... AN ORNATE HAIRPIN, HUH?
I'M SURE IT'LL LOOK GOOD WITH THE PRESIDENT'S LONG HAIR.
BRIL-LIANT, HANDA-KUN!
WOW, IT'S CUTE.
BY THE WAY...
...HANDA-SAN ISN'T MOVING A MUSCLE.
DID SOME-THING HAPPEN?
HA HA HA HA HA HA.
BUILDING: CLASS TRIP INN
HA HA HA HA HA.
NO! NOTHING AT ALL!
HA! HA! HA! WELL, I GUESS HANDA-SAN GETS LIKE THAT EVEN WHEN NOTHING HAPPENS.
HA-HA-HA-HA! YOU SAID IT!
HA HA HA HA HA...

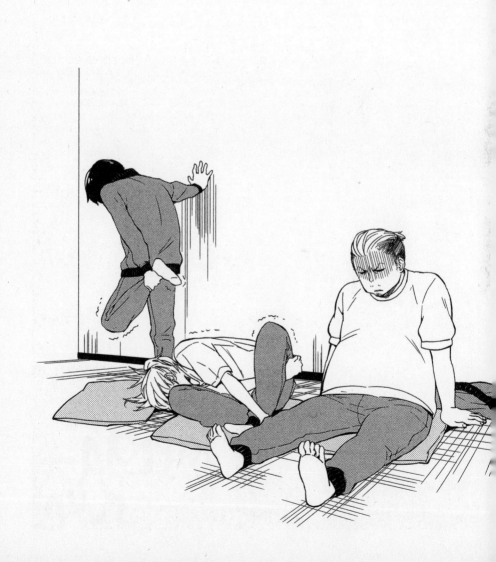

Handa-
Kun

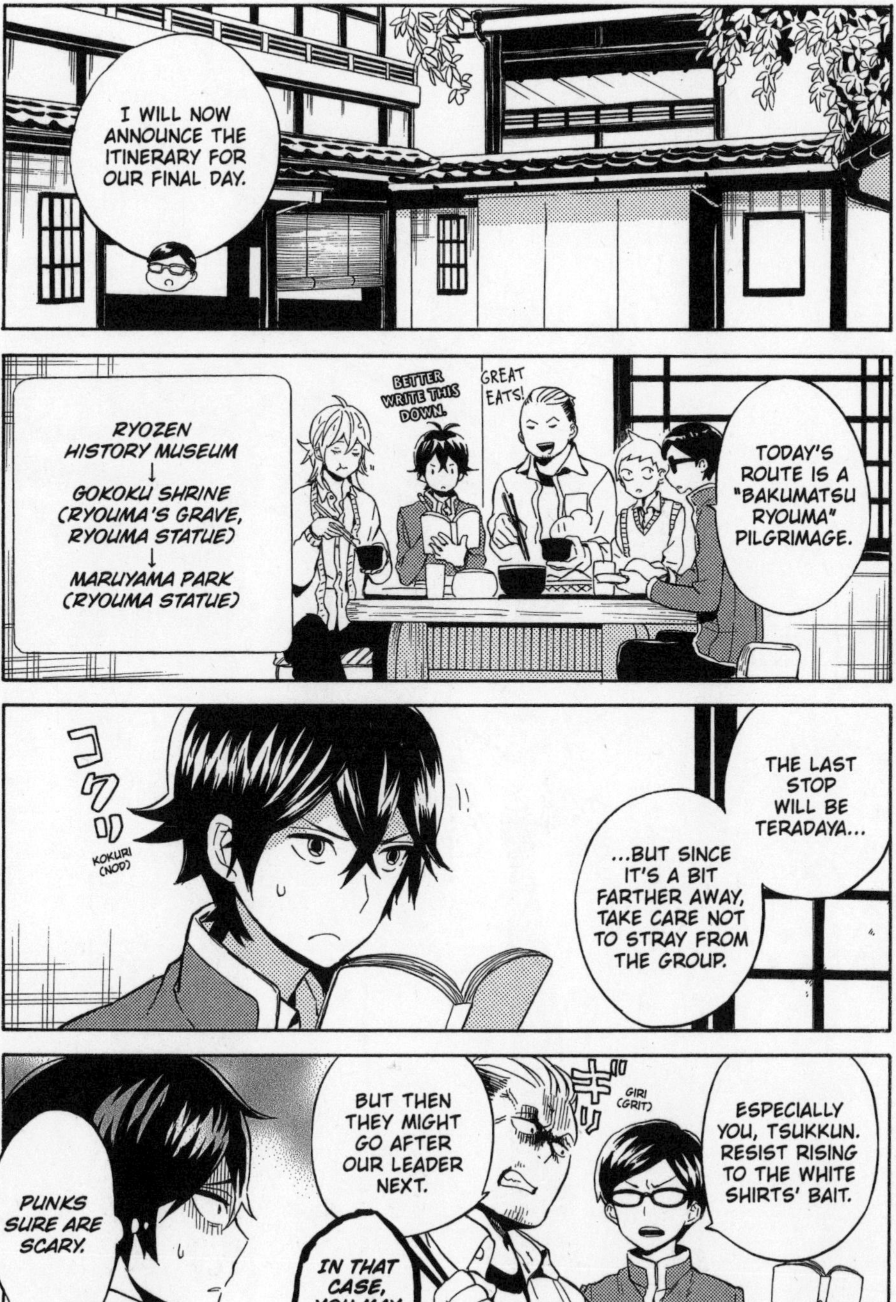
I WILL NOW ANNOUNCE THE ITINERARY FOR OUR FINAL DAY.
TODAY'S ROUTE IS A "BAKUMATSU RYOUMA" PILGRIMAGE.
GREAT EATS!
BETTER WRITE THIS DOWN.
RYOZEN HISTORY MUSEUM
↓
GOKOKU SHRINE (RYOUMA'S GRAVE, RYOUMA STATUE)
↓
MARUYAMA PARK (RYOUMA STATUE)
THE LAST STOP WILL BE TERADAYA...
...BUT SINCE IT'S A BIT FARTHER AWAY, TAKE CARE NOT TO STRAY FROM THE GROUP.
KOKURI (NOD)
ESPECIALLY YOU, TSUKKUN. RESIST RISING TO THE WHITE SHIRTS' BAIT.
GIRI (GRIT)
BUT THEN THEY MIGHT GO AFTER OUR LEADER NEXT.
IN THAT CASE, YOU MAY DO THEM IN.
PUNKS SURE ARE SCARY.

Chapter 25: Handa-kun & the Class Trip, Final Day

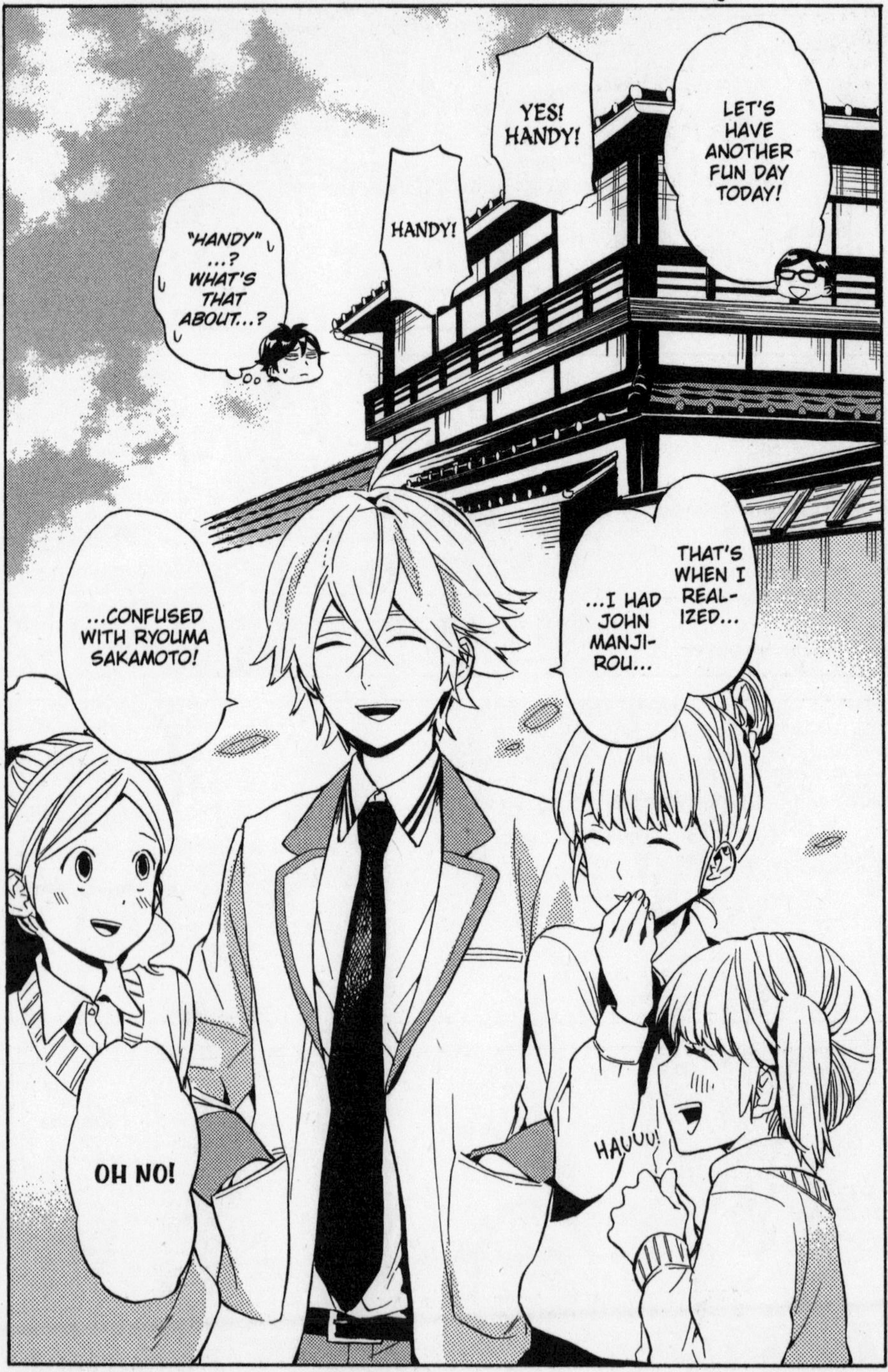
LET'S HAVE ANOTHER FUN DAY TODAY!
YES! HANDY!
HANDY!
"HANDY" ...? WHAT'S THAT ABOUT...?
THAT'S WHEN I REALIZED...
...I HAD JOHN MANJIROU...
...CONFUSED WITH RYOUMA SAKAMOTO!
HAUUU!
OH NO!

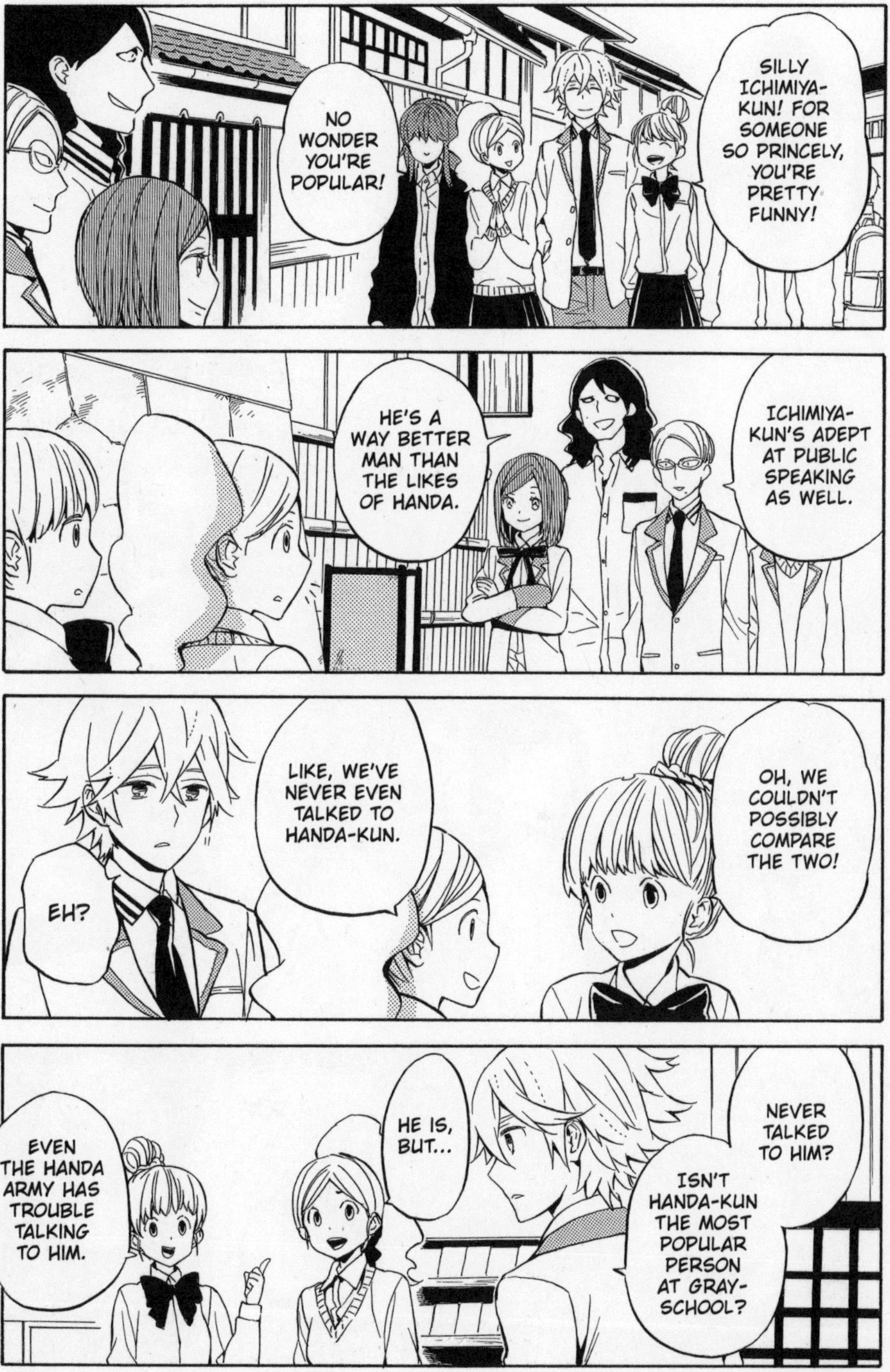
SILLY ICHIMIYA-KUN! FOR SOMEONE SO PRINCELY, YOU'RE PRETTY FUNNY!
NO WONDER YOU'RE POPULAR!
ICHIMIYA-KUN'S ADEPT AT PUBLIC SPEAKING AS WELL.
HE'S A WAY BETTER MAN THAN THE LIKES OF HANDA.
OH, WE COULDN'T POSSIBLY COMPARE THE TWO!
LIKE, WE'VE NEVER EVEN TALKED TO HANDA-KUN.
EH?
NEVER TALKED TO HIM?
ISN'T HANDA-KUN THE MOST POPULAR PERSON AT GRAY-SCHOOL?
HE IS, BUT...
EVEN THE HANDA ARMY HAS TROUBLE TALKING TO HIM.

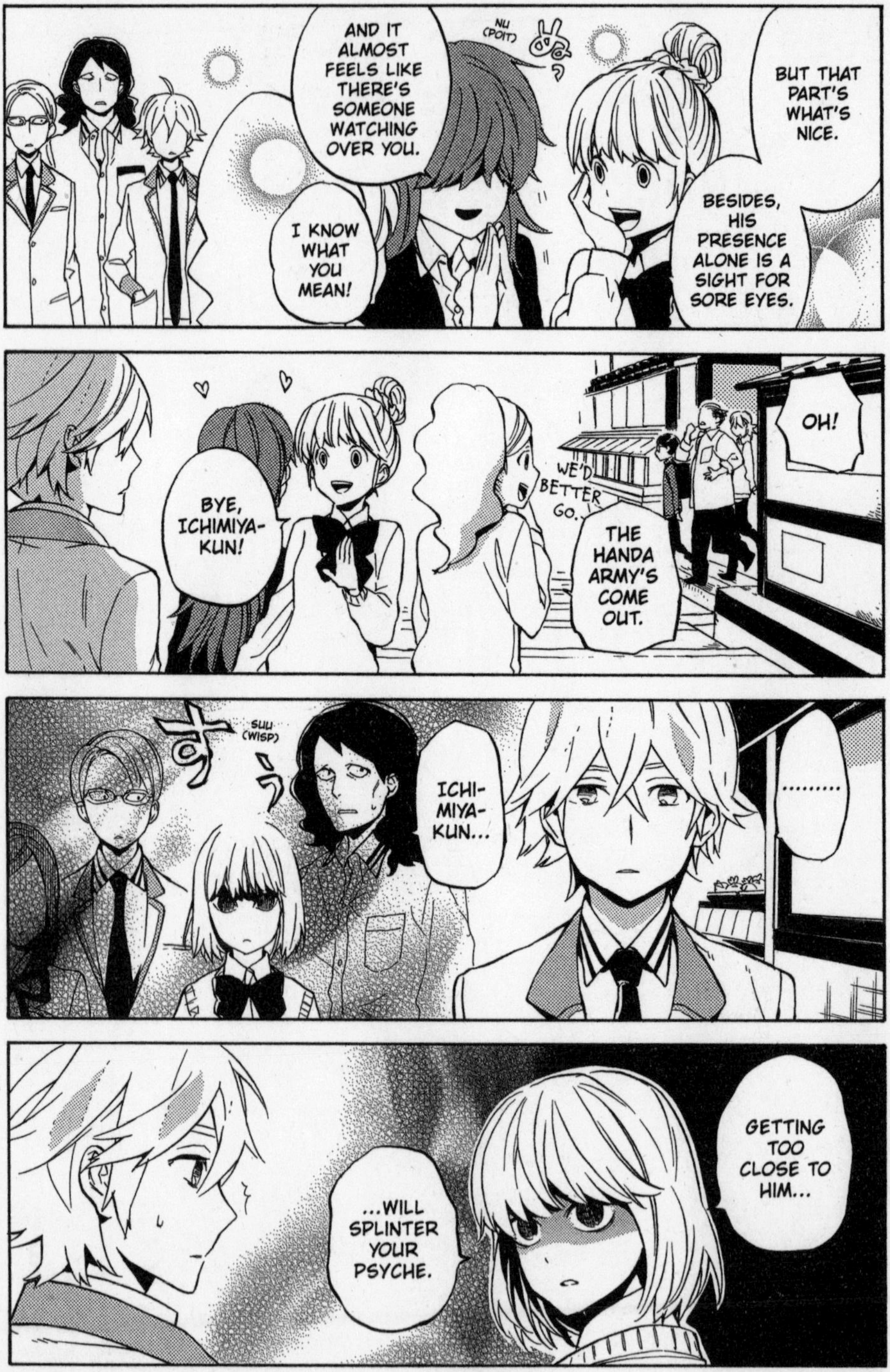
BUT THAT PART'S WHAT'S NICE.
BESIDES, HIS PRESENCE ALONE IS A SIGHT FOR SORE EYES.
ぬっ
NU (POIT)
AND IT ALMOST FEELS LIKE THERE'S SOMEONE WATCHING OVER YOU.
I KNOW WHAT YOU MEAN!
OH!
WE'D BETTER GO..
THE HANDA ARMY'S COME OUT.
BYE, ICHIMIYA-KUN!
....
ICHI-MIYA-KUN...
すう
SUU (WISP)
GETTING TOO CLOSE TO HIM...
...WILL SPLINTER YOUR PSYCHE.

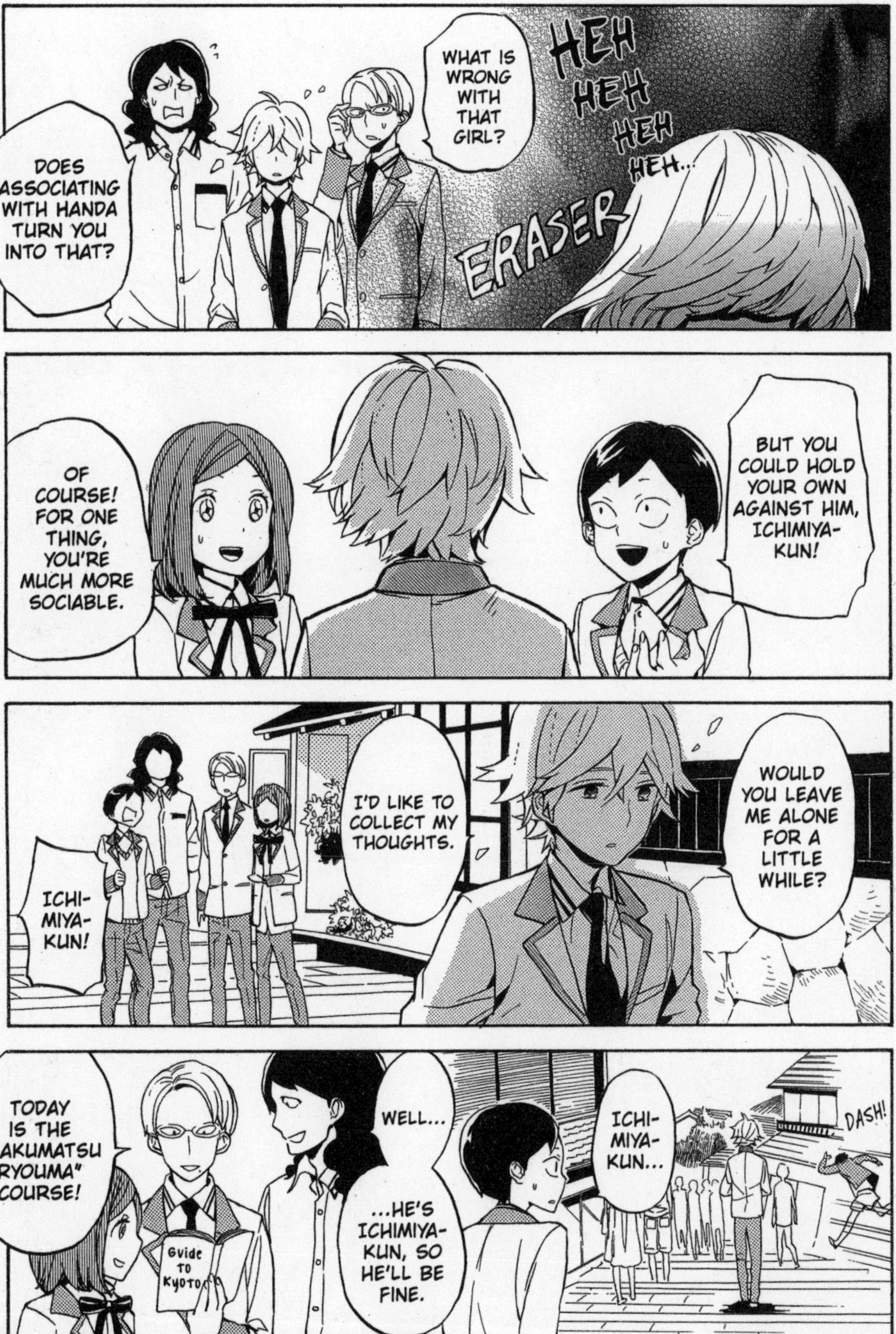
HEH HEH HEH HEH...
ERASER
WHAT IS WRONG WITH THAT GIRL?
DOES ASSOCIATING WITH HANDA TURN YOU INTO THAT?
BUT YOU COULD HOLD YOUR OWN AGAINST HIM, ICHIMIYA-KUN!
OF COURSE! FOR ONE THING, YOU'RE MUCH MORE SOCIABLE.
WOULD YOU LEAVE ME ALONE FOR A LITTLE WHILE?
I'D LIKE TO COLLECT MY THOUGHTS.
ICHI-MIYA-KUN!
DASH!
ICHI-MIYA-KUN...
WELL...
...HE'S ICHIMIYA-KUN, SO HE'LL BE FINE.
TODAY IS THE "BAKUMATSU RYOUMA" COURSE!
Guide to Kyoto

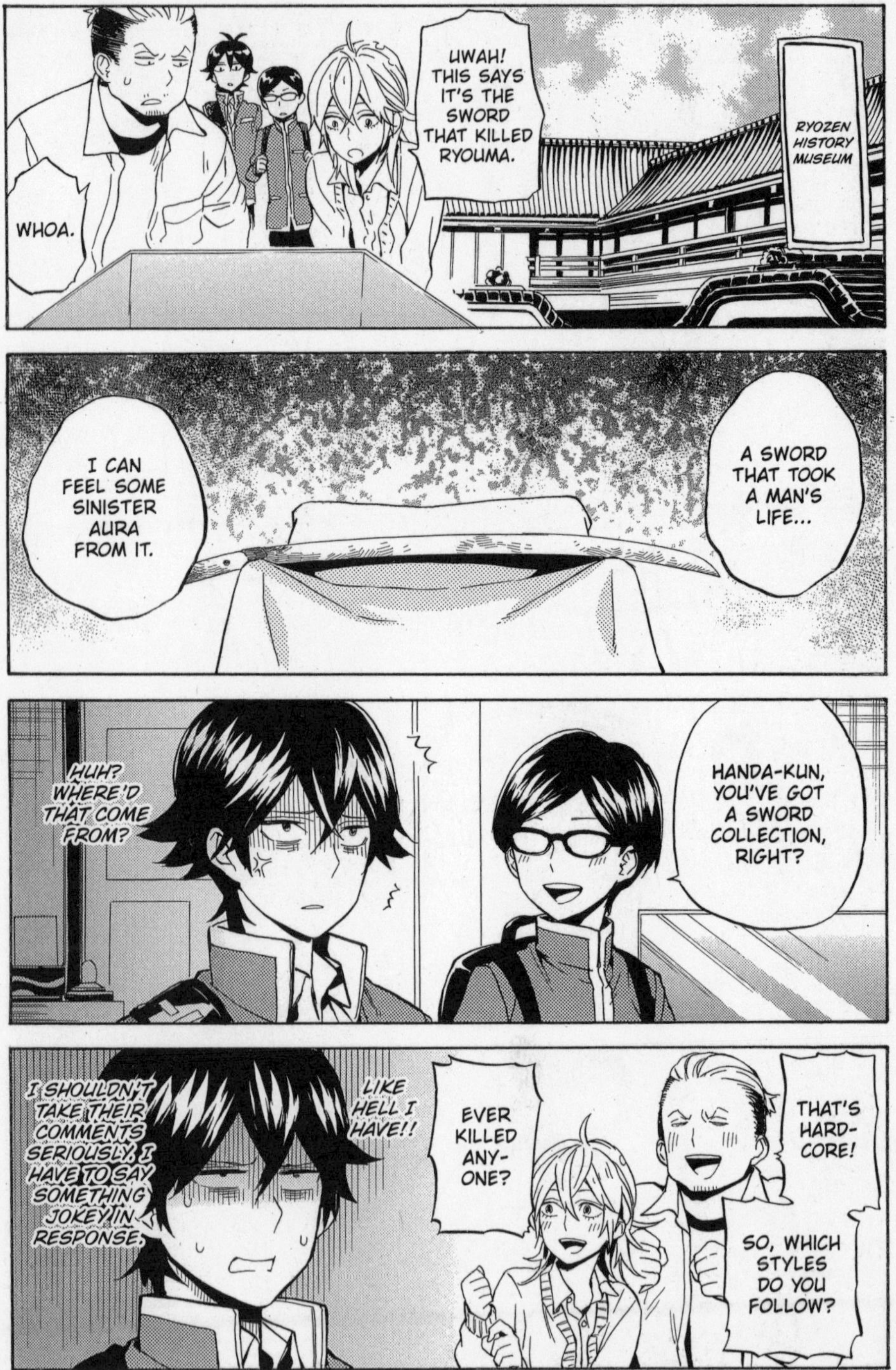
RYOZEN HISTORY MUSEUM
UWAH! THIS SAYS IT'S THE SWORD THAT KILLED RYOUMA.
WHOA.
A SWORD THAT TOOK A MAN'S LIFE...
I CAN FEEL SOME SINISTER AURA FROM IT.
HANDA-KUN, YOU'VE GOT A SWORD COLLECTION, RIGHT?
HUH? WHERE'D THAT COME FROM?
THAT'S HARD-CORE!
SO, WHICH STYLES DO YOU FOLLOW?
EVER KILLED ANY-ONE?
LIKE HELL I HAVE!!
I SHOULDN'T TAKE THEIR COMMENTS SERIOUSLY. I HAVE TO SAY SOMETHING JOKEY IN RESPONSE.

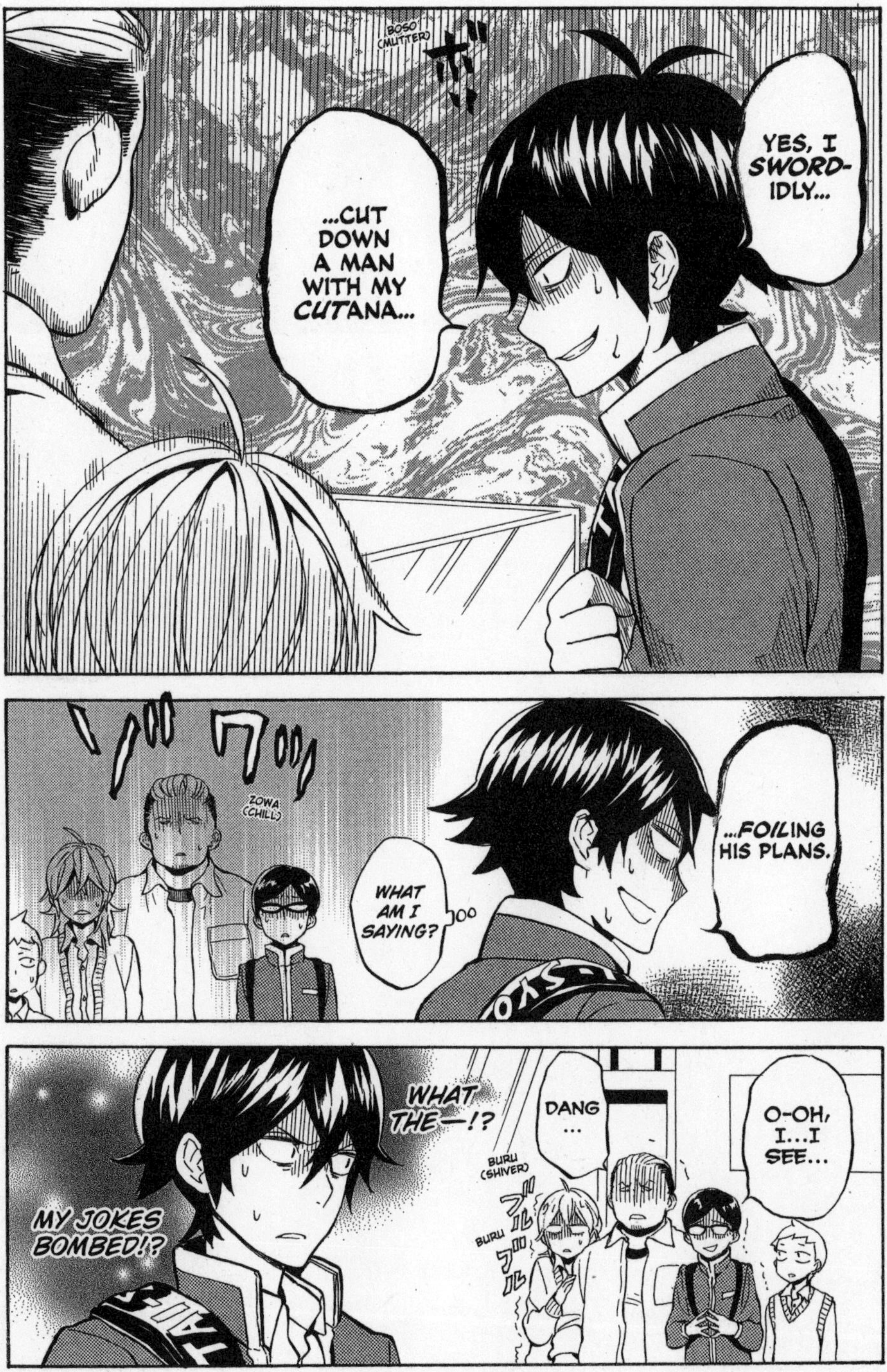
BOSO (MUTTER)
YES, I SWORDIDLY...
...CUT DOWN A MAN WITH MY CUTANA...
...FOILING HIS PLANS.
WHAT AM I SAYING?
ZOWA (CHILL)
O-OH, I...I SEE...
DANG...
BURU (SHIVER)
BURU
WHAT THE—!?
MY JOKES BOMBED!?

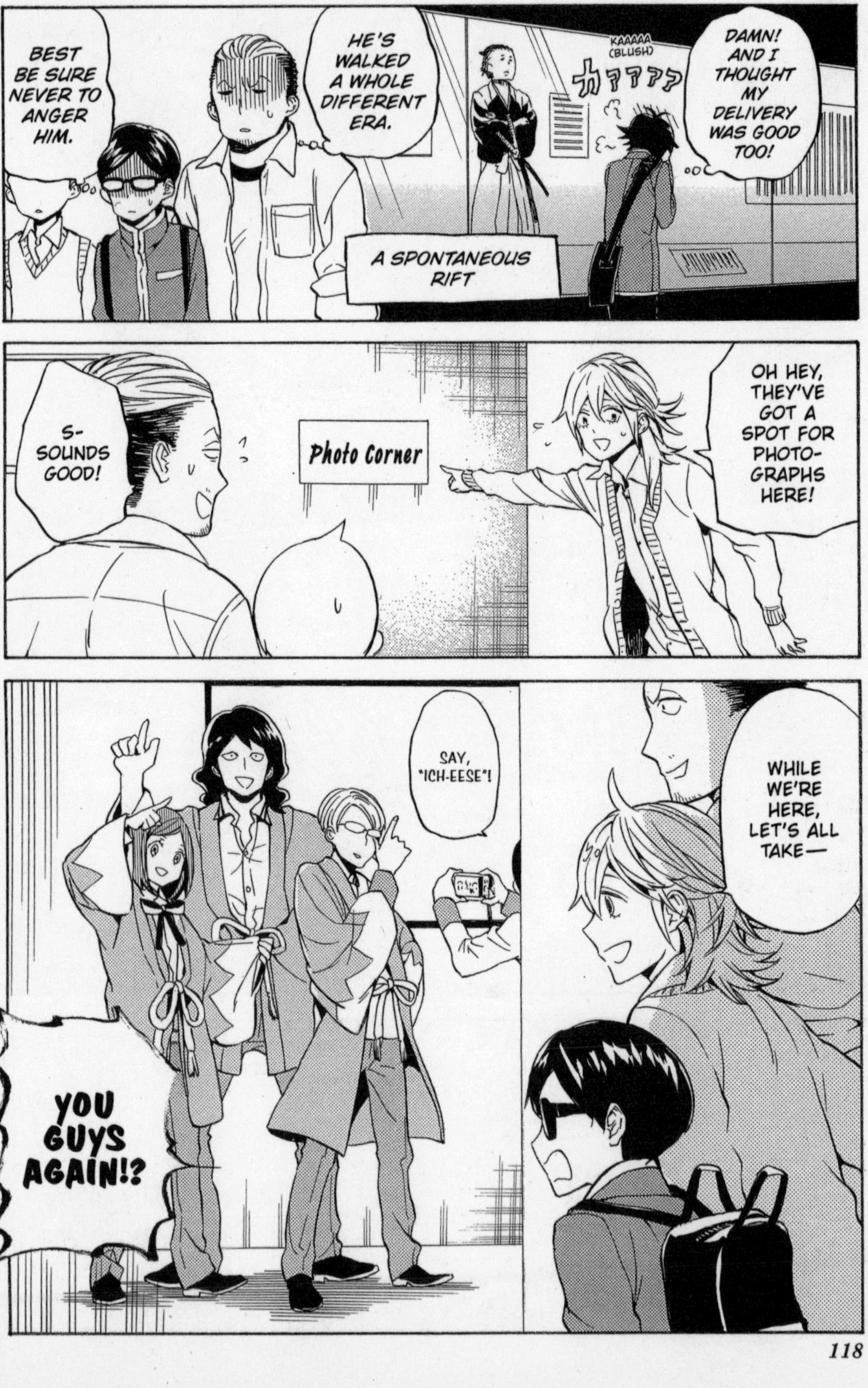
DAMN! AND I THOUGHT MY DELIVERY WAS GOOD TOO!
KAAAAA (BLUSH)
カァァァァ
HE'S WALKED A WHOLE DIFFERENT ERA.
BEST BE SURE NEVER TO ANGER HIM.
A SPONTANEOUS RIFT
OH HEY, THEY'VE GOT A SPOT FOR PHOTO-GRAPHS HERE!
Photo Corner
S-SOUNDS GOOD!
WHILE WE'RE HERE, LET'S ALL TAKE—
SAY, "ICH-EESE"!
YOU GUYS AGAIN!?

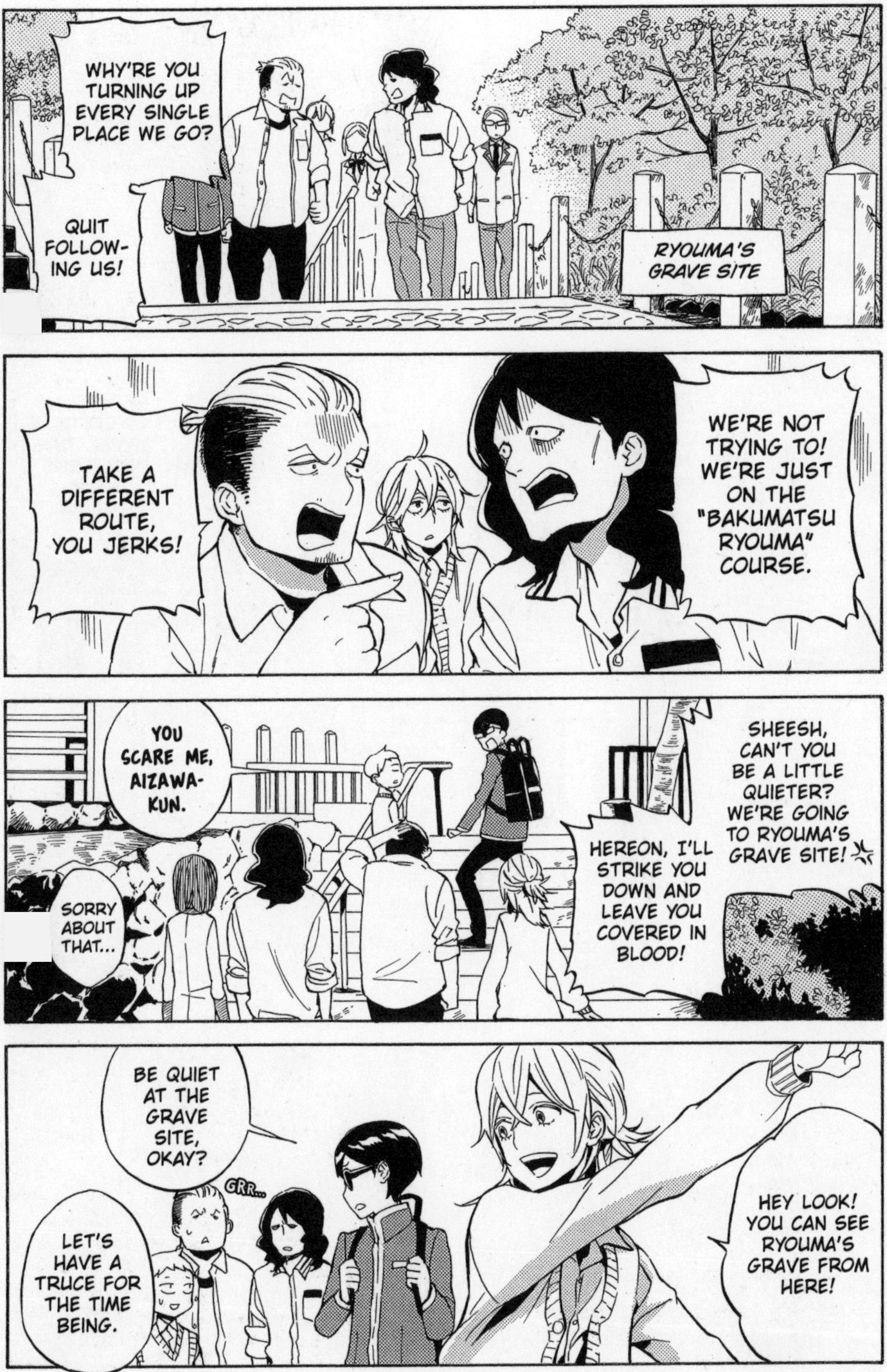
WHY'RE YOU TURNING UP EVERY SINGLE PLACE WE GO?
QUIT FOLLOWING US!
RYOUMA'S GRAVE SITE
WE'RE NOT TRYING TO! WE'RE JUST ON THE "BAKUMATSU RYOUMA" COURSE.
TAKE A DIFFERENT ROUTE, YOU JERKS!
SHEESH, CAN'T YOU BE A LITTLE QUIETER? WE'RE GOING TO RYOUMA'S GRAVE SITE!
HEREON, I'LL STRIKE YOU DOWN AND LEAVE YOU COVERED IN BLOOD!
YOU SCARE ME, AIZAWA-KUN.
SORRY ABOUT THAT...
HEY LOOK! YOU CAN SEE RYOUMA'S GRAVE FROM HERE!
BE QUIET AT THE GRAVE SITE, OKAY?
GRR...
LET'S HAVE A TRUCE FOR THE TIME BEING.

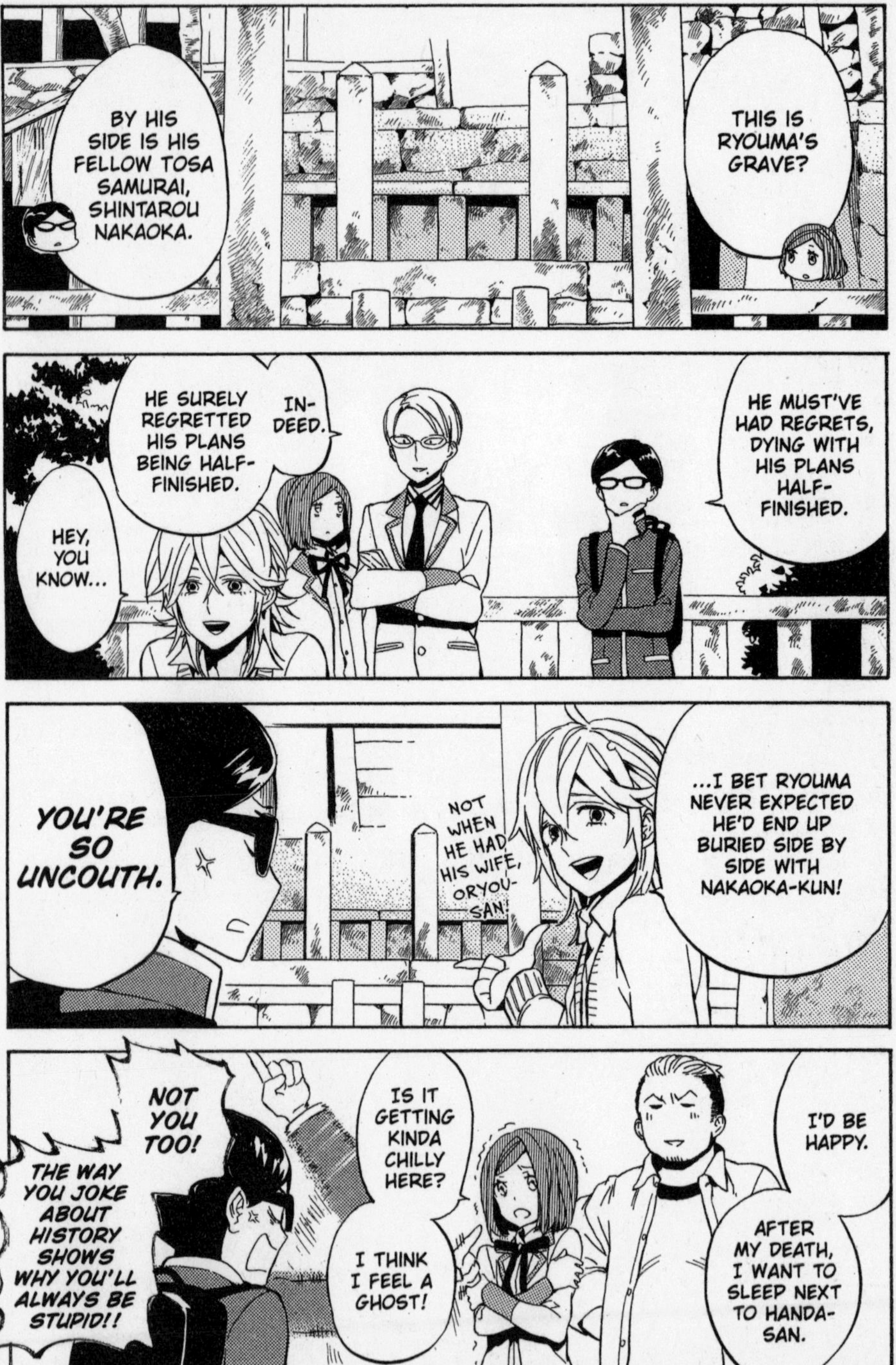
THIS IS RYOUMA'S GRAVE?
BY HIS SIDE IS HIS FELLOW TOSA SAMURAI, SHINTAROU NAKAOKA.
HE MUST'VE HAD REGRETS, DYING WITH HIS PLANS HALF-FINISHED.
IN-DEED.
HE SURELY REGRETTED HIS PLANS BEING HALF-FINISHED.
HEY, YOU KNOW...
...I BET RYOUMA NEVER EXPECTED HE'D END UP BURIED SIDE BY SIDE WITH NAKAOKA-KUN!
NOT WHEN HE HAD HIS WIFE, ORYOU-SAN!
YOU'RE SO UNCOUTH.
I'D BE HAPPY.
AFTER MY DEATH, I WANT TO SLEEP NEXT TO HANDA-SAN.
IS IT GETTING KINDA CHILLY HERE?
I THINK I FEEL A GHOST!
NOT YOU TOO!
THE WAY YOU JOKE ABOUT HISTORY SHOWS WHY YOU'LL ALWAYS BE STUPID!!

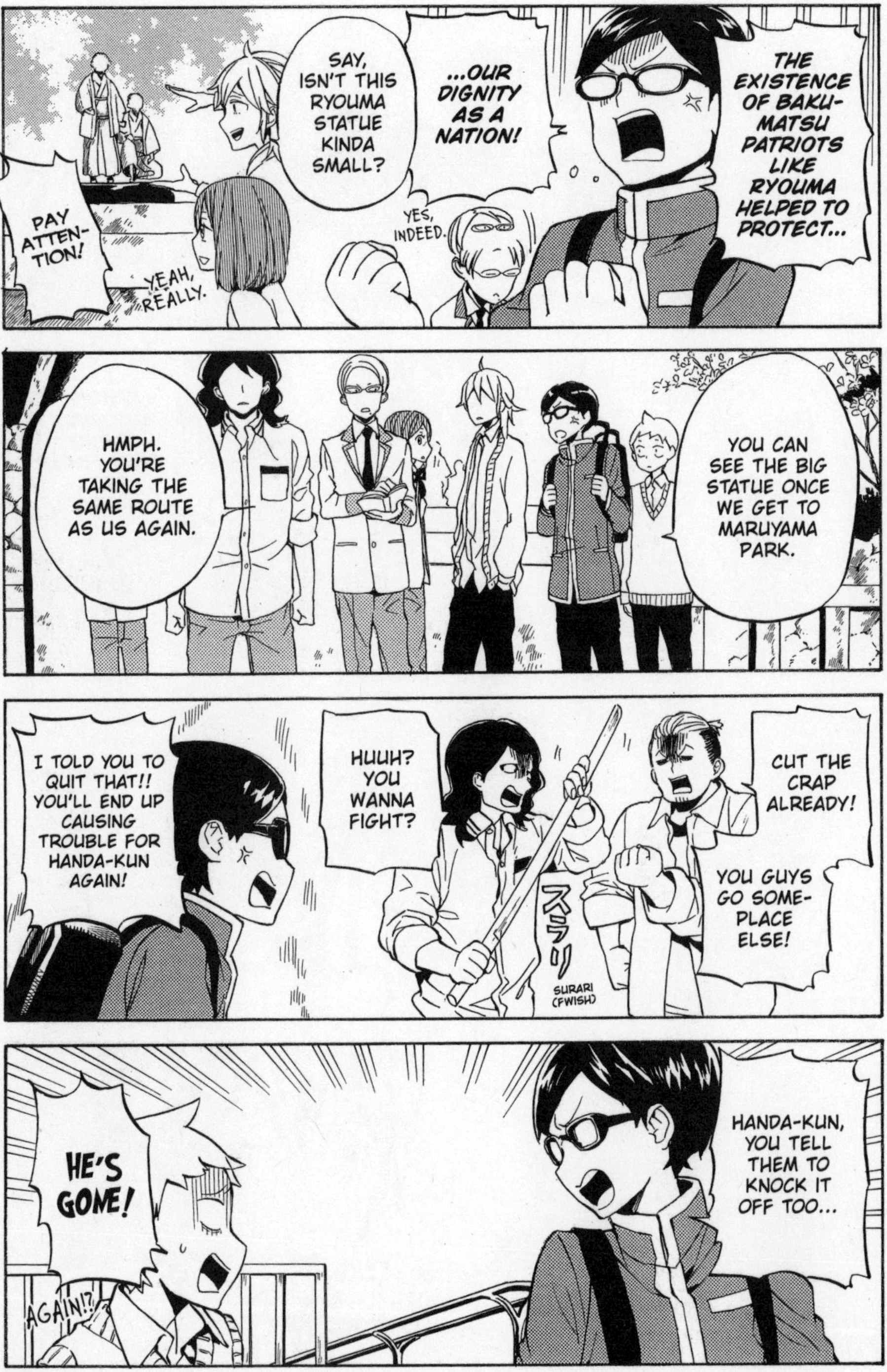
THE EXISTENCE OF BAKU-MATSU PATRIOTS LIKE RYOUMA HELPED TO PROTECT...
...OUR DIGNITY AS A NATION!
YES, INDEED.
SAY, ISN'T THIS RYOUMA STATUE KINDA SMALL?
YEAH, REALLY.
PAY ATTEN-TION!
YOU CAN SEE THE BIG STATUE ONCE WE GET TO MARUYAMA PARK.
HMPH. YOU'RE TAKING THE SAME ROUTE AS US AGAIN.
CUT THE CRAP ALREADY!
YOU GUYS GO SOME-PLACE ELSE!
スラリ
SURARI (FWISH)
HUUH? YOU WANNA FIGHT?
I TOLD YOU TO QUIT THAT!! YOU'LL END UP CAUSING TROUBLE FOR HANDA-KUN AGAIN!
HANDA-KUN, YOU TELL THEM TO KNOCK IT OFF TOO...
HE'S GONE!
AGAIN!?

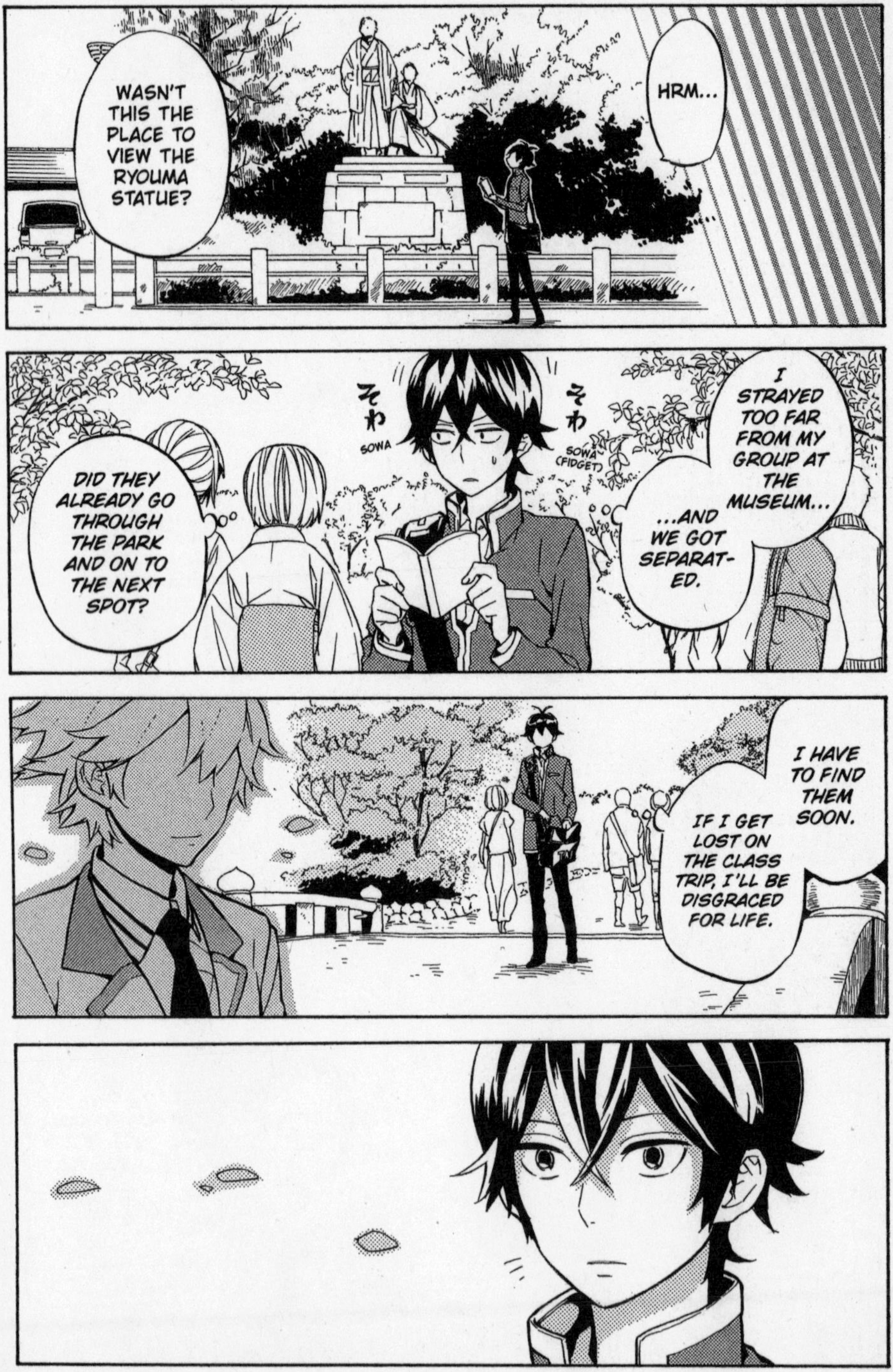
HRM...
WASN'T THIS THE PLACE TO VIEW THE RYOUMA STATUE?
I STRAYED TOO FAR FROM MY GROUP AT THE MUSEUM...
...AND WE GOT SEPARAT-ED.
そわ
SOWA (FIDGET)
そわ
SOWA
DID THEY ALREADY GO THROUGH THE PARK AND ON TO THE NEXT SPOT?
I HAVE TO FIND THEM SOON.
IF I GET LOST ON THE CLASS TRIP, I'LL BE DISGRACED FOR LIFE.

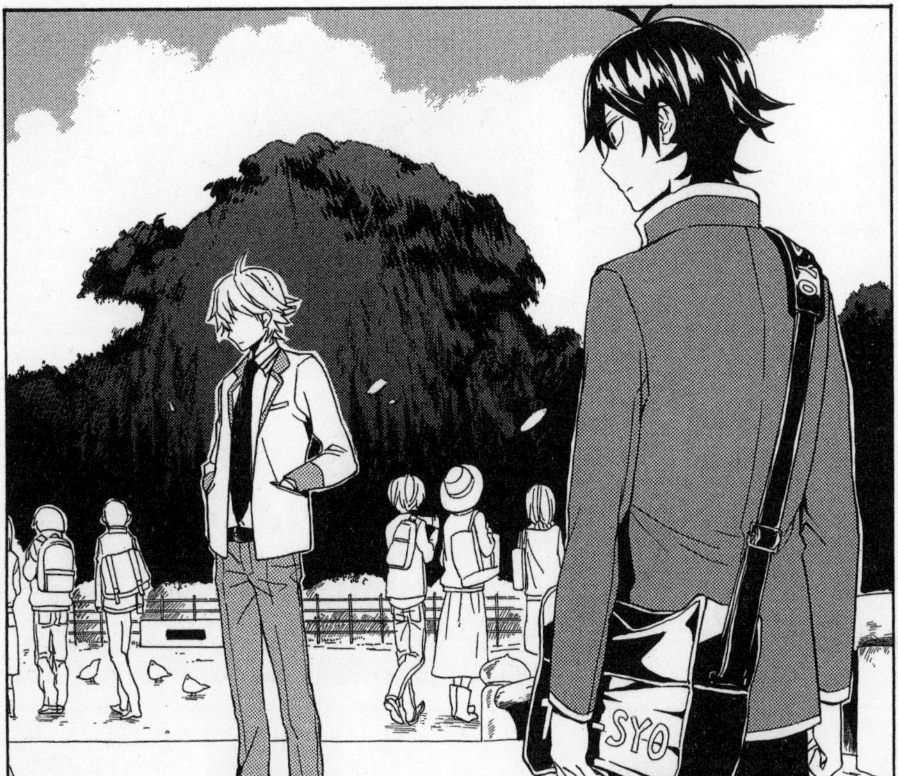

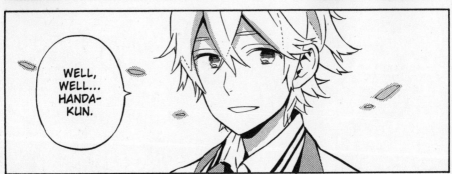

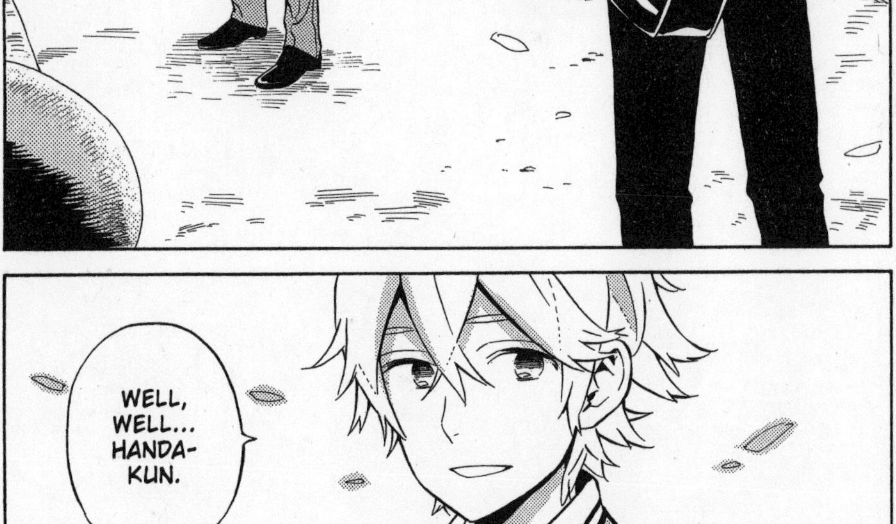
WELL, WELL... HANDA-KUN.

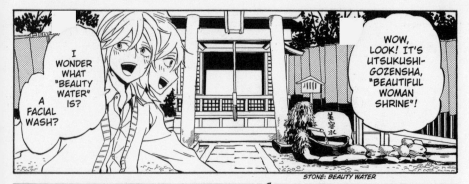

WOW, LOOK! IT'S UTSUKUSHI-GOZENSHA, "BEAUTIFUL WOMAN SHRINE"!
美容水
I WONDER WHAT "BEAUTY WATER" IS?
A FACIAL WASH?
STONE: BEAUTY WATER
MY BEAUTY SENSES ARE AT MAX!
ZABA (SPLASH)
ZABA
REO-KUN, PLEASE DON'T MAKE TROUBLE FOR PEOPLE.
HANDA-KUN ISN'T HERE EITHER...
LET'S ALL WRITE VOTIVE TABLETS!
FOR THE MEMORIES.
NURI (SMEAR)
AHH! I'VE GROWN BEAUTIFUL ALREADY!
NURI
LET'S ALL TAKE THE SEARCH FOR HANDA-KUN SERIOUSLY.
IT'S FINE AS LONG AS HE DOESN'T RUN INTO THE WHITE SHIRTS.
YEAH.
THAT'S TRUE.
MAYBE IF WE TRY A DIFFERENT PATH THROUGH THE PARK...

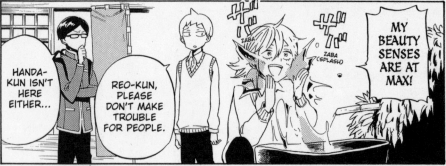

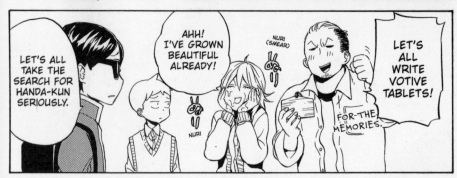

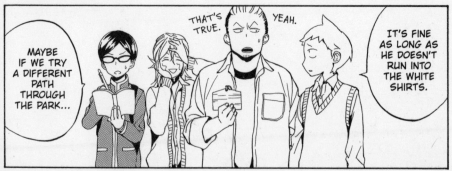

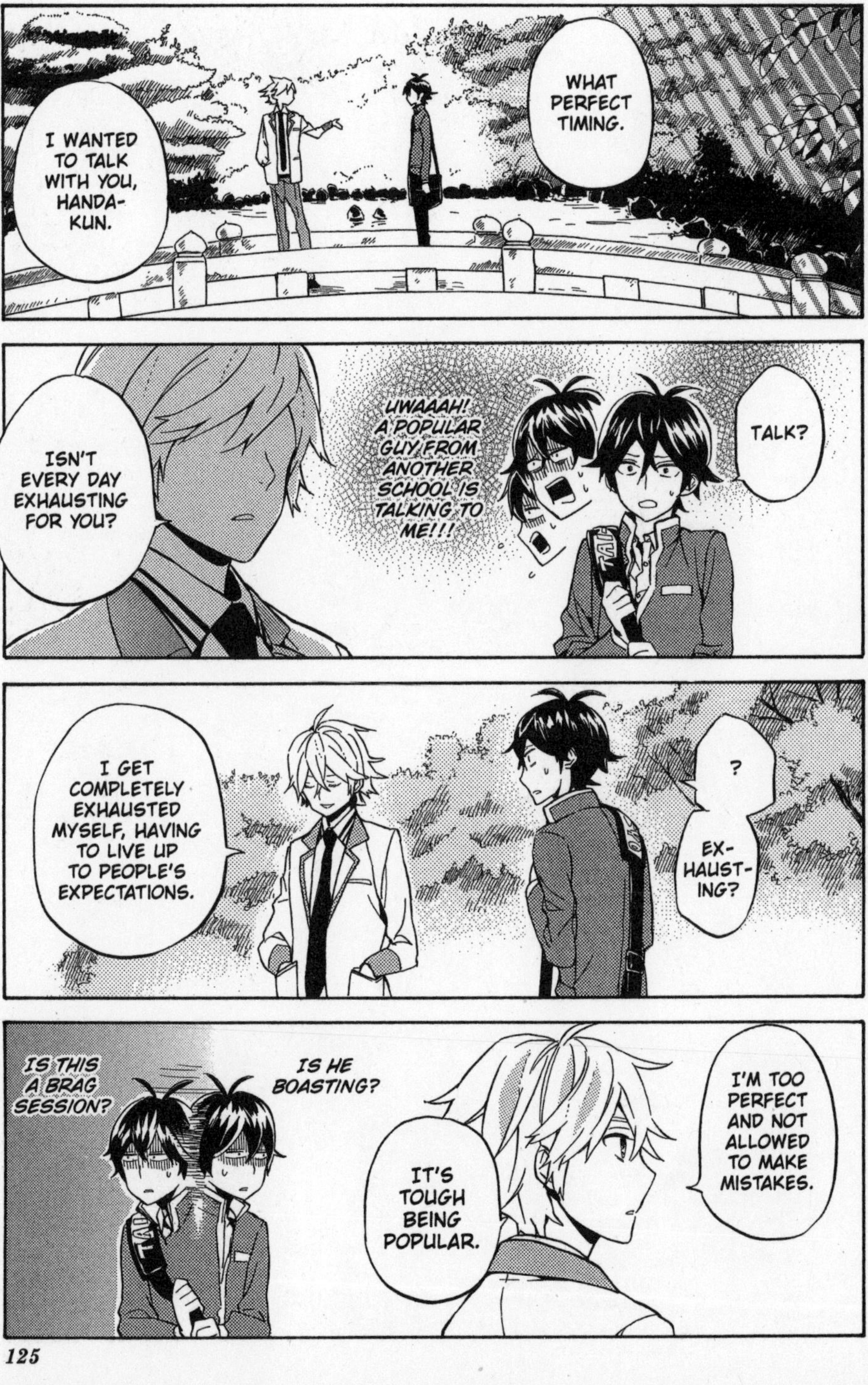
WHAT PERFECT TIMING.
I WANTED TO TALK WITH YOU, HANDA-KUN.
TALK?
UWAAAH! A POPULAR GUY FROM ANOTHER SCHOOL IS TALKING TO ME!!!
ISN'T EVERY DAY EXHAUSTING FOR YOU?
?
EX-HAUSTING?
I GET COMPLETELY EXHAUSTED MYSELF, HAVING TO LIVE UP TO PEOPLE'S EXPECTATIONS.
I'M TOO PERFECT AND NOT ALLOWED TO MAKE MISTAKES.
IT'S TOUGH BEING POPULAR.
IS HE BOASTING?
IS THIS A BRAG SESSION?

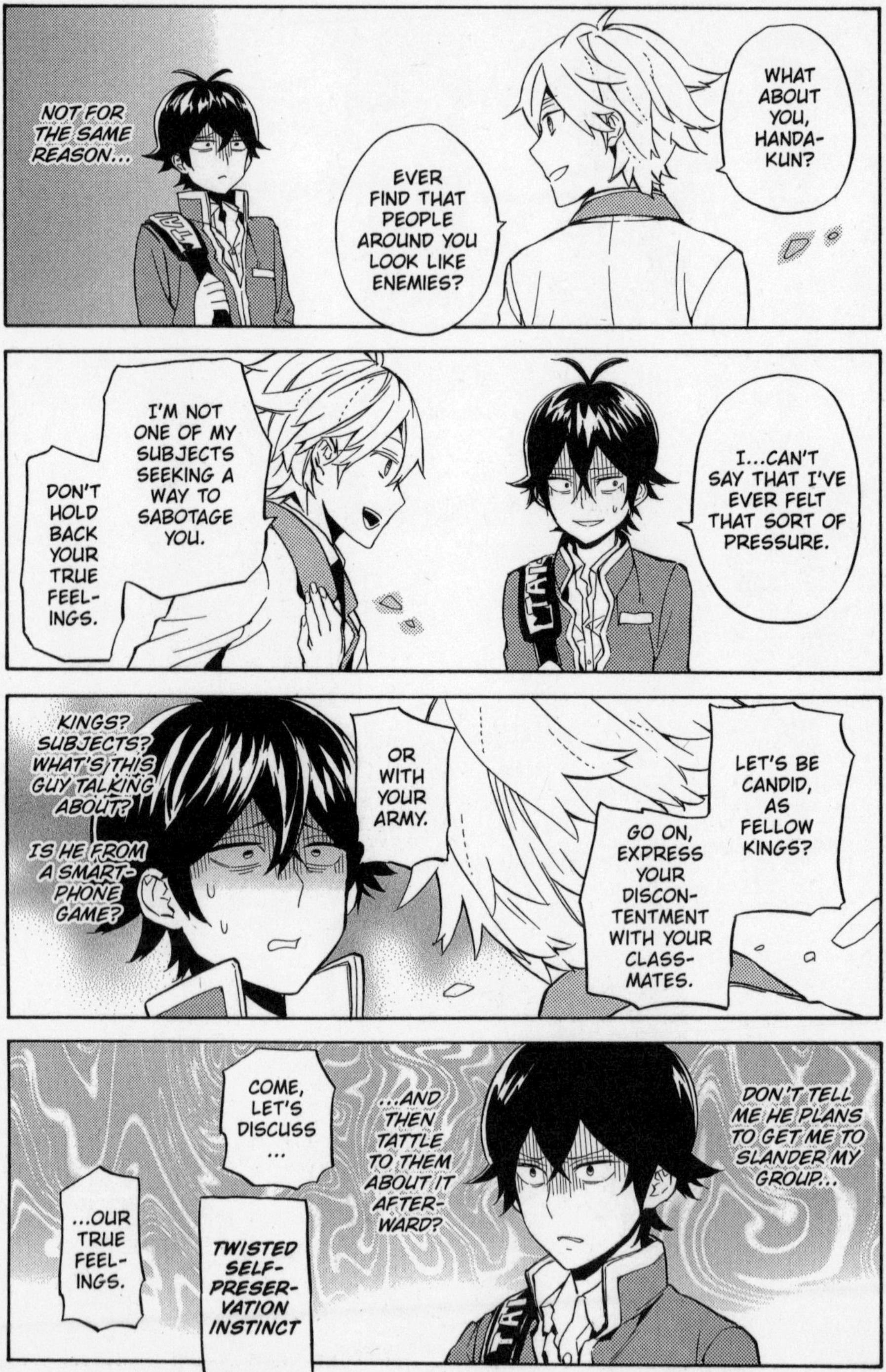
WHAT ABOUT YOU, HANDA-KUN?
EVER FIND THAT PEOPLE AROUND YOU LOOK LIKE ENEMIES?
NOT FOR THE SAME REASON...
I...CAN'T SAY THAT I'VE EVER FELT THAT SORT OF PRESSURE.
I'M NOT ONE OF MY SUBJECTS SEEKING A WAY TO SABOTAGE YOU.
DON'T HOLD BACK YOUR TRUE FEELINGS.
LET'S BE CANDID, AS FELLOW KINGS?
GO ON, EXPRESS YOUR DISCONTENTMENT WITH YOUR CLASSMATES.
OR WITH YOUR ARMY.
KINGS? SUBJECTS? WHAT'S THIS GUY TALKING ABOUT?
IS HE FROM A SMARTPHONE GAME?
DON'T TELL ME HE PLANS TO GET ME TO SLANDER MY GROUP...
...AND THEN TATTLE TO THEM ABOUT IT AFTERWARD?
COME, LET'S DISCUSS...
...OUR TRUE FEELINGS.
TWISTED SELF-PRESERVATION INSTINCT

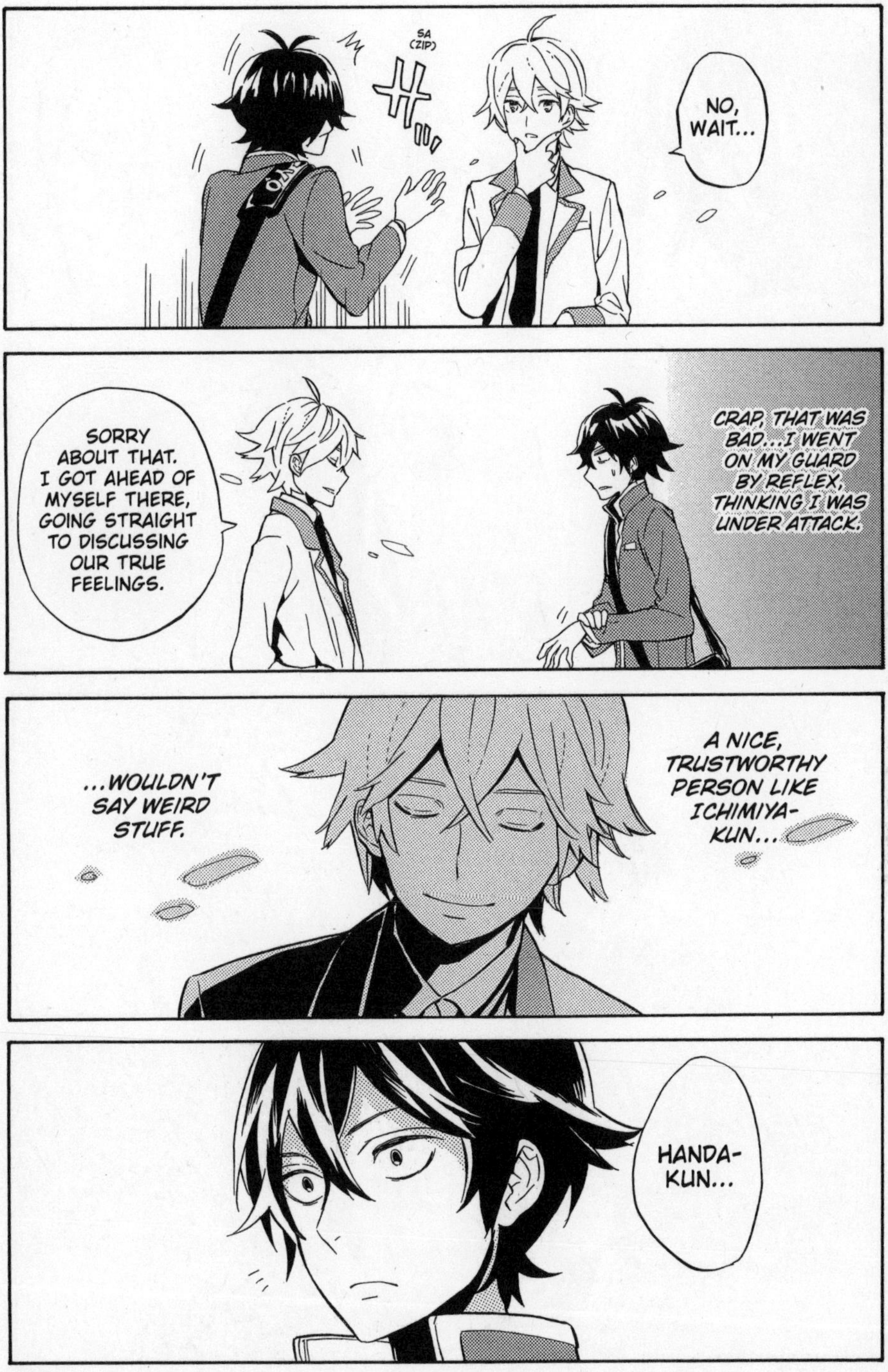
NO, WAIT...
SA (ZIP)
CRAP, THAT WAS BAD...I WENT ON MY GUARD BY REFLEX, THINKING I WAS UNDER ATTACK.
SORRY ABOUT THAT. I GOT AHEAD OF MYSELF THERE, GOING STRAIGHT TO DISCUSSING OUR TRUE FEELINGS.
A NICE, TRUSTWORTHY PERSON LIKE ICHIMIYA-KUN...
...WOULDN'T SAY WEIRD STUFF.
HANDA-KUN...

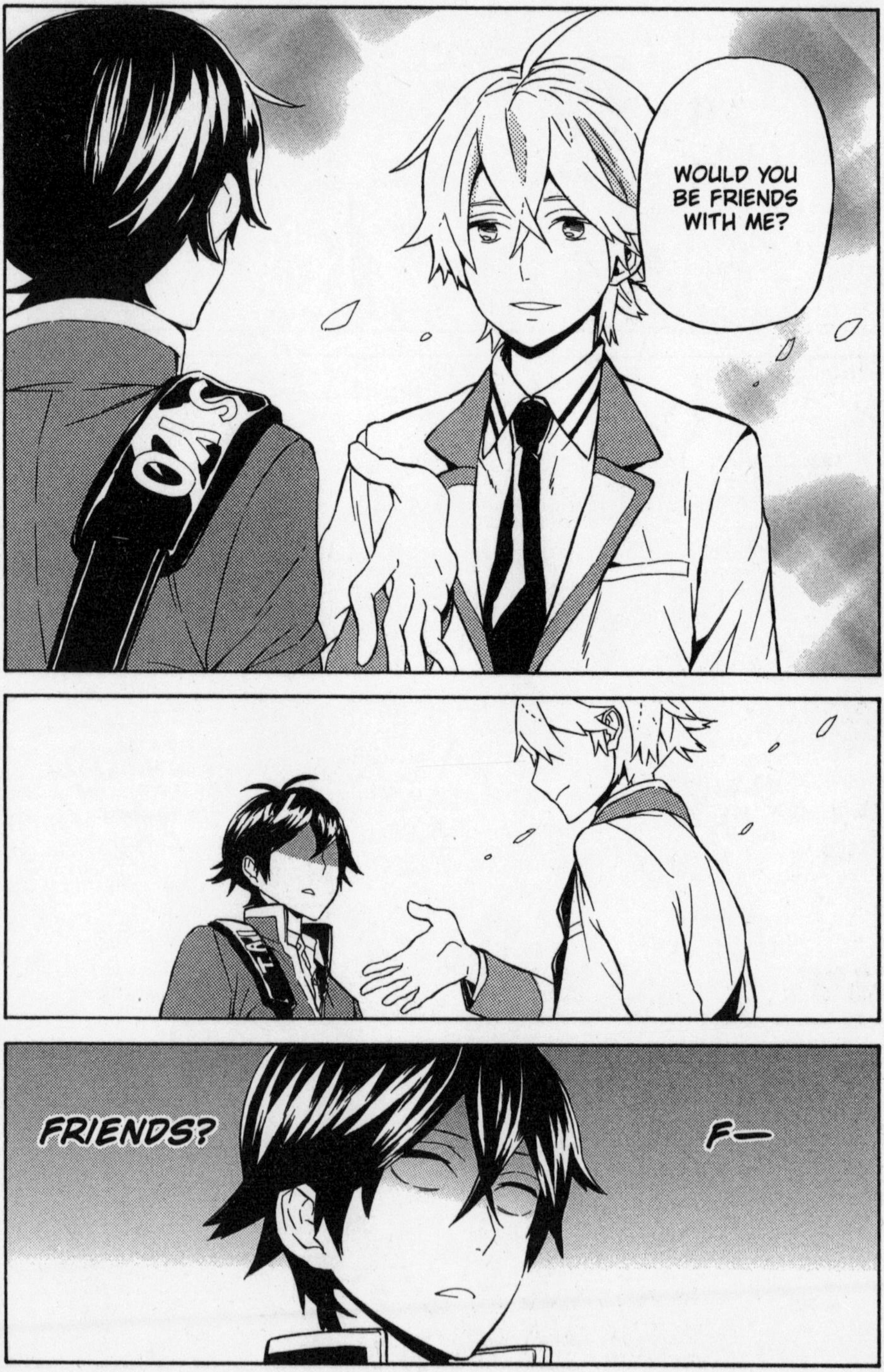
WOULD YOU BE FRIENDS WITH ME?
F—
FRIENDS?

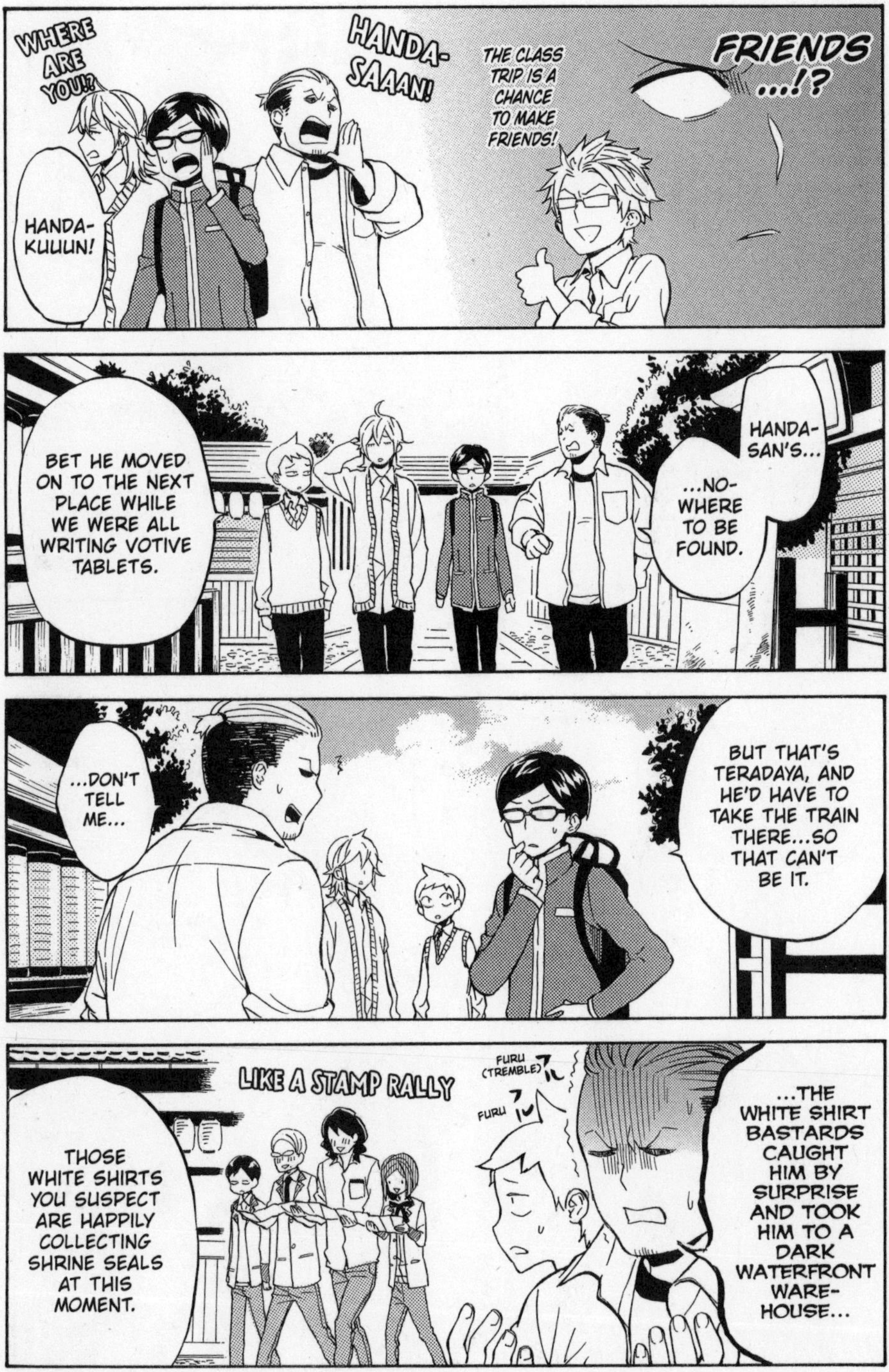
FRIENDS ...!?
THE CLASS TRIP IS A CHANCE TO MAKE FRIENDS!
HANDA-SAAAN!
WHERE ARE YOU!?
HANDA-KUUUN!
HANDA-SAN'S...
...NO-WHERE TO BE FOUND.
BET HE MOVED ON TO THE NEXT PLACE WHILE WE WERE ALL WRITING VOTIVE TABLETS.
BUT THAT'S TERADAYA, AND HE'D HAVE TO TAKE THE TRAIN THERE...SO THAT CAN'T BE IT.
...DON'T TELL ME...
...THE WHITE SHIRT BASTARDS CAUGHT HIM BY SURPRISE AND TOOK HIM TO A DARK WATERFRONT WARE-HOUSE...
FURU (TREMBLE)
FURU
LIKE A STAMP RALLY
THOSE WHITE SHIRTS YOU SUSPECT ARE HAPPILY COLLECTING SHRINE SEALS AT THIS MOMENT.

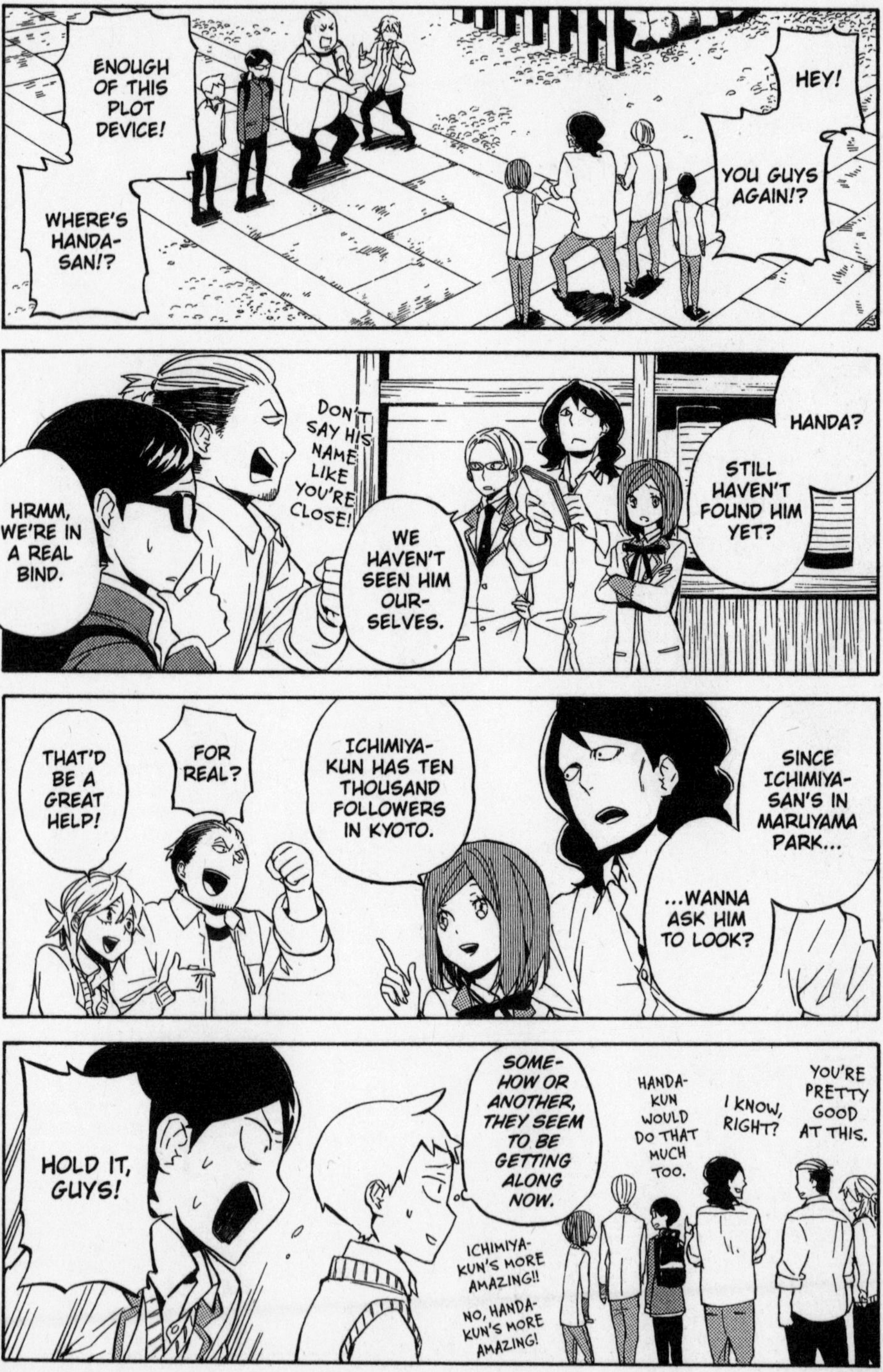
HEY!
YOU GUYS AGAIN!?
ENOUGH OF THIS PLOT DEVICE!
WHERE'S HANDA-SAN!?
HANDA?
STILL HAVEN'T FOUND HIM YET?
WE HAVEN'T SEEN HIM OURSELVES.
DON'T SAY HIS NAME LIKE YOU'RE CLOSE!
HRMM, WE'RE IN A REAL BIND.
SINCE ICHIMIYA-SAN'S IN MARUYAMA PARK...
...WANNA ASK HIM TO LOOK?
ICHIMIYA-KUN HAS TEN THOUSAND FOLLOWERS IN KYOTO.
FOR REAL?
THAT'D BE A GREAT HELP!
YOU'RE PRETTY GOOD AT THIS.
I KNOW, RIGHT?
HANDA-KUN WOULD DO THAT MUCH TOO.
ICHIMIYA-KUN'S MORE AMAZING!!
NO, HANDA-KUN'S MORE AMAZING!
SOMEHOW OR ANOTHER, THEY SEEM TO BE GETTING ALONG NOW.
HOLD IT, GUYS!

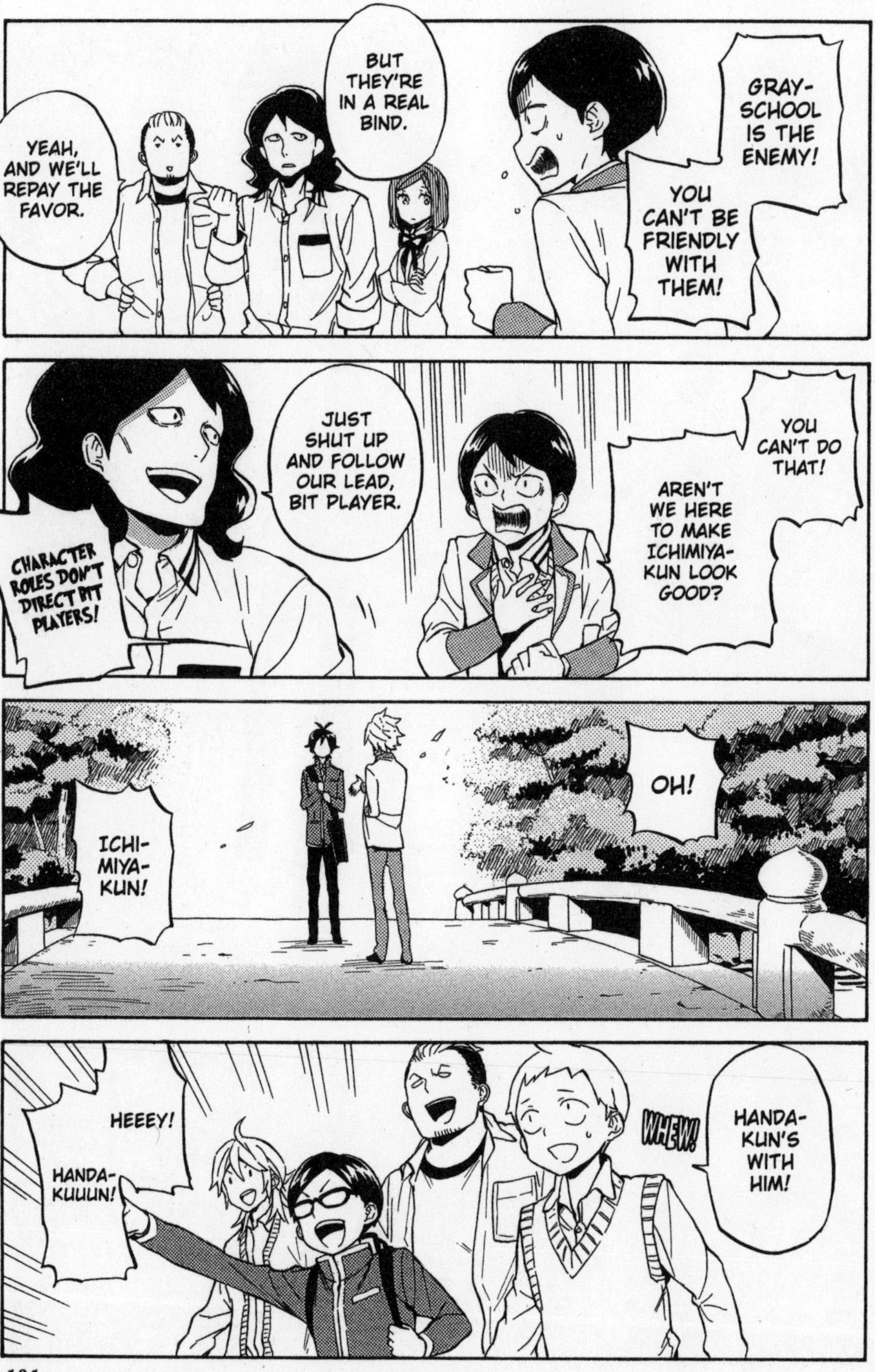
GRAY-SCHOOL IS THE ENEMY!
YOU CAN'T BE FRIENDLY WITH THEM!
BUT THEY'RE IN A REAL BIND.
YEAH, AND WE'LL REPAY THE FAVOR.
YOU CAN'T DO THAT!
AREN'T WE HERE TO MAKE ICHIMIYA-KUN LOOK GOOD?
JUST SHUT UP AND FOLLOW OUR LEAD, BIT PLAYER.
CHARACTER ROLES DON'T DIRECT BIT PLAYERS!
OH!
ICHIMIYA-KUN!
HANDA-KUN'S WITH HIM!
WHEW!
HEEEY!
HANDA-KUUUN!

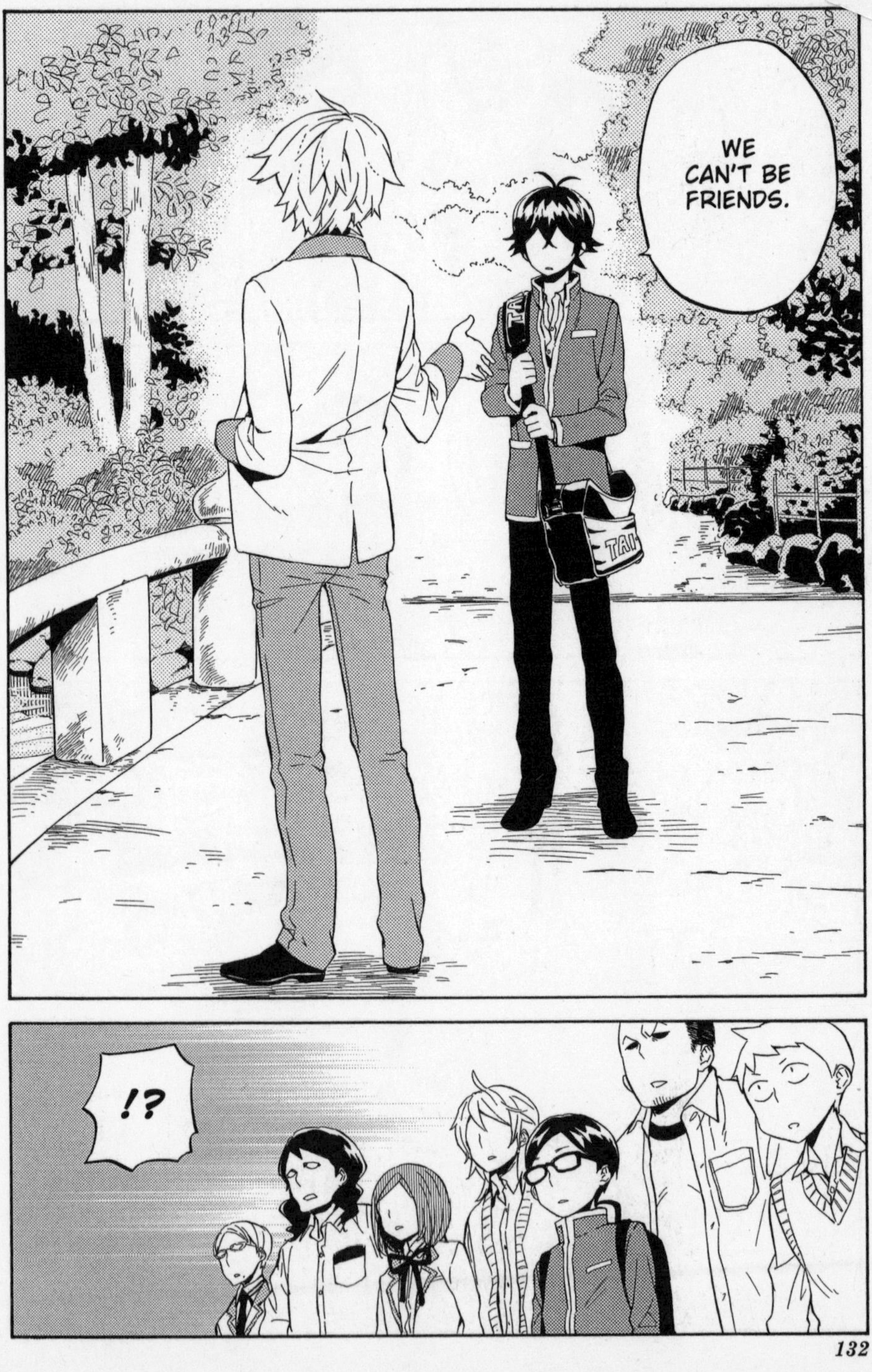
WE CAN'T BE FRIENDS.
!?

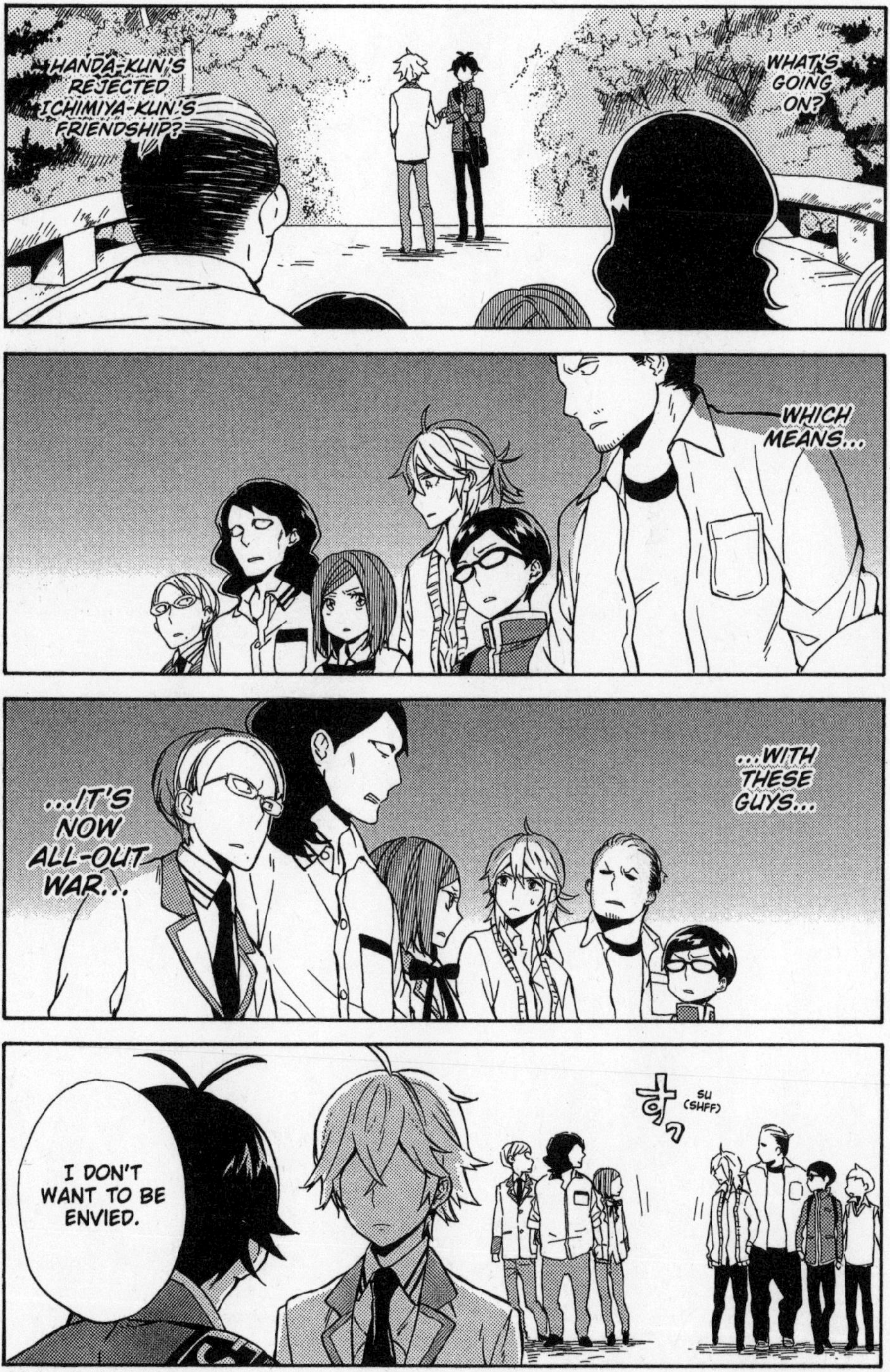
WHAT'S GOING ON?
HANDA-KUN'S REJECTED ICHIMIYA-KUN'S FRIENDSHIP?
WHICH MEANS...
...WITH THESE GUYS...
...IT'S NOW ALL-OUT WAR...
すっ
SU (SHFF)
I DON'T WANT TO BE ENVIED.

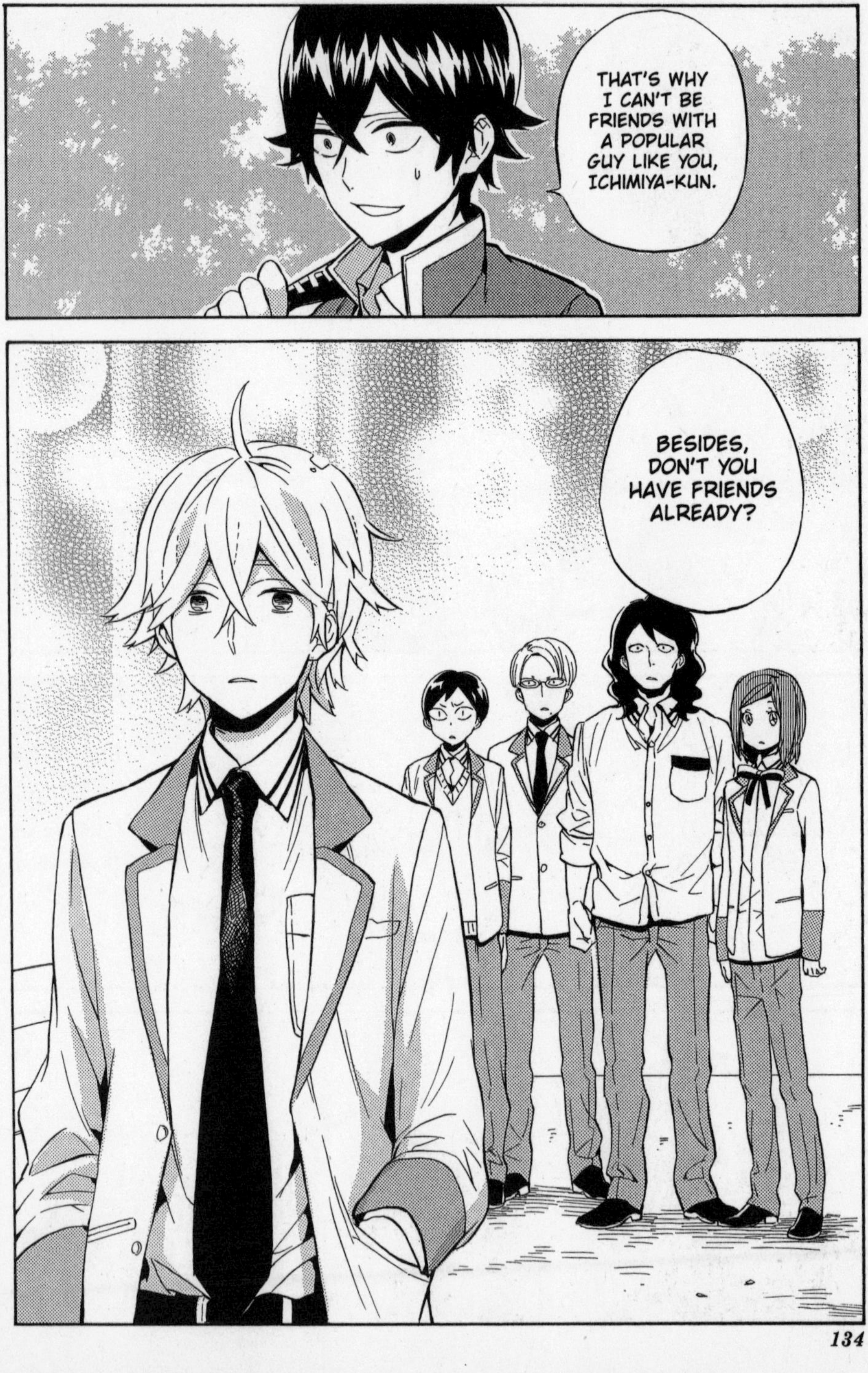
THAT'S WHY I CAN'T BE FRIENDS WITH A POPULAR GUY LIKE YOU, ICHIMIYA-KUN.
BESIDES, DON'T YOU HAVE FRIENDS ALREADY?

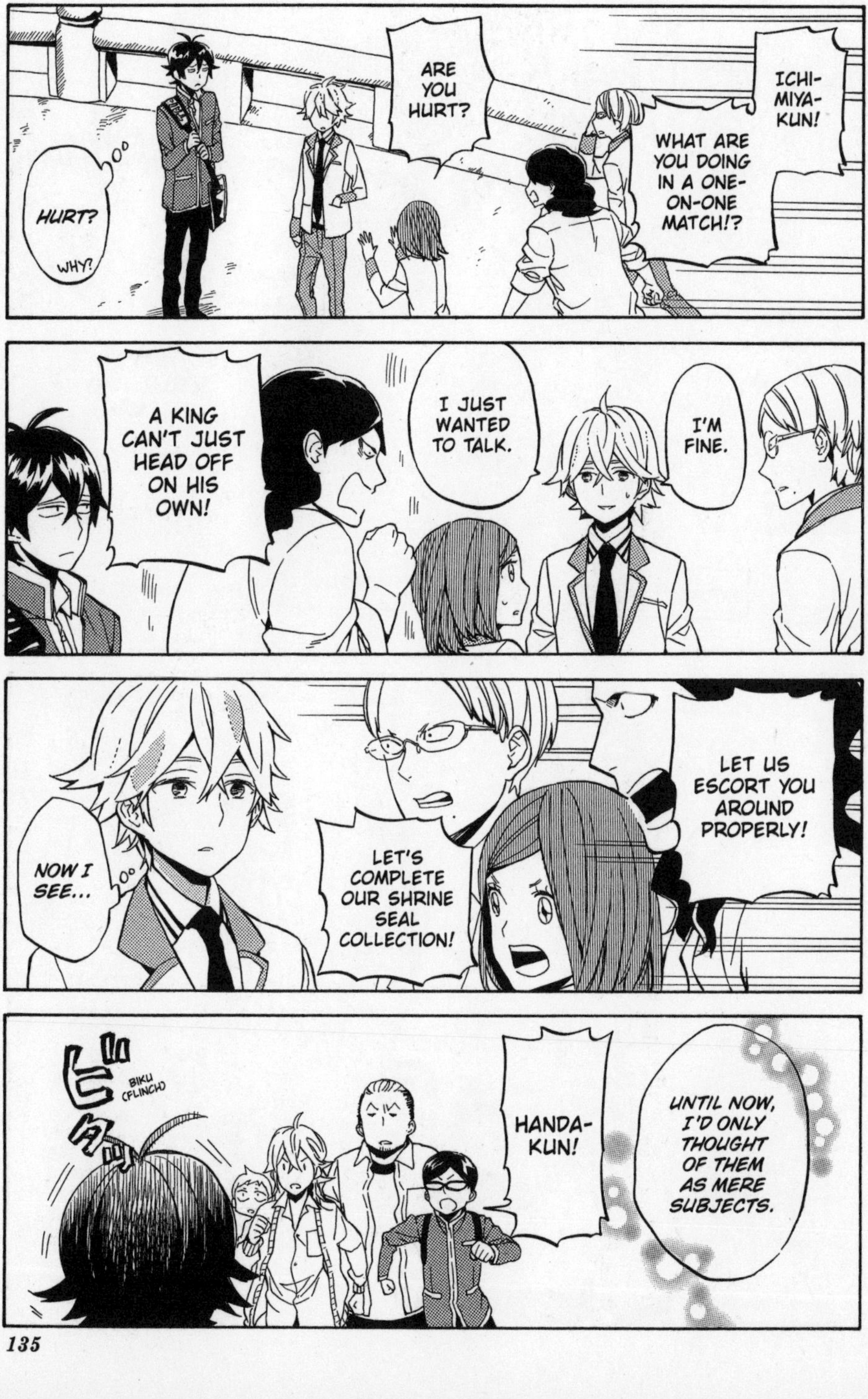
ICHI-MIYA-KUN!
WHAT ARE YOU DOING IN A ONE-ON-ONE MATCH!?
ARE YOU HURT?
HURT?
WHY?
I'M FINE.
I JUST WANTED TO TALK.
A KING CAN'T JUST HEAD OFF ON HIS OWN!
LET US ESCORT YOU AROUND PROPERLY!
LET'S COMPLETE OUR SHRINE SEAL COLLECTION!
NOW I SEE...
UNTIL NOW, I'D ONLY THOUGHT OF THEM AS MERE SUBJECTS.
HANDA-KUN!
BIKU (FLINCH)

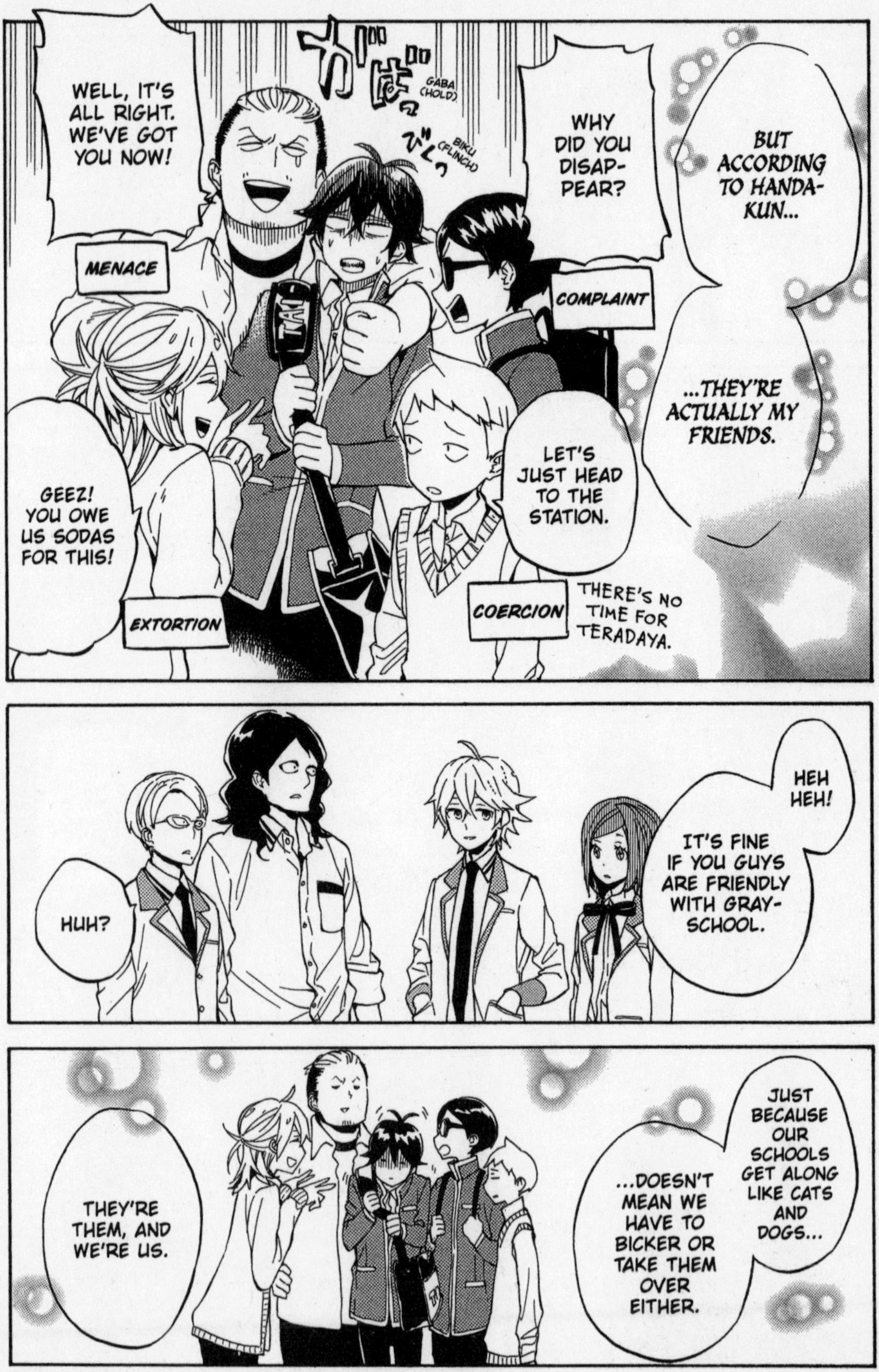
BUT ACCORDING TO HANDA-KUN...
...THEY'RE ACTUALLY MY FRIENDS.
WHY DID YOU DISAPPEAR?
GABA (HOLD)
BIKU (FLINCH)
WELL, IT'S ALL RIGHT. WE'VE GOT YOU NOW!
COMPLAINT
MENACE
LET'S JUST HEAD TO THE STATION.
THERE'S NO TIME FOR TERADAYA.
COERCION
GEEZ! YOU OWE US SODAS FOR THIS!
EXTORTION
HEH HEH!
IT'S FINE IF YOU GUYS ARE FRIENDLY WITH GRAY-SCHOOL.
HUH?
JUST BECAUSE OUR SCHOOLS GET ALONG LIKE CATS AND DOGS...
...DOESN'T MEAN WE HAVE TO BICKER OR TAKE THEM OVER EITHER.
THEY'RE THEM, AND WE'RE US.

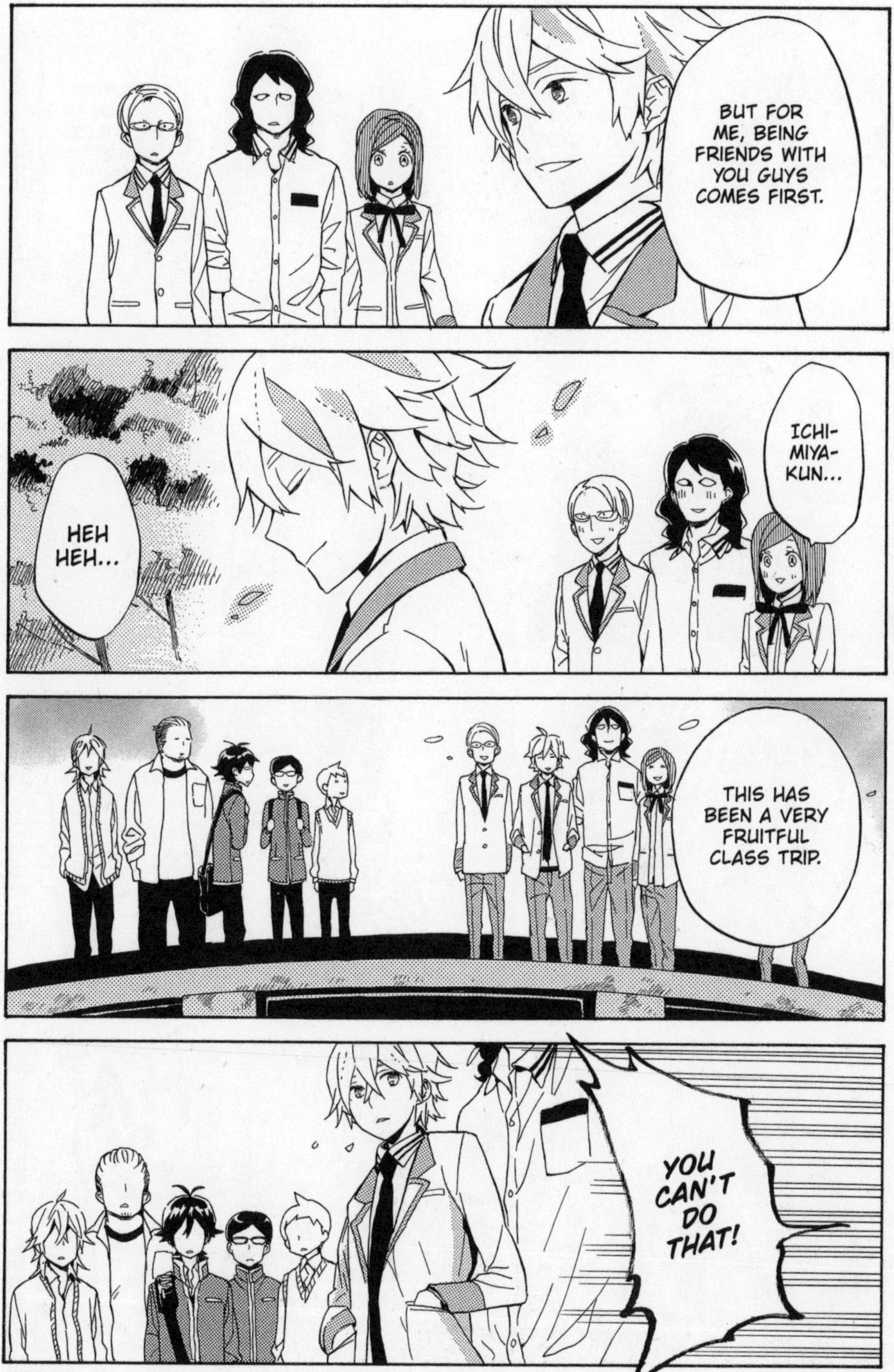
BUT FOR ME, BEING FRIENDS WITH YOU GUYS COMES FIRST.
ICHI-MIYA-KUN...
HEH HEH...
THIS HAS BEEN A VERY FRUITFUL CLASS TRIP.
YOU CAN'T DO THAT!

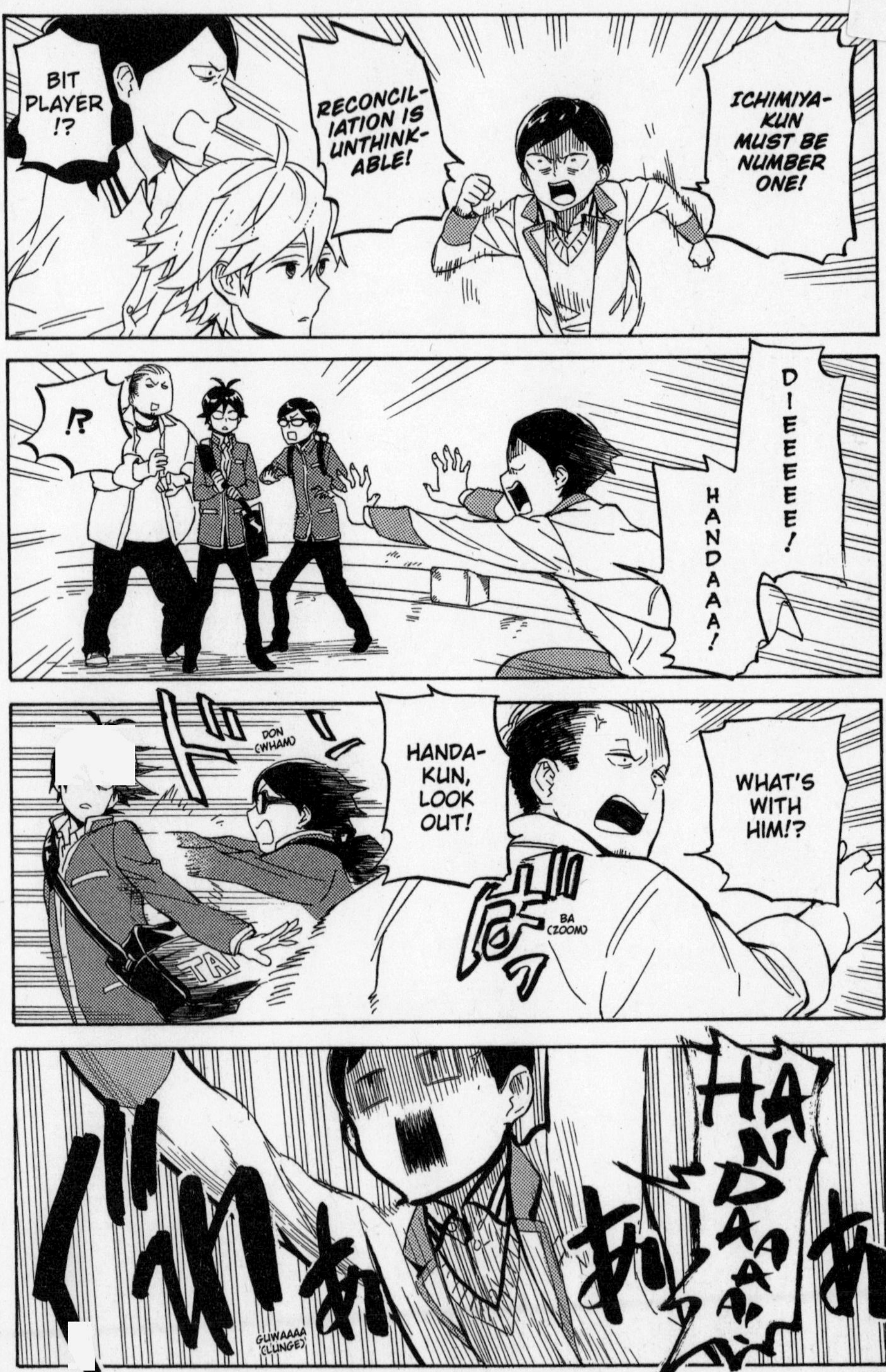
ICHIMIYA-KUN MUST BE NUMBER ONE!
RECONCIL-IATION IS UNTHINK-ABLE!
BIT PLAYER !?
DIEEEEEE!
HANDAAAA!
!?
WHAT'S WITH HIM!?
BA (ZOOM)
HANDA-KUN, LOOK OUT!
DON (WHAM)
TA!
HANDAAAAA!
GUWAAAA (LUNGE)

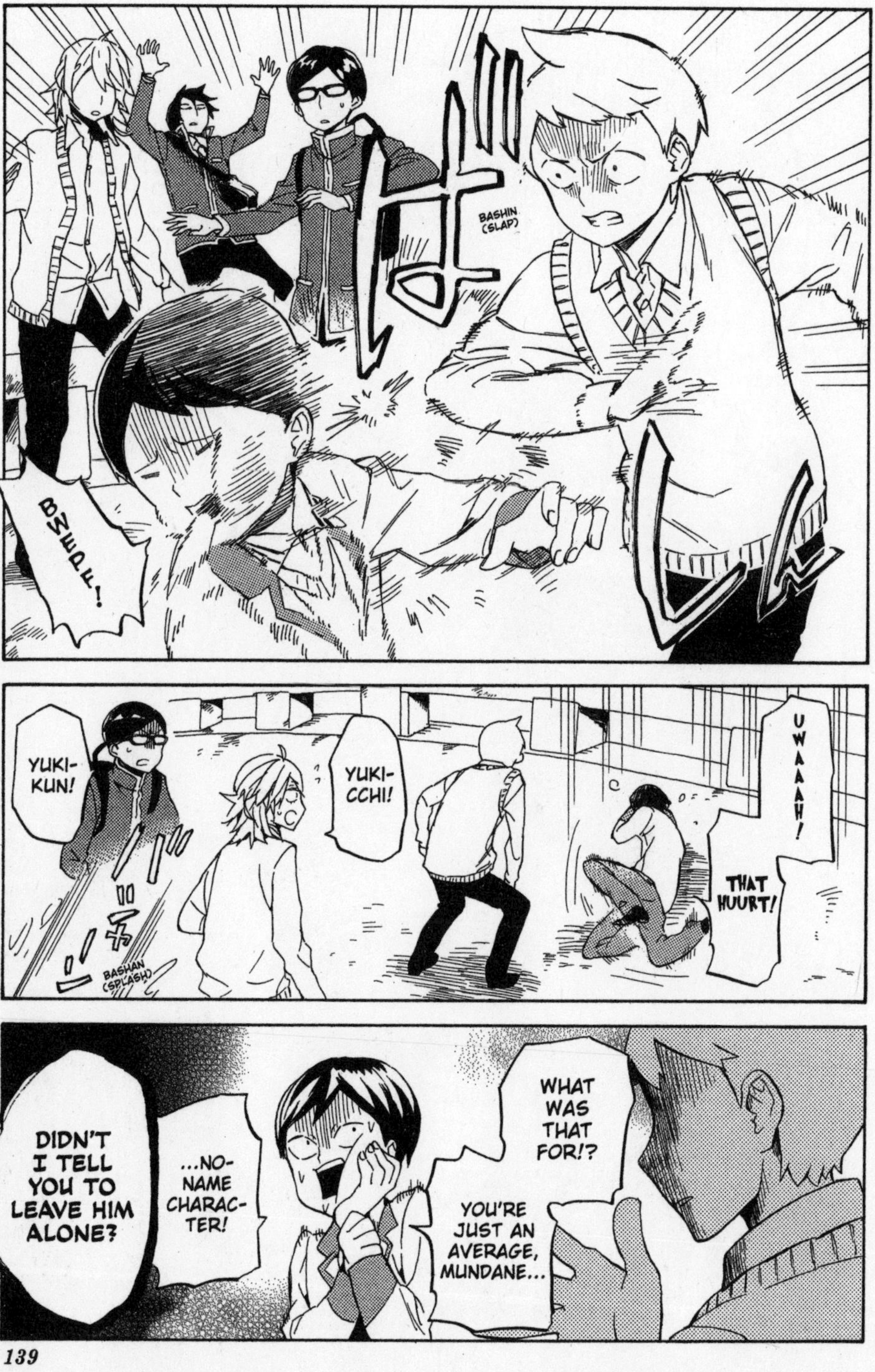

BASHIN (SLAP)
BWEPF!
UWAAAAH!
THAT HUURT!
YUKI-CCHI!
YUKI-KUN!
BASHAN (SPLASH)
WHAT WAS THAT FOR!?
YOU'RE JUST AN AVERAGE, MUNDANE...
...NO-NAME CHARACTER!
DIDN'T I TELL YOU TO LEAVE HIM ALONE?

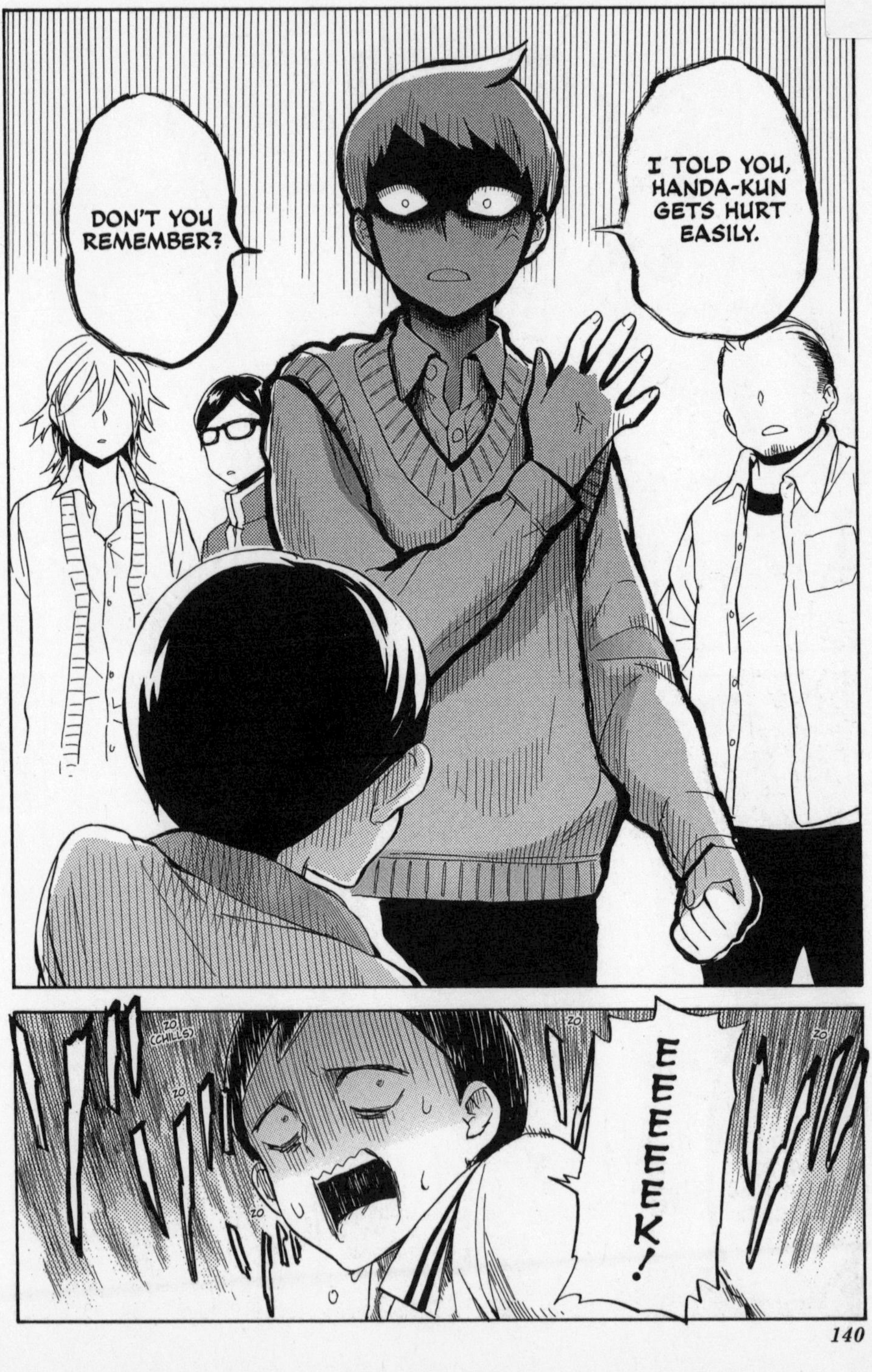
I TOLD YOU, HANDA-KUN GETS HURT EASILY.
DON'T YOU REMEMBER?
ZO
ZO
EEEEEEK!
ZO (CHILLS)
ZO
ZO

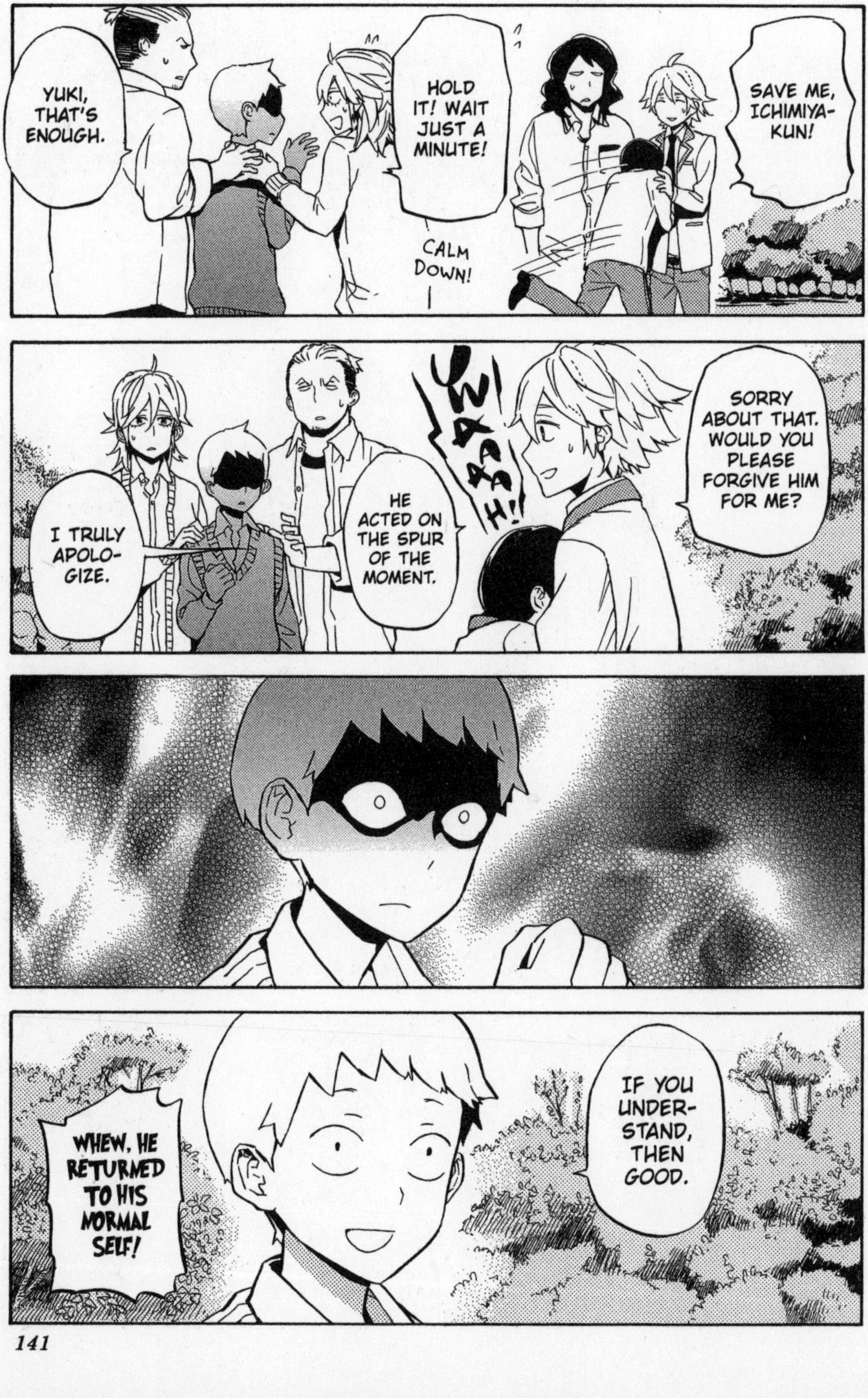
SAVE ME, ICHIMIYA-KUN!
HOLD IT! WAIT JUST A MINUTE!
CALM DOWN!
YUKI, THAT'S ENOUGH.
SORRY ABOUT THAT. WOULD YOU PLEASE FORGIVE HIM FOR ME?
WAAAAH!
HE ACTED ON THE SPUR OF THE MOMENT.
I TRULY APOLO-GIZE.
IF YOU UNDER-STAND, THEN GOOD.
WHEW, HE RETURNED TO HIS NORMAL SELF!

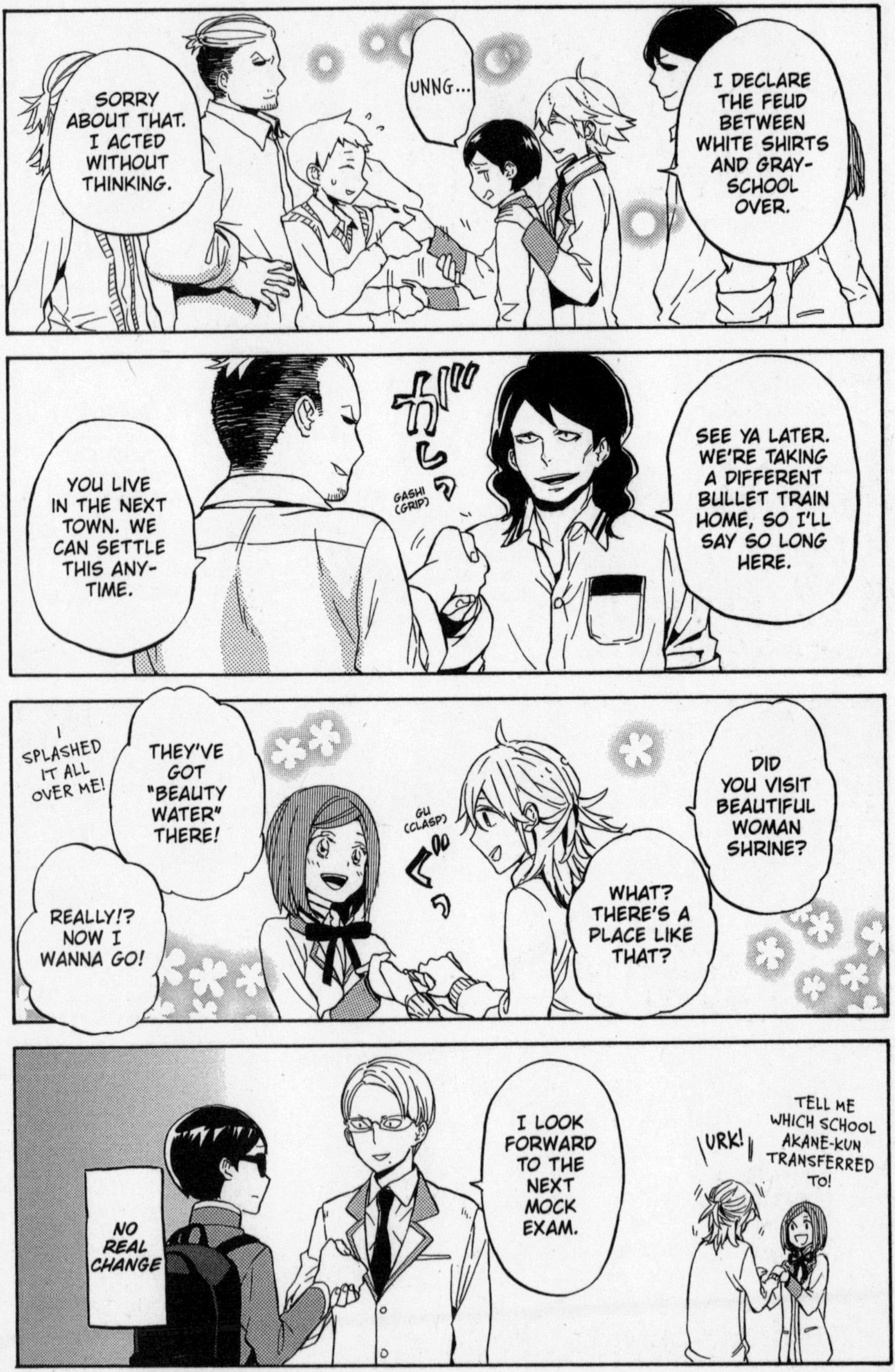
I DECLARE THE FEUD BETWEEN WHITE SHIRTS AND GRAY-SCHOOL OVER.
UNNG...
SORRY ABOUT THAT. I ACTED WITHOUT THINKING.
SEE YA LATER. WE'RE TAKING A DIFFERENT BULLET TRAIN HOME, SO I'LL SAY SO LONG HERE.
GASHI (GRIP)
YOU LIVE IN THE NEXT TOWN. WE CAN SETTLE THIS ANY-TIME.
DID YOU VISIT BEAUTIFUL WOMAN SHRINE?
WHAT? THERE'S A PLACE LIKE THAT?
GU (CLASP)
THEY'VE GOT "BEAUTY WATER" THERE!
I SPLASHED IT ALL OVER ME!
REALLY!? NOW I WANNA GO!
TELL ME WHICH SCHOOL AKANE-KUN TRANSFERRED TO!
URK!
I LOOK FORWARD TO THE NEXT MOCK EXAM.
NO REAL CHANGE

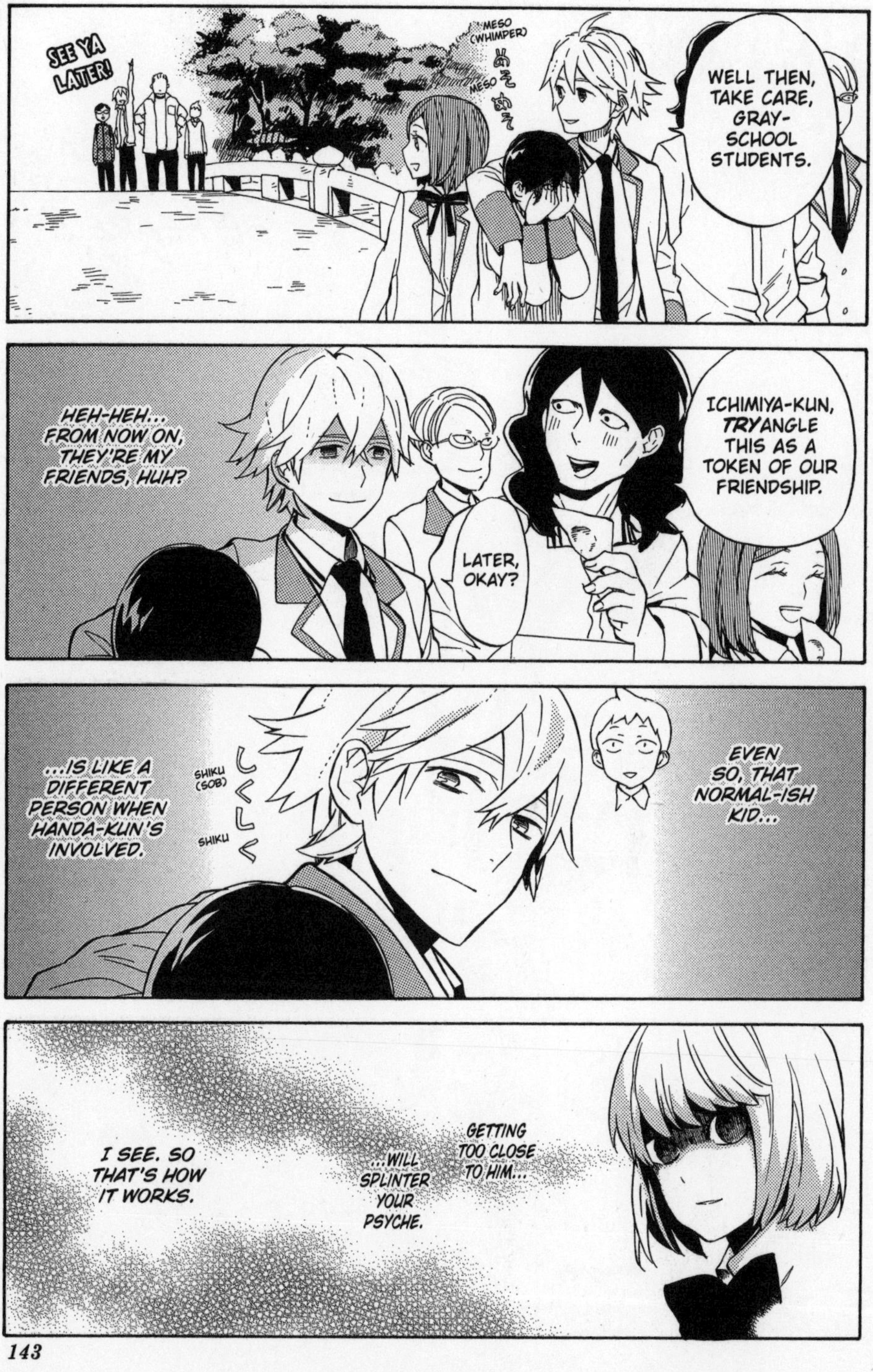
WELL THEN, TAKE CARE, GRAY-SCHOOL STUDENTS.
MESO (WHIMPER) めそ MESO めそ
SEE YA LATER!
ICHIMIYA-KUN, TRYANGLE THIS AS A TOKEN OF OUR FRIENDSHIP.
LATER, OKAY?
HEH-HEH... FROM NOW ON, THEY'RE MY FRIENDS, HUH?
EVEN SO, THAT NORMAL-ISH KID...
SHIKU (SOB) しくしく SHIKU
...IS LIKE A DIFFERENT PERSON WHEN HANDA-KUN'S INVOLVED.
GETTING TOO CLOSE TO HIM...
...WILL SPLINTER YOUR PSYCHE.
I SEE. SO THAT'S HOW IT WORKS.

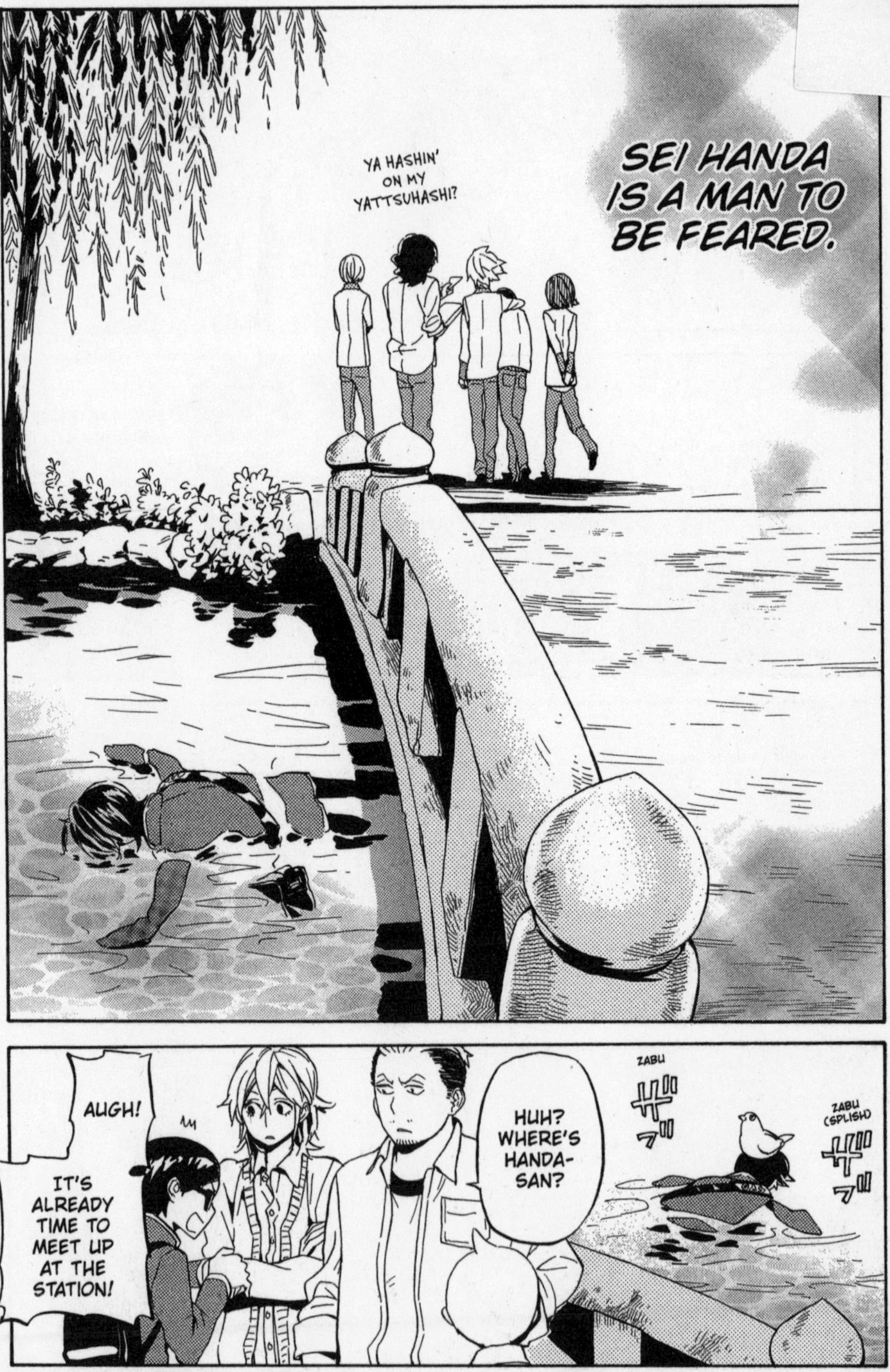
SEI HANDA IS A MAN TO BE FEARED.
YA HASHIN' ON MY YATTSUHASHI?
ZABU (SPLISH)
ZABU
HUH? WHERE'S HANDA-SAN?
AUGH!
IT'S ALREADY TIME TO MEET UP AT THE STATION!

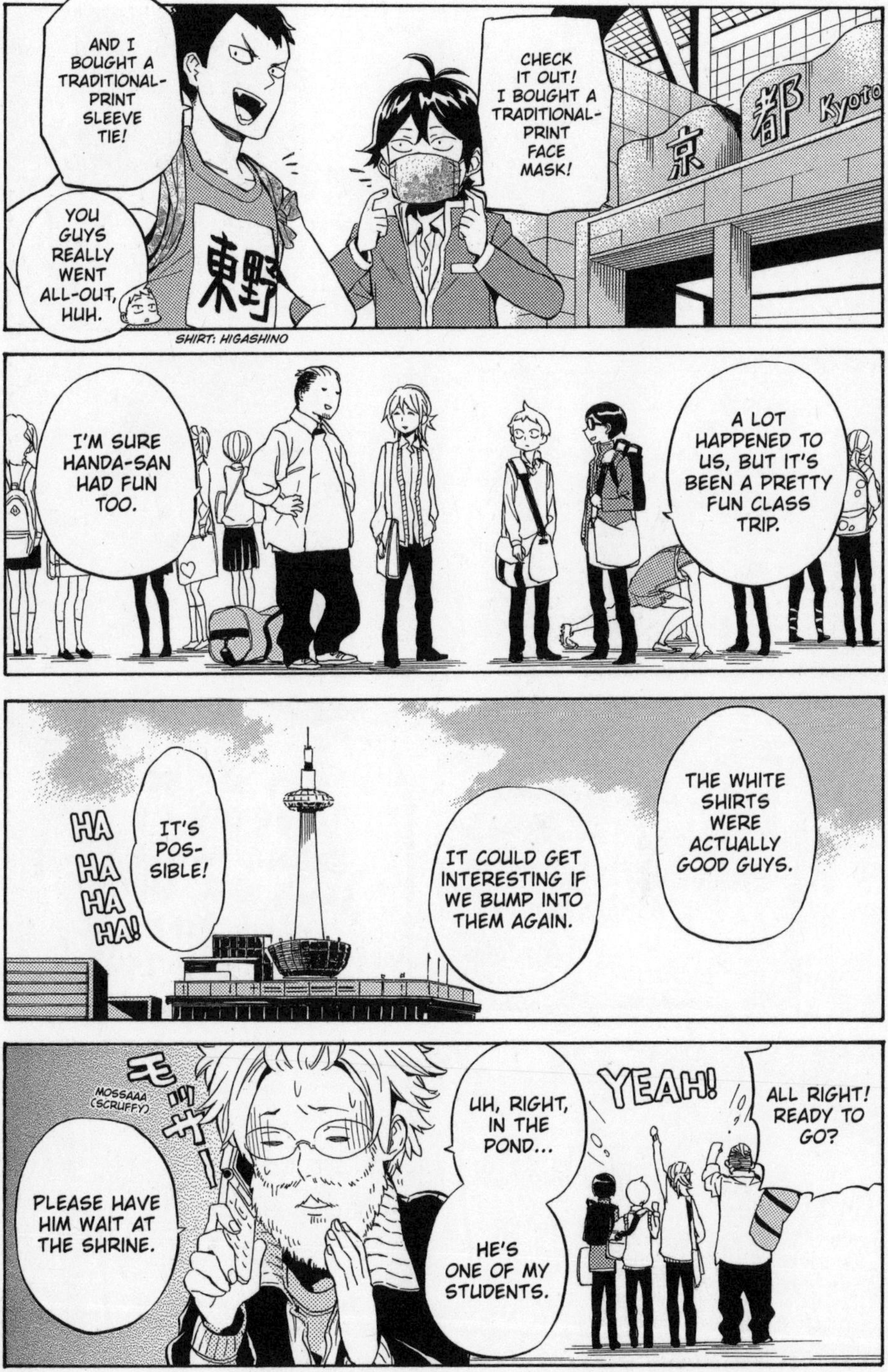
京都 Kyoto
CHECK IT OUT! I BOUGHT A TRADITIONAL-PRINT FACE MASK!
AND I BOUGHT A TRADITIONAL-PRINT SLEEVE TIE!
東野
YOU GUYS REALLY WENT ALL-OUT, HUH.
SHIRT: HIGASHINO
A LOT HAPPENED TO US, BUT IT'S BEEN A PRETTY FUN CLASS TRIP.
I'M SURE HANDA-SAN HAD FUN TOO.
THE WHITE SHIRTS WERE ACTUALLY GOOD GUYS.
IT COULD GET INTERESTING IF WE BUMP INTO THEM AGAIN.
IT'S POS-SIBLE!
HA HA HA HA!
ALL RIGHT! READY TO GO?
YEAH!
UH, RIGHT, IN THE POND...
HE'S ONE OF MY STUDENTS.
モッサー
MOSSAAA (SCRUFFY)
PLEASE HAVE HIM WAIT AT THE SHRINE.

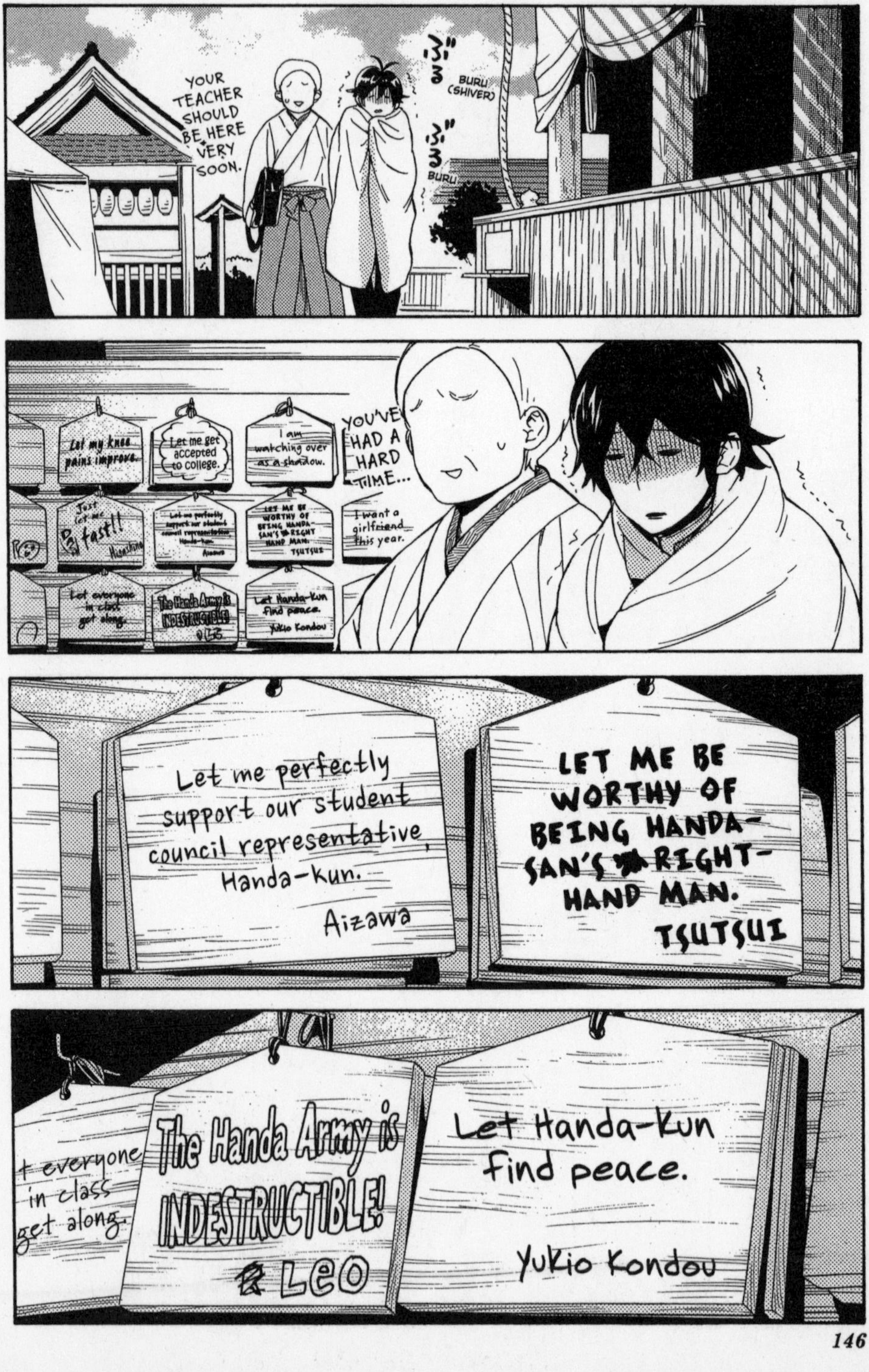
ぶる
BURU (SHIVER)
ぶる
BURU
YOUR TEACHER SHOULD BE HERE VERY SOON.
YOU'VE HAD A HARD TIME...
I want a girlfriend this year.
I am watching over as a shadow.
LET ME BE WORTHY OF BEING HANDA-SAN'S RIGHT-HAND MAN. TSUTSUI
Let Handa-kun find peace. Yukio Kondou
Let me get accepted to college.
Let my knee pains improve.
Just let me get fast!!
The Handa Army is INDESTRUCTIBLE!
Let everyone in class get along.
LET ME BE WORTHY OF BEING HANDA-SAN'S RIGHT-HAND MAN. TSUTSUI
Let me perfectly support our student council representative, Handa-kun. Aizawa
Let Handa-kun find peace.
Yukio Kondou
The Handa Army is INDESTRUCTIBLE!
Leo
t everyone in class get along.

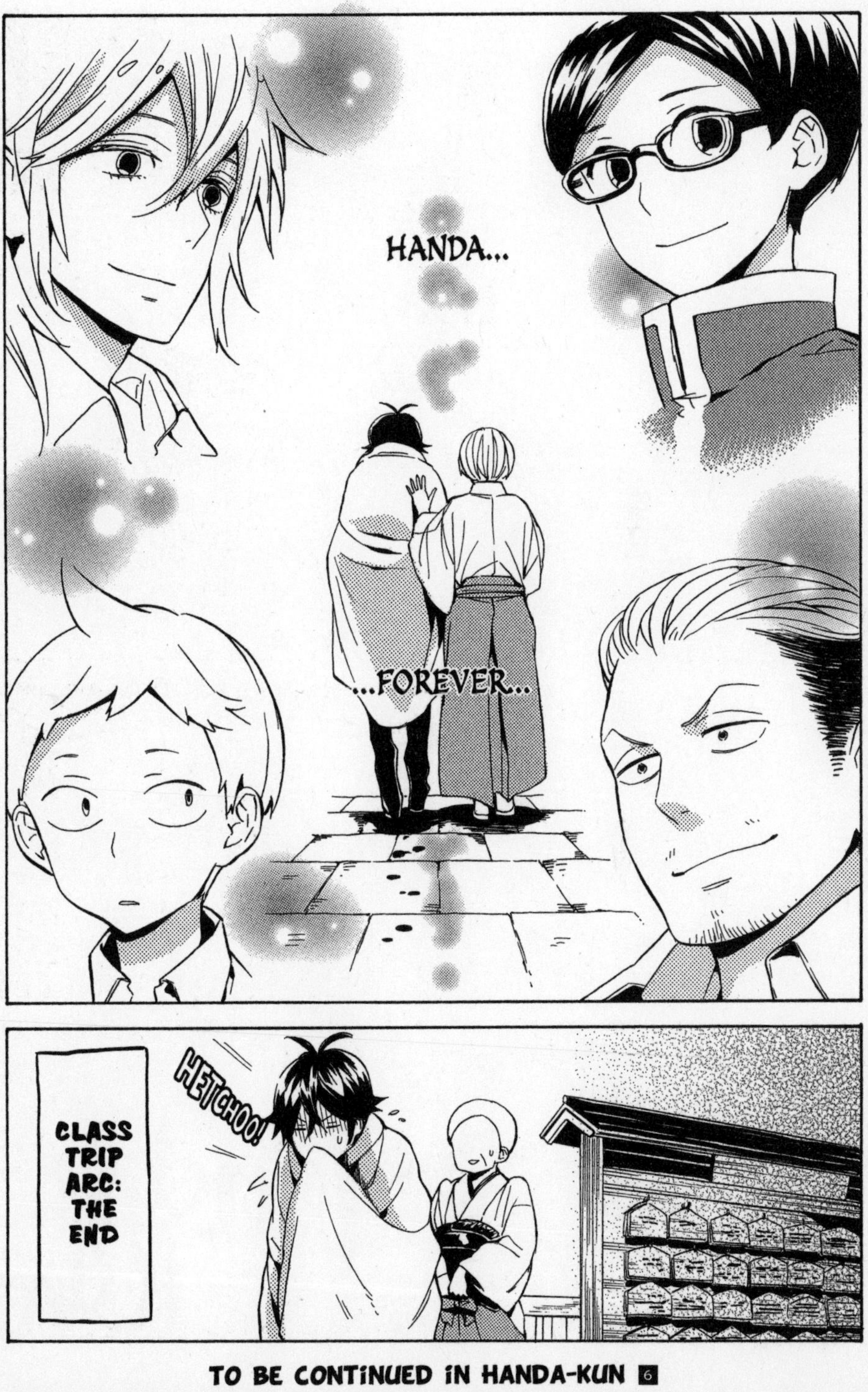
HANDA...
...FOREVER...
HETCHOO!
CLASS TRIP ARC: THE END

TO BE CONTINUED IN HANDA-KUN 6

Handa-
Kun

BONUS

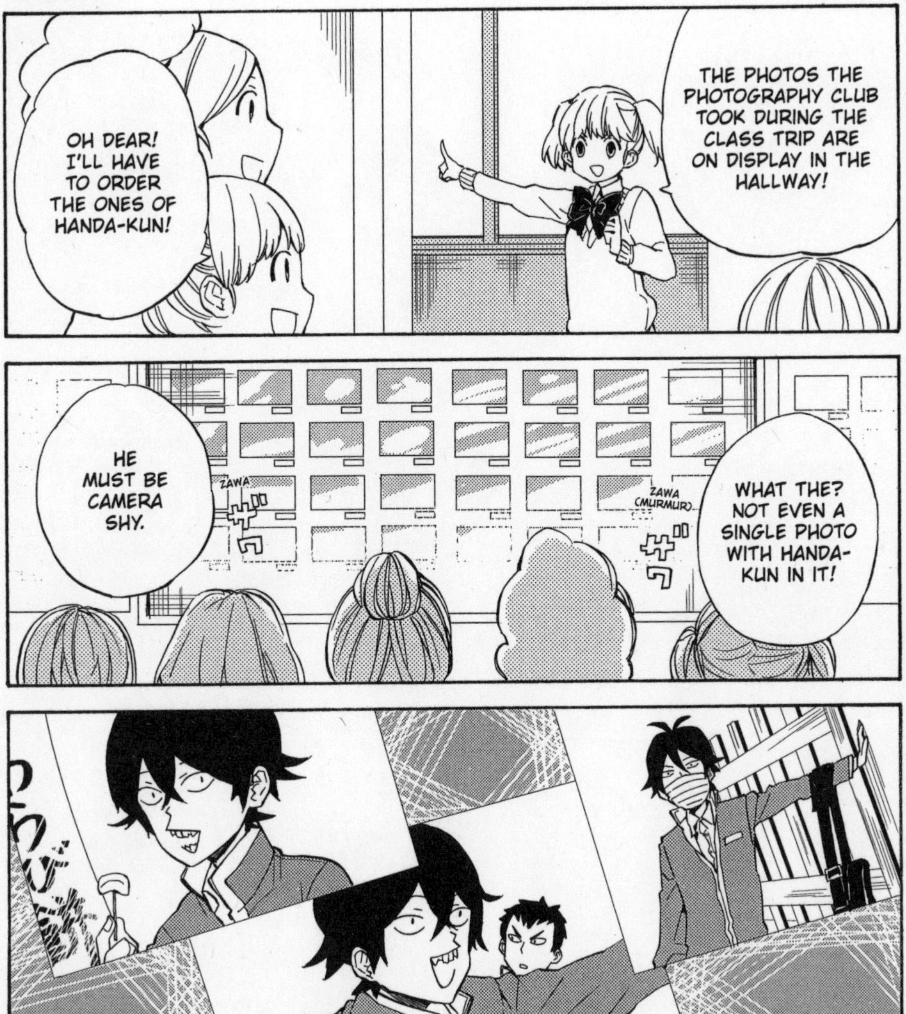
THE PHOTOS THE PHOTOGRAPHY CLUB TOOK DURING THE CLASS TRIP ARE ON DISPLAY IN THE HALLWAY!
OH DEAR! I'LL HAVE TO ORDER THE ONES OF HANDA-KUN!
WHAT THE? NOT EVEN A SINGLE PHOTO WITH HANDA-KUN IN IT!
ZAWA (MURMUR)
ZAWA
HE MUST BE CAMERA SHY.

SIGN: WARABIMOCHI

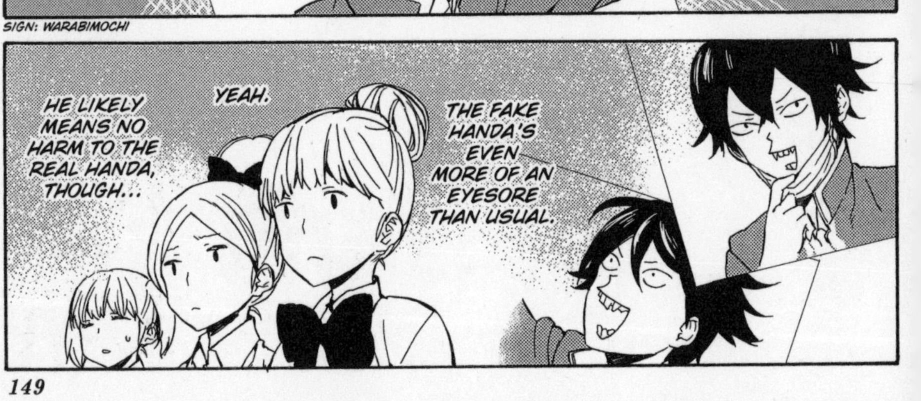
THE FAKE HANDA'S EVEN MORE OF AN EYESORE THAN USUAL.
YEAH.
HE LIKELY MEANS NO HARM TO THE REAL HANDA, THOUGH...

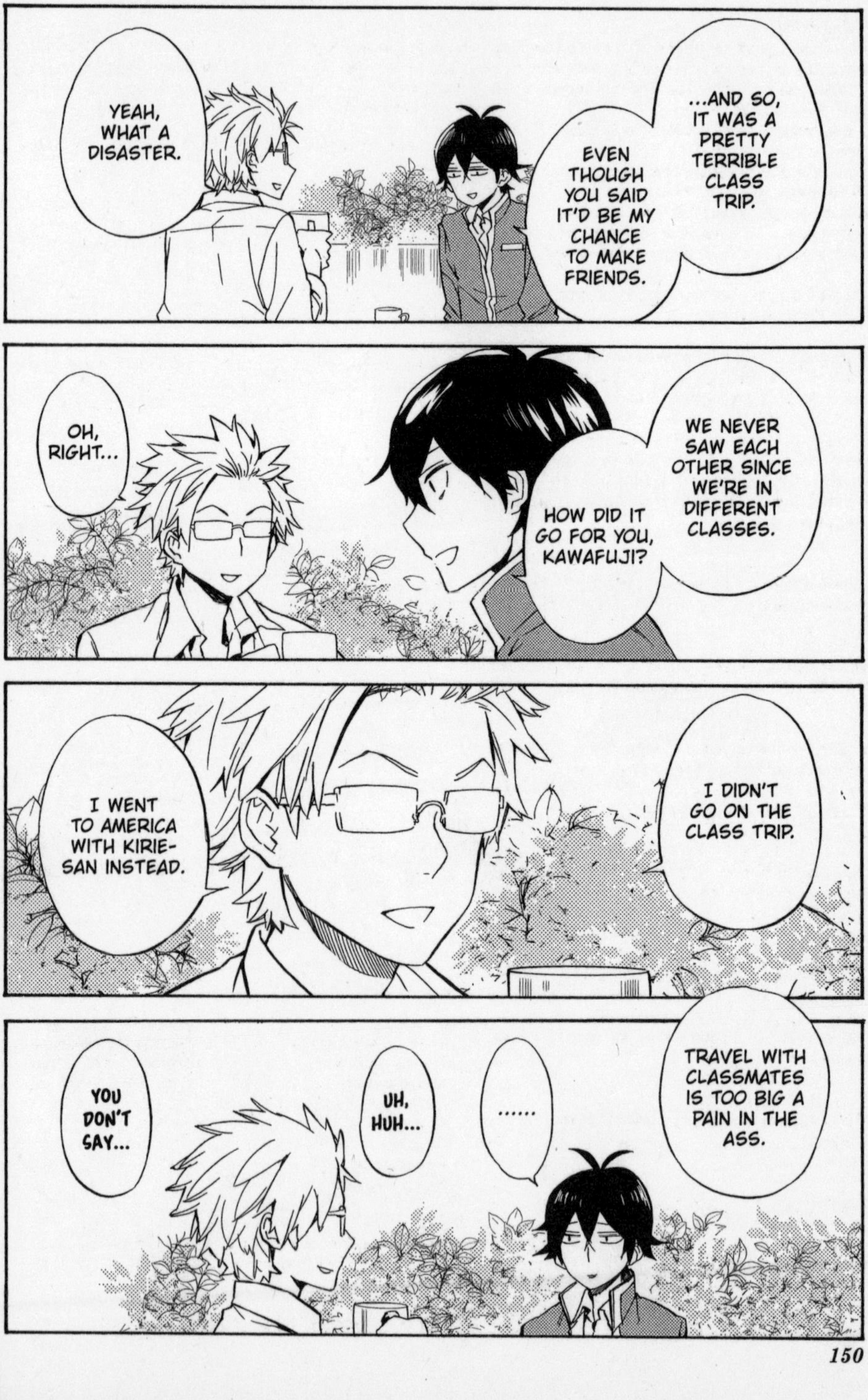
...AND SO, IT WAS A PRETTY TERRIBLE CLASS TRIP.
EVEN THOUGH YOU SAID IT'D BE MY CHANCE TO MAKE FRIENDS.
YEAH, WHAT A DISASTER.
WE NEVER SAW EACH OTHER SINCE WE'RE IN DIFFERENT CLASSES.
HOW DID IT GO FOR YOU, KAWAFUJI?
OH, RIGHT...
I DIDN'T GO ON THE CLASS TRIP.
I WENT TO AMERICA WITH KIRIE-SAN INSTEAD.
TRAVEL WITH CLASSMATES IS TOO BIG A PAIN IN THE ASS.
......
UH, HUH...
YOU DON'T SAY...

COMMON HONORIFICS

no honorific: Indicates familiarity or closeness; if used without permission or reason, addressing someone in this manner would constitute an insult.

-san: The Japanese equivalent of Mr./Mrs./Miss. If a situation calls for politeness, this is the fail-safe honorific.

-sama: Conveys great respect; may also indicate that the social status of the speaker is lower than that of the addressee.

-kun: Used most often when referring to boys, this indicates affection or familiarity. Occasionally used by older men among their peers, but it may also be used by anyone referring to a person of lower standing.

-chan: An affectionate honorific indicating familiarity used mostly in reference to girls; also used in reference to cute persons or animals of either gender.

-sensei: A Japanese term of respect commonly used for teachers, but can also refer to doctors, writers, and artists.

Calligraphy: Japanese calligraphy has a long history and tradition, with roots stemming from ancient China. One of the traditions carried over was the Chinese expression of the "Four Treasures," which refers to the brush, ink, paper, and inkstone used in calligraphy. Traditionally, an inkstick—solidified ink—is ground against an inkstone filled with water in order to produce ink with which to write. This time-consuming process helped to teach patience, which is important in the art of calligraphy. However, modern advances have developed a bottled liquid ink, commonly used by beginners and within the Japanese school system.

PAGE 11

"born after the Cold War": Tsukkun actually said "born in the Heisei era," which started in January 1989 after the death of Emperor Hirohito.

PAGE 12

"You asking for a licking, punk!?": The Japanese phrase Joumoto said is literally "Don't lick me!" which, in context, means "Don't mess with me!"

PAGE 16

Their sightseeing spot: The large temple shown is Kiyomizudera, one of the most famous and popular historical sites in Kyoto. Jishu Shrine, which the gang visits on the next page, is on the grounds of Kiyomizudera, and is a popular place for love and matchmaking fortunes.

PAGE 18

Fortunes: Here's the order of luck on the *omikuji* (paper fortunes) the characters draw or mention, from best to worst: Excellent Luck (*daikichi*), Good Luck (*kichi*), Medium Luck (*chuukichi*), Half Luck (*hankichi*), Uncertain Luck (*suekichi*), and Terrible Luck (*daikyou*). There are two reasons Handa doesn't want to show his fortune: 1) it's not very good, and 2) the kanji for "half" (*han*) is also in his name!

PAGE 31

Class Trip Inn: The hotel name, *Shuugaku Ryokan*, is a pun on the Japanese term for "class trip," *Shuugaku Ryokou*.

PAGE 35

loincloth: The Japanese word was actually "*fundoshi*," a sumo wrestler's version of a loincloth.

PAGE 41

buckwheat pillow: Hulls of the pseudo-grain buckwheat (*soba*) are a traditional filler material in Japanese pillows.

PAGE 48

onmyouji: A specialist in magic who protects people from evil spirts.

PAGE 61

Uzumasa Cinema Village: This refers to an actual place in Kyoto called Toei Uzumasa Movie Village (*Toei Uzumasa Eiga Mura*), which Toei Studios uses as a set for historical TV shows and films and as a theme park for people interested in the historical settings.

Very general historical overview (with bold terms appearing in the chapter): The historical figures that the characters are cosplaying are from a time of unrest in Japan called the **Bakumatsu**. After Ieyasu Tokugawa took control of Japan as *shogun* (military ruler) in 1603, and the country had been ruled by a series of his descendants, with a series of laws that forced people into strict social castes and disallowed entry for foreigners, especially Europeans. The Bakumatsu has long been a popular setting for works of historical fiction, and more recent works have kept the time in the popular consciousness.

Shinsengumi: A group of masterless samurai in Kyoto that fought the patriots on behalf of the shogunate. Had very distinctive sky-blue jackets with a jagged white trim pattern on the sleeves. Very popular in historical dramas.

PAGE 63

Katamori Matsudaira: Appointed as Protector of Kyoto during the Bakumatsu time, he made use of groups like the Shinsengumi among others to maintain order in the city and protect agents of the shogun.

Yoshinobu Tokugawa: The final shogun of the Tokugawa family line, which controlled Japan from 1603 to 1868.

PAGE 64

Isami Kondou: Commander of the Shinsengumi.

Souji Okita: Captain of the first unit of the Shinsengumi.

PAGE 65

Shinpachi Nagakura: Captain of the second unit of the Shinsengumi.

Kai Shimada: Vice-captain of the Shinsengumi second unit.

Toshizou Hijikata: Vice-commander of the Shinsengumi.

PAGE 66

Exclusionist patriots: The term "*joui shishi*" means "patriots for expelling the foreigners"; usually includes "*sonnou*" ("revere the emperor") before it, which is often rendered as "loyalist." Another common term for them was "*ishin shishi*," or "restoration patriots," where the focus was on restoring power to the Emperor instead of the shogun.

Ryouma: Ryouma Sakamoto was an important figure involved in many parts of the process of Japan opening to the world and changing its system of government during the Bakumatsu.

"Just so": Ryouma Sakamoto was originally from the Tosa region, now Kouchi, on the southern part of the island of Shikoku. The "just so" that the White Shirts are tacking on to their sentences is originally "*zeyo*," an old Tosa dialect version of "*desu ka* (is that?)," which has become a trademark phrase for Ryouma as arguably the most famous person from Tosa.

"I will cleanse Japan, just so!": Seems to match a famous line by Ryouma, written in a letter to his sister.

PAGE 71

"defend our Emperor from foreign impurity": "*Sonnou Joui*" was the slogan used by the *Ishin* patriots and meant "Revere the Emperor; expel the foreigners."

"The dawn of Japan is near, just so!": Another Ryouma quote.

PAGE 72
mannequin-matching: "*Manekin-gai*" is a slang term for a person who buys the exact same complete outfit that is on a mannequin at a clothing store, rather than coming up with their own outfit coordinate.

PAGE 74
Harajuku: A center of fashion in Tokyo and home to numerous trendy boutiques.

PAGE 75
purification font: A *mitarashi* is a fountain or basin of water for washing one's hands (and rinsing out one's mouth) before entering a shrine.

Sanskrit key holder: A key holder with a Sanskrit syllable written on it in the Siddhaṃ script used for Buddhist sutras in Japan.

PAGE 76
lady ninjas: Handa actually used a specific term for female ninjas, "*kunoichi*."

PAGE 77
fidelity: The flag shown is the flag that was used by the Shinsengumi.

PAGE 81
Oryou: The name of Ryouma Sakamoto's wife.

PAGE 93
Ornate Hairpins: A *kanzashi* is a long, straight hairpin with a decoration on one end.

Yattsuhashi: Yattsuhashi is Kyoto City's specialty Japanese sweet. It is made from sweet rice dough that is either baked like a cookie or left uncooked to act as a wrapper. The traditional flavor is cinnamon and sugar, but there are many other flavor options available.

PAGE 94
Goddess of Mercy: "Kwannon," or "Kannon," is the Japanese name for the Buddhist and Hindu goddess of mercy. According to legend, the Buddha granted her a thousand arms in order to save as many souls as possible. Her statue would be on sale at a Kyoto gift shop due to the famous Kyoto Buddhist temple *Sanjuusangendou*, which contains a thousand statues of the thousand-armed Kwannon.

PAGE 96
"monster parent": An egotistical or irrationally demanding parent, not dissimilar to the recent American term "helicopter parent." It was coined by educator and former elementary school teacher Youichi Mukouyama.

PAGE 104
Terada: Teradaya is the inn where (in 1866) an attempt was made on Ryouma Sakamoto's life; he was warned just beforehand by Oryou, one of the maids, whom he married soon after. Would be fitting if these items are bath towels, considering Oryou ran upstairs naked from the bath to give Ryouma the warning!

PAGE 111
Bakumatsu: A time of violent power struggles over Japan's future between 1853 and 1867, which led to the end of the Tokugawa shogunate's centuries-long feudal military rule and isolationist foreign policy and the restoration of political power to the Emperor in the Meiji Restoration.

Ryouma Sakamoto: An important figure involved in many parts of the process of Japan opening to the world and changing its system of government during the Bakumatsu period. Unfortunately, he died too soon to see the results of his work, as he was assassinated in Kyoto on Dec. 10, 1867, less than one month before the Meiji Restoration on Jan. 8, 1868. We really can't do him justice in a short translation note, but his charisma, revolutionary ideals, and varied interests make him a figure as widely adored in Japan as the Founding Fathers are in the United States.

Ryozen History Museum: A museum dedicated to the history of the Bakumatsu period and the Meiji Restoration. And yes, visitors really can dress up like Shinsengumi members for photos.

Gokoku Shrine: Gokoku shrines honor Japan's heroes. The Kyoto location, next to the Ryozen Museum, was built in 1868 to honor those from the Bakumatsu period. As noted, it houses the gravesite of Ryouma Sakamoto, which also includes his associate Shintaro Nakaoka who was fatally wounded at Ryouma's assassination.

Maruyama Park: A scenic park in eastern Kyoto city that includes a large bronze statue memorializing both Ryouma Sakamoto and his associate Shintaro Nakaoka. The park is especially popular as a cherry-blossom viewing site, but they aren't visiting during the season for that. Only a ten minute walk from the Ryozen Museum, it's an obvious stop to make for a "Bakumatsu Ryouma" tour.

Teradaya: Teradaya is the inn where an attempt was made on Ryouma Sakamoto's life on March 3, 1866; he was warned just beforehand by Oryou, one of the maids, whom he married soon after. And yes, it's roughly a thirty minute ride south from the other historical sites they're visiting that day.

PAGE 112
John Manjiro was a Japanese fisherman who got rescued by an American whaling ship after his boat was wrecked in 1841. He went on to learn American customs and technology, as well as the English language, over the next decade on various whaling ships and while living in the United States. He managed to return to Japan in 1851 with relatively little difficulty (considering that leaving Japan was a capital crime during the Edo period) and became a valuable resource for the shogun.

PAGE 117
Handa's horrible sword puns: The original Japanese lines were "*Sordosu*," a pun on "sword" and "*Sou desu* (That's right)"; "*Kubi o katta na*," a pun on "*katta* (hunted)" and "*katana* (Japanese longsword)"; and "*Katanarashi de*," a pun on "*katanarashi* (shoulder warm-up exercise)" and "*katana*" again.

PAGE 118
"Ich-eese!": Pun mixing "Ichi" from Ichimiya with the usual phrase "(Say) Cheese!"

PAGE 123
Maruyama bridge & pond: The place Ichimiya and Handa meet is an especially scenic spot in the west-central part of Maruyama Park, not far from Yasaka Shrine. Handa approached it from the east, after visiting the Ryouma statue in the south-central part of the park.

PAGE 124
Utsukushi-gozensha: Meaning "Beautiful Woman Shrine," this subshrine of Yasaka Shrine just west of Maruyama Park is visited by not only women interested in beauty, such as *geisha* or *maiko* (apprentice *geisha*) but also people in professions related to beauty, so it's not that weird for Reo to go there. He's applying the Beauty Water (*biyousui*) almost correctly: You're actually supposed to catch a little water falling from the pipe to spread on your face, rather than splashing on a bunch of water straight from the basin.

votive tablets: *Ema* are small wooden tablets, sometimes with illustrations, which people buy from a Shinto shrine to hang up there with their own written wishes or prayers. The word literally means "picture horse," since it evolved from the original custom of donating horses to a shrine for good fortune. There are examples of them hanging at this shrine on the second to last page of the chapter.

PAGE 129
stamp rally: A common Japanese way to promote tourism by providing a collection book for visitors to go around to a set of different places and get a unique rubber-stamp imprint from each one

shrine seals: *Goshuin* is when pilgrims get (frequently red) seal imprints from visiting shrines and temples in an area. Maybe this is what stamp rallies originated from?

PAGE 143
Joumoto's horrible puns: This time it's snacks instead of swords!

For the first one, he offers Ichimiya a Kyoto specialty sweet snack called *otabe*, made from soft *yattsuhashi* dough folded into a triangle over filling (usually sweet bean paste). He makes use of the fact that "*otabe*" is also the polite command form of the verb *taberu* (to eat).

For the second one, he says "*Yappashi yappashi?*": the word is an alternative form of "*yappari* (as I suspected)," and a logical (though incorrect) alternative pronunciation for the snack name *yattsuhashi*, sweet rice dough that is either baked like a cookie or left uncooked to act as a wrapper). An extra dose of groan comes from the fact that those kanji also literally mean "eight bridges," since they're leaving the bridge in the park...

PAGE 145
sleeve tie: Dash is wearing a *tasuki*, a cord used to tuck & tie up the long sleeves of a kimono. You may have seen this used when characters in traditional clothing are doing house cleaning, etc., in anime or movies.

PAGE 146
peace: There's a slight oddity with the way that Kondou wrote the word *heion* (peace). Though that kanji combination is allowed, normally the second kanji uses the meaning for "calm, quiet," while the one he used means "to hide."

Leo: Reo started to write his name with an "R," then scratched that out—because he thought it would look cooler to write his name as "Leo"!

PAGE 149
warabimochi: A Japanese sweet similar to traditional mochi, but made from starch from the bracken root instead of glutinous rice flour. It is jelly-like and often dipped or covered in *kinako*, sweet toasted soybean flour.

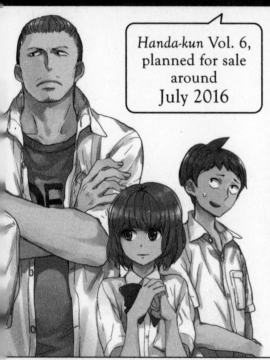

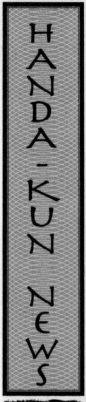

HANDA-KUN NEWS

Vol.HND

And Then the Next Volume, Unbelievably the Final One!!!

Handa-kun Vol. 6, planned for sale around July 2016

Everyone, thank you very much for buying volume 5 of *HANDA-KUN*! Thanks to all your support, *HANDA-KUN* is slated to receive a TV anime adaptation! However—would you believe it!? *HANDA-KUN* will be finishing in volume 6 (lol)! Can Handa finally bridge the distance between himself and everyone else...!? Laugh or cry, please continue to watch warmly over Handa to the very final chapter! (grovel)

TOTODON: BARAKAMON & HANDA-KUN Official Tweet Book by Satsuki Yoshino

ヨシノサツキ
ばらかもん・はんだくん
公式Tweet Book
ととどん

HAPPY HALLOWEEN 2014

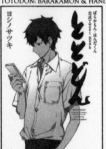

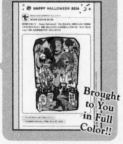

Brought to You in Full Color!!

Releasing on the same day as this book is the second *BARAKAMON* spin-off comic series: *TOTODON*! The protagonist is Seishuu Handa's father, Seimei Handa, in his younger days! This book also includes a large number of full-color *HANDA-KUN* illustrations that were previously only available on the official Twitter account, so be sure to check it out!

Contents

- >55 pages of the manga *TOTODON* (with 10 new specially-drawn pages)
- >90 illustrations not included in the volume releases
- Campaign of illustrations specially-drawn on request from followers
- Satsuki Yoshino & Editor dialogue   And Much More!

Also Including a Large Number of *Handa-kun* Illustrations! *TOTODON*, Now on Sale to Popular Acclaim!

An Anime Adaptation!!

▶▶▶ Anime follow-up reports will be released on occasion in *Monthly Shonen Gangan*, which goes on sale the 12th of each month, or in *Gangan* ONLINE, which updates every Thursday and the 1st & 3rd Monday of each month!

©Campaign Target Books (maximum of two send-away tickets per person)

On Sale Feb. 12th	● Monthly Shonen Gangan March Issue ● GC BARAKAMON Volume 5 ● GC TOTODON - Barakamon/Handa-kun Official Tweet Book
On Sale March 12th	● Monthly Shonen Gangan April Issue ● GC Online BARAKAMON Volume 13 ● GC Online BARAKAMON Official Fanbook

A Barakamon Special Box

B Reusable Baraka-Bottle

C "ば (BA)" T-Shirt

Application Deadline: valid if postmarked by Tues., April 4th, 2016

To commemorate the same-day release of this volume 5 of *HANDA-KUN* with *TOTODON*, next month's same-day release of *BARAKAMON* volume 13 with the *BARAKAMON* Fanbook, and the 100th chapter of *BARAKAMON* in March, a lottery campaign is now underway for original Barakamon merchandise!! Be sure to collect the common send-away tickets from any of the target books and send them in!

Baraka - Handa - Totodon Campaign Now Under-way!!

※ Please note that all promotional items presented in this segment were only available to readers in Japan at the time of the original volume's release.

Karino Takatsu, creator of
SERVANT x SERVICE, presents:

My Monster Girl's Too Cool For You

**Burning adoration melts
her heart…literally!**

In a world where *youkai* and
humans attend school together,
a boy named Atsushi Fukuzumi
falls for snow *youkai* Muku Shiroishi. Fukuzumi's passionate feelings
melt Muku's heart…and the rest of her?! The first volume of an
interspecies romantic comedy you're sure to fall head over heels for
is now available!!

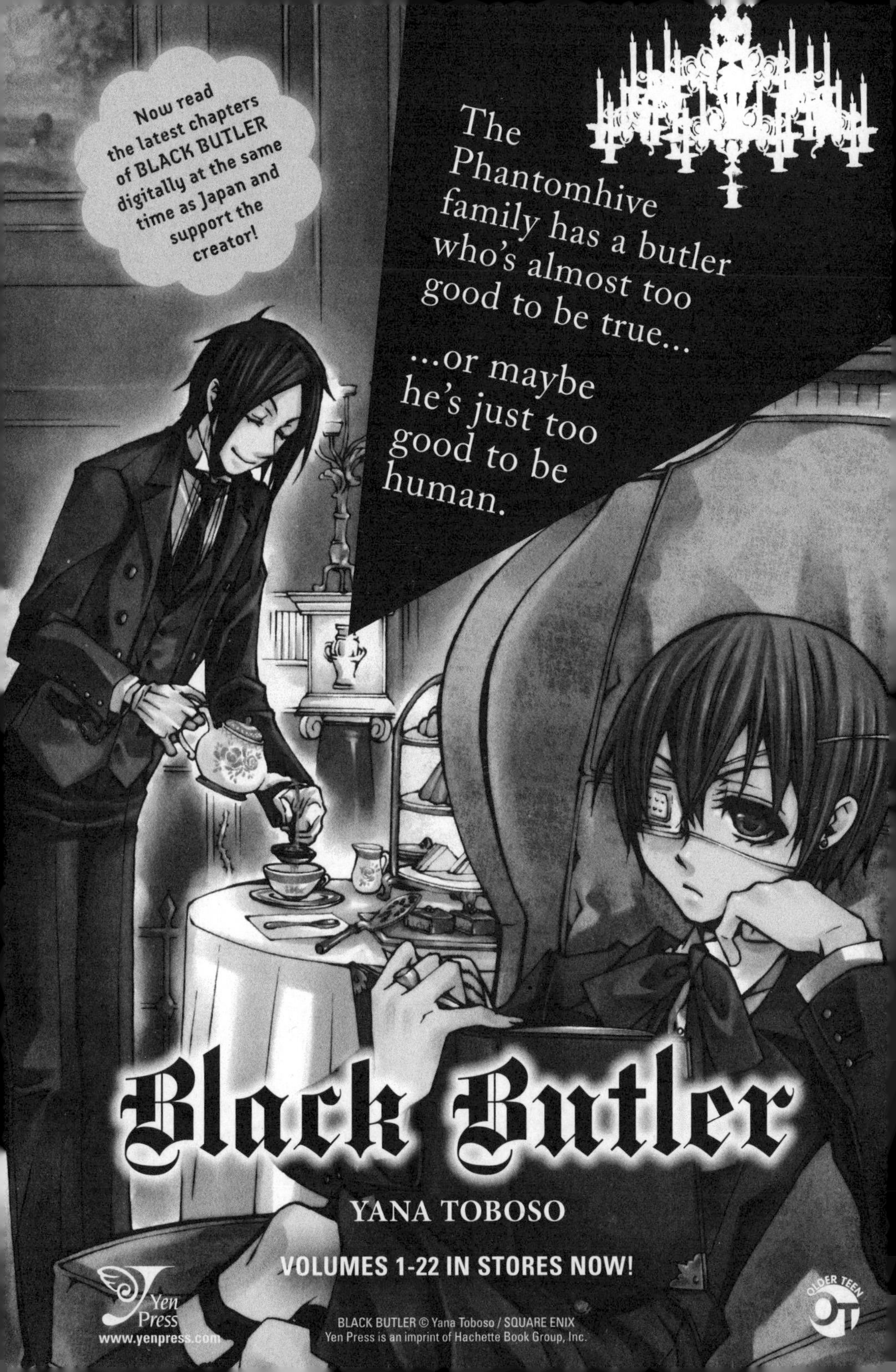
Now read the latest chapters of BLACK BUTLER digitally at the same time as Japan and support the creator!
The Phantomhive family has a butler who's almost too good to be true...
...or maybe he's just too good to be human.
Black Butler
YANA TOBOSO
VOLUMES 1-22 IN STORES NOW!
Yen Press
www.yenpress.com
BLACK BUTLER © Yana Toboso / SQUARE ENIX
Yen Press is an imprint of Hachette Book Group, Inc.
OLDER TEEN
OT

ENJOY EVERYTHING.

Hello! This is YOTSUBA!

Guess what? Guess what? Yotsuba and Daddy just moved here from waaaay over there!

And Yotsuba met these nice people next door and made new friends to play with!

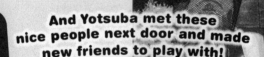

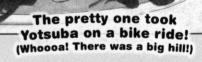

The pretty one took Yotsuba on a bike ride!
(Whoooa! There was a big hill!)

And Ena's a good drawer!
(Almost as good as Yotsuba!)

And their mom always gives Yotsuba ice cream!
(Yummy!)

And...
And...
OHHHH!

Handa-kun 5

Satsuki Yoshino

Translation/Adaptation: Krista Shipley, Karie Shipley
Lettering: Lys Blakeslee

Handa-kun Vol. 5 ©2016 Satsuki Yoshino/SQUARE ENIX CO., LTD. First published in Japan in 2016 by SQUARE ENIX CO., LTD. English translation rights arranged with SQUARE ENIX CO., LTD. and Yen Press, LLC through Tuttle-Mori Agency, Inc.

English translation ©2015 by SQUARE ENIX CO., LTD.

Yen Press
1290 Avenue of the Americas
New York, NY 10104

Visit us at yenpress.com
facebook.com/yenpress
twitter.com/yenpress
yenpress.tumblr.com
instagram.com/yenpress

First Yen Press Print Edition: March 2017
The chapters in this volume were originially published as ebooks by Yen Press.

Yen Press is an imprint of Yen Press, LLC.
The Yen Press name and logo are trademarks of Yen Press, LLC.

Library of Congress Control Number: 2015952606

ISBNs: 978-0-316-46927-2 (paperback)
       978-0-316-43918-3 (ebook)

10 9 8 7 6 5 4 3 2 1

BVG

Printed in the United States of America